THE CONSTITUTIONAL FUTURE

of the

PRAIRIE and ATLANTIC REGIONS

of CANADA

THE CONSTITUTIONAL FUTURE

of the

PRAIRIE and ATLANTIC REGIONS

of CANADA

Edited by James N. McCrorie
and
Martha L. MacDonald

Canadian Plains Research Center
University of Regina
1992

Canadian Plains Research Center
University of Regina
Regina, Saskatchewan S4S 0A2
Canada

∞

Printed on acid-free paper

Canadian Cataloguing in Publication Data

Main entry under title:

The Constitutional Future of the Prairie and Atlantic Regions of Canada

(Canadian plains proceedings, ISSN 0317-6401 ; 22)
Proceedings of a conference held in Regina,
Saskatchewan, November 8-10, 1991.
ISBN 0-88977-068-9

1. Federal-provincial relations – Canada – Congresses.*
2. Federal-provincial relations – Prairie Provinces –
Congresses.* 3. Federal-provincial relations –
Atlantic Provinces – Congresses.* 4. Canada –
Constitutional history – Congresses. I. McCrorie,
James Napier, 1936-   II. MacDonald, Martha.
III. University of Regina.   Canadian Plains Research
Center. IV. Series.

JL27.C65 1992   971.064'7   C92-098038-4

73238

Designed by Brian Mlazgar and Agnes Bray, Canadian Plains Research Center, University of Regina.

Printed and bound in Canada by
Hignell Printing Limited, Winnipeg, Manitoba.

The publication of this book was made possible, in part, by a conference grant from the Social Sciences and Humanities Research Council of Canada.

Contents

Introduction

James N. McCrorie

The struggle to amend the Canadian constitution in the hope of accommo-dating the needs and aspirations of the province of Quebec has understandably overshadowed concern about the future and indeed the constitutional require-ments of other collective realities in Canadian society. If Canada may be defined as an historic partnership between two founding nations, then there is more to this uneasy marriage than a federation of provinces. Canadian society has been, and remains, a complex network of regions.

This collection of papers focusses on two regions — Atlantic Canada and the Prairies — which have had different relationships to the central, urban industrial provinces of Quebec and Ontario, yet share common problems and have similar constitutional demands.

It may be argued at the outset that the three prairie and four Atlantic provin-ces no longer constitute "regions" in the sense that the term is often employed. It is useful, therefore, to introduce this collection with a consideration of the concept of region, with a view to providing a critical framework within which the papers that follow may be studied.

Despite the fact that the concept of region has been widely deployed in the social sciences, there is no consensus as to how it should be defined. Not surpris-ingly, different definitions have yielded conflicting results. However, it is dif-ficult to improve on Janine Brodie's review of the varied use of the concept of region in her book, *The Political Economy of Canadian Regionalism* (Toronto: Harcourt Brace Jovanovich, 1990). Brodie argues that the concept tends to fall into one of two categories, depending on the perspective that is brought to bear on the issue of regional integration:

> The formal approach ... is most often accompanied by what have been termed theories of regional self-balance. These theories assume that regions are discrete entities that are separated and isolated from other regions by some formal criteria. No linkages between regions are postulated in their definition and, as a result, factors explaining the character of the region are sought within the region itself. (Brodie, 16)

The second approach has been called "relational." Again, in Brodie's words:

> this approach differs from the formal procedure most fundamentally be-cause it does not propose concrete boundaries that isolate one region from another. Nor is it primarily concerned with discovering similarities and dif-ferences in geographic space. Instead ... regions are seen as part of an inter-connected whole in which one regional configuration is largely a function

> or an expression of another. Regions ... are not arbitrary constructs but
> effects or consequences of historical relationships. (Brodie, 17).

There are two tendencies which may be discovered in the formal tradition of conceiving regions. First, the conception tends to be static. Regions are conceived in terms of one or a constellation of characteristics. If one of them changes or disappears, the region — so defined — is either modified or ceases to exist. Second, it is possible, in this tradition, to become eclectic and to select criteria for the purpose of definition that have more to do with the intellectual predisposition of the observer than the empirical realities of the area selected for study. In such cases, regions become more the artifact of the scientist than a conception of a phenomenon in the real world.

In contrast, the relational approach conceives of regions as realities, *sui generis*. As Brodie puts it: "regions are the product of historical experience, human organization and social interaction." (Brodie, 17). This approach to the conceptualization of regions has its own tendencies. As Brodie's definition stipulates, regions can never be reduced to one variable or one consideration. There is always a constellation of interacting variables — economic, political, social, cultural — which develop and are expressed over time. Moreover, this tradition of conceptualization insists on viewing one region in relation to those others with which it interacts. While it might suffice, in the formal tradition, to conclude a study within the parameters of a region however defined, such a study would remain incomplete in the relational tradition. The study of one region must lead to an examination of those others with which it is related.

This tradition is demanding in another respect. Regions are conceived as dynamic phenomena and must therefore be studied in an historical context; an optional requirement in the formal tradition. Again, a study at a point in time might be appropriate to the formal approach to regionalism; it is merely the beginning of an investigative journey in the relational tradition.

It is in this respect that the relational tradition enjoys a theoretical advantage over the formal. In the case of the latter, a major change in one of the variables used to define the region may lead to the conclusion that the "territory" under study no longer constitutes a region. Not so in the case of the relational approach. Here one expects the characteristics of a region to change. Here one is encouraged to look behind the appearance of things in order to discover the deeper relationships which themselves are dynamic, assuming different patterns and generating new and different results.

It may be argued that this approach permits one to classify as the same region a territory whose appearance radically changes over a period of time; surely a paradox if not a contradiction. Precisely. If one will permit a human analogy, the appearances and indeed the properties and characteristics of a human at birth are quite different from the results at the moment of death. Is this still the same person? Most will reply "yes," without hesitation. Upon reflection, they will offer a more revealing answer. In one sense, they might argue, it is the same person. On

viii

the other hand it is not. What the individual was like at birth was not what she or he became at death. In other words, there is a recognition that human beings are dynamic, that they develop, that they start off as one thing and become something else. So it can be with regions.

Different traditions of conceiving of regions can therefore lead to different results — a conclusion that is evident in the different approaches to be found in the papers in this collection. However, there is one consideration which both traditions can and often do share, a consideration that has a direct bearing on the constitutional past and future of Canadian society. A distinction can and should be made between a region "in itself" and a region "for itself." In the first instance, we are dealing with an objective reality. One may prefer one tradition of conceiving that reality over another. The point remains, however, that both traditions can, and indeed endeavour to, address objective reality. In the second instance, we are dealing with whether the residents of a region are conscious of their common interests and whether they are prepared to act on and advance them.

Again, it may be suggested that the relational tradition offers a more imaginative approach to the study of regional interests and consciousness than the formal tradition. It permits variation in the degree of regional consciousness and therefore can accommodate both the presence and absence of the assertion and promotion of regional interests over a period of time. Nevertheless, the issue of regional consciousness is important to both conceptual traditions.

It is certainly central to Canadian constitutional history. Although some political leaders in British North America favoured the union of the colonies in a single, unitary state, French Canada insisted on a different arrangement — one which permitted the creation of a collective community having a measure of independence within a larger political union. The result was something more than the division of the nation into provinces with specific jurisdictions in which to govern. This assertion of collective rights found additional expression in the inclusion in the British North America Act of the Senate, a parliamentary institution created to provide a measure of protection to the regional interests of Quebec and the maritime provinces against the anticipated growth — and therefore electoral, political power — of Ontario.

There were thus two related but contrasting features built into the Canadian Parliament. Representation in the House of Commons was based on population, an affirmation of individual rights in a parliamentary democracy. Representation in the Senate was based on region, an assertion of collective rights in the political life of the nation. While it is true that the BNA Act tipped the balance of power in favour of the Commons and therefore individual rights, the provision for the legitimate expression of regional or collective concerns is to be noted.

The most dramatic and telling manifestation of this constitutional arrangement in the daily lives of Canadians first occurred in the late 1930s, when the Liberal government of Mackenzie King appointed a royal commission to inquire into the future of dominion-provincial relations, as they were then called. The government had recognized — correctly — that there was more to the economic depression than massive unemployment and the potential for explosive class conflict. There was, in addition, a regional imbalance to unemployment and poverty. It was bad enough to be unemployed in Toronto; it was worse to be so in Moncton or Brandon.

One of the tasks of the Rowell-Sirois Commission was to inquire into what steps the federal government could take under the BNA Act to ensure that growing up in one province or region of the nation did not, in respect of matters of health and education, for example, carry with it a burden not borne in other provinces and regions. One of the legacies of that commission and the government's response to its recommendations is the political acceptance of the federal government's constitutional right to take legislative and programmatic steps to address and redress regional imbalances in respect of economic development, health, education and the provision of social services, even though many of these matters fall within provincial jurisdiction.

Since Confederation, the power of the federal government and its constitutional right to become directly involved in regional concerns have been matters of considerable importance, if not controversy to the Atlantic provinces, Quebec, and the three prairie provinces. Yet it has been Quebec, and the needs, concerns and initiatives of that province, that have dominated the constitutional struggles and debates both before and since the repatriation of the constitution. Until recently, the reaction in English-speaking Canada, including the regions we are concerned with, has been largely one of indifference, with occasional expressions of annoyance. If an explanation is offered for this striking difference in attitude, a preoccupation with the economy is usually given as the answer.

This would appear to be a reasonable attitude among those who reside, and endeavour to make a living, in economically depressed and threatened regions. Yet the appearance conceals an important social premise. Residents of Atlantic Canada and the Prairies do not, in the main, view existing constitutional arrangements as an impediment to the resolution of their economic and social difficulties. Most of the residents of Quebec do.

What, after all, is a constitution? It is a human convention concerning how the residents of a community, however defined, are going to live their lives, and govern or be governed. It may be an unwritten convention or series of conventions, as in the case of the United Kingdom. It may be expressed in the form of a written document, supplemented by a series of written interpretations by a judicial body, as in the case of the United States. It may be a combination of both, as in the case of Canada. Whatever form it takes, it is clear that the provisions of the present constitution are unsatisfactory to most French Canadians, particularly those resident in the province of Quebec.

This becomes problematic when one acknowledges that within French Canada there is a body of opinion which seeks not amendments to the constitution in order to permit Quebec to remain within the Canadian confederation, but the creation of a new, independent nation-state. It is by no means self-evident that this option is attractive to most French Canadians, including those who are resident in the province of Quebec. However, it may become so if the nation cannot find a new and different set of constitutional provisions and conventions.

Put bluntly, we are being asked to change the way we live together and govern ourselves. It is pertinent and proper to inquire if the changes we are being asked to consider will address and serve, or threaten and compromise, the regional needs and interests of the Atlantic and prairie regions of the nation. The papers in this collection are being published in the hope of providing an informed basis for an answer.

The collection opens with two papers offering an historical perspective on the regional nature and characteristics of the Prairies and Atlantic Canada. Section II contains six papers dealing with economic problems and prospects, both at the provincial and regional levels. The four papers in section III examine social, cultural and political issues in the respective regions. The final section includes six papers which address constitutional issues and problems directly.

1

The Prairies as Region:
The Contemporary Meaning of an Old Idea

Gerald Friesen

In a period of political crisis, when the accustomed arrangements of the federal state are in question, it is appropriate to review historic grievances and to ask whether a revised constitutional structure might better meet Canada's needs. Canadians would acknowledge that prairie residents have often expressed discontent with Confederation. Today's political discussion — western separatism, western alienation, "the West wants in" — has made the theme familiar. Canadians are aware, too, that the points of dissatisfaction are not new. During the first half of this century, such labels as prairie protest, agrarian revolt and labour revolt were often applied to similar expressions of discontent. Métis rebellion and aboriginal resistance and provincial rights, all of which might be said to have a regional cast, dominated the last decades of the nineteenth century. Even before Confederation, the Prairies and the western interior were described as a distinct part of the globe. Visitors attributed a special status to the land, a separate identity to this striking expanse that they depicted as one of the noteworthy "wildernesses" on the globe. The talk of a single West, of a prairie region and of prairie regionalism is, therefore, part of Canadian popular expression.

My assignment is to review the idea of prairie region and to provide a context for discussions of the place of prairie residents in Confederation. I have interpreted it in the form of several questions: first, how has the concept of prairie region been used and has it been regarded as helpful or appropriate in the interpretation of prairie experience? And, second, when we invoke "prairie regionalism" in our contemporary constitutional discussions, what is the "ism" meant to convey and does it offer a relevant interpretation of contemporary prairie political experience?

There are three main approaches to the phenomenon of region — the formal, the functional and the imagined. Separately, each has been employed as a means of depicting the Canadian Prairies; together, they present problems. They tend to overlap in popular thinking, mutually to reinforce and, yet, to flee from precise definition. They are often fuzzy when utilized in debates about public policy, so it is as well that we be clear about the concept before we use it in the discussions to follow.

The simplest approach, on the surface, is the formal region: the Prairies *look* like a separate and distinct and homogeneous place — in short, like a region. When Henry Kelsey arrived on the edge of these plains in 1690, he described them as a "barren ground" and said that they offered "Nothing but short Round sticky grass & Buffillo."[1] A century later, David Thompson named this zone "the Great Plains as a general name," said they constituted a "very different formation," and placed the area in continental perspective by suggesting that they stretched from the Gulf of Mexico to the 54th parallel.[2] In the eighteenth century, European Canadian scientific observations having intensified with the extension of national boundaries and surveys into this area, an 1884 geology textbook divided the northern half of the continent in two at the "Laurentian axis extending from Lake of the Woods to the Arctic, arguing that the eastern and western halves were geologically and physically distinct."[3] These generalizations represent the first level of European Canadian regional perceptions. They rely upon land forms and climate and unity of historical experience to define a separate and distinct place on the earth's surface.

The historian Goldwin Smith best encapsulated this phase of thinking about regions in the late nineteenth century. Writing in the era when nation building and national realignment were still transforming the globe, Smith evoked the power of geographical forces to break apart the new transcontinental Canada. He argued in the opening statement of his *Canada and the Canadian Question* that, if one wished to understand Canada's national dilemma, one must turn "from the political to the physical map," from an image of a united land to one that featured "four separate projections of the cultivable and habitable part of the Continent into arctic waste," each separated from the others "by great barriers of nature, wide and irreclaimable wildernesses or manifold chains of mountains" and each "closely connected by nature, physically and economically" with the adjoining American region.[4] Such perceptions represent the physical interpretation of the western interior as a formal region. They underlie all the perspectives that follow, and they *will* linger in our minds, despite our best efforts to rid ourselves of such apparently simple interpretations of human society.[5]

The developing literature on the Prairies, whether in fiction or the social sciences, offered further variations on this interpretation of regional difference — of formal region — in the late nineteenth and early twentieth centuries. Environment, in this view, affected and perhaps even determined human character or social behaviour. Thus, Roger Pocock, a novelist of the 1880s, described mounted police returning from patrol, "their eyes bright with the reflected breadth and freedom of the plains. ... [they] have no flavour of the old tiresome life of the umbrella and the table-cloth."[6] In a novel by the immensely popular

Ralph Connor, a character exclaims: "How wonderful the power of this country of yours to transform men!"[7]

These assertions may now appear foolish but they represent a significant strain in Canadian thought early in the twentieth century. Scholars shared with novelists this preoccupation with the power of the land. The geographer Griffith Taylor, for example, built a career on his environmentalist interpretations. His major work on Canada, published in 1947, distinguished twenty Canadian regions, including the Winnipeg basin and the western prairie, and forecast remarkable population growth for both on the basis of his assessment of the future of world agricultural and energy production.[8] The great prairie historian of that era, Arthur Silver Morton, invoked similar assumptions when, in describing the crucial shift of aboriginal groups from parkland to plains in the 1700s, he wrote that the "Crees wandered over into the prairies and adopted the very different manner of living which characterized the buffalo country." In such works, an implied environmental determinism assumed as much as it explained but it also offered an explanation for the presence of formal regions.[9]

The foregoing versions of the western interior, whether depicting the area as a natural product of physical geography (David Thompson and Goldwin Smith), or as a social phenomenon introduced by environmental forces (Ralph Connor and Griffith Taylor), asserted that the Canadian Prairies constituted a definable portion of the earth's surface. No reference to other places was necessary to establish the region's character. The prairie region stood on its own, distinctive and clearly demarcated, as a "formal region" that occupied an unmistakable physical place on the map. Its boundaries would not change significantly as long as the physical environment remained unaltered. It was relatively consistent internally as measured by certain self-evident and allegedly objective characteristics. The link in this analysis between formal region and environmental interpretations of human affairs will be unmistakable.

Environmentalism, pure and simple, has since fallen into disrepute but recognition of environmental *influence* in human affairs can hardly be disputed. Ronald Rees's recent volume on the Canadian plains examines such difficult matters as the impact of an environment devoid of trees and other physical relief upon human well-being.[10] The careers of many Canadian scholars, including W.L. Morton and Harold Innis, were devoted to understanding the interplay between environment and human endeavour. Thus, environmentalism need not become determinism and emphasis upon landscape and resource differences in regional analysis must not be dismissed today as the musing of fanatics. As students of society, we run the danger, ironically, of neglecting environmental influences upon human activity while, because of some atavistic mental reflex, we retain a dogged and simple concept of formal physical region — the Canadian Prairies — that underlies our daily life and thought. My observation is that, no matter how we try, our picture of a prairie region will always retain some degree of this plain and simple thinking, of formal regionalism.

A second kind of regional definition, also important in Canada, employs a relative or relational approach. In order to have one region, in this view, one must have another. Hinterland regions exist because there are also metropolitan regions, frontiers can only be distinguished from densely settled zones, areas of staple exploitation from central markets where consumers and entrepreneurs and, often, cultural and political leadership are located. These places, shaped as much by the coherent whole of which they form a part as by internal consistency or evident boundaries, have been labelled "functional regions." As Janine Brodie has suggested, they are defined by their relationships as well as by their internal characteristics, and by social as much as "natural" elements.[11]

I will offer just two illustrations of how this approach has influenced our thinking about the Prairies. Canadians once were accustomed to describing the West as a frontier. Thus, the Queen's University academic, Adam Shortt, reported that his preconceptions about social organization had been "revolutionized" during his travels in the Northwest in 1894. He found there not the well-defined characteristics of business and social life he was accustomed to in Ontario but, rather, a society "in process of formation."[12] When Isaiah Bowman designed the multivolume scholarly project, the Canadian Frontiers of Settlement series in the late 1920s, he believed that he was creating a science of settlement that would have international application because "the pioneer belts of the world are regions of experiment — 'experimental zones' we might call them."[13] Similarly, the distinguished economist, W.A. Mackintosh, argued that "Sectionalism is always characteristic of a new and expanding country. There is always division between the frontier and the old settlements, whether exemplified in Jacksonian democracy, or in conflict between Halifax and York currencies and between established churches and Methodism, or in farmers' movements."[14] The sociologist S.D. Clark employed comparable arguments in linking the Seven Oaks incident, the two Métis resistances, the One Big Union, the People's Church, the wheat pools and Social Credit as "western movements of revolt," the expressions of "a separate people," that would recur in cycles as the predecessor movements lost their bite.[15] Each of these examples distinguishes the prairie West from more settled zones in the rest of North America. Each is an example of a functional region.[16]

Another influential approach to the prairie region has been the so-called staples or Laurentian school of Canadian history. As Janine Brodie has noted, Harold Innis's work on cod, fur, timber and wheat implies a spatial distribution of economic activity consequent upon the export of particular staples to a metropolis. Unfortunately, the staples thesis lends itself to a simplistic, dualist interpretation of Canadian experience that Innis himself would have rejected. Thus, the so-called metropolis-hinterland, centre-periphery, and regional-disparity models, so familiar among social scientists in the 1970s, are abstractions that convey sharp images of Canadian regions while simplifying the very complex circumstances in which regional differences developed. One point of

Brodie's work, indeed, is to recover some of the crucial economic and social forces that have been lost in the model building. By returning to the economic foundations of functional regions, she is restoring strength to an approach that has lacked it. Her emphasis on the uneven spatial development in capitalist economies must be treated seriously and her revival of V.C. Fowke's concern for the spatial biases of government policies must, similarly, be acknowledged as sound.[17]

Both the frontier and staple approaches to prairie history entail the use of a functional definition of region. Each assumes a relationship between at least two entities and, consequently, a larger system, one that encompasses these component parts, that can change over time. In some cases, the boundaries between the communities — and thus the identity of previously-distinct regions — may actually vanish. The Prairies need not always be the Prairies, or at least need not be distinguished as a separate place and society.

The third approach to region assumes that a place must be imagined before it can be. This approach grew out of the environmentalism associated with such early novelists as Ralph Connor. It was consolidated in the late 1940s by the critic and novelist Edward McCourt who argued that prairie literature was distinctive because of the author's association with the landscape.[18] Of course, this environmentalism has been superseded by more precise analysis in later decades but McCourt's convictions about prairie cultural differences have not been contradicted. Rather, one could argue that more convincing articulations of the same perception have won the attention of cultural scholars.

Eli Mandel, who has written of these matters in the 1970s and 1980s, views region as "a mental construct ... a myth." He argues that there is a "certain coherence or unity or identity" in the poetry and prose that we describe as *prairie* literature. This coherence is expressed through elements common to regional literatures: a local landscape pictured with startling clarity; a child's view of the world and of home — home being the place where one realizes one's *first* and most memorable vision of things; a grotesque storyteller; a regional dialect; and stories of the past. Thus, in Mandel's view, there is a distinctive regional prairie literature that creates a mythicized prairie world. Prairie storytellers project onto the land their chosen images of the environment — images of the land's redemptive powers (in the figure of a child) and of its demonic tyranny (a hostile father) — and in that choice they adapt their images to a pattern that belongs to all humankind. What images do prairie writers choose? Mandel replies that they are "images of a search for home and therefore a search for the self."[19] Mandel's conceptual language is, we would say today, more convincing, more subtle, than the environmentalism of McCourt. The conviction that drives him, and perhaps even his conclusion may be little different, but Mandel's understanding of human society and his articulation of the processes of the human imagination convince us that something about this place warrants a distinct category in the company of international social orders or, at the least, in the list of Canadian communities.

There are three fundamental approaches to region — formal, functional and imagined. Each has been used to distinguish a prairie social order. Together, over the past two centuries, these approaches have sustained an abiding belief that something marked off the prairie place or the prairie experience or the prairie expression from other places, experiences and expressions. Whether observers were describing a landscape that shaped one's interests and one's mind, or minds that shaped a landscape, or political and economic interests that dominated one's outlook, the cumulative weight of thinking, illustrating and writing about "the Prairies" asserted the distinctiveness of life on this portion of the globe. There is something here that cannot be ignored. Thus, to my first questions, how has the concept of region been used and has it been regarded as helpful, my answer is that region has been applied to the Prairies in three overlapping ways and that, yes, it has been regarded as helpful, even necessary, in discussing the prairie experience.

The second issue concerns the term *regionalism* — what has the idea of prairie regionalism conveyed to observers and does it offer fundamental insights into *contemporary political* experience?

To this point, I have been discussing the region as a place and a proper noun. One cannot have regionalism without a region or regions, presumably, but the analysis of a popular sentiment or political movement distinguished by the term "regionalism" must be different from the relatively abstract discussions about formal and functional and imagined regions. Regionalism implies protest. It speaks of injustice, of neglect, perhaps even of one community's alleged superiority or power over another. Regionalism demands that the student pay simultaneous attention to community consciousness and community behaviour; that is, regionalism speaks of outlook, on the one hand, and self-interest or needs, on the other. The term "regionalism" presumes a larger administrative, economic and political entity, of which our special "region" is a part. Regionalism, in Canada at least, also raises the problem of federalism, meaning such specialized topics as the distribution of powers, revenue sharing, and mechanisms for resolving constitutional disagreements between levels of government. As Northrop Frye once commented, it also raises the issue of national survival. Indeed, regionalism is often used to describe an alternate nationalism, a loyalty to place and people that is built upon the same foundations of sentiment as the nation. In short, regionalism is a messy concept.

Because of the overlap between region and province, between economic and social definitions of a community on the one hand, and political units on the other, such scholars as Donald Smiley and Ramsay Cook have called for an end to talk of regionalism and a focus on province in Canadian scholarly discourse concerning territory-based loyalties. Alan Cairns's landmark article on "The Governments and Societies of Canadian Federalism" probably did much to sustain this approach in contemporary political studies.[20] Nor should one under-estimate the fear of national disintegration as a force in proscribing talk of regionalism from the late 1970s on.[21]

Garth Stevenson, Ralph Matthews, Raymond Breton and Janine Brodie have rejected this conclusion. Stevenson defines region as a "natural and organic unity and community of interests that is independent of political and administrative barriers."[22] Matthews asserts the existence of "a socio-psychological factor that involves identification with and commitment to a territorial unit."[23] Breton has argued that regionalism is a political phenomenon in which other interests are ar-ticulated in spatial terms — that is, "an interpretation of social relations that gives political priority to the condition of the territorial entity" rather than to such nonterritorial conditions as gender, class and race.[24] Brodie, too, em-phasizes the political and material foundation of regions, which she defines as *"political creations* that state development strategies cumulatively impose upon the geographic landscape."[25] These scholars share a conviction that regions and regionalism exist in Canada, that they are not merely arbitrary intellectual con-structs, that their origins lie primarily in material factors (associated especially with the distribution of resources and with economic development policies), and that, in the final analysis, reference to them in public discourse is a significant part of Canadian life. In the case of the Canadian Prairies, I think it is possible to reconcile the views of advocates of regional analysis and those who believe it should be jettisoned.

The case for prairie regionalism is usually made by reference to moments of significant public protest: the Métis resistances of 1869-70 and 1885, the farm and labour and religious outbursts after 1918, the rise of third parties in the 1930s and 1940s, the emergence of provincial rights and secessionist sentiments in the 1970s and early 1980s.[26] What do these expressions tell us about prairie regionalism?

The aboriginal unrest of the late nineteenth century, whether Métis or Indian, is better described as the expression of profound cultural conflict. Moments of violence were not, in the first instance, "regional" protests but rather incidents in the painful adjustment of very different cultures. I am aware that the conflicts arose in part because of Ottawa's failure to communicate effectively and to reconsider particular policies. Seen from the aboriginal perspective, however, (and they were the people engaged in the uprisings), the refusal of the govern-ment to understand the needs of the First Nations was evidence of a failure of European Canadian cultural imagination. Moreover, the aboriginal cultures did not divide along territorial (east-west) lines. The distinction between resistance by military action and resistance by other means was less significant, in the aboriginal view, than it was in the eyes of European Canadians.

By an unusual reversal, ironically, the aboriginal discontents have been in-cluded in the tradition of western grievance. Given this contemporary confusion, it is important that we support W.L. Morton's perspective on the initial bias of prairie politics and reject S.D. Clark's inclusion of Métis uprisings in the tradition of western regional protests. Incoming settlers, mostly Ontarians, who had very little sympathy for the aboriginal cause when the spectre of violence arose in the 1880s, had no difficulty separating their grievances against Ottawa and central Canada from those of the Métis and Indians. The newcomers, often transplanted Ontarians, complained about federal control of lands and resources, the tariffs, freight rates, federal subsidies to the provinces and the Manitoba school question. They even sustained a revisionist, western-based school of historical interpretation. They did not endorse Big Bear or Riel after the shooting started. The causes of the incoming settlers, as W.L. Morton pointed out, arose from the initial bias of Confederation, the political imbalance established by the Manitoba and North-West Territories Acts and by the economic policies that followed. It was only many decades later, the precise issues having been forgotten, that aboriginal leaders became the heroes of western protest and representatives of the initial "bias" of prairie politics, as W.L. Morton named it.[27]

The second source of prairie bias, in Morton's interpretation, was the agrarian protest that peaked during the opening decades of this century. The agrarian campaign, driven by western unhappiness over tariffs, freight rates and many other farm-related matters consolidated the local and national conclusion that a distinctive prairie region had come into being. We have already noted that this is a complicated conclusion. To understand how difficult, we must return to the thorny question of territory-based loyalties.

In the decades between 1900 and 1930, Canadians came to believe that a new community had crystallized in the prairie West. A formal region, a variety of functional regions, and an imagined region had coalesced into a single image. Its characteristics, aside from the all-important lines on the political map, included frontier vitality and economic grievance and political protest. The evidence for the existence of such a regional community is incontrovertible: the secession of western members of the Presbyterian Church in such numbers that the Church (or most of it) was propelled into the United Church of Canada in 1925; the secession of many trade unions from the Canadian Trades and Labor Congress and their American craft headquarters in the events surrounding the Winnipeg General Strike and the One Big Union; the secessions from the old-line political parties that launched the Progressives; and the secessions from the grain handling and marketing system that produced the cooperatives and the wheat pools. Regionalism was the term applied to this shift in the locus of power and in the requirements placed upon certain national institutions. It was a term coined to explain the apparently collective assault upon Canada's fabric by western residents in these heady decades. A model of "the Canadian region," and an assumption about both the Prairies and all the other parts of Canada had crystallized.

Phillips, Conway and Brodie follow Morton, Fowke, Mallory, Macpherson and a host of writers on farm protest in arguing that the manifestations of regional protest during the era of the so-called first National Policy were reactions to that very body of policies.[28] This interpretation of prairie-voting patterns from 1918-26 is reasonable, as far as it goes. It does not explain, however, why the One Big Union should have been founded on a regional secession from Canadian and American unions, or why western newspaper editors seceded from the Canadian Press syndicate in favour of the Western Associated Press, or why the establishment of the United Church should have been driven by western needs, attitudes and individuals. In each case, I believe, the assumption that regions existed, and that regional interests were primary interests in community life, and that regionalism was a fundamental interpretation of social organization, underlay their dissent. This cultural perspective, a supplement to the economic and political analysis, is pivotal to our appreciation of the regional "imagined community" that had just taken shape. Not surprisingly, these "regional" characteristics coincided with the formal prairie region.

Why did the consolidation of the prairie "imagined community" occur between 1900 and 1930 and why within these boundaries? The lines on the map help to explain the boundaries. Such cultural icons shape the way we think. So, too, does the administration of the territory; boundaries are made real by the activity of civil servants who work within the map's boundaries. In prairie Canada, to a degree now forgotten, the administration was the work of the federal government and thus was a unifying force. Ottawa treated the West, especially through the Department of the Interior, as a single administrative unit for lands and forests. Ottawa established policies, too, for naturalization and tariffs and police and Indians and transportation. Another explanation of the regional boundary rests upon the work of Winnipeg, the metropolis of the Prairies in that period, which sent its decrees from the grain exchange and stock yard and newspaper print shop (the boiler plate or "patent insides" that accompanied many prairie weeklies), and by means of an army of travelling salesmen. These metropolitan forces, too, generated a sense of a single community. The prairieness of this era was also sustained by the intellectual climate, a climate composed of equal parts frontier theory, staple thesis, environmentalism, and simple boosterism, which reinforced the perception that the Prairies constituted a new society, one truly in tune with the times.

Political innovations in the 1930s and 1940s, socialism and Social Credit, have also been attributed to a distinctive prairie regional behaviour. W.L. Morton described the 1930s and 1940s as the era of utopianism and suggested the rise of the two parties was the culmination of the previous biases in prairie politics. In other words, he linked these phenomena to the National Policy era that preceded 1930. No one would wish to deny the presence of East-bashing in some of the platform rhetoric of the 1930s but, by the same measure, CCF and Social Credit owed their electoral successes to far more than regional sentiments.

V.C. Fowke introduced a different perspective by arguing that the first National Policy had been completed by 1930 and that a second was struggling into life in these decades, commencing with the introduction of "social net" or wealth redistribution measures as part of a new Keynesian approach to economic planning.[29] How could the second National Policy be interpreted as a regional phenomenon? One might argue that the devastating prairie experience of depression, unique in its impact, drove Bracken and Dafoe and Douglas and Aberhart, unlike other political leaders, to adopt distinctive approaches to political economy, including social democratic and redistributive measures. Janine Brodie takes another tack by suggesting that the Prairies, whether or not they may have contributed to the introduction of Keynesian approaches, actually were the creation of them, in the sense that the second National Policy, like its predecessor, reinforced regional interests. Indeed, by targeting regional disparities as a primary concern of national politics, according to Brodie, the second National Policy contributed a significant new source of regionalism to Canadian public life. To me, this approach seems viable, especially if we link it to events in the 1960s and 1970s. However, the arguments in favour of a sharp divide in prairie history around 1930 and of prairie continuity during the next half century will require further elaboration.

Prairie unrest during the Trudeau era was focussed especially on federal government policies. Agricultural issues such as grain sales and freight rates and the temporary LIFT program to reduce crop production, control of such resources as oil and potash — indeed energy policy in general, bilingualism, metric measures, diversification of the prairie economy into secondary and tertiary sectors, multiculturalism, all could be said to have fuelled prairie protest between the late 1960s and the mid-1980s. Of course, Trudeau was held to be responsible for everything.[30] What was especially galling to prairie residents, as David Smith has suggested, was that many of these Liberal policies denied longstanding prairie conclusions. One official language, continuity on the family farm, the Crow's Nest Pass freight rate agreement and provincial control of natural resources belonged in the category of sacred trusts in prairie political life. Thus, "prairie regionalism" in this era was a means of describing the prairie revolt against federal policies and against the Liberal party.

The regionalism of the 1970s, indeed the regionalism that had been developing from the 1930s through the 1970s, differed from its predecessor. Though it inherited the causes and the fervour of the 1870-1930 model, this next phase of prairie regionalism was actually expressed through the province. As Roger Gibbins has demonstrated, prairie society became more like Ontario society in these decades. And, as Alan Cairns has argued so effectively, provincial governments assumed an increasingly prominent part in defining their communities. Moreover, Ottawa no longer ruled a fiefdom but, rather, treated all the provinces more or less equally. Winnipeg's economic leadership was superseded by provincial metropolises and by increasingly national and international trade flows. This was the generation of province building. Prairie regionalism in the 1970s simply reinforced the prevailing "provincialism."

What does such an historical review demonstrate? Popular outbursts occurred often in the Prairies during the century after 1870. Some of these expressions of discontent had their roots in aboriginal culture and in European Canadian blindness to the imperatives of that culture; such expressions should not be described as regionalism. The later protests targetted Macdonald's National Policy and probably were reinforced by the second National Policy. The protests demonstrated the ways in which the federal structure of government and the electoral system sustained territory-based loyalties in preference to those of class, gender or ethnicity. Changes in prairie Canada's relations with the international economy, as in the 1880s and after World War I and again in the 1930s and 1970s, also lay behind the conflict. Rather than enter a debate about the relative merits of regionalism and provincialism, I would prefer to argue that both are territory-based loyalties, both can be plausibly invoked in discussions of prairie history, and one is the heir of the other.[31] The key question, in my view, is the vehicle that carries and simultaneously diffuses the prairie political protest — before 1930, that vehicle was the federal party system; increasingly, after 1930, it was the system of federal-provincial relations.[32]

Our problem is not just to decide whether regionalism, based on the formal region or on the various provinces, has existed but to estimate how important the sentiment is. Does it play a role in public opinion in 1991 comparable to its role in 1941? 1921? 1901? 1881? How much does it really matter? One way to tackle such a difficult question is to approach it from the perspective of nation and nationalism.

In Canada, discussion of region often has provoked concern about nation, especially the unity of the nation, and often is said to contradict national identity. Northrop Frye was not happy with this concatenation of the two sentiments, love of nation and love of region, and preferred to separate them. He argued that they arose out of two very different concepts, unity and identity. In this view, "unity is national in reference, international in perspective, and rooted in a political feeling" whereas "identity is local and regional, rooted in the imagination and in works of culture."[33] Frye's perspective is interesting because it distinguishes between types of feeling. He suggests that sentiments concerning political loyalty — what might be called community subjects — can be separated from sentiments concerning personal identity. If Frye is correct, Mandel's work on prairie literature and prairie region must be revisited. Mandel posits that region in literature is an expression of personal identity. However, if the discussion of "identity questions" is separated from political feelings and other such territory-based loyalties, then we must redefine the cultural or "imagined" region. In this task, some recent work on nationalism might offer assistance.

The nation offers a helpful perspective upon smaller, territory-based, community loyalties (region, province, city, neighbourhood), because, in the last two centuries, it has become the essence of community. As Benedict Anderson has suggested, "nation-ness is the most universally legitimate value in the political life of our time." The nation, in Anderson's definition, is a limited, sovereign, imagined community: limited, in that it does not, in any single instance, cover all of humankind; sovereign within the boundaries of a given state; and a community in the sense that it is "imagined" as "a deep, horizontal comradeship."[34] The strengths of this recent and, I think, fruitful approach are that it treats communities as political places and that it distinguishes these political communities by "the style in which they are imagined." It takes no great leap of imagination to place the region and the province in the same scale as nation. We all possess a hierarchy of political or civic values associated with the imagined communities in which we live. Moreover, the standings within this hierarchy and the reasons for the ranking are probably subject to investigation. If region were profoundly important in the outlook of citizens resident in the Canadian Prairies, then it would tend toward nation; if province were paramount, then it would acquire nation-like attributes; if neither was as important as nation, or some other national alternative such as continental union, then it would not constitute an alternate nationalism. What is the relative importance of the various imagined communities in prairie society? Put another way, what is the cultural context of the Canadian prairie community?[35]

"Culture" is a very difficult word these days. Many cultural scholars now assert that their subject is just as likely to be primary — and important — as economics or technology. Their purpose is to subvert the customary assumption that "base," defined as material reality, determines superstructure; instead, they assert that "the representations of the social world themselves are the constituents of social reality." One of these advocates has written that "Economic and social relations are not prior to or determinants of cultural relations — they are themselves fields of cultural practice and cultural production."[36] Culture, in this perspective, is larger than the arts or the cultural industries, smaller than an entire way of life.[37] When we discuss culture, we are discussing the sense we make of our "selves" and situating that sense within our social order.

Little has been written on prairie culture from this perspective. Let us assume, for argument's sake, that the region, whether in its 1920-era prairiewide boundaries or its 1980-era provincial boundaries, might coincide with an imagined community. Where would it find its definition or rationale? One potential source of an imagined community is kinship.[38] National identity may also be expressed through language and religion. Of course, prairie Canada and its constituent provinces do not possess such genealogical continuity nor do they share a unique religion. On the other hand, the experience of prairie citizens during the preceding hundred years constitutes a relevant and important claim to a common prairie linguistic and religious heritage, one based on shared experience of linguistic assimilation and lost or, to put it more positively, redefined faith. These historical matters that prairie citizens experienced in common might constitute a foundation for a separate nationhood and, perhaps, could work in favour of a more powerful regional identity. This argument might be built on the contention that history, appropriately interpreted, has sustained many nationalisms in the

Americas. The argument might be plausible but the fact that it has not been made suggests that it simply does not hold water.

Another foundation of the imagined community is a network of communications, originally based on print but now also on electronic means, that establishes a feeling of simultaneity, or of shared political experience, across space, time and household. Yet another foundation is the network of functionaries in the modern state whose pilgrimages and very existence outline the boundaries and educate the imaginations of the citizenry. The communications networks did develop in the late nineteenth century on the Prairies. As we have seen they helped to sustain a prairie regional consciousness between 1880 and 1930. Thereafter, they declined in favour of continental, national and provincial empires. The professions linked by this communications web, including lawmakers, mapmakers, museum builders, archivists, census takers and government administrators, also shifted from a prairiewide to a provincial constituency in this century. The Hudson's Bay Company and the Department of the Interior, two pivotal "inventors of tradition" before 1870 and 1930 respectively, gave way to provincial and city leaders in the later decades of the twentieth century. All this would suggest that a prairiewide nationalism is a little less likely in the present than is a province-based alternate nation. But it offers little guidance about the relative power of the regional perspective.

The province-based communications networks and the inventors of provincial traditions have not received a great deal of attention in prairie scholarship. The failure of any single newspaper to sustain a regionwide circulation after World War I might be seen as evidence of provincial preeminence in post-1920 cultural networks. This same trend is reflected in the absence of prairiewide electronic media. Significantly, when the CBC entered the Prairies in 1939 and 1945-46 with its own stations, it set up provincial superstations of 50,000 watts. Language and schools issues were fundamental in prairie cultural history; again, it is noteworthy that ethnic cultural distinctiveness capsized on the rocks of provincial education policy. After 1945 and especially after 1970, prairie cultural history is noteworthy for the rise of provincial museums and heritage departments and cultural policies. Thus, we might find two phases in twentieth century prairie cultural history: the first illustrates the force of prairiewide regional consciousness before, roughly, the 1920s and 1930s, and the second is marked by the ascendancy of provincial consciousness in the next half century.[39] Indeed, David Smith has argued that the cultural shift could be discerned even in the twenty-five years between Saskatchewan's fiftieth jubilee celebration in 1955 and its seventy-fifth in 1980. Thus, by 1980, "when federal policies, including even cultural ones, were perceived as a threat to provincial integrity, the diamond jubilee identified the province as a distinct society. In the 1950s the emphasis was on overcoming isolation, in the 1980s it was on maintaining or developing separateness."[40]

Territory-based loyalty has long been important to residents of the Canadian

Prairies. Geography and policy choices and cultural expressions have ensured its continuity. This loyalty was once expressed in terms of a prairiewide imagined community and later through the province but there is no law that requires the continuation of such a cultural consensus. If the Confederation of Regions Party created a single prairie province, as it claims it would do, the formal, prairiewide region and the imagined regional community would soon coincide. The power of politics, government and the communications media that feed off them would ensure this result. But whether such loyalties really matter in the 1990s is not as clear; and whether any imagined community smaller than the continent can prevail in the days of globalization is even less certain. So much will depend on the power and ability of Canadians to establish as strong an imagined community as their forebears were able to do in the preceding 125 years.

Notes

1.   Cited in B. Kaye and D.W. Moodie, "Geographical Perspectives on the Canadian Plains," in Richard Allen, ed., *A Region of the Mind: Interpreting the Western Canadian Plains* (Regina: Canadian Plains Research Center, 1973), 18.

2.   J.B. Tyrell, ed., *David Thompson's Narrative of His Explorations in Western America 1784-1812* (Toronto: Champlain Society, 1916), 183.

3.   A.R.C. Selwyn and G.M. Dawson, *Descriptive Sketch of the Physical Geography and Geology of the Dominion of Canada* (Montreal: n.p., 1884). John Warkentin employs an earlier moment in this same generation to define the West. He contends that the exploring parties of Palliser and Dawson and Hind between 1857 and 1860 laid "the basic conceptual framework for our present interpretation of the physical geography of Western Interior Canada." See John Warkentin, *The Western Interior of Canada: A Record of Geographical Study, 1612-1917* (Toronto: McClelland and Stewart, 1964), 147.

4.   G. Smith, *Canada and the Canadian Question* (Toronto: Hunter Rose, 1891), 1-3.

5.   They are not, as I will argue later, entirely "wrong." See Donald F. Putnam, ed., *Canadian Regions: A Geography of Canada* (Toronto: J.W. Dent, 1952) and William C. Wonders, "Canadian Regions and Regionalism: National Enrichment or National Disintegration?" in Eli Mandel and David Taras, eds., *A Passion for Identity: Introduction to Canadian Studies* (Toronto: Methuen, 1987), 239-62.

6.   H.R.A. Pocock, *Tales of Western Life, Lake Superior and the Canadian Prairie* (Ottawa: n.p., 1888), 56, 62.

7.   Ralph Connor, *The Foreigner: A Tale of Saskatchewan* (Toronto: Westminster, 1909), 378.

8.   Griffith Taylor, *Canada: A Study of Cool, Continental Environments and Their Effect on British and French Settlement* (London: Methuen, 1947).

9.   Arthur S. Morton, *A History of the Canadian West to 1870-71* (1939; Toronto: University of Toronto Press, 1973).

10. Ronald Rees, *New and Naked Land: Making the Prairies Home* (Saskatoon: Western Producer Prairie Books, 1988).

11.   Janine Brodie, "The Concept of Region in Canadian Politics," in David P. Shugarman and Reg Whitaker, eds., *Federalism and Political Community: Essays in Honour of Donald Smiley* (Peterborough: Broadview Press, 1989), 42; also William Westfall, "On the Concept of Region in Canadian History and Literature," *Journal of Canadian Studies* 15, no. 2 (1980): 3-15.

12.   Adam Shortt, "Some Observations on the Great North-West," *Queen's Quarterly* 2 (1894-95): 184.

13.   Isaiah Bowman, *The Pioneer Fringe* (New York: Books for Librairies, 1931), v.

14.   W.A. Mackintosh, "Current Events," *Queen's Quarterly* 29 (1921-22): 312.

15.   S.D. Clark, "Foreword," in W.L. Morton, *The Progressive Party in Canada* (Toronto: University of Toronto Press, 1950), viii-xi.

16.   For most North American historians, the shorthand version of this approach to region, an approach that assumes one can distinguish stages of social formation, has been the frontier hypothesis of Frederick Jackson Turner. After all, it is no accident that Turner spent much of his career working on sections and sectionalism in American history. See Frederick Jackson Turner, *The Frontier in American History* (1920; New York: Holt, Rinehart and Winston, 1962); Michael C. Steiner, "The Significance of Turner's Sectional Thesis," *Western Historical Quarterly* 10 (1979): 437-66. However, because the distinction between "frontier as place" and "frontier as process" has never been clear, the implications of the frontier hypothesis for analysis of prairie regionalism have been uncertain. Moreover, the idea that American theories might have relevance for Canadians has also raised the hackles of some Canadian scholars. Neither objection need detain us. Canada, like the United States, is a North American nation, after all, and the frontier is, or was in Turner's thought, *both* a place and a process. In our terms, Canadian scholars who relied upon frontier characteristics to distinguish the prairie West were thinking in terms of a functional region.

Though not often remembered today, the "frontier" assumption was once a common place in Canadian discussion. Clifford Sifton observed in 1898 that party loyalty, an important basis of the Canadian community, did not prevail automatically in the newly settled regions: "One of the difficulties in politics in the west," he told Walter Scott in 1898, "is that matters do not run in well settled grooves which exist in the older communities. There is therefore extra need for friendliness on all hands." Saskatchewan Archives Board, Scott Papers, Sifton to Scott, 20 September 1898. The region, in this view, was "the West," and was defined in relation to older communities, for which one might read "the East." The West was different — it constituted a region — because it was a "frontier." Such attitudes became a reflex in Canadian public life between the 1880s and 1930s. The West occupied a distinct and obviously different stage of social development. See Henry Nash Smith, *Virgin Land: The American West in Symbol and Myth* (New York: Vintage Books, 1959), 267.

17.   Janine Brodie, *The Political Economy of Canadian Regionalism* (Toronto: Harcourt Brace Jovanovich, 1990).

18.   Edward A. McCourt, *The Canadian West in Fiction* (Toronto: Ryerson, 1970), 125.

19.   Eli Mandel, "Images of Prairie Man," in Allen, *A Region of the Mind*, 201-9; also Gerald Friesen, "Three Generations of Fiction: An Introduction to Prairie Cultural His-

tory," in D.J. Bercuson and P.A. Buckner, eds., *Eastern and Western Perspectives* (Toronto: University of Toronto Press, 1981), 183-96.

20. Alan Cairns, "The Governments and Societies of Canadian Federalism," *Canadian Journal of Political Science* (December 1977); Ramsay Cook, "Regionalism Unmasked," *Acadiensis* 13, no. 1 (1983); Donald Smiley, *The Federal Condition in Canada* (Toronto: McGraw-Hill Ryerson, 1986), 23.

21. Lovell Clark, "Regionalism? or Irrationalism?" *Journal of Canadian Studies* (Summer 1978): 119-24; J.M.S. Careless, "Limited Identities — Ten Years Later," *Manitoba History* 1 (1980): 3-9.

22. Garth Stevenson, "Canadian Regionalism in Continental Perspective," *Journal of Canadian Studies* (Summer 1980): 17.

23. See Brodie, *The Political Economy of Canadian Regionalism,* 12, summarizing Ralph Matthews, *The Creation of Regional Dependency* (Toronto: University of Toronto Press, 1983), 22.

24. This summary is taken from Brodie, *The Political Economy of Canadian Regionalism*; she is citing Raymond Breton, "Regionalism in Canada," in D. Cameron, ed., *Regionalism and Supranationalism* (Montreal: Institute for Research on Public Policy and Policy Studies Institute, 1981), 19.

25. Brodie, *The Political Economy of Canadian Regionalism, 77.*

26. It is a little early to decide about the impact on the Reform Party phenomenon of the early 1990s.

27. W.L. Morton, "The Bias of Prairie Politics," Royal Society of Canada, *Proceedings and Transactions*, Third Series, Vol. 49 (1955); Doug Owram, "The Myth of Louis Riel," *Canadian Historical Review* 53, no. 3 (1982) and Owram, *Promise of Eden: The Canadian Expansionist Movement and the Idea of the West 1856-1900* (Toronto: University of Toronto Press, 1980).

28. Paul Phillips, *Regional Disparities* (Toronto: J. Lorimer, 1978); John Conway, *The West: The History of a Region in Confederation* (Toronto: J. Lorimer, 1983); Brodie surveys this literature in *The Political Economy of Canadian Regionalism*, chapter 5.

29. V.C. Fowke, "The National Policy — Old and New," *Canadian Journal of Economics and Political Science* (1952); Donald Smiley, "Canada and the Quest for a National Policy," *Canadian Journal of Political Science* (1975).

30. David Smith, *The Regional Decline of a National Party: Liberals on the Prairies* (Toronto: University of Toronto Press, 1981).

31. Frederick Jackson Turner preferred the term sectionalism; Michael C. Steiner, "The Significance of Turner's Sectional Thesis," *Western Historical Quarterly* 10 (1979): 437-66.

32. Roger Gibbins, *Prairie Politics and Society: Regionalism in Decline* (Toronto: Butterworths, 1980); Cairns, "The Governments and Societies of Canadian Federalism."

33. Northrop Frye, *The Bush Garden: Essays on the Canadian Imagination* (Toronto: Anansi, 1971), i-iii.

34. Benedict Anderson, *Imagined Communities: Reflections on the Origin and Spread of Nationalism* (1983; London: Routledge Chapman and Hall, 1991), 4.

35. Culture has become a point of convergence in the human disciplines. As social history has matured and displaced politics and economics as the central organizing principle of historical inquiry, it has simultaneously grown so complex and varied that its organizing principles — history from below, the story of an entire society, limited identities of class and ethnic group and gender — have lost the shock of the new. Its variety of approaches ensures that social history no longer constitutes an automatic challenge to power relations. In addition, the struggle for control in society has moved on. In a world built on service and knowledge, the wage nexus is less influential in life than is communication itself.

Culture has become a scholarly battleground. I am not using the word in the anthropological sense of all aspects of a whole and distinctive way of life. Nor am I equating culture with the arts, especially the high arts, as one would in describing a cultured individual, or the low arts, as we might in pointing to a television show as popular culture. Rather, I wish to follow a line between the two in defining culture as "the ways in which people perceive, make intelligible and organize their being." See Maria Tippett, "The Writing of English-Canadian Cultural History 1970-1985," *Canadian Historical Review* 67, no. 4 (December 1986): 548.

To follow Raymond Williams, culture in this sense should be seen as "the signifying system through which necessarily (though among other means) a social order is communicated, reproduced, experienced and explored." Raymond Williams, *Culture* (Glasgow: Fontana, 1981), 13. As John Fiske says, culture takes "the meanings we make of our social experience, ... the sense we have of our 'selves' " and "situates those meanings within the social system." See John Fiske, *Television Culture* (London: Methuen, 1987), 20.

36. Lynn Hunt, "Introduction: History, Culture, and Text," in Hunt, ed., *The New Cultural History* (Berkeley: University of California Press, 1989), 7; also Roger Chartier in ibid.

37. The fact that such an elaborate introduction is necessary demonstrates how irrelevant the present constitutional restrictions on Quebec's distinct society clause must necessarily be.

38. Perry Anderson, "Nation-States and National Identity," *London Review of Books* 13, no. 9 (9 May 1991).

39. *Prairie Forum* 15, no. 2 (Fall 1990) devoted an entire issue to "Heritage Conservation." It contains two articles by Jean Friesen entitled "Introduction: Heritage Futures" and "Heritage: The Manitoba Experience"; Don Kerr's "In Defence of the Past: A History of Saskatchewan Heritage Preservation, 1922-1983" and Mark Rasmussen's "The Heritage Boom: Evolution of Historical Resource Conservation in Alberta," each of which sustains this emphasis on the rise of provincial consciousness. Also see Gerald Friesen, "The Manitoba Historical Society: A Centennial History," *Manitoba History* 4 (1982): 2-9.

40. David Smith, "Celebrations and History on the Prairies," *Journal of Canadian Studies* 17, no. 3 (Fall 1982): 55.

2

The Politics of Place:
Regionalism and Community
in Atlantic Canada

Margaret Conrad

INTRODUCTION

I have taken as my point of departure the felicitous phrase used by John Friedmann and Yvon Forest in a paper presented to a conference on regionalism held in Grand Pré, Nova Scotia, in 1985.[1] According to Friedmann and Forest, "among academics of regional planning, a subtle but significant shift has taken place away from a predominant concern with economics to a politics of place." They argue that the politics of place demands a new model of regional planning,

> where the shift is away from an emphasis on functional regions to regions that are historically defined; from an emphasis on state and corporate action to one in which a politically mobilized regional population becomes the main protagonist; from an emphasis on reactive to proactive planning; from long-term spacial equilibrium to spacial conflict and struggle; and from an objective of simple economic growth to one of complex growth and development as an expression of regional priorities.[2]

This perspective appeals to me both as an historian and as an Atlantic Canadian. In my own work I have argued that regionalism is a highly subjective and flexible concept, sometimes used politically by Atlantic Canadians to justify demands on the federal treasury. It is also, I have argued, an economically and politically rooted phenomenon that implies, if not a unique world view, at least a peculiar angle of vision on national and international events.[3] The most obvious regional reality setting the Atlantic Provinces apart from the rest of Canada today is a persistent economic underdevelopment and consequent political impotence. This reality we now understand more fully owing to the work of scholars who have examined the centralizing tendencies of industrial capitalism and bureaucratic federalism.[4] We are also beginning to explore the political responses to underdevelopment and dependency in Atlantic Canada. In the long struggle for what Colin Howell has aptly termed a "meaningful federalism,"[5] Atlantic Canadians have experimented with a variety of strategies: threats of separation, support for third parties, demands for Maritime Rights, obsequious subservience to the party in office, and efforts to co-opt national policies. These strategies represent the politics of place manifested in its most formal sense, and will be the major focus of this paper.

At a less formal level it is also clear that the Atlantic regional identity is more than an angle of vision and a political posture. Indeed, the sense of regional identity is historically and culturally deeply rooted and remarkably resilient, having survived more than a century of dramatic and often debilitating shocks. Now, like peoples elsewhere around the world, Atlantic Canadians are being asked once again to develop strategies to preserve their regional identity, to advance regional objectives in the face of global restructuring, and to assert a greater measure of control over the forces of social and economic change. This is not an easy task. As Friedmann and Forest argue, "Subject purely to market forces, historically formed regions are constantly at risk of losing their identity" and "becoming subject to the 'logic' of global capital."[6] Given this perspective, the regional question can now be framed in another way — what role will regional identity play in efforts by people in Atlantic Canada to adjust to, shape and resist global market forces? And, ultimately, is the region's social and cultural distinctiveness worth preserving as a life space for Atlantic Canadians in the twenty-first century? The answer to the second part of this question will, no doubt, depend on the outcome of the first, given that history is written after the fact and by the winners. Nevertheless, it is imperative that we in Atlantic Canada come to terms with what it is we want to preserve as we go through the purifying fires of global restructuring. Whether we like it or not we in Atlantic Canada will face our biggest challenge of the century as we struggle to find a space in the global, as well as national, frame of reference, both of which are being radically redefined in the 1990s.

Given the emphasis that I place on context and conflict, it should come as no surprise that I do not see centralizing bureaucrats in Ottawa as exclusively the problem, local control as the only vehicle for delivering reform, or Maritime/Atlantic Union as necessarily the solution to anything. These and other policy thrusts must be assessed in the context of the social practices and political struggles which constitute our present precarious condition. Since regional identity is nothing more or less than the culture of the people living and working in a defined area, Atlantic Canadians, at any given time, will always have an identity of some kind. It is the range of human agency and the quality of our choices, in the contested terrain of the late twentieth century, that is at stake.

Having declared my own position on the question of region, I will not spend more time elaborating upon what has already become one of the most discussed concepts of our era. Nor will I focus on the various theories of regional planning which have been well documented by economists and political scientists.

Instead, I will outline briefly the contours of the Atlantic region as they have evolved historically, describe the political movements that have emanated from the region since Confederation,[7] and comment upon where our regional politics seems to be taking us.

THE ATLANTIC REGION

Like the prairie region,[8] Atlantic Canada is a geographic diversity drawn together by economic and cultural history. A miscellaneous group of islands, peninsulas and northeastern fringes of the North American continent, the region is not defined solely by its geographic heterogeneity and exposure to the North Atlantic.[9] If it were, the Magdalen and Anticosti islands, as well as St. Pierre and Miquelon and the Gaspé, would be an integral part of the region. Nevertheless, an intricate configuration of ocean and land is typical of the Atlantic region and offered early inhabitants — both North American Indian and European new-comer — easy access to the great resources of fish, timber and agricultural land, and provided them with the basis for a degree of economic and cultural cohesiveness.

The Atlantic Ocean facilitated the early penetration of the region by European explorers and immigrants, but at the same time imposed a decentralized economic development. Unlike the Prairies, where an uneasy unity prevailed under the hegemony of the Hudson's Bay Company, the Atlantic region in the colonial era nurtured diversity. Fishing, lumbering and shipbuilding flourished throughout the region, never focussing in one great metropolitan centre, rarely permitting a few individuals to dominate resources so readily accessible by na-ture. Ocean access also made the region an obvious site in the eighteenth century of the struggle between France and Britain for imperial domination. Like the Vietnamese and Poles in the twentieth century, the aboriginal peoples and Acadians were the losers in imperial battles, and British immigrants filled the "empty" spaces. The overwhelming majority of people living in Atlantic Canada today are descended from immigrants who settled — or in the case of aboriginals and Acadians, resettled in the region between 1749 and 1850. By the time of Confederation, over 80 percent of the population of the Atlantic region was Canadian-born.[10] This fact helps to explain the general discomfort with the "scheme" for political union devised by the "Canadians" in the 1860s. New-foundlanders, Islanders, New Brunswickers, Nova Scotians — and subgroups such as Micmac, Acadians, Scots and Cape Bretoners — had already carved out a social space for themselves in the Atlantic region, and were justifiably wary of a new world order based on large, centralized nation states. The rootedness of Atlantic Canadians is still a regional reality, the source for jokes and comments by "people from away." It is also the source of a complex set of regional iden-tities more easily experienced than explained.[11]

It is impossible here to discuss in detail the institutional manifestations of regional culture that had taken root in Atlantic Canada by the mid-nineteenth century; however, it is important to note that, well over a century ago, the apparatus of commercial, political, intellectual and spiritual life was in place, and has survived, with surprisingly few modifications, to the present day. In the case of universities, to take one example, more than half of those institutions now operating in the region — and presently being threatened with "rationalization" — were established prior to Confederation. It was not uncommon for many colonial institutions (those of a religious and commercial nature, especially) to have local, provincial, regional and even international dimensions. Nor was it unusual for jurisdictions to overlap and conflict. Carman Miller has pointed out that on the eve of Confederation the maritime region "resembled nothing more than a loose confederation of sub-regions which defied existing political boundaries."[12] In particular, the Bay of Fundy and the Northumberland Strait, and to a lesser extent the Gulf of Saint Lawrence, offered the basis for interregional community in the age of sail. Subregions and international linkages are still a significant feature of Atlantic Canada's complex identity.

By the time of Confederation, Atlantic Canadians had only a brief encounter with the workings of responsible government, but they already had a long and continuous history of formal political activity. Except for the New Brunswick and Labrador boundaries, and the short-lived experiment with a separate administration in Cape Breton between 1784 and 1820, the present provincial borders were in place by 1784. The small size and seeming overabundance of political units in the region have long been a cause for comment and concern. Although it has been claimed, with some justification, that the cost of provincial administrations is excessive, the politics of place is sometimes well served in national and international arenas by the diversified leadership nurtured in the region's provincial capitals. Indeed, submerged minorities throughout the world, and even the people living in our own northern territories, might well envy the degree of political autonomy exercised in Atlantic Canada.[13]

When the Fathers of Confederation met in Charlottetown and Quebec City their discourse revealed a variety of shared assumptions about the "regions" of British North America, including the Prairies and Atlantic Canada, although these were not the terms then in vogue. The deadlocked Canadians finally agreed to a course of action in 1864 which, in their words, would "pledge themselves to bring in a measure next session for the purpose of removing existing difficulties by introducing the federal principle into Canada, coupled with such provisions as will permit the Maritime Provinces and the North-West Territory to be incorporated into the same system of Government."[14] Speaking in Montreal on the heels of the Charlottetown and Quebec conferences, George-Etienne Cartier made a plea for maritime support:

> I must repeat to you what I stated while in the Lower Provinces, that while we possessed the personal and the territorial elements which go to constitute a nation, we were wanting in the maritime element. During six months of the year we had to knock at the door of our neighbour in order to carry on

our trade. I know that every citizen of Montreal will understand that at this
critical time we should look to Nova Scotia, to New Brunswick, and Prince
Edward Island for the elements wanting in Canada to make a great nation.[15]

Similarly, Joseph Howe, in arguing against Confederation maintained, somewhat
ingenuously, in 1866:

Though I have never proposed any scheme of union, I have no invincible
objection to become a unionist provided anybody will show me a scheme
which does not sacrifice the interests of the Maritime Provinces.[16]

Clearly "maritime provinces" was a term already widely used at the time of
Confederation and was synonymous with "lower provinces" for the "Upper
Canadians." These terms usually did not encompass Newfoundland, which then,
as now, stands slightly aloof from the maritime provinces. "Canada" or the
"upper provinces" in the 1860s meant exclusively the old province of Canada,
which cynics would suggest still is the focus of "Canadian" government. The
North-West Territories, at that time were still a vague concept. (As an aside to
the conference organizers, I would point out that to be "politically correct" in the
historical sense the program should have focussed upon the maritime provinces
rather than Atlantic Canada, leaving Newfoundland and British Columbia to
form the balance of our fearful Canadian symmetry.)

THE POLITICS OF PLACE

As Joseph Howe implied and historian Phillip Buckner has recently argued,
Maritimers were not opposed to Confederation *per se*; only to the terms of union
as embodied in the Quebec resolutions.[17] With the federal government in control
of customs revenues, the smaller provinces were left with per capita grants inadequate to finance growing provincial debts for such essential public services as
transportation and education. It may well have been the case that the maritime
provinces would have run into financial difficulties had they remained independent — Newfoundland, which descended into bankruptcy and was stripped
of its democratic rights during the Depression of the 1930s, offers a sobering
case study[18] — but once in the union Maritimers could not help but compare
their progress with that of their counterparts in the larger and wealthier provinces, just as Canadians tended to compare their progress with that of their neighbour to the south. Moreover, Maritimers knew that geographic size alone was not
the cause of their economic plight. In nineteenth-century Great Britain, a bundle
of islands off the coast of Europe served as a model for their development.
Japan offers a similar example in the twentieth century. What was to prevent the
Atlantic provinces from duplicating such successes?

The goals of the pro-Confederation forces in the Maritimes were clear. Nova
Scotia's much maligned Father of Confederation Charles Tupper spoke openly
about his motives in supporting the creation of a strong central government. In
1866 he declared:

> Under the Quebec scheme the power to levy an export duty on coal was left in the hands of the Local Governments. We have changed that ourselves. ... I regard them [coal mines] as the great source of Provincial wealth and prosperity. ... In fact, the possession of coal mines, together with other natural advantages must, in the course of time, make Nova Scotia the great emporium of manufactures in British America. We felt that in taking out of the power of any legislature to double the amount of royalty, we were giving guarantee to capitalists who might come in and invest their money in these coal mines.[19]

Tupper also insisted that there be a constitutional guarantee of an intercolonial railroad linking the Maritimes to the Canadas. Unfortunately, Tupper's goals of regional industrial development and British North American integration were never achieved as he had envisioned them. Indeed, as Ged Martin has recently pointed out: "Hindsight may yet conclude that while the Antis lost the battle, they won at least some of the arguments."[20]

Since New Brunswickers and Prince Edward Islanders fought elections around the issue of Confederation, it can be argued that they chose their destiny democratically. Nova Scotians, however, were manoeuvred into union. As soon as they had the opportunity to do so, they elected anti-confederate members to the provincial and federal legislatures, and introduced bills to repeal the hated union. Britain's refusal to countenance such a move, and Ottawa's timely offer of "better terms," as well as the implementation of tariff and trade policies widely supported in the Maritimes, gradually defused the first separatist movement in Canada. But resentment lingered, as did the fundamental objections to the fiscal arrangements imposed by Confederation. Meanwhile, "Canadians" dominated the federal parliament and the civil service, making it necessary for Maritimers to use extra-parliamentary pressure to secure even modest ends, and to resort to the binding glue of patronage if all else failed, which it usually did.[21] As the Dominion expanded, the relative strength of the maritime contingent in Parliament shrank even further. When, in 1905, Saskatchewan and Alberta became provinces on terms that offered them generous provincial subsidies, and in 1912 the older provinces of Quebec, Ontario and Manitoba doubled in size as a result of federal largesse, Maritimers became outraged over what seemed to them to be the unfair way in which the resources of the nation were being apportioned.

While it is true that, prior to Confederation, Maritimers were slow to propose alternatives to the Quebec resolutions, once Confederation was a *fait accompli*, they offered a variety of methods by which their needs could be accommodated. Even as they accepted the "better terms" offered in 1869 (which included a "finality clause" attached by representatives from Ontario), the anti-confederate members of the Nova Scotia Assembly defiantly passed a resolution in which they asserted the province's right to a larger subsidy, and demanded an amendment to the BNA Act that would give Nova Scotia and New Brunswick representation in the House of Commons equal to that of Quebec, and permit senators to be appointed by provincial legislatures.[22] These were not frivolous demands; they still appear on provincial wish lists of desired reforms and occasionally even in the constitutional proposals of desperate federal administrations.

Between 1884 and 1886 the Liberal government in Nova Scotia, facing a bankrupt treasury and demands for more railways, conducted a spirited campaign for better financial terms under Confederation. Macdonald stalled and then refused to make concessions, with the result that, in 1886, Premier Fielding introduced a motion in the assembly calling for repeal of Confederation and a maritime union, if constitutional reform was not forthcoming from Ottawa. Should the other maritime provinces refuse to cooperate, Fielding was prepared to go it alone. In the words of the resolution:

> That if it be found impossible after negotiations for that purpose, to secure the co-operation of the respective Governments of the sister provinces in withdrawing from the Confederation and entering instead into a Maritime Union, then this Legislature deems it absolutely necessary that Nova Scotia, in order that its railways and other public works and services may be extended and maintained as the requirements of the people need them; its industry properly fostered, its commerce invigorated and expanded, and its financial interests placed upon a sound basis, such as was the case previous to Confederation, should ask permission from the Imperial Parliament to withdraw from the Union with Canada and return to the *status* of a Province of Great Britain, with full control over all fiscal laws and tariff regulations within the Province, such as prevailed previous to Confederation.[23]

The motion passed, but the thrust of the repeal campaign was blunted by regional support for Macdonald's National Policy. In short order, Nova Scotia's demands were drowned in the growing chorus of complaints from other provinces.[24] When new financial arrangements were hammered out at federal-provincial conferences in 1902 and 1906, the Maritimes fared badly in the bargaining process.[25]

This failure was critical. While politicians were debating fiscal reform, the industrial revolution was proceeding apace. T.W. Acheson has argued that in the early years of the National Policy, maritime entrepreneurs managed to make a rather successful transition from seaward to land-based industries but, when uncoordinated growth gave way to consolidation, the head offices of businesses, banks and transportation concerns gravitated to the St. Lawrence heartland.[26] People, parliamentary seats and power followed them. Migration of as many as one in three Maritimers in the fifty year period between 1881 and 1931 testified to the inability of the region to support its own population, let alone attract newcomers from the rising flood of immigrants arriving by the turn of the century.[27]

As was the case in the 1880s, fiscal and economic difficulties of crisis proportions caused maritime politicians and businessmen to consider regional cooperation. Members of the Maritime Board of Trade were particularly attracted to the old idea of maritime union. In 1908 New Brunswick premier H.D. Hazen called for a "united Acadia," to resist further decreases in maritime parliamentary representation.[28] Despite concerted and coordinated efforts on the part of the premiers of the three maritime provinces to restore the absolute number of seats held at the time of Confederation — provincial conferences were convened in 1910 and 1913 to deal with the matter — little was achieved. The only concession to maritime concerns was an amendment to the BNA Act which guaranteed that representation in the House of Commons would not be less than the number of Senators representing a province.[29] For Prince Edward Island, this move meant that its elected representation could not be reduced to fewer than four, scarcely the contingent required for dramatic parliamentary manoeuvres.

Immediately following World War I the maritime provinces experienced a devastating economic collapse. Farmers and organized labour turned briefly to third parties in their efforts to improve their prospects.[30] Protest was soon channelled into the Maritime Rights movement which mobilized support from many sectors and all three provincial governments in the region. The Maritime Board of Trade again figured prominently in defining this brand of regional discontent. Nova Scotia once more led the way, but this time the Conservative, rather than the Liberal, party appeared in the vanguard of the campaign. With federal Liberals clinging tenuously to power, and the West well represented by its Progressive members, oppositional politics seemed like the best means of placing maritime concerns on the national agenda. Secessionist sentiment continued to be expressed, but such a notion was steadfastly opposed by the movement's leadership. The goal of Maritime Rights was the fulfillment of the promise of Confederation, not the dismantlement of the union, a point widely conceded by the various Conservative leaders who used the movement to win elections.[31]

In response to the chorus of political discontent on the east coast, the King administration established a Royal Commission on Maritime Claims, chaired by British lawyer and industrialist Andrew Rae Duncan, to investigate the situation. The commissioners conspicuously ignored any "rights" that the region may have had to a share of the nation's wealth, and they rejected the regional view of Canadian history carefully articulated in provincial submissions to the Commission. It is therefore not surprising that the Commission's recommendations fell somewhat short of what was required to meet the demand for equity within Confederation. There would be no call for major constitutional adjustments to address the issue of regional disparity. Instead, a list of modest legislative reforms — always subject to modification — were advanced, including improved provincial subsidies, reduced freight rates, harbour commissions and, tellingly, better service from the Dominion Bureau of Statistics.[32] As E.R. Forbes has pointed out, the commissioners were sympathetic to the plight of the aggrieved Maritimers and offered practical solutions, but, in the final analysis, their report was used by Ottawa and by local elites to diffuse discontent, not to solve the underlying causes of it. Maritimers thus entered the Depression at the bottom of the provincial heap, and were so strapped financially that they had difficulty participating in the new federal cost-sharing programs that might have helped to alleviate the suffering of the most disadvantaged of the region's population.[33]

Although the Maritime Rights movement achieved less than many had hoped for, it nevertheless had a significant impact. It left a legacy of regional cooperation and a collective sense of regional grievance that would continue to inform public policy and popular opinion. Maritime Rights also marked a turning point in regional strategy. Prior to the collapse of the maritime economy in the 1920s, most of the expressions of regional discontent were provincially generated and fought, in part because the developing doctrine of provincial rights seemed the most acceptable language in which to couch demands for regional assistance, and, of course, also because provincial administrations were in the best position organizationally to mount an assault on Ottawa. By the 1920s new notions about the role of the state, reinforced by World War I and progressive political thought, made it possible for the poorer provinces in Confederation to supplement the provincial rights doctrine with demands for equity and social justice. In its submission to the Royal Commission on Maritime Claims, the Nova Scotia government argued that:

> It should not be beyond the resources of statesmanship so to distribute the benefits of Canadian federation so that all the partners may have a just share. To express it in economic terms, the problem of Canadian prosperity is one of distribution, not of production. There is enough to go around if certain adjustments and compromises are made.[34]

The Duncan Commission report echoed these sentiments:

> We believe that the claims which these provinces have submitted in connection with the present condition, and the future possibilities, of their own part of the Dominion, should now be viewed with sympathetic consideration and understanding, so that in approaching the future, a better balance of territorial prosperity can be assured, and the original hope of Confederation — unity, prosperity and contentment for all the provinces, as well as of the whole of Canada — can be made capable of realization.[35]

When North America as a whole began to experience the tragedy of economic collapse during the Depression, the rationales hitherto voiced in relation to the Maritimes suddenly gained wider respect and sympathy. The report of the Rowell-Sirois Commission investigation into dominion-provincial relations released on the eve of World War II legitimized the notion of "fiscal need" as a justification for federal action, and recommended a variety of measures, including "National Adjustment Grants," as a means of maintaining an acceptable standard of services in the poorer provinces.[36]

Facing opposition from the richer provinces and preoccupied with various universal welfare programs, the federal government was slow to respond to the demand for "regional development" in the years during and immediately following World War II. Under Ottawa's reconstruction program, the unemployed, aged and dependent received the same benefits wherever they lived in Canada, while provinces were encouraged to give up their exclusive right to income, corporation and succession taxes so that the federal government could pursue its centralized planning to maximum effect. However, it soon became clear that welfare measures and centralized fiscal planning alone would not redistribute wealth on a geographic basis. University of Toronto political economist Harold Innis, writing to Nova Scotia Premier Angus L. Macdonald in January 1946, noted prophetically:

> I have always felt that these various devices for full employment implied grave dangers for the Maritimes in that full employment is apt to mean prosperity on the St. Lawrence and the continued steady drain of population and revenues from the Maritimes. It must be kept in mind that uniform monetary measures will not operate to the equal advantage of all regions.[37]

It was in this context, one in which a "new" national policy based on social and economic planning was being forged,[38] that the "Atlantic revolution" gained momentum.

In 1957 University of New Brunswick historian W.S. MacNutt used the term "Atlantic revolution" to describe events of the 1950s in the on-going struggle between Ottawa and the Atlantic provinces for a meaningful federalism.[39] As I have argued elsewhere,[40] this is a useful designation, not only because it helps us to distinguish developments in the 1950s from the movements for better terms, repeal and Maritime Rights that went on before, but also because, in the larger sense, Atlantic Canadians lived through revolutionary times in the postwar decades. Moreover, like Quebec, where the term "revolution" is more commonly applied in this period,[41] Atlantic Canada produced a class of professionals and bureaucrats who articulated the goals and coordinated the direction of the movement. Although professionals and civil servants have not always been in agreement with politicians on issues of regional policy,[42] they have become, along with local business and political elites, major players in the politics of place in Atlantic Canada.

The 1950s proved to be a relatively good time for Maritimers to launch their crusade. New ideas about regional development circulating internationally fed into maritime goals while a number of federal initiatives in other regions of the nation — the St. Lawrence Seaway and the Trans-Canada Pipeline were the most spectacular — set a positive example. The addition of Newfoundland to the regional equation in 1949 was also significant for the Atlantic revolution. It quadrupled the geographic area of Atlantic Canada, added seven seats in the House of Commons, and, under Joey Smallwood's energetic leadership, brought a fresh perspective to bear on regional strategy. From the maritime viewpoint Newfoundland's Confederation agreement was generous, including a substantial subsidy and a constitutional guarantee under Term 29 that a royal commission would be established within eight years of the Confederation agreement to review the province's financial position and determine what assistance might be needed to keep Newfoundland's level of services equal to those of the maritime provinces. Such a stipulation reflected the regional approach embedded in national policy decisions, and offered considerable incentive for Newfoundlanders to think regionally.[43]

The symbiotic relationship between Newfoundland and the maritime provinces created by their common economic plight offers a striking contrast to the western provinces where, Gerald Friesen argues,[44] region building has given way in the postwar period to province building. At one level this is also true of the Atlantic region; indeed, has always been true in this community of communities. But unlike the prairie provinces, the Atlantic provinces in the postwar period did not display widely different economic conditions or political approaches. Ottawa continued to treat the region as a unit for specialized policies, and, although provincial administrations often went their own separate ways, there was a shared sense of federal purpose. Dependency, of course, made it difficult to mount a regionally based political party, but it did not prevent the region's leaders from asserting as much power as they could muster over the federal-provincial process. Angus L. Macdonald, having spent five years in the federal cabinet during the war, was particularly sceptical of any policy emanating from Ottawa,[45] but all Atlantic premiers and an unusually high proportion of voters shared his cynicism.[46]

Unfortunately for Newfoundland and the region generally, the maritime provinces in the postwar period continued their economic decline in relation to the rest of Canada. Emerging from World War II with a per capita income 24 percent below the national average, the region sank to 33 percent in 1955 (and 37 percent when Newfoundland is included in the tabulation). Secondary industries in the Maritimes accounted for only 2.2 percent of the national increase from 1946 to 1953, while Ontario's share in the corresponding period was 56.6 percent. In 1953, the net value of secondary industry in the Atlantic provinces was $94 per capita; the national average was $405 and Ontario's, $696.[47] At the same time, the expansion of state services in the postwar period put a severe strain on provincial treasuries. In 1951 New Brunswick's administration was forced to accept an "advisor" by its creditors, Prince Edward Island continued to give annual evidence of its modest financial resources, and even the Newfoundland government which had entered Confederation with a surplus of over $40 million, found its treasury rapidly dwindling under the twin demands of social services and economic development. In Nova Scotia the collapse of the coal industry made massive layoffs and depleted provincial revenues a certainty.

The social implications of underdevelopment, dependency and rapid transformation in Atlantic Canada can be deduced from the statistical evidence. In the decade of the 1950s, the number of people engaged in primary industries in the four Atlantic provinces declined by over 50,000. (In percentage terms those engaged in agriculture declined by 49 percent; in forestry by 24.5 percent; in fishing and trapping by 37 percent; and in mining by 22.2 percent.) The manufacturing sector also showed a small decline, with 4,000 fewer people engaged in secondary industry in 1961 than ten years earlier. Unable to find jobs, some 82,000 people left the region in the 1950s, following the 93,000 who had migrated in the previous decade. Those who stayed behind found work in the expanding trade and service sectors where, in the 1950s, jobs increased by over 75,000. By 1961 direct government employment accounted for over 100,000 jobs in Atlantic Canada, not including defense activities which employed as many people (41,164) as forestry (21,089) and mining (16,030) combined. Perhaps even more revealing of deep structural transformation was the fact that the number of paying jobs held by men in the region actually decreased by 5,000 (-1.1 percent) during the decade while women in the labour force increased by 35.9 percent to 135,000.[48]

Notwithstanding the social upheaval, there was no great announcement or cataclysmic event to signal the advent of the Atlantic revolution. Only the boring succession of briefs and bylaws, annual meetings and agendas, heralded the new era of bureaucratic federalism. Once again, the Maritime Board of Trade figured prominently in behind-the-scenes manoeuvring, most notably in the creation of the Atlantic Provinces Economic Council (APEC) in 1954. This time New Brunswick, under Conservative Premier Hugh John Flemming, rather than Nova Scotia, took the lead in mounting the regional campaign against Ottawa's unwillingness to tailor national policy to the region's needs. Flemming demanded subsidies for his Beechwood power project as a *quid quo pro* for assistance to the St. Lawrence Seaway development and pressured Ottawa to support a flexible interest rate policy for regions where unemployment rather than inflation was the major economic problem.[49] Like his predecessor, St. Laurent submitted the region's plight to yet another commission. Established in 1955, it was chaired by Walter Gordon and was charged with examining the economic prospects of Canada as a whole. Meanwhile, some of the money in the vast defense budget was diverted to military bases in the region and Walter Harris's 1956 budget included an equalization formula based on the income of the two wealthiest provinces.

These measures exhausted the limits, at least for the time being, of federal thinking on the matter of regional disparities. Speaking to the Canadian Congress of Labour in Toronto on 24 April 1956, St. Laurent challenged Atlantic Canadians to produce "the initiative and ideas" to accomplish the redevelopment they were demanding.[50] St. Laurent might have chosen a more appropriate location than Toronto to issue his challenge, but his timing could not have been better. Hugh John Flemming was facing an election as well as huge provincial debts incurred by Beechwood. He could not let such an opportunity pass. Encouraged by Michael Wardell, the British-born publisher of the Fredericton *Daily Gleaner* and *Atlantic Advocate*, Flemming sent a telegram to each of his Atlantic colleagues (with a copy to St. Laurent) inviting them to a meeting in Fredericton to make plans for cooperative action. Flemming gave his telegram to the press, an action which not only put the other premiers on the spot but also brought an offer from the president of APEC to help coordinate the regional response to St. Laurent.[51] I have already chronicled the sequel to these developments — the Atlantic Premiers' Conference, APEC manoeuvres and the Conservative Party's timely Atlantic Provinces Manifesto — elsewhere and will not repeat the details here.[52] It is sufficient to point out that eventually all federal parties included concessions to the Atlantic provinces in their platforms, the report of the Royal Commission on Canada's Economic Prospects endorsed interventionist policies to rehabilitate the region, and sympathetic legislation was forthcoming, especially during the minority administrations of 1957, 1962 and 1963. In the short period from 1956 to 1965 the Atlantic revolution succeeded in winning recognition of the equalization principle, Atlantic Provinces Adjustment grants, and the Atlantic Development Board, in short, the apparatus of regional development that is still more or less in place. It also stimulated some of the most ambitious and controversial provincial initiatives in economic and social planning undertaken in this country. These include outport resettlement in Newfoundland,[53] the "equal opportunity" program in New Brunswick,[54] the industrial estates initiative in Nova Scotia,[55] and the virtual takeover of Prince Edward Island by the "planners" in the late 1960s.[56]

Like the Maritimes Rights Movement, the Atlantic revolution fell short of its aims. The average income in Atlantic Canada is still well below the national average, and much energy has been expended in analysing the reasons for the failure of regional planning to achieve the desired effect.[57] Nevertheless, the legacy of the Atlantic revolution is still very much with us. It established the goal of regional equality within Confederation which is enshrined, however narrowly circumscribed, in Section 36 of the Constitution; it created bureaucratic structures to fight the internecine battles that regional policy struggles now entail; and it sanctioned the role of the interventionist state at both the federal and provincial levels in dealing with regional disparity. It is this shaky edifice, built over a century of federal-provincial interaction, that is now being threatened with demolition as other priorities emerge to dominate national and international agendas.[58]

AFTERWORD

The foregoing chronicle suggests that Atlantic Canadians have become adept practitioners of the politics of place. At one level, surely, we can take some comfort from the fact that maritime Canadians, and Newfoundlanders, have been reasonably successful during a century of rapid economic transformation in maintaining and adapting regionally based social and political institutions. Nevertheless we can not rest on our past achievements, as modest as they might be. At present, provincial task forces in Atlantic Canada are pouring over constitutional proposals, and "rationalization" threatens to transform many of our time-honoured traditions and institutions. Meanwhile, there is talk of decentralization and even the possible dismemberment of the nation. History, it seems, can not stand still or even necessarily move forward.

Based on our previous experiences at junctures such as these, it is almost certainly the case that leaders in Atlantic Canada will seize upon any straw in the winds of change that offers survival and stability. But will this next exercise in "adjustment" be our undoing? Much, of course, depends upon whether the politics of place remains possible for small and dependent regions like Atlantic Canada — Friedman and Forest are not optimistic[59] — or whether it is only the luxury of the more favoured regions of Canada and the world. The Atlantic Revolution benefitted from a highly favourable conjunction of forces: unprecedented economic growth in Canada as a whole during and after World War II; efforts on the part of centralized industrial states to spread the benefits of capitalist development more equitably; and a naive belief in the possibility of unending human progress. In the 1990s the entrails do not offer such an auspicious reading.

It may well be the case that we in the Atlantic region can develop, and perhaps have defined, "new notions of happiness"[60] that do not make economic growth the only, or indeed the primary, end of human endeavour. Nevertheless, like old generals, we in Atlantic Canada have a tendency to go into battles fighting the last war. It should come as no surprise that the regional focus is presently on maritime and even Atlantic provinces economic union.[61] This might be an adequate response for APEC and the Council of Maritime Premiers; it will not spare the people of the Atlantic region from the adjustments now being thrust upon them, or perhaps even serve them well in the adjustment process. In a "new world order" where environmental standards, fair labour practices and humane social welfare policies — the fundamental basis of our postwar sense of community — are being steadily eroded, we must proceed with the utmost caution.

David J. Elkins had recently argued that Canada, like the strands of a rope, is becoming "unbundled."[62] Such unbundling is not unique to Canada. Since nations as we know them are relatively recent historical phenomena, it is also very likely that they are also fleeting ones. The same might be said of such informally constituted regions as Atlantic Canada. Following this line of thought, it can be argued that, while nations and regions may survive the present 'crisis' in some modified configuration, the strands of transnational interests and identities based on non-spatial values — ranging from capital and environmental concerns to gender and ethnicity — will increasingly take precedence over any particular sense of place. In short, community may become divorced from geography.

We are, then, at a curious crossroads in our history where community, region, nation and planet offer conflicting possibilities for our future direction. Atlantic Canada's long tradition of loose-jointed regionalism could serve its people well in these difficult times. If nothing else, the region's recent history suggests that community identities can survive the most drastic of "adjustments," including loss of sovereignty and even stifling economic dependency. The deep-rooted sense of community that typifies the region should not be underestimated or overromanticized. Such identities have demonstrated enormous potential, not only in Canada as a whole but also, to take another obvious example, central Europe. Indeed, I would argue that unless we succeed in developing structures that offer dignity and equality for all Canadians we may well see community, variously defined, taking precedence over the much vaunted global forces in shaping our future. In this scenario, the Atlantic region will certainly meet the test of global and national restructuring; but it will do so, if the recent election in New Brunswick is any indication, in ways that may surprise and dismay those of us struggling to establish a meaningful federalism in the northern half of the North American continent.

Notes

1.   This conference was held under the auspices of the Canadian Institute on Regional Development, and the paper was published in the conference proceedings: John Friedmann and Yvon Forest, "The Politics of Place: Toward a Political Economy of Territorial Planning," in Benjamin Higgins and Donald J. Savoie, eds., *Regional Economic Development: Essays in Honour of Francois Perroux* (Boston: Unwin Hyman, 1988), 115-30.

2.   Ibid., 116. See also Edward J. Soja, *Postmodern Geographies: The Reassertion of Space in Critical Social Theory* (New York: Routledge Chapman and Hall, 1989) and David Frank's recent review essay, "The Geography of Centralization," *Acadiensis* 20, no. 2 (Spring 1991): 190-206.

3.   Margaret Conrad, *George Nowlan: Maritime Conservative in National Politics* (Toronto: University of Toronto Press, 1986), xii-xiii.

4.   See, in the Canadian context, Ralph Matthews, *The Creation of Regional Dependency* (Toronto: University of Toronto Press, 1983) and Janine Brodie, *The Political Economy of Canadian Regionalism* (Toronto: Harcourt Brace Jovanovich, 1990).

5.   Colin D. Howell, "Nova Scotia's Protest Tradition and the Search for a Meaningful Federalism," in David J. Bercuson, ed., *Canada and the Burden of Unity* (Toronto: Macmillan, 1977), 169-91.

6.   Friedman and Forest, "Politics of Place," 116.

7.   This task has already been accomplished in vastly greater detail in G.A. Rawlyk and Doug Brown, "The Historical Framework of the Maritimes and Confederation," and Terry Campbell and G.A. Rawlyk, "The Historical Framework of Newfoundland and Confederation," in G.A. Rawlyk, ed., *The Atlantic Provinces and the Problems of Confederation* (St. John's: Breakwater, 1979), 1-81.

8.   Gerald Friesen, *The Canadian Prairies: A History* (Toronto: University of Toronto Press, 1984), 3-5.

9.   For a continental perspective on region see, Stephen J. Hornsby, Victor A. Konrad and James J. Herlan, eds., *The Northeast Borderlands: Four Centuries of Interaction* (Fredericton: Canadian-American Centre, University of Maine and Acadiensis Press, 1989).

10.   Ralph C. Nelson, Walter C. Soderlund, Ronald H. Wagenberg and E. Donald Briggs, "Canadian Confederation as a Case Study in Community Formation," in Ged Martin, ed., *The Causes of Canadian Confederation* (Fredericton: Acadiensis Press, 1990), 68.

11. According to Newfoundlander Adrian Fowler, this rootedness offers identity for a person "out of a region so dense with life of its own, so individualized that he can tell a fellow countryman by a thousand things and not know how he does it." Quoted in David G. Alexander, "New Notions of Happiness: Nationalism, Regionalism and Atlantic Canada," in Eric W. Sager, Lewis R. Fischer and Stuart O. Pierson, compilers, *Atlantic Canada and Confederation: Essays in Canadian Political Economy* (Toronto: University of Toronto Press, 1983), 83.

12. Carman Miller, "The Restoration of Greater Nova Scotia," in Bercuson, *Canada and the Burden of Unity*, 45.

13. The persistence of provincial political cultures has prompted political scientist J. Murray Beck to conclude that, "Because distinct provincial identities and loyalties constitute so important a feature of political culture, I think it is highly misleading to talk and think in terms of a Maritime or Atlantic [regional] culture. It is much more meaningful to recognize the existence of four provincial cultures having many values, attitudes and beliefs in common." I have no quarrel with this position, although I choose here to focus on the cultural traditions and political movements common to the Atlantic Region, rather than the differences separating the provinces. See, J. Murray Beck, "An Atlantic Region Political Culture: A Chimera," in David J. Bercuson and Phillip A. Buckner, eds., *Eastern and Western Perspectives* (Toronto: University of Toronto Press, 1981), 168.

14. Cited in Province of Nova Scotia, *A Submission of its Claims with Respect to Maritime Disabilities within Confederation as Presented to the Royal Commission [on Maritime Claims]* (Halifax: n.p., 1926), 7.

15. Ibid., 11.

16. Joseph Howe to the Hon. Isaac Buchanan, 20 June 1866, cited in Joseph Andrew Chisholm, ed., *The Speeches and Public Letters of Joseph Howe*, Vol. 2 (Halifax: The Chronicle Publishing Company, 1909), 464.

17. Phillip Buckner, "CHR Dialogue: The Maritimes and Confederation: A Reassessment," *Canadian Historical Review* 71, no. 1 (1990): 1-30.

18. For an insightful discussion of the comparative fates of Newfoundland and the maritime provinces see David Alexander, "Economic Growth in the Atlantic Region, 1880-1940," in Sager et al., *Atlantic Canada and Confederation*, 51-78.

19. Kenneth Pryke, *Nova Scotia and Confederation, 1864-74* (Toronto: University of Toronto Press, 1979), 41.

20. Ged Martin, "The Case Against Canadian Confederation," *The Causes of Canadian Confederation*, 49.

21. Gordon Stewart, *The Origins of Canadian Politics: A Comparative Approach* (Vancouver: University of British Columbia Press, 1986); Phillip Buckner, "The 1870s: The Integration of the Maritimes Into Confederation," unpublished paper, 15.

22. Nova Scotia, *Journals of the House of Assembly*, 12 and 25 May 1869.

23. Ibid., 8 May 1866.

24. Colin D. Howell, "W.S. Fielding and the Repeal Elections of 1886 and 1887 in Nova Scotia," *Acadiensis* 8, no. 2 (Spring 1979): 28-46.

25. For instance, while the governments of British Columbia, Quebec and Ontario received subsidy increases of 121.0 percent, 66.1 percent and 62.5 percent respectively in 1907, Prince Edward Island's subsidy increase was only 59.8 percent, Nova Scotia's 46.7 percent and new Brunswick's a miserable 41 percent. James A. Maxwell, *Federal Subsidies to Provincial Governments in Canada* (Cambridge: Harvard University Press, 1963), 113, cited in Colin Howell, "Industry, Urbanization and Social Reform in the Maritimes: 1900-1910," unpublished paper, 11-12.

26. T.W. Acheson, "The National Policy and the Industrialization of the Maritimes, 1880-1910," *Acadiensis* 1, no. 2 (Spring 1972): 3-28 and "The Maritimes and 'Empire Canada'," in Bercuson, *Canada and the Burden of Unity*, 87-114.

27. Alan A. Brookes, "Out-Migration From the Maritime Provinces, 1860-1990: Some Preliminary Considerations," *Acadiensis* 5, no. 2 (Spring 1976): 26-55 and Patricia A. Thornton, "The Problem of Out-Migration from Atlantic Canada, 1871-1921: A New Look," *Acadiensis* 15, no. 1 (Autumn 1985): 3-34.

28. Howell, "Industry, Urbanization, and Social Reform," 10.

29. Province of Nova Scotia, *A Submission of Its Claims with Respect to Maritime Disabilities Within Confederation...* , 169.

30. G.A. Rawlyk, "The Farmer-Labour Movements and the Failure of Socialism in Nova Scotia," in L. Lapierre, ed., *Essays on the Left* (Toronto: McClelland and Stewart, 1971), 31-41.

31. E.R. Forbes, *The Maritime Rights Movement, 1919-1927: A Study in Canadian Regionalism* (Montreal/Kingston: McGill-Queen's University Press, 1979).

32. Sir Andrew Rae Duncan et al., *Report of the Royal Commission on Maritime Claims* (Ottawa: King's Printer, 1926).

33. E.R. Forbes, "Cutting the Pie into Smaller Pieces: Matching Grants and Relief in the Maritime Provinces during the 1930s," in Forbes, *Challenging the Regional Stereotype: Essays on the 20th Century Maritimes* (Fredericton: Acadiensis Press, 1989), 148-71.

34. Province of Nova Scotia, *A Submission of its Claims with Respect to Maritime Disabilities within Confederation...* , 54.

35. Duncan et al., *Report of the Royal Commission on Maritime Claims*, 11.

36. *Report of the Royal Commission on Dominion-Provincial Relations*, 3 vols. (Ottawa: King's Printer, 1939).

37. Public Archives of Nova Scotia, Angus L. Macdonald Papers, MG 2, Box 898, F19 1/2 D/1D, Harold Innis to Angus L. Macdonald, 17 January 1946.

38. Vernon C. Fowke, "The National Policy — Old and New," *Canadian Journal of Economics and Political Science* 18, no. 3 (August 1952): 271-86.

39. W.S. MacNutt, "The Atlantic Revolution," *Atlantic Advocate* (June 1957): 11-13.

40. Margaret Conrad, "The Atlantic Revolution of the 1950s," in Berkeley Fleming, ed., *Beyond Anger and Longing: Community and Development in Atlantic Canada* (Fredericton: Acadiensis Press/Mount Allison University, Centre for Canadian Studies, 1988), 55-96.

41. Hubert Guindon, "The Social Evolution of Quebec Reconsidered," in Marcel Rioux and Yves Martin, eds., *French Canadian Society* (Toronto: McClelland and Stewart, 1964), 137-61.

42. R.A. Young, "'and the people will sink into despair': Reconstruction in New Brunswick, 1942-52," *Canadian Historical Review* 69, no. 2 (June 1988): 127-66; Stephen G. Tomblin, "The Council of Maritime Premiers and the Battle for Territorial Integrity," *Journal of Canadian Studies* 26, no. 1 (Spring 1991): 100-19.

43. Joey Smallwood, *I Choose Canada: The Memoirs of the Honourable Joseph R. "Joey" Smallwood*, Vol. 2: *The Premiership* (Toronto: Macmillan of Canada, 1973).

44. "The Prairies as a Region: The Contemporary Meaning of An Old Idea," presented at this conference.

45. John Hawkins, *The Life and Times of Angus L* (Windsor: Lancelot Press, 1969).

46. Mildred Schwartz, *Politics and Territory: The Sociology of Regional Persistence in Canada* (Montreal/Kingston: McGill-Queen's University Press, 1974).

47. Royal Commission on Canada's Economic Prospects, *Final Report* (Ottawa, n.p., 1957), 403.

48. T.N. Brewis, *Regional Economic Policies in Canada* (Toronto: Macmillan, 1969), 166-67; Atlantic Provinces Economic Council, *First Annual Review: The Atlantic Economy* (October 1967), 44-51; *Defence Expenditures and the Economy of the Atlantic Provinces*, APEC Pamphlet No. 9 (December 1965), 10.

49. James Lawrence Kenny, "Politics and Persistence: New Brunswick's Hugh John Flemming and the 'Atlantic Revolution,' 1952-1960" (M.A. Thesis, University of New Brunswick, 1988); Robert Andrew Young, "Planning for Power: New Brunswick Power Commission in the 1950s," *Acadiensis* 12, no. 1 (Autumn 1982): 73-99.

50. "The Fredericton Conference of Atlantic Premiers," *Atlantic Advocate* (September 1956): 28.

51. Public Archives of New Brunswick, Hugh John Flemming Papers, RS 415, C9b, R. Whiddon Ganong to Hugh John Flemming, 1 May 1956.

52. Conrad, "The Atlantic Revolution of the 1950s."

53. Noel Iverson and D. Ralph Matthews, *Communities in Decline: An Examination of Household Resettlement in Newfoundland*, Newfoundland Social and Economic Studies, No. 6 (St. John's: Memorial University, 1968). For a different interpretation of this process, see Frank W. Rowe, *The Smallwood Era* (Toronto: McGraw-Hill Ryerson, 1985), 107-28.

54. R.A. Young, "Remembering Equal Opportunity: Clearing the Undergrowth in New Brunswick," *Canadian Public Administration* 30, no. 1 (Spring 1987): 88-102; Della M. M. Stanley, *Louis Robichaud: A Decade of Power* (Halifax: Nimbus, 1984).

55. Roy George, *The Life and Times of Industrial Estates* (Halifax: Dalhousie University, Institute of Public Affairs, 1974).

56. Verner Smitheram, David Milne and Satadal Dasgupta, eds., *The Garden Transformed: Prince Edward Island, 1945-1980* (Charlottetown: Ragweed Press, 1982).

57. In addition to many of the sources already cited see James P. Bickerton, *Nova Scotia, Ottawa, and the Politics of Regional Development* (Toronto: University of Toronto Press, 1990); Anthony Careless, *Initiative and Response: The Adaption of Canadian Federalism to Regional Economic Development* (Montreal/Kingston: McGill-Queen's University Press, 1977); N.H. Lithwick, *Regional Economic Policy: The Canadian Experience* (Toronto: McGraw-Hill Ryerson, 1978); Donald J. Savoie, *Regional Economic Development: Canada's Search for Solutions* (Toronto: University of Toronto Press, 1986) and Donald J. Savoie, ed., *The Canadian Economy: A Regional Perspective (Toronto: Methuen, 1986)*.

58. Thomas Courchene, "Avenues of Adjustment: The Transfer System and Regional Disparities," in Michael Walker, ed., *Canadian Confederation at the Crossroads* (Vancouver: Fraser Institute, 1978); and *Economic Management and the Division of Powers*, Vol. 67, prepared for the Royal Commission on the Economic Union and Development Prospects for Canada (Toronto: n.p., 1986). For a commentary on these views see, Ernest Forbes, "The Atlantic Provinces, Free Trade, and the Canadian Constitution," in Forbes, *Challenging the Regional Stereotype*, 200-16.

59. Friedmann and Forest argue that the politics of place usually does not originate in the poorest regions; they therefore see Quebec (and presumably the West and Ontario), rather than Atlantic Canada or the North as the optimum places of regional politics. See "The Politics of Place," 126.

60. David Alexander, "New Notions of Happiness: Nationalism, Regionalism and Atlantic Canada," in *Atlantic Canada and Confederation*, 79-100.

61. Charles J. McMillan, *Standing Up to the Future: The Maritimes in the 1990s* (Halifax: Council of Maritime Premiers, 1989).

62. David J. Elkins, "Canada in the Twenty First Century," paper presented to the ACSANZ Canadian Studies Conference, Armidale, Australia, July 1990.

3

The Canadian Prairies —
One Economic Region or Two?:
Implications for Constitutional Change
with Particular Reference to Manitoba

Paul Phillips

INTRODUCTION: DEFINING THE REGION

The concept of region is a difficult and rather amorphous one in economics. The term is variously used to refer to international trading areas (e.g., the Pacific Rim), subcontinental geo-economic areas (e.g., the North-American Great Plains), subnational functional economic systems (e.g., the West in Canada), subnational geo-economic formations (e.g., the Canadian Prairies), or even smaller geographic features (e.g., the Interlake Region of Manitoba). Alternative defining characteristics are economic, socio-cultural, linguistic, or geographic homogeneity and contiguity, though for practical analysis the economist is usually forced to use existing political divisions or administrative units as the area of analysis whether or not they comprise theoretically defensible regional boundaries, simply because statistics are only available for such units.

In the constitutional debate, what has been considered the appropriate analytic unit for our region has usually been either Canada's four most westerly provinces, "the West," or the three prairie provinces, "the Prairies." There is justification for both. The West as a whole has played a specific functional economic role in Confederation, that of resource hinterland to the metropolitan region of central Canada (Phillips, 1973). However, neither the economic and geographic homogeneity of the western provinces nor the political reality make the west the optimum unit for analyzing the regional economic dimensions of a renewed Confederation.

The prairie provinces are also not the ideal unit for such analysis. First, since the days of the fur trade, the land area covered by the present provinces does not constitute a homogeneous economic or geographic region. In the north of all three provinces lies the Canadian Shield; to the south, the flat, arable lands that give the region its name. Nevertheless, for political, statistical and, perhaps historical, reasons we must accept it as the most appropriate unit of analysis.

However, and this is one of the central issues of this paper, the economic homogeneity and the resource base of the prairie provinces have become bifurcated not only on the north-south (Shield-Prairies) axis, but also on an east-west axis that divides the Prairies between energy- and mineral-rich western parts and the south-eastern extent (Manitoba and much of Saskatchewan) that is still largely reliant on agriculture and the transportation, manufacturing and financial service industries that developed, initially at least, as backward, forward and final demand linkages of the staple, or export, agriculture of the Prairies. This is particularly important when considering constitutional changes since, as it will be argued later, what might be appropriate for an energy- and mineral-rich region which is the recipient of significant resource rents (a region based on a "strong staple"), will not normally be appropriate for a region based on competitive export agriculture (a "weak staple"), that, far from generating resource rents, becomes dependent on at least intermittent, interregional transfers (House, 1986).

THE PRAIRIE ECONOMY: HISTORICAL DIMENSIONS

The prairie region played a particular and essential role in the mercantilist nation-building strategy that is now widely known as the National Policy (Fowke, 1957; Fowke, 1952; Phillips, 1979). With the loss of its protected position in the British economic empire by the British adoption of free-trade imperialism in the mid-nineteenth century and the repudiation of continental integration by the American decision to abrogate the reciprocity treaty in 1865 and growing American protectionism that denied Canada commercial access to the American midwest, the Canadian merchant capitalist class was forced to search out a new strategy.

This strategy was the National Policy, a group of policies designed to knit the disparate regions of British North America into a viable and complementary political and economic entity and create for the dominant class of central Canada, an internal colony, a frontier of profitable investment. The legal form this entity would take was defined by the British North America Act (BNA Act), the act of Confederation. The specific foundations of the National Policy which were gradually put in place over the next quarter century were a transcontinental railway uniting the regions, a land and immigration policy opening the West to agricultural settlement, and a system of tariffs to force commerce on an east-west basis and, simultaneously, to protect the industrial and commercial interests of central Canada.

The Canadian strategy was by and large a mirror of American mercantilist policy with respect to western expansion (Fowke, 1956). The great plains and the further western reaches were to be not only a sump for eastern manufacturers and a source of raw materials and foodstuffs for industry, the new industrial working-class, and the commercial traders, but this new frontier was also to be a source of surplus accumulation both through trade and transportation, and also through finance capital. Achieving these goals was not to be left to the "invisible hand" of the market, but accomplished by the very visible and very class conscious hand of the state. Governments were to provide, directly or indirectly, all the necessary infrastructure, in particular, the transportation systems. In Canada, this was done through a combination of direct government investments, subsidies, land grants, loan guarantees, tax expenditures and monopoly charters. This was particularly important in Canada because it did not have a continuous agricultural frontier west of the commercial and industrial heartland as did the United States. In short, the federal government was responsible for offsetting the costs of the "land bridge" between southern Ontario and the prairie region. For industrial capital, profitable investment was to be assisted through tariff protection.

Though the policies and the infrastructure were in place by the end of the 1880s, development in the Canadian west was slow to take off. It was not until the conjuncture of a rising world economy, and with it demand and prices for agricultural products, the development of dryland-farming techniques, and the filling up of the American agricultural frontier, that the Canadian "wheat boom" began. Though it has become fashionable among some "new economic historians" to depreciate the importance of the western agricultural expansion to Canadian economic growth in the first decade of the twentieth century, the undeniable fact is that the expansion in the prairie region was enormous and rapid, financial and commercial capital was accumulated, the railway was so profitable that two other transcontinental systems were built, and the metropolitan region of Canada prospered. Much of the profits and accumulation came from surplus generated in the western region but expropriated through unequal exchange (Phillips, 1985). Most of the immigration came from outside Canada, particularly eastern Europe, though there were also substantial migrations from the United States, particularly into Alberta.

The economic homogeneity of the prairie region was determined by the staple base, export agriculture with particular emphasis on wheat. This is not to say either that agriculture was the only industry or that grain production was the only form of agriculture. Livestock were raised everywhere, most notably in southern Alberta where ranching was a dominant industry (Breen, 1983). Coal mining was prominent in the Crowsnest Pass area of Alberta and stretched as far east as southern Saskatchewan. In the late 1920s, copper-zinc mining began at Flin Flon on Manitoba's northern border with Saskatchewan. Fishing on Manitoba's lakes employed many in the Icelandic and Native communities while the commercial fur trade still remained the dominant market activity of the Native population in the northern reaches of all three provinces. But, no matter the number of alternative sources of employment and income there were in the prairie region, it was agriculture and, more specifically, wheat and other export grains that determined the state of the regional economy and dictated its politics. There is no better evidence of this than the collapse of the regional economy in the 1930s as a consequence of the collapse in world grain markets and compounded by the drought that ensued in the middle years of the decade.

Agriculture not only determined the region's relationship with central Canadian capital, it also determined the internal economic and urban structure of the region, in part through the logistics of the transportation infrastructure and the geography, as enhanced by policy. Winnipeg's strategic geographic position as gateway to the West was augmented by the National Policy tariffs which reduced American competition and by the regulated transport rates which gave the city preference as a wholesale centre for the region, at least until after World War I.

The whole urban, commercial, industrial and transportation structure of the region during the agricultural period was centred on Winnipeg (Phillips, 1981). In 1910 as the expansive phase of the wheat boom was beginning to wane, almost two-thirds of prairie manufacturing took place in Manitoba, most of it within Winnipeg. Moreover, this manufacturing was both for domestic consumption and for staple export. Winnipeg and Manitoba accounted for well over half of the region's wholesale trade. The Grain Exchange and federal inspection and grading of grain were located in Winnipeg and, with the convergence of three railways and attendant shops on the city, its dominance over the grain trade and the financial and commercial supporting industries was more or less complete.

The staple boom was, by and large, played out by World War I. The wheat economy, its commercial and transportation infrastructure, and its main institutions were established and in place. The taking up of unoccupied land and investment in railway branch lines and powered farm machinery were carried on in the 1920s, but the scale and the rate of expansion were greatly reduced. At the same time, the opening of the Panama Canal and changes in railway rate structures established Vancouver as an alternative gateway to the prairie region. The successful launching of the prairie wheat pools, statutory regulation of the railway freight rates for grain, and, during the thirties, the replacement of the Grain Exchange by the Canadian Wheat Board, meant that the region was no longer the same source of accumulation for either regional or metropolitan capital.

Nevertheless, for the two interwar decades the structure of the prairie economy remained remarkably stable and, despite the first show of petroleum and gas resources in Turner Valley in Alberta in 1914 and the opening up of conventional oil wells there in the latter years of the 1930s, the dominance of agriculture in the whole region continued more or less unchallenged until after World War II. Mining output, including fuels, was 16 percent of agricultural output in the first five years of the 1930s when grain prices were greatly depressed, but this had fallen to 10 percent during the war and, even after the discovery of the Leduc field in 1947, had only risen to 14 percent in the first five postwar years. From 1936 to 1950, agriculture (not including the processing of agricultural products for domestic or export markets) consistently represented almost 60 percent of the total value of commodity production in the prairie region (Phillips, 1981: 17). Such restructuring as did occur was more within agriculture as Alberta increasingly shifted to livestock production, particularly after 1940.

The stability in the economic structure of the Prairies began to change after the war, first quite slowly and then increasing rapidly as the impact of the new petroleum staple was felt (see Table 1).

Table 1

Contribution of Agriculture and Mining to the Net Value of Commodity Production: Prairie Region, 1941-1960

Averages	Agriculture (%)	Mining (%)
1941-1950	58.0	6.8
1951-1955	45.6	10.8
1956-1960	29.0	16.4

Source: Phillips, 1963: Appendix B.

This was accompanied by a rapid decline in the proportion of rural population, reflecting not only the mechanization of agriculture but also the growth of manufacturing and the pull of the developing metropolitan centres of Edmonton and Calgary. However, while Alberta and, to a much lesser extent, Saskatchewan felt the positive impact of the new resource frontier, Manitoba saw few direct benefits and, in relative terms, declined while the economic function of Winnipeg, embedded in agriculture and its investment frontier and in the grain trade and transportation, was undermined.

POSTWAR ECONOMIC DEVELOPMENT

The new generation of export staples (oil and gas, potash and other minerals) involved a north-south and/or Pacific orientation both in terms of investment capital and markets. Even the shift in markets for agricultural products favoured a Pacific Rim orientation. As a result, Manitoba's and Winnipeg's connections with the western half of the region have greatly weakened. Indeed, as Gonick has noted, the concept of a regional prairie economy is anachronistic "since the prairie economy was really a euphemism for the wheat economy and while wheat still plays an important role, especially in Saskatchewan, it is no longer dominant" (Gonick, 1990: 40).

Throughout the 1970s and 1980s, Manitoba wheat represented 20 percent or less of the value of regional wheat production as compared with 60 percent or more for Saskatchewan and 20-30 percent for Alberta. A similar concentration in Alberta and Saskatchewan existed in livestock, though with the positions of Alberta and Saskatchewan reversed. Indeed, in terms of agricultural output, both Saskatchewan and Alberta in the last two decades have had a regional weighting of more than double that of Manitoba. This points to the further conclusion that, not only has Manitoba not participated significantly in the new staples, it is of declining relative importance in the production of the old staple.

This, of course, does not mean that Manitoba does not rely heavily on agriculture but rather that its dependence is more closely connected to its linked transportation, financial, commercial and manufacturing industries. This makes the shift of grain exports from Manitoba ports (Thunder Bay and Churchill) to west coast ports (Vancouver and Prince Rupert) somewhat more ominous. In the early 1960s, 64 percent of grain export shipments went via Manitoba ports. This declined slowly but more or less steadily through the 1970s before dropping rapidly after 1984. Recently, Thunder Bay and Churchill combined have shipped less than one-third of the prairie harvest. The possible demise of the Port of Churchill, the increasing propensity of the railways to bypass Manitoba using American routes, the diminished role of the Canadian Wheat Board, the impact of the Canada-United States Free Trade Agreement (FTA) promoting a north-south axis of trade and transportation and permitting American grain to enter Canadian markets, all threaten Manitoba's historic role within the export-based economy of the prairie region.

But it is not the weakening of Manitoba's historic function in agricultural marketing and transportation that is most significant in setting the province off from Alberta and Saskatchewan so much as it is the participation of these two provinces in the development of new resource export industries that do not have a regional integrative or east-west orientation in terms of transportation, finance, marketing or manufacturing. Moreover, as a result of the potential and realized rents, particularly in oil and gas, Manitoba does not have the same potential fiscal capacity in the medium to longer run.

Table 2
Estimated Distribution of Goods in Goods-Producing Industries

	1971-75 (%)	1975-80 (%)	1981-84 (%)	1985-86 (%)
Manitoba				
Staple	51.8	46.5	46.0	42.6
Non-staple	48.2	53.5	54.0	57.4
Saskatchewan				
Staple	77.9	73.0	73.0	65.5
Non-staple	22.1	27.0	27.0	34.5
Alberta				
Staple	64.9	63.8	69.4	68.4
Non-staple	35.1	36.2	30.6	31.6

Source: Statistics Canada, *Provincial Gross Domestic Product by Industry*, SC61-202 (1983), SC15-203 (1984, 1986).

The differential in the importance of natural resource industries between Manitoba and the other two provinces is quite marked. Regular data is only available up to 1986 on the value of goods production by province and industry. (The data on service production is very incomplete though estimates of total "gross provincial product" are available. However, since the majority of services are population- and income-related, they tend not to vary directly with goods production or international markets.) In Table 2, the goods-producing industries are divided into two major categories, "staples" and "non-staples." The "staples" category includes agriculture and other primary production (forestry, fishing, hunting and trapping, and mining), together with primary manufacturing (food and beverages, primary metals, wood products, pulp and paper, petroleum and coal products). This measure tends to exaggerate Manitoba's staple dependence much more than the other two provinces. Nevertheless, the difference is clear and unequivocal.

Although, as anticipated, the changes were not dramatic, the indication is that Manitoba has continued to move away from staple production and is much less dependent on primary industries than the other two provinces. Were it not for the decline in oil prices in 1986, the results would have been even more dramatic.

As a further measure of the difference in resource structure between Manitoba and the other two provinces, one can simply use the ratios of the value of agricultural production to that of mineral production. The comparable figures for 1985-86 are shown in the following table:

Table 3

Agricultural Production as Percent of Mineral Production, 1985-86

Manitoba	296.9
Saskatchewan	116.8
Alberta	13.0

Source: Same as previous table.

The evidence from the manufacturing sector is consistent with that of the primary sector. Manitoba's manufacturing, however, has had a difference in structure dating back to the province's role in supplying the domestic regional market. Its industry tends to be more diverse in both composition and markets, being less reliant on its immediate hinterland and on export processing. It is also differentiated by being much more characterized as a "branch plant" of Ontario manufacturing (Gonick, 1990: 41).

A final piece of evidence to support the conclusion of a substantial structural difference between Manitoba and Alberta, with Saskatchewan somewhere in between, is the composition and distribution of exports. Figures for 1989 are given in Table 4.

A number of observations can be made from this table. The first is that Manitoba is least dependent on exports. On a per capita basis, Saskatchewan exports around 60 percent more than Manitoba; Alberta 100 percent more.

Secondly, Manitoba's exports are more diverse than either of the other provinces and it is the only province to export significant amounts of secondary manufactures. Saskatchewan, on the other hand, has a more geographically diverse export market due to its heavy reliance on grain exports. With the exception of grain, however, the region's export dependence on the United States market is extremely high.

Table 4
Structure of Exports For Selected Industries and Dependence on the US Market: 1989

	Manitoba	Saskatchewan	Alberta
Exports ($000,000)	2,966	4,693	9,647
Distribution (figures in brackets = % to US)			
Animals, animal products	7.4 (82)	2.4 (93)	3.1 (78)
Vegetable products	25.5 (16)	46.8 (6)	10.3 (12)
Fats and oils	1.6 (82)	1 (23)	3 (71)
Minerals and fuels	8.4 (96)	16.5 (100)	59.7 (87)
Chemicals and fertilizer	1.8 (77)	24.0 (59)	9.1 (52)
Base metals and products	3.4 (95)	1.0 (98)	9 (70)
Vehicles/trans. equipment	13.0 (94)	.4 (95)	.8 (85)
All exports	(68)	(44)	(74)
Percent of exports from top three industries	46.9	87.3	79.2

Source: Statistics Canada, *Exports by Commodity*, SC65-004, December 1989.

Recent trends in labour force structure, employment, income, and investment are also consistent with the conclusion that the old agricultural staple-based prairie region, of which Manitoba was an integral, at times dominating, member, has been gradually overtaken by a new staple alignment with a north-south market and financial orientation (Phillips, 1988). Manitoba has participated only peripherally in these new staples and has developed an economic structure that has less and less in common with other provinces in the region, and perhaps more and more in common with Ontario.

One qualification to this general conclusion should, however, be made and this with respect to Saskatchewan. Saskatchewan has, as it were, a foot in both camps. In terms of employment and linkages, agriculture still predominates and the province's overall prosperity is still tied very closely to that of agriculture, witness the current economic problems of the province consequent on the international grain subsidy war and several years of drought. However, in terms of output and government fiscal revenue, oil and gas, potash and uranium play a disproportionate role.

ECONOMIC STRUCTURE AND FISCAL RESOURCES

The difference in economic structure and natural resource allocation among the three provinces has a profound effect upon their relative tax bases. This is manifested in a number of ways: the direct resource rents available for taxation, the level of taxable personal and corporate income, and the vulnerability of provincial industries to competition which increases the elasticity of demand for regionally produced output thereby reducing potential tax revenues. These differences can be readily demonstrated. What this reveals is that Alberta, and, to a much lesser extent, Saskatchewan, have a substantial potential resource-based fiscal capacity, particularly when it is recognized that around 40 percent of Alberta's manufactures are petroleum based. This is confirmed by provincial fiscal accounts (see Table 5).

Table 5

Measures of Fiscal Capacity: Selected Per Capita Income and Output Measures: 1986

	Manitoba	Saskatchewan	Alberta
Population (000s)	1,071	1,010	2,375
PDI/capita* ($)	12,638	12,486	14,340
GDP/capita* ($)	17,197	16,972	24,132
Manuf. shipments/capita ($)	529	300	639
Mineral prod./capita ($)	71	250	688

*Personal Disposable Income (PDI) and Gross Domestic Product (GDP) per capita

Source: Statistics Canada, 13-213.

In short, the pattern of Alberta's dependence on staple resources, Manitoba's dependence on a more diversified, but still heavily regional agricultural base, and Saskatchewan's intermediate position, are again confirmed (see Table 6).

Table 6

Resource Revenue as a Proportion of Provincial Government Revenues: 1986-87

	1986 (%)	1987 (%)
Manitoba	1.8	1.8
Saskatchewan	17.9	15.9
Alberta	38.2	23.5

Source: Statistics Canada, SC68-209.

REGIONAL PROSPECTS: TEA LEAVES AND TAROT CARDS

It is always hazardous for economists to attempt to predict the future. Nevertheless, if the purpose of this paper is to provide a basis for discussing constitutional issues, it is necessary that we project into the future our understanding of the direction of structural change in the economy. Only two assumptions are made in the following analysis; one, that we can expect no significant change in the direction of trade policy in the United States or the European Economic Community (EEC); and, two, that despite the possible discovery of new fields and the introduction of enhanced secondary and tertiary recovery techniques, petroleum and gas reserves in Alberta and Saskatchewan are nonrenewable and, in the foreseeable future, bound to decrease.

If one accepts these two assumptions, it is difficult to be optimistic about the future of the region, or to view with any equanimity Conservative policies and their vision of the direction of constitutional evolution — or perhaps more correctly, devolution.

The European market for grain is, by and large, an historical artifact. It is difficult to predict what will happen in the Soviet Union but either they will successfully reform their agriculture, in which case they may become competitors in the export market for grain, or their economy will deteriorate further in which case they will not have the foreign exchange to buy Canadian grain. In either case, the European market at best will be intermittent and dependent on Canadian government credit (perhaps more realistically, subsidy). The eastern market, though perhaps more reliable in the short run, is also problematic given Japanese agricultural protectionism and the long run potential that China will become self-sufficient. Continued massive subsidies by the United States and the EEC to grain exports, therefore, mean that the mainstay of prairie agriculture will not become independent of federal government largesse.

This leads to the conclusion that the future of prairie agriculture is tied to the domestic market and, perhaps to a lesser extent, the American market for animal products. Given United States protectionism and the FTA, this future is, at best, cloudy and uncertain. This is even more so given the evidence of soil depletion and chemical pollution consequent on remaining "competitive" in international markets. Serious attention must be given to diversifying the agricultural base away from dependence on uncertain export markets. In any case, agriculture is a "weak staple" and will, it will be argued, depend on central government support for the foreseeable future.

The future for the other nonrenewable resource-based industries of the prairie region is hardly more positive. Conventional reserves are at or near their point of decline while nonconventional reserves are presently noneconomic or dependent on government subsidy and therefore do not comprise a "strong staple" base for future development. In economic terms, there is diminishing economic rent available to capitalize regional economic development. This has been exacerbated by the wasting of the accumulated rents in the provincial heritage funds by Conservative governments, particularly in Alberta, for partisan short-term political gains and through mismanagement (*Globe and Mail*, 27-30 May 1991).

Indeed, it is difficult to conceive of a regional development policy that could prove effective in the climate of the FTA since the agreement, in effect, rules out all of the levers of regional development policy.

WEAK STAPLE/STRONG STAPLE: DEVELOPMENTAL IMPLICATIONS

In a compilation of studies of the impact of petroleum discoveries and exploitation on regional economic development in maritime (fishing) regions, House has developed the weak staple/strong staple analytic framework. It is equally applicable to the prairie region where agriculture represents the "weak" (historic) staple and oil the "strong" (new) staple. Table 7 reproduces his schematic representation here substituting agriculture for fishing.

Table 7
Agriculture and Oil: Contrasting Strong and Weak Staples

Dimension	Oil	Agriculture
Demand	Inelastic	Elastic
Substitutes	Few	Many
Prices	Control by producers	Control by consumers
Marketing	Cartel	Competitive
Locus of metropolitan control	All phases	Marketing
Organization of production	International	Local
Units of production	Dominated by majors	Various
Ownership of production	Foreign	Local
Ownership of processing	Foreign	Local/outside
Economic surplus	Large and positive	Minimal to negative
Producers' incomes	High	Mixed
Governments	Source of revenues	Subsidization
Role in economy	Dominant	Secondary
Cultural implications	International, homogeneous	Local, heterogeneous

Source: House, 1986: 135.

It is perhaps unnecessary to attempt to trace through all the implications of this analysis for the prairie regional economy. For purposes of discussing the constitutional implications, three dimensions are central — economic surplus, producers' incomes and governments. For Manitoba, economic surplus is minimal (and, in any case, largely expropriated by financial and commercial capital through unequal exchange), producers' incomes are at best moderate and subject to uncontrollable fluctuation, and government is a necessary source of subsidization, particularly in the current climate of an international subsidy war.

For Alberta, economic surplus is, at least potentially large, producers' incomes high, and governments have been a source of revenue, not of taxation. Saskatchewan lies somewhere in between. The problem is, oil has a foreseeable horizon, agriculture does not. Given the failure, at least so far, of Alberta and Saskatchewan to diversify, by utilizing their mineral bases, the region must ultimately rely again on its renewable resource, agriculture. This, therefore, is the economic reality behind any discussion of change in the Canadian constitution — always providing, of course, that there is no unforeseen shift in the economy of the prairie region.

WEAK STAPLES AND THE CANADIAN CONSTITUTION

If one accepts the argument that, in the longer run, the prairie region will again become increasingly dependent on the health of its agriculture and less and less supported by the economic surplus engendered by nonrenewable petroleum resources, then one must conclude that the regional economy — if we can still talk about the Prairies as a regional economy — will become increasingly dependent on the existence of a strong central government. That is, we must accept that Manitoba remains dominated by a "weak" staple (to the extent it has not diversified into secondary manufacturing) and that Alberta is dominated by a "strong," though eventually exhaustible, staple; and that Saskatchewan lies somewhere in between.

Given this analysis, the Conservative agenda for constitutional reform which emphasized decentralization and the transfer of responsibility for the financing of social programs to the provinces, portends economic disaster for the prairie region, most immediately for Manitoba but in the longer run for Saskatchewan and Alberta as their surplus-producing nonrenewable resources run out. This is easily demonstrated by comparing the sources of revenue of the provincial governments with their expenditures.

As noted above, a very substantial portion of provincial revenues for Alberta came from resources, a lesser but still significant amount for Saskatchewan. In Manitoba, the amount was almost insignificant. On the other hand, transfers from the federal to the provincial governments remain critical to Manitoba. In 1986-87 transfers represented 28.6 percent of Manitoba's revenue, almost double Saskatchewan's 16.9 percent and more than double Alberta's 12.4 percent.

At the same time, the proportion of essentially nonreducible social service expenditures on health, education, and social services exceeded half of the provincial expenditures in all three provinces (ranging from 57.7 percent in Manitoba to 51.4 percent in Alberta and 51.1 percent in Saskatchewan, averaged for 1986-87) — nonreducible that is, assuming we maintain the existing level of social programs that are integral to the maintenance of a distinct Canadian society.

The conclusion of this analysis is obvious. National policy made the region, and national policy, as currently conceived by the Conservatives and their neoclassical economic advisors, will destroy it. Without a national regional development policy (preempted by the FTA), a strong regional redistribution policy (opposed by the reduction in Established Programs Financing), and a strong central government presence in the setting of national economic standards (proscribed by the Meech Lake Accord), the prairie "region" will become a mere adjunct to the distressed northern plains region of the United States. But, perhaps, that is what the current Canadian government would like to see.

References

Breen, David H. 1983. *The Canadian Prairie West and the Ranching Frontier, 1874-1924*. Toronto: University of Toronto Press.

Fowke, Vernon C. 1952. "The National Policy – Old and New." *Canadian Journal of Economics & Political Sciences* 18 (August).

———. 1956. "National Policy and Western Development in North America." *Journal of Economic History* 16 (December).

———. 1957. *The National Policy and the Wheat Economy*. Toronto: University of Toronto Press.

Gonick, Cy W. 1990. "The Manitoba Economy Since World War II." In Jim Silver and Jeremy Hull, eds., *The Political Economy of Manitoba*. Regina: Canadian Plains Research Center.

House, J.D. 1986. "Fish is Fish and Oil is Oil; The Case for North Sea Comparisons to Atlantic Canada." In J.D. House, ed., *Fish Versus Oil*. St. John's: Institute of Social and Economic Research, Memorial University.

Phillips, Paul. 1963. "Structural Change and Population Distribution in the Prairie Region, 1911-1961." Unpublished MA Thesis, Department of Economics, University of Saskatchewan.

———. 1973. "The National Policy and the Development of the Western Canadian Labour Movement." In A.W. Rasporich and H.C. Klassen, eds., *Prairie Perspectives 2*. Toronto: Holt, Rinehart and Winston.

———. 1979. "The National Policy Revisited." *Journal of Canadian Studies* (Autumn).

———. 1981. "The Prairie Urban System, 1911-1961: Specialization and Change." In A. Artibise, ed., *Town and City: Aspects of Western Canadian Urban Development*. Regina: Canadian Plains Research Center.

———. 1988. "Easternizing Manitoba: The Changing Economy of the New West." *London Journal of Canadian Studies* 5.

4

Restructured Federalism and its Impacts on Atlantic Canada

Tim O'Neill

INTRODUCTION

The federal government has tabled its latest proposals for constitutional reform.[1] These are designed to sustain the Canadian Confederation while making changes that will satisfy the need for an effective economic, and a viable political, union. The proposals will dominate discussions and negotiations regarding the structure of Canadian federalism although both modifications and alternatives to the proposals have already begun to emerge.

Whatever the specific outcome of the debate over the coming months, any significant adjustments to the current constitutional structure will have impacts on all regions and segments of society in Canada. There is little doubt that different regions of the country will be affected differently. Arguably, the effects will be more pronounced in the smaller provinces, which also tend to be economically weaker. Perhaps the most profound impacts will be felt in Atlantic Canada. Whether that proves to be the case, it is important for Atlantic Canadians to evaluate the potential impacts of the changes, and to consider the responses to be made by, and initiatives to be taken within, the region.

The purpose of this background document is to provide an initial assessment of some of the most likely outcomes of the debate. It is neither exhaustive in its coverage of possible outcomes nor definitive in its direction of impacts. It is meant to provoke thought and discussion, and suggest further research. It is not a specific response to the federal proposals. There will, however, be reference to elements of the proposals where relevant.

The paper begins with an examination of the current state of the discussions and analyses carried out to date. Following an outline of the most probable constitutional outcomes, I will proceed to study the implications (primarily economic) for Atlantic Canada. The document finishes with a study of three paths that the region may choose to follow in the upcoming discussions.

CURRENT STATE OF DISCUSSIONS AND ANALYSIS

Since the failure of the Meech Lake Accord in June 1990, the future of the Canadian political union has become far less clear than may have seemed the case when the accord was initially approved by the eleven first ministers in April 1987. The most extensive and active formal discussions have been held in Quebec, with several reports containing specific proposals for constitutional change emerging.

The federal government has commissioned its own examinations of the topic and the September proposals represent its efforts to provide the basis for sustaining Confederation. Most provinces have begun public consultation processes that will provide their governments with citizens' views on the positions to be taken in negotiations.

There has also been a virtual explosion of analysis by academics and research organizations on all dimensions of Confederation — economic, political, legal, social, and cultural. They have pondered alternative structures for political decision making (constituent assembly, national referendum, senate reform); examined various mechanisms for altering the division of powers between federal and provincial levels of government (asymmetric transfer to Quebec, opting out for all provinces, interdelegation of authority); and evaluated the economic impacts of various paths that might be followed (notably separation of Quebec, sovereignty association, and significant devolution of powers to provincial governments). As important as the consideration of alternative structures and mechanisms is, this study will deal with those elements of the discussion only insofar as they have economic impacts.

A Summary of Current Analysis

Canada's latest round of constitutional wrangling began with the agreement on the constitution negotiated by the eleven first ministers at Meech Lake in 1987. Designed to make Quebec a full signatory to the 1982 Constitution Act, it required approval by legislatures in all the provinces, and by the federal government, within a certain period (three years) after the first of the eleven parliaments approved. The necessary approval was not obtained. This set the stage for a series of federal and provincial commissions, inquiries, and investigations into what shape the country would take.[2]

A legion of studies and papers has analyzed the current situation, partly building on work done during the debates of the late 1970s and early 1980s, but substantially setting it firmly in the context of the 1990s. This dictates that any outcome for Canada will eventually (probably sooner rather than later) face up to the realities imposed by the outside world. Canada's open economy cannot operate in isolation. Maintaining and improving existing living standards demands we become more competitive both to preserve our existing markets (domestic and external) and to build new ones. This alone would be a daunting task, faced as the country is with enormous debt problems at federal and provincial levels. Accommodating structural changes to the Canadian federation at the same time makes the challenge formidable.

There is a spectrum of possible outcomes. At one extreme is *preservation of the status quo*, with the responsibility for powers in current program and policy areas not significantly changing between the two senior levels of government. Few people think this likely, and that some federal powers at least must devolve to the provinces.

Opinions diverge on the extent of the devolution. Those who favour *limited decentralization* hold that the benefits and desirability of a strong central government must outweigh provincial aspirations, to maintain the Canadian system of shared values and equal access to essential services backed up by extensive income redistribution from one part of the country to another.

Others argue that we must have quite *extensive decentralization* as a minimum for keeping the country at all. Yet others see this option as a route to more effective control over provincial/regional economies. (The new federal proposals fall between limited and extensive decentralization, although are much closer to the "limited" end of the spectrum.)

Sovereignty association for Quebec assumes a relatively amicable split, with the main structures of economic union still preserved in a North American context. Sentiments in favour of this option are not confined to Quebec; it has strong adherents in the other parts of Canada (particularly the West) where feelings run strongly that costs of maintaining a bilingual (bicultural) society outweigh the benefits, or that simply the wrangling has gone on too long and that it is time to cut Quebec loose to fend for itself. Many would argue that the cost of sovereignty association to all of Canada might be prohibitive.

Separation for Quebec without economic association rounds out the spectrum at the other end. This is more likely than maintenance of the status quo, but assumes an acrimonious split that probably makes it the least desirable outcome.

Some who argue in favour of limited decentralization, such as Harris and Purvis,[3] contend that it is beyond Canada's powers to effect radical federal change while adapting to the new global order. The existing Canadian common market is an imperfect economic union, substantially short of where the Europeans are going in 1992 or where the Americans already are:

> We admit it is conceivable that further decentralization of major powers ... will lead to more efficient regional economies, greater economic opportunities and higher growth. It is conceivable, but highly improbable. ... if we go down the decentralization route, it will be like driving down a one-way street. We may appear to make some progress for a while but then we will get hit by a truck moving in the opposite direction. That truck is the global economy...[4]

Harris and Purvis recommend that a well-paced, incremental approach to renewed economic federalism will allow Canada to build on the already significant achievements of the past.

Boadway emphasizes that decentralization of federal fiscal responsibilities will severely erode the federal ability to achieve redistributional equity.[5] Whatever Quebec's reasons for not wanting to remain part of the existing redistributional web, the only federal option is an asymmetric one that decentralizes some functions to Quebec. But if most federal budgetary functions are essentially redistributive in nature, it would be very difficult to extricate Quebec from them. Decentralization of some regulatory functions might be an alternative, especially those related to cultural and language policies. Regulatory functions such as energy, transport, agriculture and capital markets are important for maintaining the common market. Where these have already been decentralized, they have frequently become the source of interprovincial friction.

Boadway's analysis may have academic and intellectual integrity, but it does not correspond to the aspirations of either Quebec or the western provinces. Quebec already administers its own income tax system for example, and the West would like to have a similar role. Atlantic Canada is naturally apprehensive about any threats to Ottawa's redistributive capacity. The region has for long been a major beneficiary of this system, and would encounter grave fiscal difficulties if it had to fulfil the same role itself. Both Quebec and the West, indeed all parts of Canada, have been at least disenchanted with Ottawa's recent management of the national economy, and base their arguments for further devolution of powers largely on this basis.

Perhaps the most prolific commentator during the current debate has been Courchene, who argues that decentralization of powers is necessary because Canada's very size (large geographically, small and dispersed demographically) is so unwieldy.[6] This makes it impossible to run everything by means of a single vision coming from the centre. In any case, there are already powerful decentralizing forces under way, such as current trends in fiscal policy, and the Canada-United States Free Trade Agreement. Even without the Meech Lake debacle, therefore, Canada would not be the same in 2000 as it was in 1990.

Decentralization of economic powers, Courchene argues further, would be offset by maintenance of strong central control over a "social policy and value system railway," an analogy to the interprovincial railway that first bound Canada after Confederation last century. The challenge is to reorganize Canada's welfare system to accommodate changing global circumstances. Inherently, this involves a change of emphasis from "assistance to places" to "assistance to people."

The dark horse in this entire process is Ontario, currently emerging, he believes, as Canada's social policy leader. As this province undergoes its own "quiet revolution" it will have to become more economically pragmatic (as, for example, Mitterand's France has become) but its endeavours will probably attract the political support of the other "have" provinces (Alberta and British

Columbia). While not dismissing the gravity of the threat of Quebec's separation, Courchene also believes this would be a Pyrrhic victory. Quebec might achieve sovereign independence from Canada, but the necessities of negotiating monetary and commercial association with the rest of Canada and with the United States would erode its economic independence to a point much further behind what it hopes to attain within a new Canadian federation. Pragmatism dictates, therefore, that Quebec remain a part of Canada.

Two reports in Quebec have moved radical reorganization of federal powers to the centre of the political stage. The Allaire report to the Quebec Liberal Party (adopted as policy by the party) argued for exclusive provincial jurisdiction over twenty-two policy areas, including many (such as unemployment insurance, communications, energy, and environment) that are now mainly or significantly federal domains. A further nine areas are to be shared with the federal government, while only four (defense and territorial security, customs and tariffs, currency and common debt, and equalization) remain federal powers.[7]

The report of Quebec's Bélanger-Campeau Commission[8] was almost as uncompromising. Although the commission appears implicitly to favour renewed federalism, it leaves no doubt as to the alternative. Citing the numerous failures to integrate the province into the Canadian federation:

> Two courses are open to Quebec with respect to the redefinition of its status, i.e. a new, ultimate attempt to redefine its status within the federal regime, and the attainment of sovereignty. Some people [in Quebec] feel that the first course must be adopted and, should it fail, that Quebec should achieve sovereignty. Other people [in Quebec] prefer to adopt the second course of action immediately.[9]

Extensive decentralization was also the recommendation of a group of twenty-two prominent Canadians, both English- and French-speaking.[10] The group agree with Courchene that federalism is a highly flexible, modern system of government with an almost infinite capacity to adapt as necessary. It is essential to overcome our constitutional problems quickly to allow us to channel our collective energies on the other pressing challenge, competing effectively in world markets not only as individuals but as a nation. Decentralization can be accommodated, according to the group, as long as safeguards (such as national standards) are put in place.

The "Group of 22" recommends that federal responsibilties in certain social and cultural areas be transferred to the provinces, including income security and health. The group, is not quite as radical as Allaire/Bélanger-Campeau with regard to economic powers, in which federal powers (fiscal and monetary policy especially, and also trade and commerce) should be strongly retained to assure the integrity of the economic union. Some economic powers, however, should become the exclusive domain of the provinces, including intraprovincial transportation and natural resources (including energy, but with special considerations for fisheries). Regional economic development should be the responsibility of the provinces, with the federal government powers under Sec. 36 of the Constitution Act being retained to address regional disparities.

There is a "fundamental conundrum" in the constitutional debate. This is how, simultaneously, to recognize symbolically and substantially (that is, with transfer of powers) Quebec's distinctiveness; to treat all provinces equally; and to maintain a strong central government for national standards and desired redistributive activity. There is a strong argument that achievement of all three would be very difficult if not impossible. Any combination of two would be possible.

Alternative Paths

In the studies, reports, and policy statements emanating from Quebec in 1990 and 1991, it appears that the province is interested in two options: 1) a significant transfer of power, authority and fiscal capacity over a range of policies/programs currently handled either solely by the federal government or shared with the provinces; and 2) failing that option, political sovereignty for Quebec preferably incorporating economic association with the rest of Canada.

Appearances can, of course, be deceiving, and positions can change. The extensive decentralization called for in the Allaire report[11] may no longer be seen in Quebec as a "reasonable" reallocation of powers. It is unclear where on the spectrum from the current division of authority (status quo) to the Allaire proposals (virtual provincial autonomy) Quebec would set its minimum acceptable degree of devolution. Most informal evidence suggests that the Meech Lake Accord is an absolute minimum.

Quebec clearly requires formal acceptance of distinct status within Confederation. However, the substantive recognition of such status in the form of a transfer of powers to the province does not need to be exclusively for Quebec. It is likely that, on the devolution issue, the province is indifferent between symmetric and asymmetric federalism — that is, between all provinces being offered the same transfer of powers or only Quebec being made the offer.

The impetus for Quebec's demand for greater autonomy comes from several sources. The emergence of a strong, indigenous entrepreneurial class has fostered considerable self-confidence (at least among the business, professional and intellectual classes) in the province's capacity to prosper economically while becoming more independent politically. Improvement in the Quebec economy and less dependence on a strong federal redistributive system has enhanced feelings of self-assurance. When coupled with a perception of economic policy mismanagement by the federal government (the Allaire report is an unremitting litany of this) it is little wonder that Quebec believes its economic prospects would be better with greater autonomy.

Many in western Canada also feel federal policy has been mismanaged, with very damaging effects.[12] This also justifies transfer of policy responsibility to the provinces along with taxing power to finance it. In that respect, there is common ground with Quebec's position. Two important points distinguish the Quebec and western views. First, there is far from a uniform view in the West on the devolution of powers. Many would argue that if decentralization is likely to weaken the federal government significantly it would not be an unmixed blessing. This is particularly the case for the two smaller and weaker economies in the West — Saskatchewan and Manitoba. A strong central government much more responsive to regional concerns would be acceptable.

Second, many who favour a transfer of powers to the provinces see it as a means of reducing the role of government at all levels. In Quebec, greater autonomy is unlikely to be accompanied by a diminished role for the public sector but rather a change in the focus of that role.

There are other economic factors contributing to the pressure to decentralize economic policy making. Two in particular have received prominence. First, federal fiscal restraint implies a diminished capacity at the centre to "purchase" harmony or unity. It also is an indication of the degree of past federal economic mismanagement. Second, increasing integration of the international economy (GATT, the Canada-United States Free Trade Agreement and European economic integration) is argued by some to have reduced the capability of national governments to exercise control over economic events. Some of this loss of capability implies a *de facto* transfer of responsibility to subnational or "local" areas. That is, greater international integration means a lessening of the economic ties among the constituent parts of a national economy. This, in turn, leads to greater economic autonomy of those constituent parts.

The extent of the influence of these external factors is debatable. It may not be inevitable that the process of international economic integration necessarily and irrevocably reduces the role of the national government. It may change the kind of role it can play (less macroeconomic stabilization but more redistribution and/or greater microeconomic efficiency, for example). As well, it is an empirical issue whether increased international trade and investment activity has actually reduced intracountry (interprovincial) trade and capital flows to any significant degree. Since successful fiscal restraint is inherently "self-destructive" (it eliminates the problem that gave rise to the restraint) the pressure to sustain it will diminish over time. This will permit, if desired, a greater role for government.

At the heart of this discussion are the future prospects for the Canadian economic union. Of all the issues that have been and will be raised, this is clearly central. The *economic* rationale for a continued Canadian Confederation is based on the existence of net benefits for the participants in the economic union. How those benefits are affected by Quebec's possible separation or greater provincial autonomy is the focal point of the next section. We will focus on the extensive decentralization and separation options not because we are expecting or predicting either will happen, but because they represent the most significant departures from the status quo. It is to these more radical changes that more modest constitutional changes may effectively be compared.

The Canadian Economic Union

Economic integration involves the establishment of interaction and interdependence among distinct economic units. Although usually applied to countries, it is appropriate in a discussion of provincial economies. Any form of economic integration (the free trade area, for example) involves reducing barriers and harmonizing policy. In the Canadian economic union, there is relatively free movement of goods and services, of capital and people. There are, however, a number of impediments or barriers to completely free movement derived mainly from provincial policies and regulations. Any proposal to eliminate interprovincial trade barriers is a step in the direction of increasing the degree of economic union and, therefore, enhancing the economic efficiency gains from the union. This is the backbone of the federal proposals, combined with some devolution of powers to the provinces.

In the Canadian economic union, there are also a number of policies designed to redistribute gains from the union. These "risk-pooling" programs involve transfers to persons (such as unemployment insurance and pensions); transfers to provincial governments (such as equalization and Established Programs Financing [EPF]); and transfers to businesses (such as agricultural and energy capital assistance programs, and subsidies to companies). These redistributive activities are not inherent in all forms of economic union/integration but are extensive in Canada's. Boadway, as well, believes that a much wider array of federal spending than this is inherently redistributive in nature.[13]

The components of the Canadian union also benefit from sharing public infrastructure and public goods (national defense, interprovincial transportation systems) and from participating in international agreements negotiated on their behalf by the national government. The former provides goods and services at a lower cost than would prevail if the individual provinces attempted, on their own, to provide them to their citizens. The latter allow greater market access, improved terms of trade, or protection against countervail activities in other countries.

The efficiency gains from the economic union arise because of the cost-reducing economies to scale and gains from specialization that are the result of operating and selling in a larger market area than in an individual province. The fewer impediments there are to movements of traded goods and services and of inputs, the greater are the gains.

When the market fails to allocate resources in an efficient manner (because of what economists call externalities) there is a role for government action to correct the market failure. This has been used to justify government policy in areas ranging from the environment, transportation and communications, to the provision of labour-force training.

Many economists contend that the extensive integration of the international economy implies that the gains from economic union among the provinces are diminished *in relative terms*. That is, the advantages of belonging to the Canadian common market decline relative to the advantages of being part of a larger international economy. In that context, the activist role for a national government may be weakened since the impact of external economic factors are less readily modified or influenced in a more open economy. This means that authority over policy areas should logically be transferred to provinces where they can deal (as effectively as possible) with the local effects of these factors.

The more common argument made for the shift in responsibility for economic policy from federal to provincial governments is that the former has had a record of ineffective and inefficient policy decisions that have diminished the gains from economic union. This is most forcefully argued in the Allaire report. It also underpins arguments of many in the West — the Canada West Foundation, for example[14] — for more policy control by the provinces.

This view usually goes further to contend that mismanagement has had (intentionally in some instances, unintentionally in others) distinct regional impacts. In particular, it is argued that the West has suffered from policy failures, and shifting responsibility to the provinces will rectify this.

The proposals for transferring authority to the provinces are given added impetus by the *de facto* transfer of fiscal responsibility for important programs from federal to provincial governments, as part of the efforts to reduce federal debt. Some provinces argue that, in these circumstances, the federal government should also transfer both fiscal capacity (tax revenue reallocation) and political responsibility (constitutional reallocation of powers).

With respect specifically to the gains from the economic union, decentralization or devolution of powers may increase efficiency gains but at a cost to other benefits of the Canadian economic union. This is most obvious in the case of the redistributive policies — those intended to make economic welfare more equally accessible to all Canadians. Some of these involve transfers to individuals irrespective of location — Canada Pension Plan benefits, family allowance payments, Canada Assistance Plan, and unemployment insurance. Others involve transfers to provincial governments — equalization payments and EPF being the most notable. The capacity to redistribute, especially along geographic lines, depends on the fiscal (and constitutional) strength of the federal government. Significant decentralization is likely to hamper such efforts.

Less obviously, it may also hinder the capacity to provide national infrastructure and to establish international agreements. The former is essentially a fiscal matter, and a weaker federal government would be less capable of financing national infrastructure requirements. The impact on establishment of international agreements is more complex. In essence, the need for multiparty consent in areas where the federal government has acted on its own in the past could hamper progress in international agreements.

The Decentralization Option

Since the division of powers influences the gains from economic union, any reallocation of powers should be contemplated only if it results in a net gain. It makes little sense to reduce the benefits of Canadian economic integration by reassigning policy responsibilities. That fundamental principle raises a number of questions about the case for significant decentralization.

If the performance of the Canadian economy has been negatively affected by federal policy mismanagement, the question is whether this is due to an inappropriate division of powers. More bluntly, will it necessarily be the case that provincial governments will manage economic policy better — be more efficient, more effective, more equitable — than the federal government has?

One compelling argument used to justify greater provincial control over a range of policy areas is that, where the needs and "tastes" of citizens vary from one jurisdiction to another, local (provincial) decision making is important to ensure that those needs and tastes are appropriately reflected. This does not necessarily imply a wholesale shift of responsibility from the federal to provincial governments.

If the current allocation of responsibility for policy is tilted too much in the direction of the federal government, the appropriate adjustment might involve a reallocation of task or function while still sharing responsibility for the overall policy area. We can, for example, distinguish between the formulation, coordination and implementation components of policy. For certain policies (monetary policy, national defense, customs and excise) all activities should be carried out by the central government. Others (culture, municipal affairs, recreation) could be the exclusive domain of the provinces. The rest could be shared but with evaluation of whether current arrangements are working effectively and whether more authority ought to be transferred to the provincial government (or in some cases to the federal government). Effectiveness in delivery, and avoidance of wasteful duplication of effort would be two criteria for judging appropriate shifts of responsibility.

If this sounds very much like what we already have, it is not accidental. Canada is already a significantly decentralized federation, perhaps the most decentralized in the world. We have, over a number of years, developed mechanisms for sharing responsibility between the provincial and federal governments. These should not be abandoned unless it is reasonably clear that alternative arrangements will generate an improvement in effectiveness and efficiency.

One of the risks associated with significant decentralization of policy responsibility is the potential for increasing interprovincial barriers to trade in goods and services and to movements of people and capital. At a time when there is impetus to remove such impediments, wholesale policy devolution could create new ones. This might occur especially in the areas of regional development, environment, and industry and commercial policy — all of which involve shared jurisdictions.

There is also the danger that, intended or not, inconsistency or direct conflict could emerge in a range of policies carried out separately by provinces where previously some coordinating element was provided implicitly or explicitly by the federal government. The (transactions) costs imposed by this disharmonization of policy could be substantial. These could include inefficiencies in resource allocation as well as much higher costs for interprovincial negotiations designed to harmonize policy.

There are also policy areas with significant interprovincial spillovers. In education, for example, students who are educated in one province and move to another to seek employment transfer the benefits of their education to the recipient province. Externalities exist in other fields such as the environment (air and water pollution), fisheries, and transportation. In a significantly decentralized system, we lose some of the capacity to internalize and hence enhance (diminish) positive (negative) spillovers.

A further difficulty with the decentralization option results from having to transfer a considerable portion of federal taxing power to the provinces. If current federal spending on goods and services (exclusive of transfers) is neutral with respect to geographic allocation, the regional impact of reallocating taxing powers will be relatively benign. However, it is unambiguously clear that the redistributive activity of the federal government is not neutral. In fact, equalization payments are deliberately allocated on a geographic basis. Unemployment insurance payments also involve a considerable interregional transfer (premiums collected are less than benefits paid) to provinces and regions with unemployment rates higher than the national average. There is also a slight equalization element in EPF transfers made to have-not provinces.

In a significantly decentralized federal system, the fiscal capacity of the central government to engage in redistributive policies would be diminished. This would apply with special force to those programs which deliberately or *de facto* transfer wealth from richer to poorer provinces. It also puts at risk interprovincial consistency in benefits from social programs in health, education and welfare. With no established national standards (health care is an exception) the federal government's contribution to cost-shared programs is the only lever available to setting implicit norms across the country. With significant devolution even those protections would disappear.

This points to a fundamental difference in the inherent economic interests of "have" and "have-not" provinces. Net recipient provinces (Atlantic Canada, Quebec, Manitoba, and Saskatchewan) have a vested interest in the maintenance of national redistribution policies. The less they "have," the stronger this interest. The decline in net transfers to Quebec over the past decade resulting from improvements in its relative economic performance is an important factor in its increasing desire for policy autonomy.

Net contributory provinces (Alberta, British Columbia, and Ontario) have a stronger interest in focussing more on allocative policies and would be more oriented towards improving efficiency and on moving away from equity (redistribution) policies. This does not mean that they have no interest in redistribution but that, on balance, they would likely prefer "people-based" equity programs rather than "place-based" ones. The former provide benefits to at least some of their citizens, the latter do not.

The implications of these considerations for Atlantic Canada are dealt with at greater length below. But the potential impact of significant decentralization on the region is reasonably clear. As individual provinces and as a region, we receive the largest per capita infusions of redistributed wealth in Canada. If these were to drop dramatically, it would cause a major decline in standards of living.

The Separation Option

So much has been written over the last twenty years about both the politics and the economics of Quebec sovereignty that another foray into the territory is doomed to say too little or to say it too simplistically. In the current discussion, there have been further attempts to quantify the economic consequences of separation. This time it is different, however, in that there is almost as much work going into estimating the impacts on the rest of Canada (ROC) as for Quebec.

Rather than attempt a survey and evaluation of the research that has been done, we will confine ourselves to outlining the main areas of agreement and debate regarding the economic consequences of separation. The likelihood of a declaration of independence and the factors that could cause it will not be dealt with here. We assume throughout that ROC remains as a single federal country after separation.

There is general agreement within and outside Quebec that independence will entail significant transitional (short-term) costs for all parts of Canada. There are, however, differences of view about the size and duration of costs and the proportional impacts on Quebec and on ROC. Key areas of impact include:

1) *Financial markets and credit ratings*: Quebec (almost certainly) and ROC (probably) would face the reaction of financial market unease and uncertainty about the ultimate outcome of the split. Concerns about political stability and economic performance would cause premiums to be charged on Canadian public sector borrowing.

2) *Investor uncertainty*: The prospects for a flight of capital from Quebec are much higher than for Canada as a whole. Nevertheless, delays and reduction of investment activities are likely in both Quebec and ROC with the more pronounced impact in Quebec.

3) *Interest/exchange rate impact*: There would likely be a temporary loss of confidence in the Canadian dollar. Significant downward pressure on the dollar could force the Bank of Canada to raise interest rates to halt this

downward trend. This could well prove to be temporary or to occur gradually in advance of an independence declaration.

4) *International trade agreements*: A separate Quebec is, as Courchene has pointed out,[15] virtually certain to run into a major problem negotiating a trade deal with the United States. Its freedom to pursue "Quebec Inc." policies to foster economic development (for example, business transfers, energy subsidies) which are acceptable as a province of Canada would not be acceptable if it were a sovereign state. There is also the possibility that the United States will press to reopen the Free Trade Agreement with the remnant Canadian federation. Where regional/provincial interests diverge within ROC, there may be a receptive audience in Canada for renegotiation. The uncertainty created by these possibilities could influence both trade activities and investment prospects.

The extent of the impact would vary considerably depending on the atmosphere surrounding negotiations over division of assets and liabilities, trade and other commercial relations, and common monetary policy (as well as currency). It is reasonable to assume that the more acrimonious the atmosphere, the higher would be the transitional costs.

A big imponderable in the debate is how to divide federal liabilities (principally the debt) and assets in the event of a breakup. How much of the debt burden would a sovereign Quebec assume? Boothe and Harris begin with four simple methods of allocation:

1) by person, on the simple premise that it is the individual who should bear the costs and benefits of past federal spending;

2) by employed worker, which would benefit high unemployment regions of Canada;

3) by citizen, which would correct for recent immigrants on the basis that they were not direct recipients of past federal spending;

4) by regional share of gross domestic product, which would correct for regional differences in income but may not correctly account for past benefits.[16]

The precise formula will be subject to rigorous negotiation. Quebec has already partially staked its territory. Instead of a share equivalent to its 25 percent of national population, the Bélanger-Campeau report claimed only 18.5 percent. This is equivalent to Quebec's share of federal assets that would revert to the new sovereign state's ownership.

The potential for bickering and frustration both in deciding the division of the debt, and in the actual administration of any agreement, is significant. The division itself could trigger significant migration of people and capital. Canada would still be responsible for actual repayment of foreign creditors, but would rely on regular installments coming from Quebec. Any balance of payments crisis in the new state could interrupt these payments.

Long-term impacts are more difficult to project. Investor uncertainty will dissipate and financial markets will settle into a pattern related to the real underlying economic conditions of the newly separated economies. Trade and other international agreements will be adjusted to the new realities. The nature and reliability of a political and economic union forged out of the remaining provinces and territories is far less certain. The dominance of Ontario in terms of both population and economic activity would certainly test interprovincial relations. It could well lead to balkanization tendencies — efforts to forge separate regional and interregional alliances with other provinces and possibly with contiguous areas of the United States. The pressures for decentralization in a ROC federation (to avoid being overwhelmed by Ontario, among other things) could prove stronger than the forces pushing in the direction of centralization (to ensure the maintenance of the economic and political union).

The capacity for structural adjustment in response to international competitive pressures is likely to be impaired for some time. National efforts to improve productivity through revised training and education programs, or by way of enhanced research and development activity, will be difficult to establish. It is hard enough in the most harmonious interprovincial and federal-provincial environment to initiate and implement coordinated policy efforts. In an atmosphere where centralizing and decentralizing forces are pulling in opposite directions, cooperative action may be impossible.

IMPLICATIONS FOR ATLANTIC CANADA

Neither extensive decentralization nor separation will have positive impacts on Atlantic Canada. Both are likely to impose substantial interim net costs on the region. The outcome of constitutional discussions and negotiations, therefore, is crucial for the region. Impacts may be more profound here than in any other part of the country because of our greater economic vulnerability. A large part of that vulnerability results from the greater dependence on external transfers, rather than indigenous wealth creation, to support public and private spending in the region.

Federal Spending Patterns

Much of Atlantic Canada's dependence on federal transfers relates to disparities in economic activity and federal programs that help compensate for this. Some programs (like equalization and unemployment insurance) compensate for lack of an industrial base and economic opportunities. Others (EPF) represent the federal government's commitment to national objectives. A small portion related to subsidies and regional development spending attempts to stabilize and expand the economic base. Federal spending on goods and services is no less important. Atlantic Canada receives a significant share of spending on operations and management, which helps stabilize a rather weak economic base.[17]

These programs reflect the notions of equity and fairness that have been

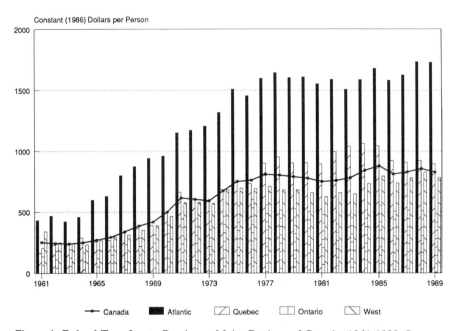

Figure 1. Federal Transfers to Provinces, Major Regions of Canada, 1961-1989. Source: Statistics Canada 13-213.

central to the Canadian federation. Provisions for equalization and regional development programs are cemented in Sec. 36 of the constitution. The two major forms of transfers (support/access, and development) should not be confused. If anything, they are substitutes; the more the Atlantic economy expands through regional development spending, for example, the less will be the requirement for equalization or unemployment insurance.

Federal spending on various programs (excluding debt payments) is expected to total $115.8 billion in 1991-92. Of this amount about 35 percent is in the form of transfers to persons. Another 21 percent is accounted for by payments directly to other levels of government. Other transfers (foreign aid, employment programs, money for Natives and agriculture, transportation, regional development and science) are another 13.7 percent. National defense and Crown corporations take 11 percent and 4.4 percent respectively, while operating and capital spending account for 14.6 percent.

Federal Transfers to Provinces

Transfers from the federal to provincial governments are in three main categories: equalization ($8.4 billion in 1991-92); EPF ($7.7 billion in 1991-92); and CAP ($5.7 billion in 1991-92). All have been affected by fiscal restraint measures in the late 1980s and early 1990s. In terms of constant dollars per person, spending has not varied substantially since 1977, and has declined since

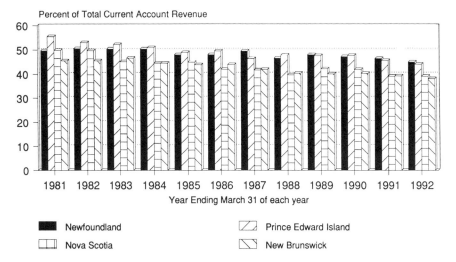

Figure 2. Federal Transfers to the Atlantic Provinces as a Proportion of Provincial Revenues, 1980/81-1991/92. Sources: Canadian Tax Foundation; Provincial Budget papers.

1985 (Figure 1). Atlantic Canada depends more on these types of transfers, mostly because of its equalization entitlements. Some $3.1 billion of the $8.4 billion paid out in equalization in 1991-92 will flow to the Atlantic region.

A corollary of this is that governments in Atlantic Canada rely more on federal transfers for their budget revenues (Figure 2). The proportion of Atlantic provincial revenues coming in the form of federal transfers in 1991-92 ranges from 37 percent to 44 percent. This compares with 12 percent in Ontario and 20 percent in Quebec. Equalization as a proportion of provincial revenues has been declining in recent years, however.

Equalization is important in the constitutional discussions on two counts. First, dramatic change to the nature of the federation could threaten it. The most likely consequences would be a significant reduction in services provided by provincial governments in Atlantic Canada, greatly lower incomes, and increased emigration. Second, equalization could also be the mechanism used by the federal government to provide Atlantic provincial governments with the fiscal capability to manage newly acquired powers.

EPF provides equal per capita grants to provinces as part of the federal commitment to provincial health care and postsecondary education programs. Growth in EPF has been reduced during the 1980s, and this will continue well into the 1990s as part of federal deficit control efforts. The CAP shares the costs of provincial spending on social assistance on a 50:50 basis. Growth in CAP has also been restrained well into the 1990s as part of deficit control efforts, but only in nonequalization-receiving provinces.

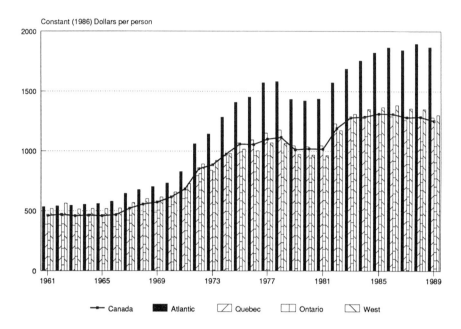

Figure 3. Federal Transfers to Persons, Major Regions of Canada, 1961-1989. Source: Statistics Canada.

Transfers to People

Transfers to individuals are the largest single component of federal program spending. They include benefits to the elderly, unemployment insurance (UI), family allowances, and veterans' benefits. They amount to $40 billion in 1991-92. Transfers to persons have declined in real terms since 1985, although this trend reversed significantly in 1990 as UI payments increased sharply in response to changes in eligibility requirements, and recession.

Federal transfers to persons totalled almost $38 billion in 1989. Atlantic Canada accounted for $4.7 billion of this total. Transfers to persons are relatively more important in Atlantic Canada (Figure 3). UI is mainly responsible for this, due to a combination of high unemployment, region-specific benefits, and some sector-specific benefits (fishermen). Atlantic Canada generally accounts for about one-fifth of all unemployment payments. Provincial administration of UI would be difficult to accommodate in Atlantic Canada. The region's residents receive more in benefits than they pay in premiums. For example, UI payments were about $1,500 per person in Newfoundland in 1990 compared to an average of $500 a person in Canada.

Transfers to Business

Federal transfers to business, particularly capital assistance, have a role in

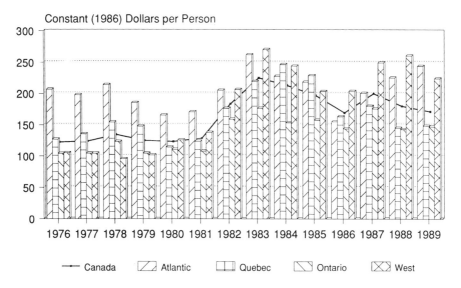

Figure 4. Federal Transfers to Business (Excluding Energy and Agriculture), Major Regions of Canada, 1976-1989. Source: Statistics Canada 13-213.

promoting economic growth. Across Canada, total direct transfers to business were $7.5 billion in 1989, down from $9 billion in 1987. Figure 4 shows federal transfers to business in the major regions in Canada in constant (1986) dollars per person from 1961 to 1989·.[18] Spending peaked in 1983 at $224 per person. Atlantic Canada generally received higher transfers per person up to the early 1980s, but has since consistently fallen behind other parts of Canada, especially the West. In 1989, the West received $224 per person versus $169 for Canada. Transfers to Atlantic Canada, in real terms, have increased steadily since the fall-off of the mid-1980s, with large increases in 1988 and 1989 due to the activity of the Atlantic Canada Opportunities Agency (ACOA).

Regional Development Spending

Figure 5 shows another estimate of regional development spending in Atlantic Canada over time in constant (1986) dollars. Spending levels were estimated from departmental annual reports and the public accounts. There is also an estimate of regional development spending relative to total program spending. (Program spending does not include debt servicing.)

Real regional development spending began to decline soon after the Department of Regional Economic Expansion (DREE) began operations in 1969. The decline continued through several reorganizations of DREE and its successor agencies. Spending levelled off in the mid-1980s as various attempts to develop new regional mechanisms in Atlantic Canada were tried. Only after the

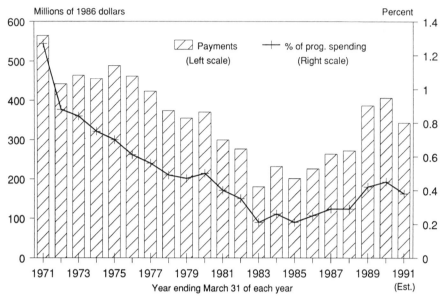

Figure 5. Assistance to Businesses in Atlantic Canada, 1970-71-1990/91. Sources: Departmental Annual Reports (1971-84); Department of Finance estimates (1985-88); APEC estimates (1989-90).

establishment of the ACOA in 1987 and the activation of its "action program" a year later did spending levels swing upward in a meaningful way.

Regional development spending in Atlantic Canada has never regained the prominence it had in the early 1970s. Regional development spending as a percent of total program spending was as high as 1.3 percent in 1970-71 and fell as low as 0.2 percent in 1981-82. ACOA spending helped regional development spending rise to levels not seen since the late 1970s but this commitment seems to have been very short-lived; the relative importance of regional development spending in Atlantic Canada began to slide again after 1989-90.

Federal Spending on Wages and Salaries

Federal departmental and Crown corporation employment has declined nationally and regionally over the last few years. Atlantic Canada, with more than its share of federal public servants is particularly sensitive to these changes.

Federal spending on goods and services (the day-to-day operations of government) has an important effect on the economy. About 545,000 federal public servants and employees of Crown corporations accounted for almost $20 billion in wages and salaries in 1989-90. About 75,000 of these were in Atlantic Canada where wages and salaries topped $2.8 billion. Federal employment (excluding Crown corporations) declined by only 0.7 percent from 1985-86 to 1989-90 across Canada, but by 3.7 percent in Atlantic Canada (including a 6.5 percent decline in Nova Scotia alone). Privatization accounts for the bulk of the national decline in employment.

Cuts in federal employment, particularly when they are concentrated in poorer provinces, can be harmful. Closure of military bases since 1989 affected Atlantic Canada especially. Total closure of CFB Summerside in Prince Edward Island, for example, caused great adjustment problems in the local community, compounded by actual loss of provincial population (as military personnel were relocated outside Prince Edward Island) that reduced entitlement to federal transfers.

What Would Loss of Transfers Entail?

The preceding sections demonstrate how much Atlantic Canada depends on federal transfers and general spending. Complete elimination of the gap between federal revenues collected from, and federal spending in, Atlantic Canada would cause a drastic drop in total economic activity levels and in living standards.

A simple order of magnitude measure is to take the difference between spending and revenue as a percentage of gross provincial output. The result is an approximate calculation of the drop in economic welfare. It varies within the region from about a 20 percent decline in Nova Scotia to a 35 percent drop in Prince Edward Island.[19] Even this crude approximation indicates that the drop in living standards would be dramatic.

The discussion of the decentralization and separation options suggested that federal transfers to Atlantic Canada were at risk in either instance. In the first case, significant decentralization would reduce the capacity of the federal government to effect redistribution of wealth. The interests of the larger, wealthier economies in reorienting policy focus from redistribution (especially geographic) to increasing efficiency will be important in this respect. The decline in net transfers to Quebec have also reduced that province's interest in sustaining transfers at the expense of greater provincial autonomy.

In the separation options, both the willingness and capacity for transfers are likely to be impaired. This will be especially true for region-specific transfers in what may become an increasingly balkanized and decentralized ROC federation. Given the unsettled political and economic atmosphere inherent in this option, the rapidity and extent of the decline in transfers may well be greater than in the decentralization case. This would leave less scope for gradual adjustment in Atlantic Canada and for attempts to restructure the regional economy to produce more wealth. There may be a counterforce to this, however. If there is a strong desire to maintain a union even at high cost, retention of most transfers may be the price the "have" provinces would be willing to pay.

Under either option, a significant reduction in transfers will lower standards of living. This will almost certainly lead to substantial emigration from Atlantic Canada. Mobility of people is an important adjustment mechanism for dealing with differences in income levels and employment opportunities. However, the history of emigration from Atlantic Canada (dating back well before substantial federal transfer programs were in effect) does not suggest that this is a simple remedy for dealing with regional disparities.

Without revisiting the debate on the role of migration as a mechanism of structural adjustment, when disproportionate numbers of the better educated and more skilled members of the labour force move, the impact on the overall quality of the labour force is negative. This may be both a disincentive for investment and a hindrance to productivity growth.

The drop in living standards in the separation option is likely to be larger and faster than in the decentralization case. As a result, emigration would be more rapid and more extensive. Major losses of population would have deleterious political, social and cultural impacts on both local communities and provinces. The consequences would also be negative for business enterprises engaged primarily in local markets. Companies confined to such markets will suffer from a decline in their market base, profits and capital asset values.

Considerable uncertainty will arise over the physical separation of Atlantic Canada from ROC. The more acrimonious the "divorce settlement," the greater the risk of temporary disruption to movements of goods and people through Quebec. Combined with the decline in living standards and the migration of the best and brightest, this could severely dampen any normal investment prospects.

This suggests that of the two options, Atlantic Canada has more to fear, at least in the short term, from the separation of Quebec. It is nothing short of incredible that public opinion polls in the region have indicated more than half the population feels that a declaration of independence by Quebec will be neutral to positive in its impact on the region. In fact, exactly the opposite is certain to occur.

This analysis also suggests that significant decentralization is not in the best interests of Atlantic Canada unless we are prepared to argue that the crisis created by elimination or drastic reduction in federal transfers will spontaneously generate positive structural adjustments. There is no doubt that adversity can be a positive influence on entrepreurial spirit, and can stimulate an aggressive search for alternatives. How rapid and extensive such a turnaround is likely to be is open to serious question.

This does not preclude the value of searching for alternatives to transfers as a buttress for regional economic activity. But that search is potentially more fruitful in an environment of gradual adjustment rather than radical change. We should also remember that the search for alternatives, for real development that reduces reliance on transfers is not a new topic for Atlantic Canadians. In the current context, however, it is more critical than ever before. We turn therefore, to consideration of what the region will have to do if faced with either of the paths outlined above.

OPTIONS FOR ATLANTIC CANADA

Faced with the prospect of substantial declines in access to social programs, and in standards of living, there are several paths which Atlantic Canada may choose to follow:

1) Negotiate flexibly but firmly for retention of the equalization structure and for maintenance of support for social programs (including UI and CAP).

2) Recognizing that other forces will cause ongoing reduction in fiscal transfers to the provinces, follow strategies designed to restructure the regional economy effectively.

3) To strengthen both the negotiating position of the region in constitutional discussions and the efforts to restructure the economy, pursue the option of regional economic integration more aggressively.

These are not mutually exclusive paths but do warrant separate consideration.

The equalization structure has existed for more than thirty years. It extends considerable financial support to poorer provinces to help them provide public goods and services. There has always been a strong equity basis to equalization — equals should be treated equally irrespective of where they live.[20] Someone living in a small town in Prince Edward Island should have access to public services roughly comparable to someone living in Toronto or Winnipeg. Equalization attempts to achieve this by transferring financial resources to provinces whose own sources of revenue are inadequate for these purposes.

A less well-known argument for equalization contends that such transfers also promote economic efficiency. If people moved from one locale or province to another because of significant differences in quality and availability of public goods and services, this would detract from the efficient allocation of resources. These resources should be employed where they are most productive. Movement induced by other factors would reduce their productivity and hence their contribution to the economy. Equalization inhibits such inefficient movement.

There have been counterarguments regarding the efficiency effects of equalization-type transfers, however. One is the fostering of a "transfer dependency" whereby payments from Ottawa are a disincentive for provinces to pursue economic development on the grounds that every extra "own-source" dollar of revenue means one dollar less from Ottawa. This has been a concern in hydrocarbon developments off both Newfoundland and Nova Scotia. There is scope to correct the disincentives by appropriate measures, as the development agreement for oil and gas development off Nova Scotia has attempted. In general, it is highly questionable whether governments would deliberately refrain from economic development efforts on these grounds.

The dependency argument, in part, also holds that transfers impede the movement of factors of production out of a receiving region, and therefore inhibit or reduce economic efficiency. This is the opposite position to the efficiency effects argument just outlined. It would be difficult to use this argument to justify reduction of transfers, however, as this would encourage the "desirable" emigration not only of low productivity factors, but also the "undesirable" outward movement of higher productivity factors that it would be better to retain. In fact, the economic history of Atlantic Canada over the past century (going back well before modern transfer systems) suggests that factor emigration did not improve efficiency as measured by income and employment performances.

THE DEBATE AND ATLANTIC CANADA:
AN ASSESSMENT AND SOME FURTHER CONSIDERATIONS
    The fate of federal transfers is central to the debate, especially in Atlantic Canada. Most research indicates strongly that Atlantic Canada has been the biggest net beneficiary of transfers, and Alberta has been the biggest net donor.[21] Mansell's analysis indicates broader inequities in the process, however.[22] At a macroeconomic scale, he believes, the policies have focussed on redistribution at the expense of efficiency; parts of Canada may have been supported or their viability maintained, but the overall economy has suffered. At the regional level, policies have destabilized rather than stabilized regional economies. Thus, one of the main reasons Alberta has contributed much more than it has withdrawn over the years has been the inequitable impact of the National Energy Policy.
    It is evident that the federal-provincial relationships that have governed transfer payments for thirty years have already changed. It is also clear that more radical change would ensue if Canada were to divide. This would cause a fundamental rethinking of the whole basis of confederation, with "have" provinces much less inclined to support "have-not" provinces, at least to the extent that they have in the past.[23]
    The point is that the seven provinces that receive equalization payments need not apologize for this. There has long been an acceptance in Canada of an implicit "social contract" in which individual (and sectoral or regional) risks are pooled and insured through a system of social programs including health care, unemployment insurance and income support for the poor. This would justify firmness in the negotiating stance.
    To avoid the high costs to the region of a disintegration of Canada and recognizing the diminished role of the federal government which has already occurred with fiscal restraint, the region will probably need to be flexible in the economic demands it makes in such negotiations. Acceptance of financial responsibility for policy devolution that will further strain fiscal capacity may well be required. The ideal situation would be for transfers of responsibility and taxing power to be fiscally neutral — current federal spending in the province would equal the revenue value of tax points transferred. There is no certainty that the ideal will occur. In any event, efforts at both federal and provincial levels to reduce accumulated debt imply an overall lowering of public spending.
    The changes in the federal role will continue with or without a constitutional

negotiation. Restructuring of the federal system will be speeded up by such a process. However, as the Atlantic Provinces Economic Council (APEC) has argued, international competitive forces, decline in the relative returns to primary resource industries, and the increasing importance of knowledge- and technology-based economic development will put considerable pressure on the regional economy to transform or decline.[24]

We further suggest that a strategy for development would require several key components: 1) a focus on human resource development to improve management and labour skills, and to enhance adaptability to technological change; 2) greater emphasis on expanding export markets for goods and services; 3) improvement in the climate for entrepreneurial development whether exercised by individuals or community development groups; and 4) considerable movement towards regional economic cooperation.

This is much easier said than done. However, such an orientation in development strategy at least forces recognition of some fundamental truths about economic development. The standards of living in this region will decline as external transfers are reduced. Wealth creation will be required to replace such transfers if income levels are to be maintained.

Whatever the myriad of mechanisms for doing so, there are only a handful of basic components to achieving economic growth. Earnings from external trade must increase (net exports increase) and/or the resource base must expand (through capital investment, labour force growth or both) and/or existing resources must be used more efficiently. Any strategies adopted must be oriented to achieving one or more of those objectives.

More recently, APEC contended that greater regional economic integration should be an important element of any strategy for restructuring the region's economy and improving its performance.[25] The gains from enhanced economic integration are well established. Reduced costs of government services may result from several types of cooperative action including elimination of restrictions on government procurement, sharing the costs of infrastructure, and joint formulation of policy and delivery of programs. Lower costs can be passed on as lower taxes, better services, or a reduced public debt. Gains also come from lower costs of production as regulations that restrict movement of goods and services, people and capital are removed. A coordinated infrastructure policy (highways, ports and so on) can potentially lower transportation and energy costs to producers. Consumers benefit from lower prices of goods and services with the sharing of producer gains. There are also potential "dynamic" gains over the long term as improvements in the productivity and competitiveness of firms translate into larger markets, more employment, and an expanded economy.

Economies also become more integrated or interdependent through harmonizing public sector policies. Where provinces have significant authority there is a potential for initiatives to work at cross purposes at a significant cost to the region. Policy harmonization can involve adjusting existing policies or regulatory regimes to make them compatible among jurisdictions; eliminating direct competition in areas such as industrial promotion; informal coordination of policy development and implementation; and formal coordination of policy development and joint implementation through an agency or commission. Benefits from increased cooperation are available in several policy areas: trade promotion (including tourism); investment (industrial development) promotion; and technology transfer and diffusion. There is role for the federal government both in promoting harmonization through regional initiatives and enhancing sensitivity of national policies to local concerns.

The APEC has never contended that regional economic cooperation would, by itself, correct the problems of the Atlantic economy or preclude the need for transfers to support living standards. Cooperation can, however, increase the effectiveness of public sector policies, reduce costs of government services and improve the climate for business and economic development.

Notes

1.   Canada. *Shaping Canada's Future Together: Proposals* (Ottawa: Supply and Services Canada, 1991). An accompanying document, *Canadian Federalism and Economic Union: Partnership for Prosperity* (Ottawa: Supply and Services Canada, 1991), explores the economic union aspects of the proposal.

2.   For a brief history of Canada's constitutional debate in recent decades, see Robert A. Jenness, "How We Got to Where We Are," in Economics of Confederation Series (Ottawa: Informetrica, July 1991).

3.   Richard G. Harris and Douglas D. Purvis, "Constitutional Change and Canada's Prospects," paper prepared for the Business Council on National Issues, March 1991.

4.   Ibid., 24-25.

5.   Robin Boadway, remarks for a panel discussion, "Politiques économiques fédérales," ASDEQ Congrès, Montreal, May 1991.

6.   See Thomas J. Courchene, *In Praise of Renewed Federalism* (Toronto: C.D. Howe Institute, July 1991); "The Community of the Canada's," an invited submission to Quebec's Commission sur l'avenir politique et constitutionel du Québec, November 1990; and "Canada 1992: Political Denouement or Economic Renaissance?" paper presented to the Economic Dimensions of Constitutional Change Forum, Kingston, Ontario, June 1991.

7.   Constitutional Committee of the Quebec Liberal Party, *A Quebec Free to Choose: Report of the Constitutional Committee* (Montreal: Quebec Liberal Party, 1991). Jean Allaire was chairman of the committee.

8.   Commission on the Political and Constitutional Future of Quebec, *Report of the Commission on the Political and Constitutional Future of Quebec* (Quebec City: Government of Quebec, 1991). Michel Bélanger and Jean Campeau co-chaired this commission.

9.   Ibid., 73.

10.   *Some Practical Suggestions for Canada*. Report of the "Group of 22," June 1991.

11. *A Quebec Free to Choose.*

12. See Canada West Foundation, "A Strategy for Canadian Nationalists," *Western Perspectives*, March 1991.

13. Boadway, remarks for a panel discussion.

14. Canada West Foundation, "A Strategy for Canadian Nationalists."

15. See Courchene, *In Praise of Renewed Federalism*, 30-34.

16. Paul Boothe and Richard Harris, *The Economics of Constitutional Change: Dividing the Federal Debt.* The Economics of Constitutional Change Series, No. 1 (Edmonton: Western Centre for Economic Research, University of Alberta, May 1991).

17. The disproportionate share relates to programs to decentralize government offices in the late 1970s and early 1980s, and the large numbers of military personnel stationed in the region. This applies more to the Maritimes, less to Newfoundland and Labrador.

18. Assistance for energy and agriculture is excluded from this analysis because amounts of transfers have been substantial, but inconsistent over time. Energy assistance, for example, includes large payments during the 1970s and 1980s under the Petroleum Incentive Program, and the Petroleum Compensation Fund, both of which no longer exist. Subsidies to farmers increased greatly in the late 1980s to compensate for a series of bad grain crops. In the course of this review APEC uncovered inconsistencies in the way Statistics Canada allocated capital assistance in its Provincial Economic Accounts (the source of many of these numbers). Numbers for 1988 and 1989 are APEC estimates, that are subject to further change.

19. See Alasdair Sinclair, "Atlantic Canada in the Post-Meech Era," *APEC Newsletter* 34, no. 5 (June 1990).

20. This, and the efficiency aspects of equalization that follow, are discussed by Paul Hobson, in "Equalizing Transfers and Provincial Fiscal Capacities in Canada," the revised version of a paper presented to the Federalism and Atlantic Canada Group, Acadia University, Sackville, New Brunswick, July 1991.

21. Measurement of fiscal transfers tell only part of the story of Canada's mammoth redistributive system; this is the part that public accounts cover. As transfers, whether to other governments, individuals, or businesses are spent and respent to buy goods and services, the final beneficiaries include, for example, southern Ontario where much of Canada's consumer manufacturing sector is located, or where many products that find their way to markets in Atlantic Canada, for example, are distributed.

22. Robert Mansell, "The Economics of Canadian Federalism," paper presented to the New Brunswick Commission on Canadian Federalism, May 1991.

23. Sinclair, "Atlantic Canada in the Post-Meech Era."

24. See APEC, "Strategies and Options for the Atlantic Economy in the 1990s," paper presented to the APEC annual conference, St. John's, Newfoundland, October 1990.

25. See APEC, "Atlantic Economic Cooperation: An Exploration of the Concept, its Benefits and Costs," paper presented to the APEC annual conference, Dartmouth, Nova Scotia, June 1991.

5

Section 92A, Policy and Economic Development

Isabel B. Anderson

INTRODUCTION

The complaints were clear at the annual conference of the premiers this year. All of them, with the leaders from the Territories, joined in calling for reform of the Bank of Canada. Their complaint — interest rates and the value of the Canadian dollar have been too high (*Financial Post*, 28 August 1991). The western Canadian premiers called for reform of Canadian monetary policy at the 1988 Canadian Premiers Conference in Saskatoon. Their position on the matter then was clear — high interest rates and an appreciated Canadian dollar, the product of Bank of Canada policy designed to solve central Canadian economic problems, had produced adverse effects on the western Canadian provincial economies.

Economic problems in Ontario may indeed be at the root of the western Canadian complaints. A recent Statistics Canada report showed that 74 percent of the jobs lost during the recent recession in the country were lost in Ontario, suggesting that the recession had been an Ontario-based phenomenon (*Globe and Mail*, 6 September 1991). A report in August showed that the new government of Ontario had increased public servant wages by 14.5 percent during its first year, a substantially higher rate of growth than in previous years (*Globe and Mail*, 31 August 1991). To the extent that a substantial portion of wage settlements in Canada occur in Ontario, Canadian monetary authorities could well be concerned about the effect on the national price index. Nevertheless, it is not clear whether the western Canadian complaints are any more than "fed bashing," although some new literature on the European monetary union scheduled for 1997, suggests that the macroeconomic adjustment mechanism in areas like Canada, in fact, could produce adverse effects in some, but not all parts of a common currency area (CCA).

This paper shows that Sec. 92A of the Constitution Act, 1982, formally separated the responsibility for implementing several types of government policy from the responsibility for the outcome of it, especially as it affects the process of economic growth and development. It left the implementation with the federal government, and the outcome with the provincial government. It set the stage for more conflict between the federal and provincial governments over revenue sharing, especially conflict between Ottawa and the nonrenewable natural resource-based provinces. It is not easy to dismiss out of hand, western Canadian complaints about policy that can affect the process of economic growth and development.

The remainder of the paper is divided into five parts. The first contains a brief description of the process of economic development, showing that it can be affected by interest and exchange rate policies. The federal government's responsibility for those policies is explained in the second part. The provincial responsibility for economic development is explained in the third part of the paper. The fourth contains an analysis of the spillovers of macroeconomic policy in open CCAs to show how policy designed to solve problems in one part can have adverse effects elsewhere in the area.

THE PROCESS OF ECONOMIC DEVELOPMENT

The purpose of economic development is to create a structure of economic activity which assures persistently high levels of productivity, and thus, high levels of income, or welfare per person in the community. Economic development itself is a process, the process by which the structure which assures persistently high levels of productivity and income per person, is put in place.

Interest rates, the cost of borrowing, and the rate of exchange, the price of the domestic currency relative to the currencies of the country's trading partners, affect the process of economic development. Changing an economy from one in which there are low levels of productivity to one in which there are high levels, usually requires growth in the existing, or in new industries; the diversification of economic activity beyond agriculture to include the processing of raw materials and manufacturing of capital equipment; and the development of a service sector, particularly the facilities to provide financial services. It requires the availability of credit. It requires investment expenditures, the development of an infrastructure for transportation and communications, social overhead capital in the form of housing, education, and health care, and often, technological change. It requires a growing demand for the output of the community's economic resources, and a growing demand in foreign markets if the development of the economy is to be based on growth in the export sector.

The case of Saskatchewan illustrates how a dichotomy between government policy making and the responsibility for the outcome of that policy, was created in 1982 by Sec. 92A of the Constitution Act. That section, the Resource Amendment, put the responsibility for promoting economic growth and development largely in the hands of the province in the case of the nonrenewable natural resource-based provincial economies. Saskatchewan is one of these. It is very much an economy open to international trade in goods, services, and financial assets.

Until the late 1960s, economic growth and development in Saskatchewan was based entirely on the development of the renewable natural resource sector — grains produced for foreign markets. Now, that agricultural economy is mature. Although it is as competitive as any in the world, it contains few avenues for developing new opportunities from technological change, or capital accumulation, or an extension of the land area under cultivation, and thus, few opportunities for growth and development. Economic development associated with agriculture must now come from manufacturing machinery and equipment used to produce the raw materials, and from processing those raw materials. With relatively small provincial and Canadian markets, the latter requires the liberalization of world markets for processed raw materials, a matter not high on the agenda of the multilateral trade negotiations.

During the 1970s and 1980s, substantial economic growth and development in Saskatchewan came from the nonrenewable natural resource sector, from the production of fuels, potash, and uranium. With international markets for potash, and uranium expected to grow substantially in the future, and with a market for processed heavy oil, these industries could well provide the basis for future development of the provincial economy. Together with diversification around the production of grains, heavy oil, potash, and uranium, there is considerable promise of high rates of economic growth and population in the years to come.

High costs of borrowing funds — high interest rates — discourage capital formation and thus, the shift in the structure of economic activity which is required for change. Consumption is discouraged when credit is not readily available. An appreciated domestic currency discourages expenditures by foreign consumers on export goods, although it encourages the inflow of investment funds from abroad. Low interest rates and a depreciated Canadian dollar encourage the growth and development of an export-oriented economy like the one in Saskatchewan.

INTEREST AND EXCHANGE RATE POLICY

The Constitution Act gives the federal government exclusive power in matters of the money supply and the operation of the Canadian financial system, as well as in matters of the regulation of trade and commerce. In particular, Sec. 91 states that the Parliament of Canada has exclusive powers over:

2. The Regulation of Trade and Commerce.

...

14. Currency and Coinage.

15. Banking, Incorporation of Banks, and the Issue of Paper Money.

...

18. Bills of Exchange and Promissory Notes.

19. Interest.

20. Legal Tender. (Canada. Department of Justice, 1986: 29-30)

This formally created a CCA for the Canadian provinces and left the federal government exclusively responsible for monetary policy, that is, the provision of liquidity and the level of interest rates for the confederation as a whole.[1] The founding of the Bank of Canada in 1935 assured that this central monetary authority would also be responsible for exchange rate policy which would focus on assuring relative price stability. In particular,

> practical policy leading to the establishment of central banking in Canada was oriented to international trade and ... its goal was internal and external price stability, with internal price stability being relative to external conditions... A central bank was established because, both from an administrative and a political point of view, it was seen to be the best way to achieve a particular practical policy [namely, internal, and internationally relative, price stability] (Neill, 1991: 17).

More recently, Canada's participation in the International Monetary Fund assures that domestic price stability and the stability of the domestic currency relative to the currencies of its major trading partners, are the objectives of monetary policy. In particular, under Article IV of the Articles of Agreement of the International Monetary Fund,

> Recognizing that the essential purpose of the international monetary system is to provide a framework that facilitates the exchange of goods, services, and capital among countries, and that sustains sound economic growth, and that a principal objective is the continuing development of the orderly underlying conditions that are necessary for financial and economic stability, each member undertakes to collaborate with the Fund and other members to assure orderly exchange arrangements and to promote a stable system of exchange rates. In particular, each member shall:
>
> (i) endeavour to direct its economic and financial policies toward the objective of fostering orderly economic growth with reasonable price stability, with due regard to its circumstances;
>
> (ii) seek to promote stability by fostering orderly underlying economic and financial conditions and a monetary system that does not tend to produce erratic disruptions;
>
> (iii) avoid manipulating exchange rates or the international monetary system in order to prevent effective balance of payments adjustment or to gain an unfair competitive advantage over other members (de Vries, 1985: 381-82).

At the same time, however, economic activity in Ontario, alone, and certainly economic activity in Ontario and Quebec together, tends to dominate the patterns described by the statistical indicators of economic activity in the country as a whole. These are used to define the needs of monetary policy for the country. Ontario alone accounts for some 40 percent of the Canadian Gross Domestic

Product and Canadian employment, while it also accounts for the largest proportion of wage settlements. A policy assuring price stability for the country is a response to price and wage conditions in central Canada. A policy assuring international price stability for Canada, is also a response to the needs of central Canada.

PROVINCIAL RESPONSIBILITY FOR ECONOMIC DEVELOPMENT

Economic growth and development in Canada has been the outcome largely of private initiative, but it has often been promoted through public policy in a variety of ways, as in the 1860s and 1870s through national policies related to immigration, railways, and tariffs. Since then, especially since the 1960s, responsibility for public policy to promote economic growth and development has come to rest primarily with the provinces.

The only reference to it in the Constitution Act is in Schedule B, Part III, Equalization and Regional Disparities, where,

> Parliament and the legislatures, together with the government of Canada and the provincial governments, are committed to
>
> a) promoting equal opportunities for the well-being of Canadians;
>
> b) furthering economic development to reduce disparity of opportunities; and
>
> c) providing essential public services of reasonable quality to all Canadians (Canada. Department of Justice, 1986: 70).

Each province is responsible for building infrastructure, transportation and communications, as well as social overhead capital like education which is required for economic growth and development within the province. Each is responsible for the way in which the natural resources within the province are developed. Each provides "assistance to agriculture, fisheries, forestry, and mines and mineral resources activities to the extent that each is significant in the provincial economy." Each has become increasingly involved in promoting the development of industry within the provincial boundaries, and each usually does the administration required for federal and provincial joint programs to promote industrialization within the province. (Canadian Tax Foundation, 1989, 8:7 and 8:10).

Sec. 92A of the Constitution Act, 1982, goes even further in the case of the provinces with nonrenewable natural resources, forestry resources, and electrical energy. In particular,

> In each province, the legislature may exclusively make laws in relation to
>
> a) exploration for non-renewable natural resources in the province;
>
> b) development, conservation and management of non-renewable natural resources and forestry resources in the province, including laws in relation to the rate of primary production therefrom; and

c) development, conservation and management of sites and facilities in the province for the generation and production of electrical energy.

...

In each province, the legislature may make laws in relation to the raising of money by any mode or system of taxation in respect of

a) non-renewable natural resources and forestry resources in the province and the primary production therefrom, and

b) sites and facilities in the province for the generation of electrical energy and the production therefrom (Canada. Department of Justice, 1986: 33).

Federal government participation in promoting economic growth and development is provided for by a series of acts of Parliament. For example, the Department of Western Economic Diversification was created in 1988. It is responsible for federal policies which promote "the development and diversification of the economy of Western Canada and the advancement of the interests of Western Canada in national economic policy, program and project development and implementation." (Canada. House of Commons, 1988: 2). The Department of Industry, Science and Technology replaced the Department of Regional Industrial Expansion and provided for federal policies designed to promote regional economic development in Ontario and Quebec (Canada. House of Commons, 1990: 3). In practice, the federal government does not implement a development program in a province without the consent of the province. Thus, federal programs typically are designed to exploit the opportunities for economic development which exist within the province, and as the province wants them exploited.

A provincial government's interest in having what it sees as the best process of economic development selected comes from its need for a broadly based, steady flow of revenues which can be used for social programs like health care, education, and social services; from the fact that increasingly, it is being expected to take on more of the financial responsibility for social programs and policies designed to promote economic activity; and from already having much of the responsibility for building the infrastructure needed for resource development and industrialization (Anderson, 1991a). Just as it objects to the federal government using its funds for ill-conceived development projects in the province, it is likely to object to federal government interest and exchange rate policies which discourage the development of economic activity in the province.

SPILLOVERS OF FEDERAL POLICY

Policy designed to control inflation and to assure stability of the domestic currency, that is, monetary policy, affects the cost of borrowing, the availability of credit, and the rate of exchange. Its objective is to change economic activity in such a way that prices change at an acceptable rate, and the value of the currency in international markets remains consistent with international trade in goods,

services, and assets. The macroeconomic adjustment mechanism in an open
CCA, shows how adverse spillovers of monetary policy can be created.

Consider a simple example of a multi-economy world which is composed of
three separate economies, S, T, and U. Two of them, S and T, are members of a
CCA. There is free trade between each of them and the third, U. Capital flows
freely among the three economies. Economy S is the focus of attention.[2]

Being in a CCA, the currencies of S and T, in effect, are converted by means
of a fixed exchange rate. The currencies of each of S and T are exchanged for the
currencies of U by means of a flexible exchange rate system. For simplicity, it is
assumed that there is a separate monetary authority in each economy. Thus the
liquidity needs in each can be met in response to the real changes occurring in
each economy.[3]

There are four sectors in each economy: the goods sector; prices; the
monetary sector; and international economic relations. A fifth set of relationships, describing the total multi-economy world, closes the system. All of the
variables are in terms of real values. The adjustment mechanism within each of
the economies can be illustrated in qualitative terms by tracing the effects of a
particular policy introduced in one of the them.

Consider the case in which monetary policy is designed to control inflation in
T. It may be a situation in which the rate of inflation in T actually is unaccept-
ably high, threatening the stability of the home economy and the value of the
home currency in international markets. Alternatively, it may be a situation in
which there is a recession in T, but there is considerable fear that the introduction
of a new tax scheme, like the Goods and Services Tax, and high wage settlements in T, will create expectations of inflation in the future and that that, in
turn, will exacerbate the recovery of economic activity.

Consider, too, the bilateral adjustments which occur in S. They come from
two sides, from the fixed exchange rate side, from T, and from the flexible exchange rate side, from U. Suppose that to begin, there is general equilibrium in
all three economies so that interest rates are at the same level in each economy
and the levels of income and employment are at their natural levels, that is, the
levels that are consistent with no inflation in any of the economies.

The policy is restrictive monetary policy in T. In the short term, before there
is time to change prices, levels of income in T fall while interest rates rise. With
incomes falling, imports from S fall (exports from S to T fall). With interest rates
rising, capital flows out of S into T. There is, therefore, a deficit created in S's
balance of payments with T. With the fixed exchange rate, net claims on foreigners in S (on T), fall and the real money supply in S falls, as long as the impact on
the money supply is not sterilized.

The decrease in the money supply leads to lower incomes and higher interest
rates in S. Imports from U fall, therefore, and capital flows into S from U (with
the relatively higher rates of interest in S). Both contribute to a surplus in S's
balance of payments with U. In turn, with flexible exchange rates, the S currency

appreciates relative to the U currency. That, in turn, discourages exports from S to U, and encourages imports. It also encourages more capital to flow from U into S because foreign investment is affected by the expected value of the currency in the economy where foreigners are investing.

Restrictive monetary policy in T, therefore, discourages exports from S to T, encourages capital flows out of S into T, and changes the real money supply in S. It then discourages imports into S from U, and encourages the flow of capital into S from U. Both of these lead to the appreciation of the S currency relative to the U currency which then discourages exports from S to U and encourages the further flow of capital into S from U. Capital flowing out of S into T is replaced by capital flowing out of U into S.

In the longer term, as prices change during the adjustment process, S may or may not gain a competitive advantage over T depending upon which set of prices fall more quickly. S could gain a competitive advantage over U, however, because prices in S fall while those in U remain unchanged. Thus, over the longer term, S's exports to U increase while its imports decrease back toward their long run equilibrium levels.

The costs of borrowing rose in S during the initial adjustment process because of policy in T. It cost more to borrow to build plants, or to buy machinery and equipment, or to hold inventories than it did before the policy was implemented. It cost more to borrow to build infrastructure and social overhead capital. Funds flowed out of S and into T. The process of economic growth and development in S was adversely affected by policy to control inflation in T. Similarly, the appreciation of the S currency relative to the U currency affected exports from S to U and imports into S from U. It too, therefore, adversely affected the process of economic growth and development in S. The process of creating incomes and employment in S was discouraged; the process of developing infrastructure for an economy with persistently high levels of productivity was discouraged.

There is a similar adjustment in S to expansionary fiscal policy in T, except that in that case there is a possibility of higher incomes in T leading to more imports into T from S and, thus, more exports from S to T. Then, the surplus in S's balance of trade could offset the effect of capital flowing out of S into T leaving a small, perhaps negligible effect of funds flowing out of S into T on S's money supply. However, where S does not ordinarily export to T, or exports very little, as in the western Canadian case, the effect of expansionary fiscal policy in T on capital flows between S and T dominates the adjustment process in S. Thus, expansionary fiscal policy in T, like contractionary monetary policy in T, discourages the creation of incomes and employment in S and the development of infrastructure for an economy with persistently high levels of productivity.

Each of these cases illustrates how adverse spillovers of economic policy in an open CCA can be created. Policy makers in the recipients are then likely to look for a means of offsetting them in addition to using their own policy tools to achieve the policy objectives in their own economies.

SUMMARY AND CONCLUSION

While the western Canadian premiers may be pursuing the popular sport of "fed bashing" when they support criticisms of monetary policy in Canada, it is more likely that they are expressing the frustration which comes from having the process of economic growth and development, a process for which they are primarily responsible, and upon which they depend for the steady flow of future sources of public funds, affected by spillovers of federal government policy implemented to solve economic problems elsewhere in Canada. Growth and development requires changes in the structure of economic activity, in infrastructure, and in social overhead capital, all of which are affected by the cost of borrowing, by the availability of credit, and by the rate at which the domestic currency is exchanged in foreign exchange markets.

The provinces are primarily responsible for defining the process of economic growth and development in Canada, especially provinces like Saskatchewan, where a considerable part of economic activity is derived from the natural resource sectors. They are also responsible, in practice, for initiating it. Interest rates and exchange rates in a CCA where there is a central monetary authority, on the other hand, are changed by the federal government. Spillovers of policy like monetary policy, or fiscal policy, in an open CCA like that in Canada, can adversely affect the process by which economic growth and development occurs.

The provinces then, especially those where the development of economic activity rests primarily with the nonrenewable natural resource sector, have an incentive to search for ways to offset the adverse effects of national policies. The conflict between the federal and provincial governments which led to Sec. 92A, the Resource Amendment, was difficult enough. It is not too early to begin thinking about how to devise a mechanism by which adverse spillovers of macroeconomic policy can be contained, perhaps to begin developing a mechanism by which compensation can be paid to those provinces which have to bear the extra burden of policy designed to solve economic problems elsewhere in the union defined by a common currency and a central monetary authority.

Notes

1. A common currency area may be created for political reasons and is not necessarily an optimum currency area. See Krugman, 1990.

2. The details of the model used here are described in Anderson, 1991b. For those interested in the technical relationships used to describe multi-economy models of this sort, see Masson, *et al.*, 1990, for example. Copies of the Anderson paper in which that mode was modified for the type of analysis done here are available upon request from the author.

3. The counterpart to this in a country like Canada where there is a central monetary authority, is the shift of liquidity within the commercial banking system in response to what is needed because of real changes in economic activity in the different parts of the country.

References

Anderson, I.B. 1990a. "Macro-economic Adjustment in a Spatially Disaggregated Open Economy with Alternative Internal Patterns of Trade." Paper presented to the 24th Annual Meeting of the Canadian Economics Association, University of Victoria, 1-3 June.

———. 1990b. "Macroeconomic Adjustment in a Spatially Disaggregated Economy with Alternative Monetary Policies." Paper presented to the 65th Annual Western Economic Association International Conference, San Diego, California, 29 June-3 July.

———. 1991a. "Canada's Section 92A of the *Constitution Act* and Policy for Economic Development." Paper presented to the Annual Conference of the British Association of Canadian Studies, University of Nottingham, 12-14 April.

———. 1991b. "Macro-economic Spill-overs in Open Common Currency Areas." Paper presented to the 66th Annual Conference of the Western Economic Association International, Seattle, Washington, 29 June-3 July.

Bruce, Neil and Douglas D. Purvis. 1985. "The Specification and Influence of Goods and Factor Markets in Open-economy Macroeconomic Models." In Ronald W. Jones and Peter B. Kenen, eds., *Handbook of International Economics*. Volume 2. Amsterdam: North-Holland, 807-57.

Canada. Department of Justice. 1986. *A Consolidation of the Constitution Acts, 1867-1982*. Ottawa: Supply and Services Canada.

———. House of Commons. 1988. *An Act to promote the development and diversification of the economy of Western Canada, to establish the Department of Western Economic Diversification and to make consequential amendments to other Acts*. Second Session. Thirty-third Parliament. 35-36-37 Elizabeth II, 1986-87-88.

———. House of Commons. 1990. *An Act to establish the Department of Industry, Science and Technology, to repeal the Department of Regional Industrial Expansion Act and to make consequential amendments to other Acts*. 38 Elizabeth II, 1989-90.

Canadian Tax Foundation. 1990. *Provincial and Municipal Finances, 1989*. Toronto: Canadian Tax Foundation.

de Grauwe, Paul, and Lucas Papademos, eds. 1990. *The European Monetary System in the 1990s*. London: Longman Group UK Limited.

de Vries, Margaret Garritsen. 1985. *The International Monetary Fund, 1982-1978: Cooperation on Trial*. Volume III: *Documents*. Washington, D.C.: International Monetary Fund.

Financial Post. 15-17 June, 28 August, 29 August, 1991.

Gandolfo, Giancarlo. 1986. *International Economics*. New York: Springer-Verlag.

Globe and Mail. 31 August, 6 September, 1991.

Helliwell, John F., and Tim Padmore. 1985. "Empirical Studies of Macroeconomic Interdependence." *Handbook of International Economics*. Volume 2, 1107-51.

International Monetary Fund. *World Economic Outlook*. Washington, D.C.: International Monetary Fund. Semi-annual.

Krugman, Paul. 1990. "Policy Problems of a Monetary Union." In de Grauwe and Papademos, *The European Monetary System in the 1990s.*

Masson, Paul, Steven Symansky, and Guy Meredith. 1990. *MULTIMOD Mark II: A Revised and Extended Model.* Occasional Paper No. 71. Washington, D.C.: International Monetary Fund.

Neill, R.F. 1991. "The Policy Significance of the Founding of the Bank of Canada." Paper presented to the Canadian Economics Association, Kingston, Ontario.

Selody, Jack. 1990. *The Goal of Price Stability.* Technical Report No. 54. Ottawa: Bank of Canada.

6

Some Issues of Concern
in the Economic Union:
A Western Canadian Perspective

Edward J. Chambers
Michael B. Percy

We begin with caveats. The existence of economic ties are necessary in defining a nation. However, they are not in themselves sufficient. We therefore want to make clear at the outset that what makes a country is more than economics. There must be synergy; a country to be healthy and viable must exceed the sum of its interest groups. Vision, trust, give-and-take, and a supportive political structure are essential foundations to maintaining a national community. What follows in this paper is a discussion of regional conditions, with particular reference to western Canada. It is offered to promote a better understanding of regional economic circumstances which, in turn, may be a means to strengthening national ties.

A second caveat concerns the practice in constitutional discussions to refer to Canada as consisting of Quebec and the "rest of Canada." Obviously, Ontario, the Maritimes, and the West are hardly homogeneous in either their respective economic structures, or in their socio-demographic characteristics. Provinces in the West — even within the prairie west — and in the Maritimes do have distinguishable features. Further within each of the provinces there is a degree of heterogeneity that makes generalization difficult at the provincial, let alone at the regional level.

In this paper we consider first the economic arguments that have been advanced in favour of a confederation. We then turn to an examination of the employment structure of the four western Canadian provinces. The third and fourth sections of the paper are closely coupled. The former examines the international composition of western Canadian trade and that of the four provinces, and the latter deals with the degree of price volatility inherent in these exports and their effect on the terms of trade. In the fifth section of the paper we address the problem of regional economic instability within the federation by considering three matters: a) the optimum currency area question; b) labour mobility within the economic union; and c) transfers for income stabilization. The final section of the paper concerns western Canada's trade position and the exercise of market power.

In raising these issues we believe it neither feasible nor desirable to overburden a constitution. Our preference is a minimalist approach to constitution writing. The constitution of a federation should identify the powers of provincial units, the powers of the central government, the institutional arrangements governing their relationship, and the rights and privileges of the individual relative to the state. We do not believe it appropriate for economic policy to be imbedded in a constitution lest the very act of inclusion create major dysfunction in the ability of the national economy and individual economic sectors to respond to changing circumstances.

ECONOMIC JUSTIFICATIONS FOR A FEDERATION

The work we have undertaken relies heavily on the sources of welfare gains from the economic integration of the political units that establish a federation. These have been explicitly enumerated by Maxwell and Pestieau (1980: 13-20), who in their analysis suggest four basic sources of gain, using as a baseline an autarkik condition for each of the member units. The specified sources of gain are: 1) the wider market provides the opportunity for increased factor specialization and the exploitation of scale economies; 2) the potential for risk pooling at the national level to provide some offsets to the consequences of regional instability that may itself be intensified by specialization; 3) the sharing of overhead expenditures such as the maintenance of defense forces, the justice system, and provision of a communications network; 4) the likelihood that the market power of the federation will be greater than that of any member unit. There is an implicit concern running throughout the paper about three of the positive arguments for economic integration, viz. 1), 2), and 4) as they apply to western Canada, and to each of the four western provinces.

THE EMPLOYMENT STRUCTURE OF WESTERN CANADA

Table 1 presents the industrial composition of employment in the four western provinces for 1988. Addressing western Canada as a quasi-homogeneous unit, particularly in a political context when economic policies concerning the resource sector are formulated, is belied by the comparative structures revealed in the table. The notable features are: 1) the dominance of agriculture in Saskatchewan relative to its sister prairie provinces of Alberta and Manitoba, and the importance of this industry in all prairie provinces relative to its place in British Columbia; 2) the greater relative importance of extractive

Table 1
Industry Distribution of Employment (%), 1988

	B.C.	Alberta	Sask.	Manitoba	Ontario	Canada
Agric.	2.8	7.9	17.3	7.4	2.3	3.6
Oth. prim.	4.4	5.9	2.7	2.0	1.2	2.4
Manuf.	14.0	8.0	6.0	12.7	21.1	17.2
Constr.	7.2	6.1	5.5	4.6	6.0	5.9
Transp.	9.0	7.8	7.5	9.5	6.7	7.4
Trade	21.4	18.0	17.9	17.6	17.5	17.8
Finance	7.7	5.1	5.1	5.3	6.7	6.0
Service	40.7	33.8	31.2	32.9	32.3	33.3
Pub. Ad.	7.0	7.3	6.9	7.9	6.1	6.7

Source: Statistics Canada, *Labour Force Annual Averages*, 71-220.

industries (energy-based) in Alberta; 3) the greater relative importance of manufacturing in Manitoba and British Columbia.

In Saskatchewan more than 17 percent, and in Alberta and Manitoba between 7.5 and 7.7 percent of the labour force are in farming, figures many times more than in British Columbia and the country as a whole.

In Alberta almost 6 percent of employment is in extractive industry, a figure larger than in other provinces. In Manitoba and British Columbia, though about 12 percent of employment is in manufacturing compared with only 7 percent in Alberta, this proportion is still significantly less than the national average of some 17 percent and much below the 21 percent of total employment represented by manufacturing in Ontario. Though the proportion of manufacturing employment in British Columbia exceeds slightly that in Manitoba, manufacturing in Manitoba is quite diversified in contrast to British Columbia where it remains highly concentrated in the forest products industry. Direct employment numbers understate the respective provincial impacts of agriculture in Saskatchewan, forest product industries in British Columbia, and energy in Alberta. Measures of the indirect and induced employment effects from these respective industries in the three provinces indicate that up to one-third or more of total employment is linked to them (Statistics Canada, *Provincial Estimates of Input-Output Tables for 1984*). Hence, in western Canada, there are four quite distinctive provincial economic profiles: a relatively diversified economy; an economy dominated by energy production; an economy in which the health of the forest products industry simply cannot be dismissed; and an economy which is still fundamentally based on agriculture.

In summary then, in western Canada it is apparent from the distribution of employment that a high degree of specialization exists in three of the four provinces. Manitoba is the exception. This points to the need for constitutional arrangements which can provide stabilization against potential cycles inherent in a highly specialized, resource-based economy.

Table 2
Leading Six Commodity Exports as % of Total Foreign Exports by Province
(1986-89 averages)

Alberta	% of Foreign Exports
Crude petroleum	26.9
Natural gas	20.8
Sulphur	5.2
Wheat	5.0
Coal	3.3
Polyethylene	2.9
Total	**64.1**
British Columbia	
Sawn and planed lumber	23.6
Woodpulp	17.8
Coal	9.0
Newsprint	5.8
Copper ore and concentrates	4.4
Paper and paperboard	2.4
Total	**63.0**
Manitoba	
Wheat	17.4
Machinery and mechanical appliances	11.2
Vehicles, excluding rail	7.7
Flax	3.8
Canola	3.3
Live animals	2.8
Total	**46.2**
Saskatchewan	
Wheat	33.8
Potash	17.0
Crude petroleum	15.9
Canola	4.6
Woodpulp	3.1
Barley	2.5
Total	**76.9**

Source: Statistics Canada, *Exports by Country*, 65-003.

PROVINCIAL EXPORT PERFORMANCE

This section builds on knowledge of the industrial composition of employment by addressing: 1) how important are exports to provincial GDP?; 2) what is
the commodity profile of international merchandise exports originating in each

of the four provinces?; 3) what are the geographical markets, foreign and domestic, for provincial exports?

Table 2, reporting estimates of the 1986-89 annual averages, demonstrates the highly specialized commodity export base of the three westernmost provinces. In each of Saskatchewan, Alberta, and British Columbia six raw materials and/or commodity grade manufactured items amounted to from two-thirds to three-quarters of the value of total provincial export shipments to foreigners. With such narrowly specialized, commodity-based exports, provincial economic conditions are highly sensitive to income and price shocks, a matter whose constitutional implications we will consider later. Further, the dependence of their governments on stumpage and royalties exposes provincial budgets to the hazards of potentially large annual swings in tax-expenditure balances (Smith, 1990). Manitoba is the outlier among the four provinces with the ranking six exports representing just over 46 percent of foreign shipments. The fact is, Manitoba's export base is relatively diversified and contains products with greater value-added content. In British Columbia there is value added to raw materials, particularly forest resources, with the manufacturing work force engaged in their conversion to construction materials or into processed intermediate inputs, themselves subject to further processing by foreign customers. However, more than 90 percent of forest-product exports are low-value added.

In Alberta energy exports dominate, but in Saskatchewan, though heavy crude oil is still in the top group, wheat is primary. Unlike the profiles of Manitoba and British Columbia, the major exports of Alberta and Saskatchewan can properly be placed in the crude materials category with little in value-added content, a fact underlying the smaller share of their respective labour forces in manufacturing.

EXPORTS RELATIVE TO PROVINCIAL GDP

How important are exports relative to a standard measure of provincial output? Goods shipped beyond the borders of any province may have either a domestic or a foreign destination. Since the relative size of domestic to foreign shipments differs across provinces (Canada. Department of Finance, March 1991). Table 3 contains two export ratios: the first is derived from an estimate of total out-of-province shipments (domestic and foreign), and the second from shipments to foreigners. The table summarizes, for each province, the relation of total goods exports and goods exports to foreign countries from 1986 through 1989, to the GDP. Total export ratios range from just over 30 percent in the case of Manitoba to slightly more than 40 percent in the case of Saskatchewan. While some caution must be used in interpreting this table, it is indicative of differences in the domestic links of each of the provinces. For example, in the case of British Columbia while total exports amounted to some 33 cents per dollar of GDP, some 24 cents or about two-thirds were accounted for by sales to foreigners. In

Table 3
Commodity Exports: Total Out-of-Province Exports and Exports to Foreign Countries as a Share of Provincial GDP (Annual averages 1986-1989)

Province	Foreign Exports as % of GDP	Total Exports as % of GDP
British Columbia	24.5	33.1
Alberta	19.5	39.0
Saskatchewan	27.4	40.4
Manitoba	13.4	30.4

Source: Statistics Canada, *Provincial Economic Accounts: Annual Estimates*, 13-213 *Exports by Country*, 65-003; total exports from the economic accounts of the respective provinces.

contrast, Alberta exports were about equally divided between foreign sales and those to the rest of Canada.

In the case of Manitoba and Alberta interprovincial exports are a considerably more important part of total exports; the variation across provinces in relative importance of foreign vs. domestic markets is clear.

A COMPARISON OF FOREIGN SPATIAL MARKETS

Table 4 contains a summary of the spatial or geographic distribution of international export markets for each province, for western Canada as a whole, and for Canada. Figures in the table are aggregated across all commodities and represent percent market shares derived from 1986-88 annual averages. The table reveals the contrast in geographic markets for western Canadian exports compared with the national, and the distinctions in the geographic destination of shipments from each of the four provinces.

An important difference in the geographic destination of western Canadian compared to Canadian exports is the smaller relative importance of the American market, and the larger relative importance of Japan and other Pacific Rim countries. For western Canada, the value of shipments to the American market represented some 54 percent of total shipments compared with a national figure of 75 percent. However, the aggregate figure is tempered by the vast importance of the American market for western nonagricultural commodities compared to its relative unimportance as a destination for agricultural exports. And further, if motor vehicle exports which account for about one-third of countrywide exports, and all of which go to the American market, were removed from the Canadian numbers, the remaining spatial export markets would bear greater resemblance to those of western Canada.

The Japanese and Pacific Rim market represents on average only 8.5 percent of Canadian exports, the comparable figure for western Canada is almost three times as great at 21.5 percent. If China is included within the Pacific Rim category, western exports rise to one-quarter of national shipments. Countries in the region offer significant markets not only for grains but for a range of non-agricultural commodities including coal, metals, and forest products but there is

Table 4

Geographic Markets: Percent Share for the Four Provinces, Western Canada, and Canada, Based on Averages of 1986-88 Export Values

Spatial Market	Alberta	B. C.	Manitoba	Sask.	Western Canada	Canada
U. S.	71.55	44.97	57.07	39.74	54.06	75.30
Japan	6.54	26.30	7.63	10.63	15.93	5.78
Pacific Rim	4.68	7.19	2.36	4.64	5.59	2.72
W. Europe	2.59	13.40	10.45	6.23	8.50	8.33
Latin America	1.65	1.36	2.00	3.79	1.86	0.82
Central America	1.16	0.66	2.73	3.34	1.36	1.26
USSR/ E. Europe	2.87	0.20	6.16	10.75	3.13	1.07
China	2.94	1.61	5.87	11.41	3.82	1.36
Middle East	1.34	0.25	2.84	4.25	1.40	0.43
Africa	2.31	0.35	0.96	2.60	1.38	0.78
Other Asia	0.74	0.66	1.02	1.66	0.86	0.72
Austral./N.Z.	1.60	2.97	0.88	1.01	2.09	1.12
Total*	100.00	100.00	100.00	100.00	100.00	100.00

*Totals may not add to 100.0 because of rounding.

Source: Statistics Canada, *Exports by Country*, 65-003.

also a strong desire in these markets to have as much as possible from the region in relatively unprocessed form. Effectively a very substantial proportion of national exports to the Pacific Rim are sourced in western Canada and are made up of purchases of relatively unprocessed resources.

A second feature of the spatial profile is that markets in eastern Europe (including the former USSR), the Middle East, and third world countries are of greater relative importance to western Canada. These shipments, largely but not entirely grains, are a primary basis of Canadian export relations with many of these countries.

Just as western Canadian spatial markets show characteristics that distinguish them from the national, so there is notable variation across provinces. Based on aggregates the province whose geographic pattern of exports, at least in the aggregate, most closely resembles the national in its dependence on the American market is Alberta, with some 71 percent of shipments, largely energy or energy-related items, going to that country. However, if the commodity composition of exports together with their destination in the American market is considered then Alberta is scarcely typical of the national situation. Japanese and Pacific Rim markets are somewhat more important to Alberta, and west European markets somewhat less significant, than for the country as a whole.

Both British Columbia and Saskatchewan stand in considerable contrast to Alberta. In the case of British Columbia some 45 percent of exports go to the United States, largely forest products and metals, while some 35 percent, dominated by coal, forest products and metals, go to Japan and other Pacific Rim countries. Western European shipments amount to more than 13 percent of exports with other spatial markets of minor significance. Though the proportion of Saskatchewan-sourced exports going to the American market is around 40 percent, the figure is accounted for largely by potash, crude oil, and woodpulp. Japan and other Pacific Rim countries including China account for about one-quarter of Saskatchewan exports. Another one-fifth is found in eastern Europe, the Middle East and third world countries. Some countries, such as Japan, South Korea, and a number in southeast Asia, represent fairly stable markets for grain but in the case of others, such as China and the former USSR, export sales constitute a residual supply to the domestic market and therefore may vary enormously from year to year.

Manitoba's proportion of exports to the American market of 55-56 percent corresponds closely to the western Canada figure. Yet if one excludes agricultural exports, approximately three-quarters of nonagricultural exports including commodities such as paperboard together with a variety of higher value-added manufactured products go to the American market.

DOMESTIC MARKET LINKS

It is worthy of comment that the most recent data available on interprovincial trade flows in goods relates to the year 1984, an unfortunate fact in light of the present debate over constitutional arrangements (Department of Finance, March 1991). Results are summarized in Table 5. These show that interprovincial trade flows between the four western provinces and the Maritimes are very small. These 1984 data are pre-FTA, a year characterized by recession in the West, most notably in British Columbia and Alberta. Another feature of the table is the importance for any western province of exports to adjacent provinces. In the case of British Columbia, Alberta is its most important domestic market. Alberta's interprovincial exports, though dominated by shipments to Ontario and a lesser extent Quebec, are nevertheless composed of substantial flows to British Columbia and

Table 5

Summary of % Distribution of Interprovincial Exports of Goods by Destination, 1984

	B.C.	Alberta	Sask.	Man.	Ontario	Quebec	Maritimes
B.C.	—	43.4	9.6	5.1	29.2	9.8	2.9
Alta.	17.0	—	11.2	6.4	44.9	17.5	3.0
Sask.	3.5	15.1	—	14.1	36.0	30.2	1.1
Man.	7.4	17.5	15.1	—	41.1	15.3	3.6

Source: Adapted from *Quarterly Economic Review*, March 1991.

Saskatchewan. Manitoba and Saskatchewan's merchandise shipments to the other western provinces were just about equal in importance to those to Ontario. Given the fact that western provinces export products with low value-to-weight ratios explains some of the importance of market proximity evident in the table.

The need for regular availability of current data to elucidate constitutional discussions is readily apparent. What the FTA has done is to increase the importance of present north-south provincial/state linkages that are already a matter of priority throughout the West. We need to know more about how patterns of interprovincial and provincial/state trade have been influenced by the FTA.

PRICE VOLATILITY AND THE TERMS OF TRADE

Recent papers by the authors make clear the degree of price volatility accompanying the major exports from western Canada, and its effect on the terms of trade (Chambers and Percy, 1991a, 1991b). For the research underlying these papers, a western Canadian commodity price index was constructed for the period since 1972, containing both agricultural and nonagricultural commodities, and based almost entirely on American dollar prices of the region's principal exports. The items contained in the index include wheat, barley, canola (rapeseed), softwood lumber, newsprint, woodpulp, natural gas, crude oil, coal, copper, zinc, nickel, aluminum, potash, salmon, and sulphur. The breadth of commodity coverage contained in the index suggests not only wide variation in the channels through which marketing occurs, but also that the factors influencing specific commodity prices are diffuse. For example, commodity futures trading in highly developed markets occurs in agricultural products and metals, while in the case of forest products and energy these markets are, if not absent, then still quite limited. It is well known that fluctuations in agricultural prices are determined in large part by the influence of annual changes in production and on the willingness of market participants to hold existing commodity stocks. These annual changes represent year to year shocks on potential supply, occasioned by changing weather conditions, as well as the effect of lagged price change on producer planting decisions. In effect, prices in these markets are strongly affected by supply shocks. Market forces in the case of metals are quite different. Weather is unimportant and supply responsive in the short run to market price variations. Because manufacturers, primarily durable manufacturers, are the basic users of metals and these industries are indeed sensitive to the business cycle, the role of demand is much more pronounced. In the case of copper about 40 percent of world consumption is accounted for by the United States, Japan, and Germany, and their share of world consumption is comparable for the other base metals. In the forest product industries, as in metals, supply can respond quite quickly to market conditions so that the role of residential construction, a dominant sectoral user of sawn lumber, is of primary importance in determining price. Woodpulp and newsprint prices reflect longer cycles in the growth of industry capacity, but also respond to demand conditions in the economy. In energy, throughout the

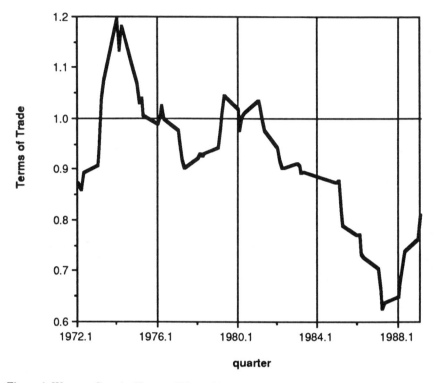

Figure 1. Western Canada: Terms of Trade (1981 = 1.0).

Source: Statistics Canada, *Industrial Products Price Index* and *Western Centre Index of Western Canadian Commodity Prices*.

period covered by the index, OPEC cartel actions to influence supply have been the significant influence on prices. For coal exports, prices are set by contract. In the case of sulphur and potash, prices are also largely set by contract and spot sales, though they occur, have been of substantially less importance.

The bottom line is that over the period from the second quarter of 1972 to the second quarter of 1990 the standard deviation of quarterly price change in the western Canadian commodity index was four times that in the CPI and 2.6 times that in the IPPI (Chambers and Percy, 1991a). The volatility in this index was reflected in a "terms of trade" index constructed for the West and defined as the ratio of the commodity price index to import prices represented by the IPPI, a proxy for the prices of manufactured goods. Figure 1 depicts the movements of the terms of trade for the period. The high degree of volatility of export prices discussed previously is evident. While the choice of time period in any calcula- tion of this sort is important, the period chosen does capture at least a full cycle in most resource price series. For western Canada as a whole the net barter terms of trade over the period 1972.1 to 1990.2 as defined declined at an annual rate of 0.31 percent.

REGIONAL INSTABILITY WITHIN A FEDERATION

Previous work covering the years 1961 through 1987 has demonstrated that Alberta, Saskatchewan, and British Columbia are economically the three most unstable provinces in Canada whether the criterion is employment, output, per capita personal income, or population change (Mansell and Percy, 1990). Manitoba is the exception; measures of instability for that province are very close to the Canadian average. Further, real capital goods expenditures in western Canada, particularly in Alberta, British Columbia, and Saskatchewan are substantially more variable (from two to three times) measured by the standard deviation of annual percent changes in outlays than for those in the rest of Canada (Chambers and Percy, 1991a). From our perspective, these findings arise out of the underlying economic structure of each of the provinces, previously sketched. Of critical importance to the West is the presence of instruments, market or otherwise, to deal with problems arising from regional instability in the Canadian economic union. In this section we address three matters: 1) the optimum currency area question; 2) labour mobility within the economic union; and 3) transfers for income stabilization.

The Currency Area Question

High degrees of regional specialization in economic activity lead to the conclusion that Canada is not an optimal currency area. Under a monetary union there is, however, the issue of what exchange rate regime would be the least injurious to regional economies. (We define the exchange rate in the subsequent discussion as the value of the domestic currency per unit of foreign currency, so that a depreciation of the foreign exchange rate therefore means a depreciation of the dollar, and an appreciation of the foreign exchange rate an appreciation of the dollar.)

In the post-1973 years, following adoption of a regime of floating exchange rates by the international economy, volatility in the external value of the currency has been added to the commodity price volatility facing Western producers. Variations in the external value of currency can, of course, be positive if they serve to offset fluctuations in commodity prices. Thus, a reasonable generalization about western Canada's major exports is that they are sold on world markets at prices determined in those markets. Perhaps in the case of sulphur, potash and natural gas the volume of exports may have some influence on market prices (we take up the constitutional implications of this in a subsequent section), and though there is some product differentiation in other goods (e.g., wheat with its high protein content and rigorous grading standards), there nevertheless must be strict adherence to international prices if market shares are to be retained. Consequently changes in the external value of the dollar directly affect company gross margins. Appreciation of the foreign exchange rate reduces the proceeds in Canadian dollars of sales occurring in those commodity markets where price is predetermined. The result is a reduced profit margin. In a similar fashion, depreciation of the foreign exchange rate increases the proceeds in Canadian dollars of sales at these predetermined prices. Net effects on profitability may be somewhat less than gross effects since the latter, in limited degree, will be offset by whatever impacts appreciation or depreciation may have on producer-unit costs. In sum, when commodity prices are falling the adverse effects of the decline on the operating position of western Canadian producers can be countered, in some degree, by a depreciation in the external value of the Canadian dollar, and when commodity prices are rising the boom effects of higher gross margins may be tempered by an appreciation. Needless to say exchange rate changes will have adverse effects on producers if appreciation accompanies commodity price declines and depreciation accompanies commodity price increases. It is therefore apparent why the level and the rate of change in the external value of the currency bring such expressions of concern in western Canada.

It is also evident that since the region competes internationally, the exchange rates of all major currencies, not just the American dollar rate, matter to the western Canadian economy. Though the United States is Canada's major trading partner, and also the major trading partner of the four western provinces, it is far from the region's only trading partner, and certainly not its only foreign competitor. Measures indicative of the effects of exchange rate movements on western Canadian export competitiveness are therefore required to interpret how changes in the external value of the currency have affected the region.

At the Western Centre for Economic Research we have constructed and maintain a nominal and real exchange rate index for western Canada in recognition of the fact that a national index can utter misleading signals about regional impacts where the product composition of the region's foreign exports and the relative importance of its trading partners clearly differ from the national (Chambers, 1991). The specific commodities included in the Western Centre index are crude oil, natural gas, copper, softwood lumber, woodpulp, newsprint, sulphur, coal, zinc, potash, wheat, canola, and barley. The countries included in the index are the United States, Australia, Japan, the United Kingdom, Sweden, France, Germany, Italy, South Korea, Finland, Norway, New Zealand, Portugal, Spain, Belgium-Luxembourg, the Netherlands, Switzerland, Austria and Denmark. The index takes account of third-country effects with multilateral weights based upon two-market share measures. The first is a set of ratios showing the distribution of the given product market in each country between domestic production in that country, and imports of that commodity from each of the other currency-basket countries. For example where the product is coal, the market shares for Japan represent the relative contributions of domestic production and imports from each of the other currency-basket countries in satisfying Japanese requirements.

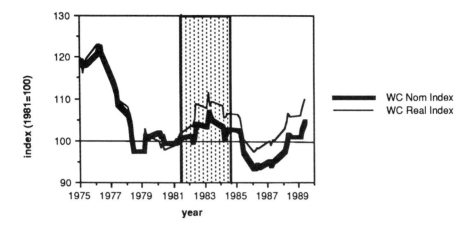

Figure 2. WCER Nominal and Real Exchange Rate Indexes, 1975.1 to 1989.4.

Source: Western Centre for Economic Research.

A similar calculation is made for each commodity in each country. The second ratio applied to each commodity is the share of each currency-basket country as a market for western Canadian exports. This is essentially an export share ratio for each commodity. The set of country weights for the final index is calculated by applying to the country weights for each individual commodity the relative importance of that commodity in total western Canadian exports, and summing across the results. In this index the American weight is .6209, the Australian .0955, and the Japanese .0830. The next highest weight is that for the United Kingdom at .0487.

Data limitations required the use of a fixed weighting scheme, and those estimated and applied were derived from trade data averages for 1986 and 1987. This poses some difficulty and permits but an interpretation of index behaviour in earlier years. Figure 2 shows the quarterly nominal and real effective exchange rate index measured by this method for the period from 1975 through 1989. The real index is obtained in this case by deflating the nominal index by the relative CPIs of Canada and the currency-basket countries.

These indexes clearly show the adverse effects on western Canada of the exchange rate path during the late 1970s and early 1980s. The index depreciates by some 25 percent between the third quarter of 1976 and mid-1980, and is followed by an appreciation of 16 percent through late 1983. The evidence from the Western Centre indexes is that the exchange rate accentuated boom conditions in the West over the first period when resource real prices were rising (by 9 percent), and when employment was rising by 25 percent, compared with a rate of

12 percent in the rest of Canada. Highlighted in Figure 2 is the evidence of exchange rate appreciation which served only to worsen difficulties in the the early 1980s, a period when resource real prices initially weakened, and then declined by 16 percent from mid-1981 through the fourth quarter of 1983.

In summary, apart from underscoring the fact that Canada is not an optimal currency area, the time path traced by the Western Centre indexes presents a different picture of economic impact than either the American dollar rate or the G-10 index of the Bank of Canada. One must reluctantly conclude that one of the strongest arguments for a flexible exchange rate, namely its role in ameliorating fluctuations in commodity prices, did not apply to western Canada in the decade following 1975. In the years through 1981 exchange rate depreciation exacerbated the boom in the region, while appreciation worsened the subsequent economic collapse from 1982 through 1984. Only in the 1987-89 period did a rising exchange rate moderate the expansionary effects in the region of sharply rising commodity prices. However, the rising external value of the currency in the 1990-91 period in the face of falling western Canadian commodity prices once again acted pro-cyclically.

Based on the empirical evidence, we feel that flexible exchange rates have not served the interests of western Canada, and we have increasing doubts, inferred from the IMF index of real and effective exchange rates for Canada, that they have had positive effects on the national economy. This leads us to conclude that the preferred option for Canada is a fixed exchange rate regime in which the Canadian dollar is pegged to the American dollar. Of course, it is well known that a fixed exchange rate regime means that Canadian monetary policy becomes a "handmaiden" to fixed rate maintenance. Domestic monetary policy must accommodate to maintain the "rightness" of the exchange rate. Hence, Bank of Canada policy must adjust to the policies established by the United States Federal Reserve.

For us, this raises an important consideration concerning north/south, as opposed to east/west, trading axes. One of the developments inherent in the FTA is increased north/south regional trade in goods and services with the effect of tying more closely together regions in Canada with adjacent areas in the United States, such as British Columbia and the coastal states, Alberta and the states of the Rocky Mountain slopes, Saskatchewan and Manitoba and the upper Mississippi basin states, the maritime provinces and the New England states, and the like. As these linkages emerge and evolve, economic conditions characterizing north/south (American and Canadian) regional axes will possess greater commonalities.

With these changes the question is whether Canadian regions would be better served by a monetary policy made by the Federal Reserve System than monetary policy as imposed by the Bank of Canada. Regional federal reserve banks with their in-depth complement of expertise play an important role in the making of American monetary policy. Much of that expertise is directed to the analysis and evaluation of business conditions and economic issues that are regional/state in character. And in the Federal Reserve system there exist legally based institutional arrangements, through which the Federal Reserve District Banks participate in the making of monetary policy. Of particular significance is the representation of five of the twelve regional Federal Reserve District Bank presidents as voting members of the twelve member Federal Open Market Committee. This committee sets monetary policy. Further, the other seven bank presidents attend meetings of the Federal Open Market Committee and freely present their views. The bringing to the table of economic and business conditions experienced by different regions of the country are thus integral to monetary policy making. This presents a stark contrast with the Bank of Canada whose research arm, to our knowledge, has never had an interest in regional problems, and whose provincial representation on the board of directors is mere tokenism. The recent document *Canadian Federalism and Economic Union: Partnership for Prosperity* (September 1991) contains suggestions about how regional input might enter Bank of Canada policy formulation. In our judgement these suggestions do not provide effectively for regional input and we conclude that western Canada, at least, would be better served by an adjustable peg system at a fixed parity with the American dollar. Such an arrangement would require domestic adjustments to a made-in-Washington monetary policy. This is preferable to a Bank of Canada policy based on regional tokenism.

Labour Mobility and the Economic Union
Interregional migration is a key mechanism of adjustment to swings in levels of regional activity. During the 1981-86 years Census data reveal that 19.5 percent of the Canadian population 5 years of age and older moved from one census division to another, and 4.5 percent moved interprovincially. In the maritime provinces approximately 90 percent of migration was interprovincial, and in the four western provinces the average was approximately 75 percent. In previous papers we have emphasized the positive role of internal migration to residents of regions characterized by high degrees of income and employment instability, or by secular decline due to erosion in the quality of the resource base, to technological changes, or to changes in tastes and preferences adversely affecting resource-based economies (Chambers and Percy, 1991b, 1991c). For households, particularly in highly specialized regional economies with a low value-added export sector such as those in the three western provinces, the freedom to seek a greater degree of employment and income stability elsewhere within the economic union, without regard to border clearances or immigration visas, is an option that many may regard as highly valuable. Options to pursue more stable job opportunities spatially within a federation have an opportunity value.

Some results from a survey of 1,045 households undertaken in March 1987 allow estimation of option values. The survey itself which contained equal representation from Calgary, Edmonton, and the rest of the province, is described, and the full results reported elsewhere (Mansell and Percy, 1990). Questions solicited respondents' attitudes to diversification, a term used to typify greater stability. Some measure of the value placed on an option to seek freely and accept work elsewhere may be gleaned from responses to the following question: "How much of an increase in your annual taxes would you be willing to pay to finance diversification?"

Just over two-fifths (41.5 percent) of those responding to this question indicated that they would accept a tax increase. The weighted average acceptable increase in taxes by those indicating a willingness is 7.5 percent. Household tax payments in Alberta in 1987 amounted to approximately $8.7 billion. Assuming, for purposes of rough approximation, that the tax bill of the average household willing to pay a tax increase was the same as that unwilling to do so, the value attached to the option is $271 million (.415)(.075)($8.7). By any standard this is a nontrivial number, amounting to approximately 0.5 percent of the Alberta GDP in 1987. The crude approximation is suggestive of potential value assigned in any one year by households to the option of labour mobility within a federal union.

Transfers for Income Stabilization

A recent paper by Reed and Snoddon (1991) uses the data from Table 6 to suggest that there is already considerable risk sharing and insurance provision across provinces provided by the Unemployment Insurance program. As they point out different cyclical behaviour in unemployment over time permits a national insurance program which allows regions and provinces to insure each

Table 6
Correlations of Deviations of Provincial Unemployment Rates from the
Canadian Unemployment Rate, 1961-89

	Nfld.	P.E.I.	N.S.	N.B.	Que.	Ont.	Man.	Sask.	Alta.	B.C.
Nfld.	1.00	0.16	0.53	0.82	0.36	-0.59	-0.45	-0.10	-0.09	0.22
P.E.I.		1.00	0.51	0.38	0.07	-0.48	0.37	0.54	0.25	0.11
N.S.			1.00	0.68	0.39	-0.50	-0.34	-0.02	-0.06	0.17
N.B.				1.00	0.48	-0.52	-0.41	-0.06	-0.21	0.05
Que.					1.00	-0.02	-0.45	0.46	-0.65	-0.46
Ont.						1.00	-0.08	-0.44	-0.62	-0.70
Man.							1.00	0.78	0.51	-0.02
Sask.								1.00	0.66	0.22
Alta.									1.00	0.74
B.C.										1.00

Source: Reed and Snoddon, "Redistribution under Alternative Constitutional Arrangements for Canada," in Western Centre for Economic Research, *Alberta and the Economics of Constitutional Change* (in press).

Table 7
Western Canada's Shares of World Production and Exports:
Selected Commodities, Volume Basis

Commodity	% Share of Production	% Share of Exports
Copper ores and conc.	5	9
Natural gas	5	*5
Crude oil	2	*8
Sawn and planed lumber	10	38
Paper and paperboard	1	4
Woodpulp	3	14
Sulphur (all forms)	12	45
Zinc ores and conc.	11	11
Potash	25	40
Wheat	5	20
Canola	17	43
Barley	8	24

* Represents percent share of the United States market.

Sources: **Copper:** Data on Canadian and world production and exports of copper ores and concentrates from UNCTAD, *Commodity Yearbook 1987*, and the U.S. Bureau of Mines, *Minerals Yearbook, 1987*; western Canada production from Energy, Mines and Resources, *Statistical Summary of the Mineral Industry in Canada 1987*, Table 5; western Canadian exports from Statistics Canada, *Exports by Country* (65-003); **Crude Oil:** Data on Canadian and world production from OECD, *Annual Oil and Gas Statistics, 1985, 1986*. and U.S. import data from OECD, *Imports by Commodity*, 1986 and 1987; **Natural Gas:** Data on Canadian and world production, and on imports from Canada as a share of the U.S. market from OECD, *Annual Oil and Gas Statistics, 1985, 1986*; **Sawn and Planed Lumber (Coniferous):** Data on Canadian and world production and exports from FAO, *Yearbook of Forest Products 1984*; western Canadian production estimated from Statistics Canada, *Sawmills and Planing Mills and Shingle Mills 1984* (35-204); western Canadian exports from Statistics Canada, *Exports by Country* (65-003); **Newsprint:** Data on Canadian and world production and exports from FAO, *Yearbook of Forest Products 1984*; western Canadian production estimated from Statistics Canada, *Pulp and Paper Industries 1984* (36-204); western Canadian exports from Statistics Canada, *Exports by Country* (65-003); **Woodpulp:** Data on world and Canadian chemical woodpulp production from FAO, *Yearbook of Forest Products 1984*; western Canadian production estimated from Statistics Canada, *Pulp and Paper Industries 1984* (36-204); western Canadian exports from Statistics Canada, *Exports by Province* (36-204); **Paperboard:** Data on Canadian and world production and exports from FAO, *Yearbook of Forest Products 1984*; western Canadian exports estimated from share of western Canadian value added in Canadian paperboard production in Statistics Canada, *Pulp and Paper Industries 1984*, (36-204); **Sulphur:** Data on Canadian and world production and exports from UNCTAD, *Commodity Yearbook 1987*. Data on western Canadian exports from Statistics Canada, *Exports by Country* (65-003); **Zinc:** Data on world and Canadian production of ores and concentrates and alloys from U.S. Bureau of Mines, *Minerals Yearbook 1987*. Data on western Canadian exports from Statistics Canada, *Exports by Country* (65-003); **Potash:** Data on Canadian and world production and exports from U.S. Bureau of Mines, *Minerals Yearbook 1987*, Volume I; **Wheat:** Data on Canadian and world production and exports from FAO, *Yearbook of Agricultural Production, 1988* and FAO, *Yearbook of Trade and Commerce in Agricultural Products 1988*; **Rapeseed/Canola:** Data on Canadian and world production and exports from FAO, *Yearbook of Agricultural Production 1988* and FAO, *Yearbook of Agricultural Trade and Commerce 1988*.

other. As they point out, the main features of this matrix are "the relatively large and always negative correlation coefficients between Ontario and the Maritime provinces and Ontario and the western provinces, the positive correlations between the provinces comprising the maritime region, the positive correlations between the provinces in the west, and the virtually zero correlation coefficient between Ontario and Quebec." (p. 34). They conclude that with the tendency for unemployment in the Maritimes and the West to move in the direction opposite to that in central Canada, the results of pooling the provinces into one unemployment insurance scheme provide positive evidence of risk sharing in support of stabilization. We have considered elsewhere agricultural support programs as an instrument for income transfers (Chambers and Percy, 1991c).

WESTERN CANADA'S TRADE POSITION AND MARKET POWER

The western Canadian share in world production and exports assembled from a variety of sources, for several of the region's important agricultural and non-agricultural commodity exports is in Table 7. The evidence is that except for potash and sulphur, and possibly in canola and natural gas relative to the United States market, the region accounts for a relatively small share of world production. However, for a number of these commodities the region's importance as an exporter is greater, suggesting that the potential to exercise some market power cannot be dismissed. In a trading environment where exporter and importer both possess a degree of market power, the potential for trade conflicts are high, and economic influence key in determining the magnitude of any potential for income redistribution between trading partners. The ability of a federation to protect its exporters, whatever their regional domicile, from the the application of monopsony power by major trading partners is a function of economic size, and of diversification in product and spatial markets. Further, a larger country will more easily provide the institutional framework to convey market power internationally, not only because of size but also because trade policies specific to one sector are integrated into the whole set of precepts governing its foreign trade. It may well be that the potential for the nation to apply market power is more meaningful in the case of some commodities rather than others. For example, would individual producers in British Columbia have achieved the same outcome in the softwood lumber dispute had either that province, or western Canada, or a non-G-7 Canada been the sovereign authority responsible for negotiations with the United States? Or, would potash producers in Saskatchewan be able to exert the same degree of market power if there was a reduction in the level of national sovereignty as we presently know it? Or, would grain producers in the three prairie provinces be in better or worse position if represented by a diminished federal jurisdiction in international trade negotiations? We do not know the full answers to these questions. But we do suggest that the preferred inference is that exporters in trade disputes over products such as softwood lumber, hogs, potash, grain subsidies, or the fisheries are better served when represented by a federation with membership in the G-7 than by any single province, by an independent western Canada, or by a "Canada" minus Quebec, and minus membership in the G-7.

CONCLUSION

We have drawn a number of conclusions from our studies of the western Canadian economy that are important to the ways in which a federal union might be reconstituted. These follow from the degree of specialization within the economies of at least three of the four western provinces. More generally, the western economy remains surprisingly dependent on, and specialized in, the exploitation and utilization of its natural resource bases. Resource markets do differ in certain respects from markets for services and highly differentiated manufactured products: they are sensitive to trade disputes centring around the definition of subsidies; they increase economic variability; they affect the mechanisms of regional adjustment to economic shocks; and they underscore the value of labour mobility in an economic union.

Our conclusion is that the West should place priority on the following issues in constitutional discussions: 1) the potential benefits from more effective provisions for insurance/stabilization measures in the economic union; 2) the recognition that Canada is not an optimal currency area — a fixed exchange rate regime would be preferable to the present situation; 3) the potentially large benefits to an economic union from labour mobility; 4) the market power advantages of an economic union compared to a fragmented Canada.

References

Boothe, Paul. 1991. "The Economics of Association: A Regional Approach to Constitutional Design," Research Paper 91-11, Department of Economics, University of Alberta.

Canada. Department of Justice. 1991. *Quarterly Economic Review*. March 1991.

Chambers, E.J. 1991. "Indexes of Effective Exchange Rates for Western Canada." Information Bulletin No. 2. Edmonton: Western Centre for Economic Research, University of Alberta.

Chambers, E.J. and Michael B. Percy. 1991a. *Western Canada in the International Economy* Western Studies in Economic Policy No. 2, Western Centre for Economic Research and the C. D. Howe Institute. Edmonton: University of Alberta Press, forthcoming.

——. 1991b. "Natural Resources and the Western Canadian Economy: Implications for Constitutional Change." Article No. 5 in The Economics of Constitutional Change Series. Edmonton: Western Centre for Economic Research, University of Alberta.

——. 1991c. "Structural Characteristics of the Alberta Economy: Implications for Constitutional Scenarios." Paper prepared for the Western Centre for Economic Research Conference, Alberta and the Economics of Constitutional Change, Edmonton, September 1991.

Courchene, T.J. 1978. "Avenues of Adjustment: The Transfer System and Regional Disparities," in *Confederation at the Crossroads*. Vancouver: The Fraser Institute.

——. 1990. "The Community of Canadas," a submission to Quebec's La Commission sur l'avenir politique et constitutionel du Québec.

Lipsey, R. G. 1991. "Trade Issues Involved in Quebec 'Separation'." Paper prepared for the meeting of Western Economists on the Constitution, Simon Fraser Harbour Centre.

Mansell, Robert and Michael B. Percy. 1990. *Strength in Adversity: A Study of the Alberta Economy*. Western Studies in Economic Policy No. 1, Western Centre for Economic Research and the C.D. Howe Institute. Edmonton: University of Alberta Press.

Maxwell, J. and C. Pestieau. 1980. *Economic Realities of Contemporary Confederation*. Montreal: C.D. Howe Institute.

Norrie, Kenneth, Richard Simeon and Mark Krasnick. 1986. *Federalism and the Economic Union*. Vol. 56, Royal Commission on the Economic Union and Development Prospects for Canada. Toronto: University of Toronto Press.

Reed, Brad and Tracy Snoddon. 1991. "Redistribution under Alternative Constitutional Scenarios for Canada." Paper prepared for the Western Centre for Economic Research Conference, Alberta and the Economics of Constitutional Change, Edmonton, September 1991.

Smith, R.S. 1990. "Spending and Taxing: The Recent Record of Western Canadian Provincial Governments." Information Bulletin No. 1. Edmonton: Western Centre for Economic Research, University of Alberta.

7

A Regional Approach to Monetary and Fiscal Policy

Harold Chorney

It is time for a change in the way we run our monetary and fiscal policy. The last sixteen years have witnessed a radical experiment in policy regression. The supposed failures of the Keynesian consensus to foresee and overcome the stagflation of the OPEC price shock permitted this return to older and previously discredited policies. Monetarism and rational expectations theories with their emphasis upon policy impotence and laissez faire have wreaked enough havoc. Coupled with the neoconservative conceptions of public choice theory with their explicit hostility to public expenditure and the ideological attack upon social intervention as inherently unproductive we have regressed back toward public policy stances that resemble the 1920s and 1930s. It was also the case in this epoch that balanced budgets were seen as the key to economic recovery, deficits were the cause of all problems, government intervention was unwise and expanding the money supply to lower interest rates was inflationary (Chorney, 1989; Howson, 1975).

It is therefore no surprise that we face similar problems to those experienced sixty years ago.The conventional wisdom is now so far to the right that many sensible people, including those who fancy themselves as reformers and social democrats, believe in views and policies that helped create and prolong the Great Depression of the 1930s and directly contributed to the rise of fascism and ultimately to World War II. It is therefore urgent that we return to the wise and sensible policies that placed full employment and price stability at the top of our priorities. This does not mean that we cannot improve upon the way these policies worked in practice.

There is no shortage of ways of improving the operation of our society to ensure that both equity and efficiency are respected. It should be obvious to all but the most ideologically blinded observers that inequitable distributions of wealth and income that became common place during the 1980s are no guarantee of economic efficiency. Michael Milken, Ivan Boesky and their imitators do not promote economic efficiency. In fact such practices and values undermine both the legitimacy and efficiency of the market system.

There is much talk these days of globalization and productive competitiveness. But the reality is that a competitive economy that is globally efficient requires an economy that is devoted to the full utilization of its human resources and industrial plants. Furthermore it requires that this utilization take place under conditions that respect the environment and the right of all citizens to a decent living standard and fair work place practices. The citizenry will accept nothing less. In a liberal democracy such as Canada where the nordic values of social justice and cooperative responsibility are deeply embedded in the society this fact should be welcomed and celebrated. It is in this spirit that I approach the problem of bringing our monetary and fiscal policy up to date with socio-political, and regional realities of our vast continental economy.

It is essential, therefore, that we get our policies right and harmonize them to the needs of our epoch. To do this we must tailor these policies to meet the truly regional nature of our country and the realities of our federal system. Neoclassical economic theory does many things, some of them even well. It is elegant and to the trained professional even aesthetically pleasing; but it fails miserably when it comes to incorporating notions of space and time and social justice into its theoretical apparatus. Canada is clearly a space- and time-dependent economy that places a high premium upon achieving a certain measure of social justice in the workings of its political economy. Indeed two of our most brilliant analysts, Harold Innis and his more famous follower Marshall McCluhan, established this point clearly in their work (Innis, 1972; Kroker, 1984; Molloy, 1992). It is time to harmonize our monetary and fiscal policy with the space and time realities of the Canadian economy. In doing so we can also promote as a more realizable goal the accomplishment of a certain high measure of social justice in our society.

It is patently unjust in a market-driven society to deny unnecessarily a substantial fraction of the population the right to earn a reasonable living in a relatively secure and stable economic environment. By this I mean a goal of full employment at the 4 to 5 percent range of unemployment. A number of our trading partners such as Japan, Sweden and Germany regularly accomplish even better performance on the employment front. Those who disagree with this goal of full employment and emphasize instead the goal of zero inflation claim that the benefits of their policies outweigh the temporary costs of higher unemployment. If this is true they must prove that: a) the unemployment at rates that are now above 10 percent (see Table 1) is only temporary (all available evidence suggests that this is false); and b) that those who lose their jobs on account of the policies followed will receive full compensation, including the shadow price for psychological stress and ill health and family disruption that unemployment creates (Pareto optimality with compensation). None of the zero-inflationists, including our central bank Governor Crow, have yet to even mention this possibility. It would seem therefore that the zero-inflation camp are incapable of defending their policy advice. This makes the advocacy of it by the Bank of Canada and the federal Department of Finance all the more illegitimate.

Table 1

Unemployment Rates for Canada and the Provinces, Selected Years

	1991 (Sept.)	1990	1989	1988	1986	1984	1982	1980
Manitoba	9.3	7.2	7.6	7.8	7.7	8.4	8.5	5.5
Saskatchewan	7.5	7.0	7.5	7.5	7.7	8.0	6.1	4.4
Alberta	8.0	7.0	7.2	8.0	9.8	11.1	7.7	3.7
B.C.	9.7	8.3	9.1	10.4	12.5	14.7	12.1	6.8
Nfld.	17.8	17.1	15.8	16.4	19.2	20.2	16.7	13.3
Nova Scotia	12.6	10.5	9.9	10.2	13.1	13.0	13.1	9.7
P.E.I.	17.3	14.9	14.1	13.0	13.4	12.8	12.9	10.6
N. Brunswick	12.8	12.1	12.5	12.0	14.3	14.8	14.1	11.0
Ontario	9.2	6.3	5.1	5.0	7.0	9.0	9.7	6.8
Quebec	12.1	10.2	9.3	9.4	11.0	12.8	13.8	9.8
Canada	10.2	8.1	7.5	7.8	9.5	11.2	11.0	7.5

Source: Statistics Canada, *The Labour Force Historical Statistics.*

What exactly do I mean by the space and time character of our economy? Investments that drive our economy do not occur in a vacuum, rather they occur in a spatial dimension in which regional difference plays an important role. Furthermore, the calculation of the expected rate of return must be projected far off into the future and discounted to the present value in comparison to the cost of capital under conditions of uncertainty. The fact that this calculation is often made by investors external to the region preoccupied by a comparative calculus that is intrinsically different from the one employed in the region by local interests further complicates the problem of harmonization. The degree of uncertainty is greatly increased by the vastness of the Canadian economy and its strong regional character. Therefore it is essential that we use fiscal and monetary policies as creatively as possible to overcome the inevitable uncertainties that flow from such an economy. Otherwise there will be a chronic tendency toward risk avoidance and under-investment which will in turn lead to higher unemployment and undermine our values of distributive justice.

In the past, and in particular in western Canada and the Prairies, the macroeconomy revolved around the exploitation of a staple commodity by capital interests at a distance for markets at a distance. Deprived of a local perspective the investments associated with these kinds of staple developments, wheat, grain, potash, oil, precious metals and nickel and copper, were usually undertaken according to an investment perspective whose timetable diverged from the needs and priorities of the local population (Watkins, 1991; Mackintosh, 1991; Innis, 1991; Drache, 1991; Naylor, 1987).

Eventually backward linkages and spread effects that flowed from these staple industries, as well as to a degree forward linkages, were formed that deepened the impact of these staples upon the economic development of the region. (Hirschman, 1958) But inevitably the financial wealth that accumulated because of these investments flowed for the most part outside of the regions of their production.

This was particularly so because of the relatively weak forward linkages that were established in the regions of origin. The largely external financial institutions that were fed by these activities did not contribute much to the economic development of the region. This fact spurred the development of indigenous financial institutions like the credit union movement, the Alberta government treasury banking system and the heritage funds that were established in all three provinces.

The growth of prairie-based venture capitalists like I.H. Asper, the Germazians, the Mannixes, the Southerns, the Lougheeds and the Belzbergs and older moneyed groups like the Richardson family, transferred some of the wealth that had previously leaked from the region to the metropole in central Canada and even abroad (Pratt and Richards, 1979; Francis, 1986). But the mark of any mature economic region that has escaped from its staple base and colonial heritage is not only local financial institutions but also access to and managerial influence over a central bank. This has been absent in western Canada from the very beginning.

It is time to remedy this absence. The experience of the maritime provinces, with the destruction of their indigenous banking system and decline of their region that followed upon Confederation, is a classic case study of the importance of control over banking for ensuring the economic health of a region (Acheson, 1991).

The prairie region now accounts for 4.6 million people, 17 percent of the population of Canada and an equal percentage of the GDP. It is clear however from Table 2 that even over the past decade there has been a substantial decline in the prairie region's share of the national economy. Its share of the GDP has fallen by almost 20 percent from 21.2 percent to 17 percent from 1983 to 1990. Part of this decline is attributable to the damage sustained by inappropriate monetary policy directed by the Bank of Canada centred in central Canada. Another aspect of the problem lies in the underdeveloped fiscal policy tools available to the prairie provinces to enable them to promote economic development of necessary infrastructure and to counter the downward pressure of the business cycle. Finally, part of the explanation for this development lies in the changing terms of trade between Canada and its principal trading partners and the relative decline in commodity prices such as for oil, wheat and potash over the past decade. Ultimately a region's relative share of an economy declines because it has a growing share of a declining industry or a declining share of growing industries.

Table 2

Provincial Distribution of Gross Domestic Product at Market Prices (%)

	1983	1984	1984	1986	1987	1988	1989	1990
Newfoundland	1.3	1.3	1.3	1.3	1.4	1.3	1.3	1.3
P.E.I.	.3	.3	.3	.3	.3	.3	.3	.3
Nova Scotia	2.4	2.4	2.5	2.6	2.5	2.5	2.5	2.5
New Brunswick	1.9	1.9	1.9	2.0	2.0	2.0	1.9	1.9
Atlantic Region	5.9	5.9	6.0	6.2	6.2	6.1	6.0	6.0
Manitoba	3.7	3.7	3.7	3.7	3.6	3.6	3.6	3.5
Saskatchewan	3.8	3.7	3.7	3.4	3.1	3.0	3.0	3.0
Alberta	13.7	13.3	13.7	11.4	10.9	10.2	10.2	10.5
Prairie Region	21.2	20.7	21.1	18.5	17.6	16.8	16.8	17.0
B.C.	11.9	11.6	11.4	11.4	11.4	11.5	11.7	12.0
Yukon	.1	.1	.1	.1	.1	.1	.1	.1
N.W.T.	.3	.3	.3	.3	.3	.3	.3	.3
Ontario	37.7	38.6	38.5	40.2	40.8	41.6	41.9	41.4
Quebec	22.9	22.8	22.6	23.3	23.6	23.6	23.2	23.2
Canada	100.0	100.0	100.0	100.0	100.0	100.0	100.0	100.0

Source : Statistics Canada, Provincial Economic Accounts.

During this same period of time the relative weight of the Ontario economy has grown significantly, while that of the Atlantic region has changed only marginally, and the same is true for both Quebec and British Columbia. Clearly the current recession which has hit hardest in Ontario and Quebec may change these relative weights in the near future. But it must be seen that the period that followed the last great recession of 1981 to 1982 worked to the disadvantage of the prairie region and to the advantage of central Canada. Part of the problem lies in the inappropriateness of our monetary and fiscal policy tools and the relative backwardness of the Bank of Canada in adapting to the regional nature of our federation and its refusal to take seriously its mandate to work for both price stability and low unemployment.The preamble to the Bank of Canada Act makes this responsibility quite clear. The preamble states:

> Whereas it is desirable to establish a central bank in Canada to regulate credit and currency in the best interests of the economic life of the nation, to control and protect the external value of the national monetary unit and to mitigate by its influence fluctuations in the general level of production, trade, prices and employment, so far as may be possible within the scope of

monetary action, and generally promote the economic and financial welfare of the Dominion.

The current proposal of the federal government to change the bank act to eliminate this responsibility for ensuring both price stability and low unemployment is a clear step in a regressive direction. It is the consequence of the triumph, for the moment at least, of rational expectations, monetarism and the notion of the natural rate of unemployment and the vertical Phillips curve in macroeconomic theory. This doctrine, which dovetails rather smoothly with neoconservative political doctrine, argues that stabilization policy of any kind is ultimately impotent and even perverse.

There is, according to the exponents of the doctrine, a specific rate of inflation that is compatible with the underlying natural rate of unemployment in the economy. The transition from a high inflation rate to a low one is accompanied either by no increase in unemployment because of the instantaneous adaption of expectations in a rational way to the new climate of low inflation (the "cold turkey" approach) and the "fact" that well-informed economic actors armed with the appropriate model of the economy (i.e., the rational expectations monetarist approach) behave as required; or that through gradual movement to a low inflation rate the rise in unemployment is only a temporary episode and well worth the slight discomfort involved when compared with the benefits of the new low inflation climate. It is this bizarre and historically discredited doctrine that lies behind the zero-inflation concept that John Crow has been touting since his elevation to the head of the Bank of Canada in 1987.

It must be said that this approach to macroeconomic policy and theory is identical with the pre-Keynesian classical approach to the management of industrial economies that prevailed in the 1920s and 1930s. Its last major accomplishment was the Great Depression. I fear there is a danger it may help bring about the Great Depression of the 1990s since the current doctrine calls itself the new classical macroeconomics. While I cannot discuss this question at great length in this paper it is essential to understand this doctrine in order to make sense of what has happened in the Bank of Canada and the Department of Finance. (For an elaboration of this doctrine and a thorough critique of it and its origins see Chorney, 1991.)

The proponents of the doctrine assert, with the same dogmatic rigidity of those who defended the treasury view during the late 1920s and early 1930s, that teaching the public the virtues of zero inflation through clearly enunciated goals and harsh but short recessions is worth the savings in "shoe-leather costs" that low or even zero inflation brings about. In so doing they have completely forgotten the lessons of the Great Depression and the critical importance of overall aggregate demand and the tragic waste of potential output and human beings that occurred in the Great Depression. They also forget that the public and many entrepreneurs are quite likely to be more Keynesian than monetarist in their thinking and respond to a short sharp shock by lowering their marginal propensity to consume and their "animal spirits" for investment sufficiently to precipitate a drastic fall in employment and a situation of chronically depressed demand.

Given the current very low birth rate in Canada, the lowest since the 1920s, and the extremely low rate of investment in capital infrastructure, also the lowest in a number of decades, there is a great danger that the zero-inflation strategy will result in a 1990s variant of the Depression of the 1930s. There is already considerable discussion of such a possibility in the financial press. (See the discussion, for example, in Harris, 1991.)

INCREASING FISCAL FLEXIBILITY:
PROVINCIAL ACCESS TO THE BANK OF CANADA

Without clear access to a central bank it is not possible for provinces to use creatively the tools of fiscal policy to enhance economic development. Without any willingness to sensitize monetary policy through a system of regionally sensitive credit controls, such as compensating balances upon loans, it is not possible to adjust policy to the real differences that exist and will continue to exist in the regionally based economic cycle.

The fact that the original conception of the Bank of Canada did not build in this access, although the bank act of 1935 clearly stated that the bank could purchase the paper of a province, as well as that of the federal government, reflected probably more of the unitary state influence of the Macmillan committee that recommended its establishment than it did any specific bias against provincial development.

In the testimony of Graham Towers, the first governor of the bank, before the House of Commons Committee on Banking and Commerce dealing with the Bank of Canada in 1939, it was clear that the bank was willing to act as the fiscal agent of the provinces:

> While I am on the subject of relations with the government I feel I should mention our position in respect to provinces. Our Act says that "The bank shall act as the fiscal agent of the government of Canada without charge, and, subject to the provisions of this Act, by agreement may also act as banker or fiscal agent of the government of any province." It has been, and is, our view that a relationship with a province should be entered into, on the understanding that it would be of a continuing character such as would normally be needed for the bank to acquire that full knowledge of a province's position which would enable it to give the province the best service of which it is capable in the matter of expert advice and frank opinions. ... If a relationship of such a character were established, the bank could perform for a provincial government much the same kind of services as it undertakes for the dominion government. I should add that no province has ever requested the Bank of Canada to act for it in this way. (Fullerton, 1986: 311-12)

In a similar sort of way the German Bundesbank has shared responsibilities for debt management and monetary policy with the Landernzentralbanks that exist in each of the German states. Because of the stringent attitude towards deficit finance and the extraordinary good fortune of postwar Germany up until the unification of Germany, debt has not been a major concern (Maycock, 1977; Moine, 1981; Deutsche Bundesbank, 1976; Reuss, 1963).

The uncertainties that surround the investment process affect the investment process in Canada more than in other national economies and make more fragile, than would otherwise be the case, the stability of our business cycle. Furthermore, because of the colonial history of development our banking structure is relatively less mature than other countries. Hence, we have a greater problem with unemployment than other capitalist countries. To maximize our potential output and capacity utilization and minimize unemployment it is essential that we tailor our public policy to attack these problems directly.

Entrenching the goals of zero inflation and restricting the central bank to worry only about price stability and ignore unemployment is a prescription for very high unemployment and exacerbating uncertainties around the investment decision. These uncertainties are exacerbated because more than 50 percent of our fiscal capacity is allocated to provincial and local governments who have no access to the central bank to help finance their expenditures and manage the domestic money market for their debt instruments. This in itself is a major structural weakness of the Canadian policy-making apparatus. Hence any policy designed to stimulate aggregate demand is bound to be hampered. I propose to remedy this in a fundamental way. In so doing not only will the efficacy of our policy making be enhanced but the degree of satisfaction with our federal structure will also be enhanced.

The proposal that I am making is not new. Clarence Barber, in his study for the Ontario government in the 1960s, made a similar sort of suggestion (Barber, 1966). I am proposing that each of the provinces have access to the central bank in the sale and management of their debt. While prevailing bank policy will determine the extent of the debt that is acquired the upward limit on this amount should be a weighted share of the debt monetization capacity of the central bank. Hence, if the province of Alberta's gross provincial product constitutes 14.6 percent of the national GDP then it should be entitled to 14.6 percent of the provincial share of total central bank debt-financing capacity. Since the provinces and local governments account for roughly 54 percent of total government expenditure in Canada then 54 percent of the total debt capacity of the central bank would be available to them.

This means that Alberta would be entitled to .54 x 14.6 = 7.9 percent. Since I suggest the general policy rule that monetized debt not exceed 20 percent of the total money stock broadly defined this means that Alberta would be entitled to sell to the central bank $64.2 billion x 7.9 percent = $5 billion at the maximum take-up position ($64.2 billion accounting for 20 percent of the current broadly defined money stock). I use the figure of 20 percent as the maximum constraint

Table 3
Monetized Government Debt as % of Broadly Defined Money Supply
and Rate of Inflation

Year	Percentage	Rate of Inflation G.N.E. Deflator
1989	7.5	3.6
1988	8.3	4.0
1987	9.1	4.5
1986	8.7	2.9
1985	8.3	3.2
1984	9.6	3.5
1983	9.8	5.4
1982	8.8	10.4
1981	10.1	10.6
1980	10.9	11.4
1979	10.3	10.3
1978	10.6	6.4
1977	10.7	7.0
1976	9.9	9.5
1975	11.1	10.7
1974	11.6	15.3
1973	12.0	9.1
1972	12.7	5.0
1971	13.0	3.2
1970	13.6	4.6
1969	14.3	1.1
1968	14.4	3.3
1967	15.8	4.0
1966	16.4	4.4
1965	17.5	3.3
1964	17.6	2.4
1963	18.6	1.9
1962	19.2	1.4
1961	19.4	.4
1960	19.7	1.3
1959	20.3	2.0
1958	20.2	1.5
1957	20.6	2.1
1956	21.5	3.7
1955	21.2	.6
1954	22.0	1.6
1953	23.7	- .2
1952	23.9	4.4
1951	25.0	11.3
1950	22.9	2.4

Source: Calculated from the Bank of Canada *Monthly Review* and Department of Finance Quarterly and Annual Review.

because on the basis of the historical record there appears to be no necessary correlation between debt monetization and inflation at rates below 20 percent of the broadly defined money stock (see Table 3). Of course, the central bank would decide in its open-market operations what amount of debt to purchase, presuming that the debt were issued in the form of bonds and treasury bills. But it would have to take the priorities of the province into consideration because I am proposing that the board of the bank have provincial input.

The alternative is to issue the debt in terms of fixed-interest instruments like Canada Savings Bonds and negotiate the level of take-up beween the central bank and the province directly. However, in this case since the issuance of debt and its monetization would equally affect the money stock the overall question of the appropriate monetary policy is still an issue. I have suggested in an earlier paper (Chorney and Bouska, 1989) that it ought to be possible through the use of regionally sensitive credit controls such as compensating balances on loans to have a more flexible and regionally sensitive monetary policy. The two approaches together would considerably increase flexibility.

Of course, because of the Bank of Canada's current commitment to the zero-inflation rational expectations monetarist theory the bank is no where near the maximum 20 percent monetization level today. Instead it holds roughly $28 billion of federal debt which constitutes a monetization level of about 8 percent in relation to M2B. The more restrictive a monetary policy one operates with and the more unemployment and inadequate aggregate demand there is the greater the size of both public and private indebtedness. Indeed, if there is a true debt crisis today it is that of private indebtedness. The severity of the recession is largely due to the credit crunch that has come about from the very high interest rates that prevailed until recently and the disinflation and possibly deflation that these policies have promoted.

If the provinces financed their debt with debt instruments such as bonds clearly the central bank would not automatically purchase all the bonds on offer. Rather just as it does in managing the federal government's debt it would act as the reserve purchaser of the bonds in the money markets, purchasing more debt when it wanted to drive down interest rates, selling more debt when it wanted to raise rates. Clearly so long as all provinces operate with the Canadian dollar it is not possible for the interest rate on the debt to diverge very far from the central tendency of interest rates that the Bank of Canada would be promoting. However, the fact that the bank would now act on behalf of all the provinces, as well as the federal government would mean that the interest rate structure would reflect the priorities of the provinces as well as those of the federal government. To ensure this there would have to be changes in the governing board of the bank to reflect the interests of the provinces in a way that is not the case currently. If the federal government were committed to tight money but the provinces committed to stimulation the net result would be somewhere in between in terms of the interest rate that prevailed.

I have suggested in an earlier paper a way in which a system of compensating balances on loans and regionally sensitive credit controls might permit increased flexibility in the operation of our monetary system (Chorney and Bouska, 1989). Despite all the criticism, almost all of which was directed at something I did not suggest — regional variations in the discount rate — I continue to believe that my original proposal along with what I am proposing in this paper offers an improvement on our existing monetary and fiscal policy instruments. These are currently a product of the unitary state model found in Britain and like many of our British-inspired institutions are inappropriate in a federal state such as Canada.

The interest that would accrue to the central bank from the purchase of provincial debt would belong to the given province in the same way that the benefits of central bank-acquired federal debt belongs to the central government. Clearly there are some accounting procedures and careful federal-provincial negotiations that would have to be developed in order to sort out start-up and operating difficulties but the end result would be to considerably increase the flexibility of provincial governments to stimulate their economies in times of an economic downturn.

Because once a province's allotment was fully utilized it could not resort to the monetization route until the economy grew sufficiently to create further room for further debt capacity there is no likelihood that the increased flexibility would remove the prudent discipline of fiscal responsibility. The reform is simply intended to modernize the fiscal and monetary system so that the benefits of central bank management of the debt is available to both levels of government. If the smaller provinces objected to the formula, I am proposing small adjustments could be made to reflect the relative weight of population in order to advantage the poorer provinces.

Now, of course, the monetarists in all political parties and in the intellectual establishment will immediately raise the alarm cry of inflation. But if they wish to be taken seriously they must explain why in the past when the rate of monetization in proportion to the money stock equalled this ratio of 20 percent inflation problems did not automatically materialize. Table 3 makes it vey clear that there is no correlation between percentage of the broad money stock that is monetized below the 25 percent level and the rate of price inflation. Relatively low inflation appears to be compatible with rates of monetization below 10 percent and rates above 20 percent. Clearly something other than monetization of debt must explain the inflation process. Since greater monetization of debt reduces the burden of debt and permits lower interest rates and a more stimulative fiscal policy it would seem a desirable policy option to resort to when stagnation appears, subject to the 25 percent constraint.

It would be a wise and prudent policy to establish a system of tripartite price and incomes review and possibly controls if and when the situation merited it. Once there was a general commitment to reestablishing full employment as a top priority and to discarding the discredited monetarist model I am confident that the labour movement of this country would be a willing participant in such an exercise. Given the historical record, however, there is nothing to suggest that a switch to the policies I am advocating would mean a sharp rise in the rate of inflation particularly if the appropriate price- and income-monitoring system were in place. The shocking waste of human potential and productive output that Canada has witnessed over the past decade because of the pursuit of these old and discredited policies from the 1920s and 1930s should be enough of an incentive to try the alternative.

The fact is that the crude quantity theory of money that lies behind this charge of inflationism simply does not explain the inflationary process. Inflation is, in reality, a very complex phenonemon that must be disaggregated in order to make sense out of it. Price increases are due to a number of factors including: tax increases; supply bottlenecks in specific key industries; profit push and wage push in certain industries that are oligopolistic and have powerful trade unions; quality improvements in products in both the private and public sectors — obviously colour televisions and medicare represent advances over black-and-white sets and limited medical coverage — sociological factors such as status and prestige competion among workers in given industries; rises in the cost of imported and difficult to substitute key commodities; rise in prices due to consumers' ignorance which permit prices to be charged in excess of competitive market norms.

The problem with monetarism is that it reduces these complex phenomena to one crude factor, the rate of increase in the money stock. Aside from the obvious problem of which money stock one should monitor, there is also the problem of endogeneity of the money stock and instability of the velocity of money. In addition the monetarists rely upon the natural rate of unemployment argument to explain why the economy always tends to full employment, despite all the evidence to the contrary. Even after eighteen months of very elevated unemployment there are relatively few monetarists (Thomas Courchene is an important exception) who are willing to admit that the zero-inflation model is a disaster. The approach that I am suggesting for understanding the inflationary process can be illustrated in the following way.

Assume that the economy can be represented by a production possibility curve representing all the various sectors. In some of these sectors where there are trade unions and oligopolistic firms and inelastic demand for the product, price rise due to profit and wage push and supply bottlenecks occur at relatively low rates of capacity utilization. In other sectors, more competitive in nature and without trade unions, these price rises only occur when the economy is much closer to 100 percent capacity. Over time sectors change their character and new products and services are introduced with quality improvements that embody price rises but not for equivalent products or services. The overall impact upon prices can be determined only when we take the weighted average of the rise in prices for the economy as a whole and add tax increases and imported commodities into the picture. The point that I am trying to establish is that price rises in a modern economy such as Canada are far more complex and disaggregated than the picture suggested by the quantity theory of money. It is no less than tragic that such a simplistic theory of price inflation coupled with a dogmatic belief in market clearing and natural rates of unemployment has come to govern economic orthodoxy in Canada.

If the argument is made as Milton Friedman and his supporters often allege that economic stimulation has an effect upon prices, and not ultimately unemployment, and that this was a lagged effect that only appeared after a period of years then this criticism is easily dealt with. Long before the inflationary effect of a stimulative policy shows up, generally at the price level, the beneficial results will appear in a lowered unemployment rate. Once the unemployment rate drops sufficiently and the stimulus affects the price level more than it does the output or employment level, and these price rises are not quality improvements or tax increases but pure price rise, then but only then is it time to institute strict anti-inflationary policies.

In other words, stimulative deficits work efficiently when they are accompanied by an accomodating monetary policy of low interest rates. Otherwise, what happens is that tight money unduly restricts the effectiveness of fiscal policy. The result is excessive unemployment, inadequate aggregate demand, excessive payments on the debt and even with a balanced primary deficit, growing expenditures on the secondary deficit due to the high interest cost of carrying the debt. These payments, unlike the expenditures associated with a primary deficit, are not stimulative, as they tend, on the whole, to increase the incomes of savers rather than those with a high marginal propensity to spend. Furthermore, since savers and investors are not the same people, excessive savings leads to depressed aggregate demand which reinforces pessimistic expectations about rates of return among investors. The result is essentially what we have now in Canada — a severe recession with depressed investment and chronically elevated unemployment.

The policy alternative that would make a contribution to overcoming this state of affairs is one that would permit the maximum stimulus from a coordinated attack on unemployment by both the federal and provincial levels of government. Combined with an accomodating monetary policy, we would experience a much more rapid return to significantly lower rates of unemployment. The emphasis upon global competitiveness, because it ignores the problem of inadequate aggregate demand in the Canadian economy and depressed levels of domestic capital investment, does not speak to the fundamental problem. An industrial strategy that emphasizes technical innovation, science-based research and development and investments in education and training is also flawed if it is not accompanied by a return to demand stimulation for the economy as a whole. Otherwise whatever gains it contributes will simply come at the expense of our trading partners and ultimately reduce our export markets. A demand stimulation policy, on the other hand, will benefit not only ourselves but also our trading partners. As such it can help promote world economic recovery. There is no better place to begin than at home. The prairie provinces and the Atlantic region have a clear opportunity to place the issue of making the central bank more responsive to their needs by placing the issue of regionalizing monetary and fiscal policy on the table for intergovernmental negotiation. When they do I hope they consider seriously the proposals I have outlined in this paper.

References

The author wishes to thank Deppy Papandreou for research assistance. Financial assistance from the Social Sciences and Humanities Research Council of Canada is gratefully acknowledged.

Acheson, T.W. 1991. "The National Policy and the Industrialization of the Maritimes, 1880-1910." In G. Laxer, ed., *Perspectives on Canadian Economic Development*.

Barber, C.L. 1966. *Theory of Fiscal Policy as Applied to a Province*. Ontario: Queen's Printer.

Binhammer, H.H. 1988. *Money and Banking and the Canadian Financial System*. Toronto: Nelson Canada.

Charles, K.J. 1967. *The Myth of Inflation*. Winnipeg: University of Manitoba Press.

Chorney, Harold. 1989. *The Deficit and Debt Management: An Alternative to Monetarism*. Ottawa: Canadian Centre for Policy Alternatives.

——. 1991. "The Economic and Political Consequences of Canadian Monetarism." Paper presented to the British Association of Canadian Studies, University of Nottingham.

——. 1992. "The Deficit in Ontario: Fact or Fiction." In D. Drache, ed., *The Way Ahead: Social Democracy in Ontario*. Montreal/Kingston: McGill-Queen's University Press.

Chorney, Harold and Bernard Bouska. 1991. "Regionalizing Monetary Policy: An Alternative to Monetarism, Learning from the Japanese Example." Paper presented to the Eastern Economics Association, Baltimore, 1989; reprinted in *The COMER Papers*, Vol. 2, 59-83. Waterloo: University of Waterloo Press.

Dermine, J. 1990. *European Banking in the 1990s*. Oxford: Basil Blackwell.

Deutsche Bundesbank. 1976. *Wahrung and Wirtschaft in Deutschland: 1876-1975*. Frankfurt: Deutsche Bundesbank.

Drache, D. 1991. "Harold Innis and Canadian Capitalist Development." In G. Laxer, ed., *Perspectives on Canadian Economic Development*.

The Federal Reserve. 1963. *The Federal Reserve: Purpose and Functions*. Washington, D.C.: Board of Governors.

Francis, Diane. 1986. *Controlling Interest: Who Owns Canada*. Toronto: Macmillan.

Fullerton, D. 1986. *Graham Towers and His Times*. Toronto: McClelland and Stewart.

Goodhart, C.A. 1984. *Monetary Theory and Practice: The U.K. Experience*. London: Macmillan.

Grieder, W. 1987. *Secrets of the Temple: How The Federal Reserve Runs the Country.* New York: Simon and Schuster.

Harris, Anthony. 1991. "Hedging Against the Risks of Low Inflation." *British Financial Times*, 4 November 1991.

Hirschman, Albert O. 1958. *Strategy of Economic Development.* New Haven: Yale University Press.

Howson, S. 1975. *Domestic Monetary Management in Britain: 1919-1938.* Cambridge: Cambridge University Press.

Innis, Harold A. 1972. *Empire and Communication.* Edited by Mary Quayle-Innis. Toronto: University of Toronto Press.

———. 1991. "Conclusion to the Fur Trade in Canada." In G. Laxer, ed., *Perspectives on Canadian Economic Development.*

Laxer, Gordon, ed., 1991. *Perspectives on Canadian Economic Development.* Toronto: University of Oxford Press.

Lipsey, R. 1990. *The Goal of Price Instability.* Ottawa: C.D. Howe Institute.

Mackintosh, W.A. 1991. "Economic Factors in Canadian Economic History." In G. Laxer, ed., *Perspectives on Canadian Economic Development.*

Martin, Peter. 1989. *Inside the Bank of Canada's Weekly Financial Statistics: A Technical Guide.* Vancouver: Fraser Institute.

Maycock, James. 1977. *European Banking: Structure and Prospects.* London: Graham and Trotman.

Moine, Gerald. 1981. *Le Deutschemark.* Paris: Documentation française.

Naylor, R.T. 1987. *Canada in the European Age.* Vancouver: New Star Books.

New York Institute of Finance. 1988. *How the Bond Market Works.* New York: New York Institute of Finance.

Parkin, Michael. 1982. *Modern Macro-economics.* Scarborough: Prentice-Hall.

Perkins, J.O.N. 1973. *Macro-economic Policy: A Comparative Study: Australia, Canada and New Zealand.* Toronto: University of Toronto Press.

Pratt, Larry and John Richards. 1979. *Prairie Capitalism: Power and Influence in the New West.* Toronto: McClelland and Stewart.

Reuss, Fredrick. 1963. *Fiscal Policy for Growth Without Inflation: The German Experiment.* Baltimore: The John Hopkins Press.

Ritter, L. and W. Silber 1991. *Principles of Money and Banking and Financial Markets.* New York: Basic Books.

Robertson, D.H. 1946. *Money.* Cambridge: Cambridge University Press.

Samuelson, A. 1971. *Le mark: Histoire de la monnaie allemande.* Paris: Didier.

Watkins, Mel. 1991. "A Staple Theory of Economic Growth." In G. Laxer, ed., *Perspectives on Canadian Economic Development.*

8

The Future of the Newfoundland Fishery

William E. Schrank, Noel Roy,
Rosemary Ommer, Blanca Skoda

INTRODUCTION

The inshore fishery of Newfoundland is in a state of crisis. This fact in itself is not, or at least should not, be surprising; despite moments of optimism, the inshore fishery of Newfoundland has been in a more-or-less chronic state of crisis since the final quarter of the last century, by which time overpopulation had led to a serious decline in fishermen's productivity.[1] The question of what is to be done about excess labor in the inshore fishery has been recurring ever since, despite various attempts to solve the problem.[2]

Twenty-five years ago, the Newfoundland government's Pushie Commission favoured the then current trend away from the inshore fishery and towards a more specialized, capital intensive, offshore fishery. In a report prepared for and accepted by the commission, Day commented (with emphasis) that "the number of people dependent on the inshore fishery should be reduced and ... efforts made to raise substantially the productivity and earned income of those remaining."[3]

As we will make clear, the Newfoundland fishery suffers from continual crises, four since the publication of the Pushie report. While the crises have economic and biological causes, the inshore fishery is hypersensitive to such stimuli because of the fundamental structural problem which was so clearly enunciated in that report. This problem has no simple, painless, short-term solution. Nevertheless, a solution must be found because it is most unlikely that the federal government of Canada will forever be willing to provide the heavy subsidies and transfer payments that are necessary to keep the industry alive. That solution, regardless of the form it takes, will involve the "downsizing" of the inshore fishery. If effective action is not forthcoming soon in Newfoundland, and the subsidies are not stopped, natural forces may "solve" the provincial problem over the next generation.

While this paper is specifically concerned with Newfoundland after it became

122

a province of Canada (i.e., post-Confederation), the generic problem of un-economic excess labour in a traditional industry is much broader, and includes many industries in a variety of developed and less developed countries. The example of, and current policy debate in, Newfoundland is of interest in this broader context.

We discuss the historical background and structure of today's fishery, focussing on the moments of optimism and crisis that the industry has faced since the Pushie report and we consider the policy options available to government in the context of the structure of the Newfoundland economy. There have been several important studies of the economy in general and the fishery in particular, and there are sharp differences of opinion between the federal and provincial governments on fisheries policy. The recurring crises seem, at last, to have focussed public opinion on the problems of the fishery and the concept of downsizing has entered the discussions. We close with consideration of specific options that are available, drawing their implications.

HISTORICAL BACKGROUND AND STRUCTURE OF THE FISHERY

When one thinks of Newfoundland in a historical or economic context, one naturally thinks of fish — in particular, codfish and the Grand Banks of the northwest Atlantic. The dominant role of the fishery in the early history of Newfoundland is amply demonstrated in the works of Innis[4] and Lounsbury.[5] During the nineteenth century, Newfoundland's population and its fishery increased (for instance, from 38,500 fishermen in 1857 to 60,400 in 1884).[6] By the final quarter of the century it was already clear that Newfoundland was relatively overpopulated given that its economic base rested on a single industry; population out-migration followed and, with the construction of the transisland railroad, development of alternative industries, particularly mining and forestry. The Great Depression of the 1930s hit the Dominion very hard and, in 1933, the quasi-independent status of Newfoundland was surrendered and a government commission was established to deal with the crisis.[7] The allies' needs during World War II stimulated and in some respects modernized the economy.

With confederation of Newfoundland as a province of Canada in 1949, the Smallwood administration (which lasted until 1972) tried to restructure the economy, continuing the wartime modernization. There was a de-emphasis on the inshore fishery, a resettlement program was introduced which led to the abandonment of many small fishing villages (or "outports"), an industrial program was established deliberately altering the provincial economic focus away from fishing into small-scale manufacturing of a variety of products (e.g., rubber boots, candy bars, cement) and large scale projects (e.g., the Come-by-Chance oil refinery, Stephenville linerboard mill, and the Churchill Falls power project). The resettlement program, which led to the concentration of population in "regional growth centres," was, on balance, a failure, many formerly "independent" fishermen ending their days as unemployed welfare recipients. In some cases, as in that of Marystown where a shipyard and a large fish processing plant were established, the results were more successful. This program has, a quarter century later, left a residual feeling of bitterness against the government and a suspicion of any programs that might work to the detriment of the inshore fishery, not without reason. Nearly all the small manufacturers were out of business in a very short time and most of the large projects ended up bankrupt, although some have been revived on a smaller scale and with lowered expectations. One area of success was the opening of the Labrador iron mines in the early 1960s. Iron ore production continues to dominate the mining sector of the province, but its employment potential could never cope with the excess labour supply available, and the industry itself is vulnerable to technological and market changes. In fact, employment in the iron mines and pelletization plants have been declining since the recession of the early 1980s.

After Confederation, the fishery was reorganized. Frozen fish products (fillets and blocks of cod and other species) were developed for export to the United States and the old saltfish industry which produced a more labour-intensive product for export to Europe was de-emphasised. By 1970, salted cod production was only one-fifth as great as it had been twenty years earlier.[8] With the development of a frozen fish products industry came the need for freezing facilities, and the Smallwood government encouraged the establishment of small fish plants in many outports. Thus, while earlier the men of an outport were fishermen and their wives and families helped with the salting and drying of the fish, now the salting function was largely gone, replaced in a limited way (and in the more fortunate communities) by employment in the local fish plant.

While the industrial diversification program of the Smallwood administration made hardly a dent on the economy, an important consequence of Confederation was the great expansion of the government sector in the province (both federal and provincial), a major part of which was the development of the health and education sectors. The retail sector was stimulated by the introduction of federal transfer payments, which substantially increased the purchasing power of households at the same time as the North American consumer culture made inroads into the desires and expectations of a rural population which had, until then, been relatively insulated from mass consumer sales and advertising.

At the time of the Pushie Commission report, the volume of fish landings in Newfoundland was slightly over 300,000 metric tons, of which half was cod and the remainder primarily flounder, redfish, and herring. The offshore catch was 45 percent (compared to only 20 percent in the late 1950s) and the report predicted a total catch by 1975 of nearly 625,000 tons. The total fisheries labour force was a little over 20,000, of whom about 1,000 were employed on offshore vessels (vessels of more than 25 gross tons). Earned fishing income from the offshore was about $4,000 per year, as opposed to only $700 from the inshore.[9]

The catch level predicted by the commission was never reached; the report appeared just as a major crisis was to hit the fishery — the crisis generated by

Table 1
Newfoundland Gross Domestic Product at Factor Cost
(Millions of Canadian Dollars and Percentage of GDP)

Sector	1971		1989	
	($)	(%)	($)	(%)
Agriculture	5.7	0.47	30.0	0.40
Forestry	14.6	1.21	59.0	0.78
Fishing & trapping	25.1	2.08	178.0	2.37
Mining	133.1	11.04	482.0	6.41
Manufacturing:				
Fish prod.	33.5	2.78	218.0	2.90
Pulp & paper	27.9	2.31	144.0	1.91
Other	49.8	4.13	256.0	3.40
Construction	219.6	18.21	577.0	7.67
Power	39.3	3.26	383.0	5.09
Service industries	670.0	55.56	5,083.0	67.57
GDP at factor cost	1,206.0	—	7,523.0	—

Source: *Historical Statistics of Newfoundland and Labrador*, 1990, F-4. (Details do not add to total because of rounding and the omission of a residual error term.)

uncontrolled foreign overfishing on the Grand Banks. Total seafish catch peaked in 1970 at 475,000 tons, fell to a little more than a quarter of a million tons in 1975, rose back to 569,000 in 1979, fell to half a million the next year and has remained in that neighbourhood ever since. Of the 464,000 ton seafish catch in 1978, groundfish accounted for 325,000, and cod for 173,000 of that. While the total groundfish catch was nearly equally divided between the inshore and off-shore fisheries, 80 percent of the cod catch was taken inshore. Twelve years later, the total seafish catch in 1990 was 426,000 metric tons, groundfish accounted for 331,000 and cod for 238,000 of that with about 46 percent of the cod being caught inshore. In 1988, there were approximately 1,000 trawlermen and a total of 14,000 full-time and 15,000 part-time inshore fishing licenses held.[10]

In 1990, of groundfish, only cod (at $118M), turbot ($13M), flounder and sole ($15M) and of other species, only caplin ($16M), shrimp ($43M) and queen crab ($13M) had landed values of more than $10M. In 1987, the most recent year for which product data are available, only frozen round or dressed caplin ($23M), frozen cod ($151M), haddock ($12M), redfish ($16M), flounder and sole ($74M), and turbot fillets ($28M), frozen cod blocks ($139M), salt cod ($55M), fish meal ($11M), pickled lumpfish roe ($15M), frozen shrimp in shell ($38M), frozen crab in shell ($12M), and fresh and frozen crab meat ($22M) were produced in values of $10M or more.[11]

FOUR CRISES

There are good reasons why the Pushie Commission overestimated future catch. The major change occurring in the fishery off Newfoundland at that time was the rapid expansion of the large foreign distant water fleets that operated unrestricted beyond the twelve-mile limit of Newfoundland's coast. Spain, Portugal, USSR, and Poland were among the countries represented. Some countries, such as the first two, had been fishing Newfoundland waters for centuries, others were new arrivals. Technologies were also being modernized; 1969 was the last year the Portuguese "white fleet," a fleet of wooden-hulled sailing vessels, operated off Newfoundland. The large vessels were converted to diesel operation, and the small dory-carrying vessels were replaced over the next few years with modern trawlers.

The effects of foreign fishing on Newfoundland stocks are perhaps most clearly shown by noting the catches of northern cod, a stock caught from mid-Labrador to the northern half of the Grand Banks and one which has, over the past fifteen years, been the focus of much policy discussion in Canada and of much dispute among Canada and the countries of the European Economic Community (EEC). Total northern cod harvests were 393,600 tons in 1960, rose with uncontrolled foreign fishing to 807,500 tons in 1968, then fell rapidly due to the effects of overfishing to 432,500 tons in 1971.[12] These effects were sufficiently obvious that they led the International Commission for the Northwest Atlantic Fishery (ICNAF) to introduce a global quota (total allowable catch — TAC) in 1972 and national quotas the following year.[13] There was no effective enforcement mechanism, however, and harvests continued to fall until they reached a low of 138,600 tons in 1978. During the same year that the national quotas were introduced, the third United Nations Conference on the Law of the Sea[14] was convened, one of the first results of which was that maritime nations, acting on the proposal that was to become Part V of the Law of the Sea Convention, declared exclusive economic zones of up to 200 miles. Canada declared such a zone effective 1 January 1977, the intention being to displace the foreign fleets.

The first major (sustained, multi-year) fisheries crisis, therefore, occurred in the late 1960s as a result of overfishing by foreign distant water fleets.

The next crisis arose just as the ICNAF quotas were being introduced. The oil price increases of early 1974 led the world into a severe, but brief, recession which affected the fisheries along with everything else. We have shown that the demand in the United States for Newfoundland fish products is income elastic with the result that the market for Newfoundland products is highly sensitive to economic conditions in the United States.[15] In addition, the market is also price inelastic so that demand cannot be stimulated by the modest price reductions the fish producers might be able to afford. As would be expected from this combination of factors, in 1974 the bottom dropped out of the market for those products creating another fisheries crisis. In addition, the economic pressures of the worldwide recession led to the first strike by Newfoundland's trawlermen, members of the Newfoundland Fish, Food and Allied Workers Union which had been founded in 1971. In September 1974, the strike was suspended when a conciliation board under Dr. L. Harris of Memorial University was appointed. Two months later the report was submitted, the board noting that all trawler/processor companies at the time were taking heavy losses even though a year earlier the firms had been profitable because of an extremely buoyant market. It was clear to the board that the companies could not afford to pay what the union was asking but that the 1,000 trawlermen deserved substantial increases in pay — an interesting and apparently insoluble dilemma. However, they thought that the increased pay could be gained by partially abandoning the "co-adventurer" system whereby fishermen were paid only a share of the value of the catch — nothing if catches were sufficiently low on any trip. The recommendation was that a substantial per diem allowance be paid plus a share of the catch. The federal government, they recommended, should make up any remaining difference that the companies could not meet. They warned: "it is our view that for several years to come ... the viability of the industry will remain in doubt," adding that

> The implications of total collapse are, however, so horrendous that we can hardly imagine a situation in which government would permit it. Thus we are recommending to Government that immediate action be taken to establish a mechanism through which the companies can continue to operate while assuring the fishermen a fair return for their labours. If the recommendation is accepted then two important questions will require answering. The first, what level of subsidy is required? and, the second, how is the subsidy to be applied?[16]

And it was done. The Temporary Assistance Program (TAP) was put in place, with subsidies paid both to the processing companies and to inshore fishermen. Not surprisingly, less than two years later, American fish processors filed a petition with their government to have countervailing duties placed on Canadian fish exported to the United States on the grounds that the fish were being unfairly subsidized — the result of the TAP program. Ultimately, the Canadians won the case but only because by 1978 the TAP program was being phased out.[17] Adoption of the TAP program marked the end of crisis number two.

In 1976 cod catches returned to the level of 1972, total seafish landings rose to their highest level since 1971,[18] cod prices rose, and Extended Fisheries Jurisdiction (EFJ) — the adoption of the 200-mile exclusive economic zone for the fishery — was announced, effective at the start of the next year. The response was nearly hysterical — with the stroke of a pen, foreign fleets would, after hundreds of years, be replaced by Canadian fleets under conditions of conservationism which would permit a rejuvenation of the depleted stocks. There was a mad rush to expand — from $74M in 1976-77, government expenditures on the fishery rose to $104M in 1977-78, an increase of 41 percent. Net unemployment insurance benefits paid to inshore fishermen rose from $9M to $15M, an increase of 67 percent in the year, and they continued to rise for the remainder of the decade, reaching $35M by 1980-81, a nearly fourfold increase in as many years.

Outstanding loans of the provincial Fisheries Loan Board, which finances small boats, rose from $12M in 1976-77 to $16M in 1977-78, an increase of one-third in the year and these loans continued to increase until by 1980-81 they reached $44M, again a nearly fourfold increase in four years. The overwhelming proportion of the $70M increase in the value of Newfoundland's fishing fleet was paid for directly, or through bounties, or through loans, by the two levels of government. The number of registered inshore vessels rose from 9,447 in 1976 to 19,498 in 1980. The number of licensed fishermen increased by one-third from 1976 to 1977 and more than doubled from 15,000 in 1976 to 35,000 in 1980 — a number that has since fallen by more than five thousand with no one seeming to know (or care) where the extra fishermen came from, or where the five thousand went. The number of fish freezing plants increased from 61 in 1976 to 84 in 1981, an increase of 38 percent since the declaration of EFJ.[19]

There are two major reasons for this incredible expansion — the historical role of the fishery and the concomitant false expectation that the fishery would permanently solve Newfoundland's economic problems while keeping its culture alive, and the traditionally poor state of the Newfoundland economy. Here was a hope that something was finally going to be done to create a good life and good living for Newfoundlanders. Perhaps it could have had that effect for a limited number of fishermen and their families if growth had been regulated and controlled — but such was not to be.

The optimism of the period was rudely shattered when the United States markets collapsed completely in response to the American economic recession of the early Reagan years. This was post-Confederation crisis number three, the worst thus far. Prices were falling, processing plants were closing, the processing companies were facing bankruptcy. Kirby describes the state of the fishery in detail in the report his task force prepared at the request of the federal government to point the way out.[20] Kirby's report led to a major financial restructuring of the industry, with most of the medium-sized companies being absorbed into two giant fish processing firms — Fishery Products International Ltd. (FPI) and National Sea Products Ltd., only the former being primarily a Newfoundland company. These companies are now among the largest 250 Canadian companies.[21]

Kirby was basically optimistic. In 1982, predictions of future harvests were grand, once again. The Kirby Commission believed that the combination of quality improvements and a financial restructuring of the industry would result in an economically viable fishery. FPI was formed by the provincial government, absorbing a number of previously independent firms, and receiving $281M from the two levels of government between 1983 and 1985, and selling about a dozen of its potentially least profitable plants. With cash available, United States markets improving as the economy improved, a doubling of world cod prices, and increasing catches (in 1986), FPI turned from losses of $35M in 1984 and $20M in 1985 to a profit of $46.6M in 1986. The atmosphere of the fishery was again excessively buoyant and the company was privatized in 1987, the governments recovering a large part of the special subsidy they had paid over the previous few years.[22] But quality improvements were never implemented, at least not in the inshore sector and the fish products market continued to be sensitive to the economic health of the United States; catches remained disappointing, and by 1989 FPI had once again taken a loss (of $22.2M).[23]

The recession of the early 1980s was sufficiently severe that another problem was overlooked, becoming critical only with the mid-1980s economic recovery. Fisheries and Oceans Canada had predicted in 1979 that, by 1985, with Extended Fisheries Jurisdiction, the total allowable catch of northern cod would be 365,000 tons,[24] a figure comparable with the catch in 1960, before foreign overfishing strained the bioeconomic system to the limit, and a catch level that had not been reached since 1974. Munro, in an aptly named book, *A Promise of Abundance*, had predicted a year later that ultimately the northern cod catch might even approach 450,000 tons per year.[25] He was here assuming a rather conservative management plan since the maximum sustainable yield, previously used as a basis of fisheries management policy but then under attack,[26] was believed to be approximately 100,000 tons higher.[27] Actual post-EFJ cod catches were disappointing, however, leading to the fourth post-Confederation fisheries crisis.

The total northern cod catch fell from 214,200 tons in 1976 (the year before Extended Fisheries Jurisdiction) to 138,600 tons in 1978. But after this initial (and desirable) drop, the catch rose again, reaching 251,500 tons in 1986. During this period, foreigners were displaced (foreign catch falling from 151,200 to 61,200 tons); but the easing of the foreign burden on the fish population was more than compensated by the Canadian expansion (inshore catches up from 59,900 to 72,400 tons and the offshore catch up from 3,100 to 118,000 tons).[28] The total (inshore and offshore) annual Canadian northern cod catch under Extended Fisheries Jurisdiction has never even reached 260,000 tons. By 1989 the figure was once again around 215,000 tons and in 1990 it was even less.

By the end of 1988, Munro's original projections, and the more conservative Fisheries and Oceans projections, seemed excessive and the entire biomass estimation procedure used by Fisheries and Oceans Canada, the scientific basis for setting the total allowable catch, had been thrown into doubt. Dr. L. Harris was called upon again, and this time given a limited mandate — to report on the quality of the scientific assessment of fish stocks. His interim report, delivered in mid-May 1989, supported the scientists' belief that current fish stocks are lower than was previously believed. Further, he suggested that the method used by biologists to estimate the current stocks is susceptible to serious error:

> whereas cohort analysis (VPA) is an accurate method of hindcasting, the results from the original analysis and from tuning techniques designed to give current estimates are only as valid as are the data sets used in the analysis. Thus, underreported catches by fishermen in one year would result

in underestimating fishing mortality in that year and possibly in overestimates for preceding years. By the same token, errors in catch at age data will result in output errors in respect both of population size and mortality. Again, biased trends in CPUE [catch per unit effort] data are particularly serious since they lead directly to biased estimates of current mortality and population size. ... we are somewhat concerned that the analytical process is being over-emphasized while insufficient attention is given to the quality of data inputs.[29]

The cause of the fourth crisis, then, was the likelihood of a long-term shortage of fish. By the fall of 1989, there was no question that at least a short-term crisis was at hand. While the 1989 total allowable catch (TAC) for northern cod had originally been set in late 1988 at 266,000 tons.[30] this figure had been reduced to 235,000 in February 1989, at the time the Harris Task Force was established. CAFSAC, the scientific unit that recommends allowable catches, had suggested a cutback to 125,000 tons for 1990 and in his interim report issued in May 1989, Dr. Harris suggested a more modest cutback to 190,000 as the TAC for 1990, this to be considered as a compromise, interim, figure subject to careful monitoring.[31] The final report of the Harris panel stated that maintaining annual catches at 190,000 tons would only continue the decline of the northern cod stock, that the catch should be reduced to the CAFSAC level as soon as possible. The report noted, however, that lowering the catch to the CAFSAC level would "precipitate social and economic repercussions of a particularly drastic nature"[32] and that even a precipitate drop would require that this low level of catch be maintained for more than a decade before the stock would have recovered to the extent that the long-term sustainable catch of 300,000 metric tons could be harvested. In 1989, the Canadian catch was 215,000 tons and Fisheries and Oceans Canada accepted the Harris approach to gradually phasing in lower northern cod TACs, setting figures of 187,860, 183,002, and 178,145 for 1991, 1992 and 1993, respectively.[33]

Once the interim Harris report became public, rumors of disaster were rampant. The St. John's *Evening Telegram* for 10 October 1989 carried an article in which a National Sea Products Ltd. vice-president denied that a decision had been made to close the large (500 employees) St. John's fish plant, but he acknowledged that the company would close some of its eight Newfoundland and Nova Scotia plants in 1990. On 11 December, National Sea announced that it would, in fact, permanently close the St. John's plant in three months, citing sharp drops in the enterprise allocations (specific company quotas) awarded by the Canadian government to the company in recent years. The plant remains in operation, with a much reduced work force, functioning as a specialized shrimp processor.[34]

While the Harris Commission was functioning, the federal government had established a separate Federal Task Force on Northern Cod to devise more general fisheries policies. In its 13 December 1989 edition, the *Evening*

Telegram carried a report that Ken Stein, chairman of the task force, had stated that there is no doubt that the number of people involved in the inshore fishery must be reduced. Significantly, the Pushie Commission's comments were still being repeated, although no action had been taken in the intervening twenty years. On 2 January 1990, Fisheries and Oceans Canada finally released its 1990 Atlantic Groundfish Management Plan, announcing that the total allowable catch for northern cod would be decreased to 197,000 tons. FPI then announced on 5 January that, considering that its enterprise allocation had fallen by 28 percent in two years, it would permanently close three of its plants (employing more than 1,300 workers), each the only significant source of employment in its town. These announcements came at a time when not only was the Newfoundland economy in trouble but the Canadian economy was weakening as well.

Earlier crises in the post-Confederation Newfoundland fishery had two causes — poor markets (the result of a weakened United States economy) and poor fish harvests (the results of overfishing). In 1989 the fishery was, probably for the first time, facing both problems simultaneously. The *Evening Telegram* of 6 January 1990 reported, in addition to the FPI closings, that the province was paying the company $11.5M to keep the plants open on a seasonal basis through 1991. The periods during which the plants would be open would be adequate to permit plant workers to qualify for unemployment insurance. Further, it also reported that only a day earlier the premier had rejected the idea of outright subsidies to the plants because "subsidizing the plants could jeopardize the entire fishing industry ... but ... in the government's opinion the [$11.5M] funding is not a form of subsidization and should not be subjected to countervail action by the United States." The provincial government also offered National Sea Products Ltd. $3M to keep the St. John's plant in operation. The St. John's *Sunday Express* of 7 January editorially recognized that the industry had grown so large that it could not be sustained by existing resources. The crisis was deepening and government and press were showing signs of tiring of the constant struggle to keep the fishery, or at least its labour-intensive inshore component, afloat.

Not only is the Newfoundland fishery perennially in a state of crisis, but the existing level of economic activity in the fish and fish products industry is obtained only under very heavy subsidies. In 1981, even before the government poured money into the financial restructuring of the Atlantic fishing industry, government expenditures in the Newfoundland fishery — including administrative expenditures, transfer payments to fishermen, and subsidies to fish processing companies — amounted to $125M, a figure nearly equal to the total value of fish landings.[35] In 1981 there were 28,587 licensed fishermen in the province, about half of them considered to be full-time. The figure fluctuates slightly; by 1986 it had fallen to 26,944 while by 1988 it had risen again to 29,851. If the Newfoundland fishery were operated on a commercially viable basis, conservatively defined, that is without government subsidies, with processing firms taking no losses, and with fishermen living on at least a poverty line income before transfers, it could employ only about 6,000 fishermen, mostly on an expanded offshore fleet.[36] There is every reason to believe that the heavy subsidization has continued to the present. For how long, then, will the federal government of Canada be willing to provide the various subsidies and transfer payments that keep the industry alive? Given the background described above, the question has to be answered in two parts: first, an explanation of why the subsidies have been tolerated for so long; and second, a consideration of whether the federal government can or will continue subsidizing the Newfoundland inshore fishery into the indefinite future.

POLICY OPTIONS

There are historical, social and cultural reasons which generate an inertia with respect to the fishery — people are hesitant to change their lifestyle, are hesitant to give up the occupation they have grown up expecting to follow and which was followed by parents, grandparents and further into the past. They are hesitant, in short, to abandon their "roots." But societies do change, and it must be now asked what economic stimulus remains to keep the inshore fishery alive when it is so susceptible to dramatic cyclical fluctuations and is maintained only with heavy government funding?

Table 2
Unemployment and Participation Rates

Year	Canada		Newfoundland	
1967	3.8	57.6	5.9	45.0
1970	5.7	57.8	7.3	45.0
1973	5.5	59.7	10.0	49.2
1976	7.1	61.1	13.3	49.4
1979	7.4	63.4	15.1	52.3
1982	11.0	64.1	16.7	52.2
1985	10.5	65.3	20.8	53.2
1988	7.8	66.7	16.4	54.6
1990	8.1	67.0	17.1	56.0

Source: Statistics Canada 71.201.

The short answer is serious long-term unemployment — the population of the province has grown from 361,000 in 1951 (the first census after Confederation) to an estimated 573,000 in 1990. The labour force during this period grew from 102,000 to 242,000, the disproportionate increase resulting from an increasing participation rate (from 45.1 percent to 56.0 percent — largely the result of women entering the paid labour force) and a demographic change towards smaller families.[37] The changing demographic structure requires the creation of new jobs; yet the industrial structure of the province limits such growth. Table 2 shows the average annual unemployment and participation rates for Canada and

Newfoundland for selected years, years representing periods of both weak and strong economies. It is clear from the table that the unemployment rate in Newfoundland is much higher than the Canadian average, that the participation rate is much lower, and that the unemployment problem is chronically worse now than it was at the time of the Pushie Commission report (1967). If anything, measured unemployment as represented in the table understates the depth of the problem: discouraged workers are excluded; and one reason for the chronic difference in participation rates between Newfoundland and the Canadian average is likely to be the general shortage of jobs so that people (particularly mature women) simply never enter the labour market. Under these conditions, it is hardly surprising that government, and society in general, are willing to support the commercially unviable inshore fishery with its generally depressed characteristic and its subsidy requirements. But will they continue to do so into the indefinite future?

In 1980, fully cognizant of the failure of the resettlement program, the Economic Council of Canada proposed what can be interpreted as a mild deemphasis of the rural economy. Their first recommendation was:

> We recommend that the Newfoundland government adopt a strategy for the island of Newfoundland that aims to provide services and employment opportunities within commuting distance of most outports on major peninsulas, so that rural people can participate in the market economy without giving up their homes and moving families. Within each peninsula, the services, infrastructure, and related employment opportunities should generally be located in one or two urban centres.[38]

Furthermore, they recommended that "migration be neither encouraged nor discouraged" — and therefore that existing preferential income support programs, such as the program of regionally differentiated unemployment insurance benefits, be reconsidered — and that "government not force the creation of jobs in outports or smaller urban centres."

The provincial government's reaction was sharply negative.[39] In response to the first recommendation, the provincial government stated that its "clearly enunciated policy is to foster rural economic development in *all* communities" (our emphasis), and they insisted that since "for many communities, the sole economic base is the fishery, and the northern cod stock is most significant. ... Government's policy is that the fishermen residing in coastal communities adjacent to the resource should have first claim." The government did, however, express agreement in principle with the concept of not interfering with migration, but took sharp issue with any reconsideration of the existing unemployment insurance benefit scheme. At the same time they voiced their belief that "rural areas have unique advantages for certain types of economic activity, and that they offer for many people a superior way of life. ... viable opportunities can be found in most rural areas to maintain and improve the lifestyle to which our people have become attached."

This is why, despite the protestations of the Pushie Commission and others that such policies are unwise,[40] when viable opportunities have not been found in the outports (small fishing villages), the provincial government has seen it as logically necessary (in order to maintain a traditional "lifestyle") for the inshore fishery to continue to be the "employer of last resort." Against this was set the Economic Council of Canada's recommendations that bioeconomic research into the fishery be expanded, that a transferable license system for fishermen be introduced (but that the transfer system operate in a way that protects the inshore fishery), and that "gear, boat, and other subsidies to the fishery be discontinued,"[41] and Kirby's recommendation that the first priority of Atlantic fisheries policy should be that the fishery "be economically viable on an ongoing basis, where to be viable implies an ability to survive downturns with only a normal business failure rate and without government assistance."[42] Nonetheless, the Kirby Task Force recognized the realities of the Atlantic provinces economic situation and the ineffectiveness of the Economic Council of Canada report, and understood that the subsidies would not be withdrawn in the near future.

In 1986 there followed the federal government's "Nielsen" Task Force report on natural resources which was strongly against subsidies,[43] arguing that the fishery is not economically viable in many parts of Canada [read: Newfoundland, and possibly other provinces] and that Fisheries and Oceans Canada should focus on "protecting the fisheries resource and maintaining a viable fishing industry" without the encumbrance of "socio-economic burdens." All direct grants or subsidies to the fishing industry should be terminated since "an artificially large employment factor and unnecessarily large capital investment in vessels and plants, dissipates total economic returns and reduces the international competitiveness of Canadian products." This statement was symptomatic of a major change in the attitude of the federal government of Canada, away from the interregional income redistribution plans of the Trudeau administration. The Mulroney government was, and continues to be, fundamentally opposed to such schemes, although it has found that its ability to change them is limited. The Nielsen reforms were politically unpalatable for their time, the government had to abandon them, and the report quickly disappeared without a trace. Nonetheless, the political ambience emphasizing international competitiveness and dislike of subsidization continues, placing pressure on the Newfoundland fishery.

Also in 1986, there appeared the report of the provincial Royal Commission on Employment and Unemployment (the House Commission). The commission claimed to reject "both a romanticized yearning for the past and an unrealistic expectation of becoming a heavily industrialized society," but stressed "a balanced approach to economic development [which] ... encourages medium- and small-scale enterprises and takes advantage of modern forms of communication and technology, in order to build upon the latent strengths of all parts of our society, including our small outports, our resource towns, and our regional service centres."[44] With regard to the inshore fishery, they encouraged further biological research into inshore cod stocks; "revitalization and development [for the inshore] ... consistent with sound economics"; conversion of fishermen's debt to government equity; and generalizing the fishermen's licensing system to allow the fishermen greater flexibility. There was no implication that the inshore fishery is overpopulated, nor that subsidies should be withdrawn except as they became irrelevant in the strengthened fishery of the indefinite future.

The background report underlying the commission's recommendations explicitly states that the authors were not recommending that "governments be expected to prop up inefficient industry in perpetuity" but it is clear that they were assuming that a "revitalized" inshore fishery would be the "cornerstone of rural development in Newfoundland" and economically viable, albeit within a rural economy in which expanded opportunities for diversification would have been created.[45] Nonetheless, the report failed to confront the problem of excess capacity, saying only that while "it may be desirable to reduce the numbers of fishermen in the long-term, too little attention has been given to the meagre alternatives that face Newfoundland fishermen and the plant workers who process their catch."[46]

Comparison of the final report of the House Commission with that of Kirby, or even with the more extreme Nielsen report, shows the differences in approach between the federal and provincial governments. The former believes employment in the fishery should be smaller than it is and that subsidies should be lowered or abandoned. The provincial government believes there should be greater reliance on a diversified rural economy, that the number of fishermen may drop, and that subsidies will ultimately be unnecessary. How exactly the rural economy will be diversified to render it economically self-sufficient remains an open question. That the provincial government essentially supports the recommendations of the House Commission is materially demonstrated by the fact that for several years Dr. House has been the chairman of the province's Economic Recovery Commission, and as such is deputed to "revitalize" the Newfoundland economy.

THE PUBLIC DEBATE

By the start of 1989 it was clear that the fishery was again in a major crisis and the current situation was forcing a fundamental re-evaluation of the Newfoundland fishery. In June 1989, two conflicting editorials appeared in the St. John's newspapers. In an editorial entitled "Too Many Fishermen?", the *Evening Telegram* of 1 June 1989 concluded that "Newfoundland's fishery must eventually be expanded and diversified so that it can employ more people, not fewer ... Aquaculture and making gear may be possibilities, and they should not be discounted. But they can never be a substitute for a vibrant fishery." In contrast, the *Sunday Express* of 4 June stated that:

> It is not fair to rural Newfoundland towns to keep their hopes up about a viable fishing industry based on pipe dreams of huge fish quotas. In the boom year of 1987, with groundfish prices high and northern cod quotas above

250,000 tonnes, FPI plants were operating at only 65% of capacity. This year, plants are operating at 55% capacity. And with further cuts, some plants will not likely be able to operate at all...

The choice is clear for the governments of Canada and Newfoundland — either the fishery must be downsized and made viable, or the industry must become a social fishery, operating from year to year with the help of government subsidies.

This was a courageous statement for the popular press to make, but it was directly to the point. The following day, the *Evening Telegram* printed several articles on the lack of alternative employment in Newfoundland for the soon to be displaced National Sea workers and included an editorial in which it took strong issue with both the federal and provincial governments, arguing that they should not acquiesce in the closure but rather that they should adopt the position of the Newfoundland Food Fish and Allied Workers Union — "that is, 'sharing the pain' of offshore quota reductions by having downtime at all plants, instead of allowing permanent closures." In the same editorial, they quoted St. John's West MP John Crosbie as saying that "it is clear that the size of the reduction in TAC of Northern Cod forces us to recognize that the Atlantic fishery cannot sustain existing employment levels," and the premier, Clyde Wells, as commenting that Newfoundlanders have to "stop burdening the fishery with the responsibility to be the employment opportunity of last resort," though the editorial added that "it is not easy to conceive of much else to have 'resort' to."

Today, the provincial government shows some signs of recognizing the need for a smaller fishery, as does the fishermen's union, and much of the recent discussion during the past several years has revolved around the issues of restricting the number of part-time fishermen (through more stringent licensing systems), plant closures, and the general downsizing of the fishery.

Fishermen's licenses fall into two categories, full- and part-time. The distinction in terms of qualifications is not nearly as clear as it could be. Kirby noted, for instance, that one-quarter of licensed part-time fishermen earn revenues from fishing comparable to that generated by full-time fishermen.[47] A full-time fisherman is one who will have fished as a registered fisherman in his area for a specified number of years, and who will not have worked for pay outside the fishery for more than thirty days during the previous fishing season, but who may work for pay outside the fishing season. A part-time fisherman is a registered commercial fisherman who does not satisfy the requirements of a full-time fisherman. Young fishermen obviously must start as part-time fishermen.[48] It becomes clear that to ban part-timers without redefining some of them as full-timers, would amount to closing the fishery to the next generation. This aspect of the debate, which started as a search for a means of restricting the number of fishermen, in 1990 disintegrated into a narrowly focussed attack on what the fisheries background paper to the House report had referred to as a widespread hostility on the part of fishermen towards "moonlighters," people who hold part-time licenses and full-time employment outside the fishery. The report noted that there are actually very few people in this category.[49] An *Evening Telegram* editorial writer commented, however, that while "in the overall scheme of things part-timers don't take a massive amount of fish out of the sea, but every fish they catch is another one a full-time fisherman can't take."[50] The author of this piece refers to support given by Walter Carter, the provincial minister of Fisheries and by Richard Cashin, the president of the Fishermen, Food and Allied Workers Union to the concept of removing moonlighters from the industry.

The debate continued into 1991, with the fishermen's union calling for greater restrictions on part-time license holders.[51] Among the union's suggestions was one that fishermen permanently downgraded to part-time status not be permitted to retain licenses for limited entry fisheries. By April 1991, the recommendation of the federal Dunne Committee[52] on the implementation of the Harris report that part-time licenses be restricted to crew members and therefore, in essence, to individuals entering the fishery who have not served the necessary time to qualify for full-time licenses, was accepted.[53] Removing moonlighters will perhaps help slightly to control pressure on the fish stocks and marginally increase the catch and income of remaining fishermen, but a focus in this area has clearly distracted from the more fundamental problems of the industry.

In response to the crisis created by the late 1989 announcement of plant closures, amid much fanfare an emergency fisheries aid package of $584M was disclosed by Fisheries and Oceans Canada on 7 May 1990 — yet another round of emergency subsidies to the industry. In a useful year-end summary of year's events in the fishery, the *Sunday Express* of 30 December 1990 noted that the money was largely taken from existing programs, that it was to be applied over five years to the four Atlantic provinces. The money was being spread very thin. As new initiatives, Fisheries and Oceans Canada declared a moratorium on the issuance of new licenses and restricted some holders of part-time licenses from catching groundfish.[54] As an extension of existing initiatives, the government announced that Industrial Adjustment Service (IAS) committees had been set up for a number of communities and various inshore and offshore fleets. To illustrate the operation of these committees, the report noted that in one, "municipal leaders are participating on the IAS Committee. All parties are being encouraged to work together to develop solutions to the problems" of the community.[55] We note that this is a community about to lose its fish plant — its only employer of any significance. The IAS program (and the accompanying worker adjustment and community development funds of $130M over four years to aid displaced workers) clearly does not address the fundamental difficulties of the fishery. It should be clear by now that the major structural problems of the fishery cannot be corrected with band-aid solutions.

Robert Sheppard, in the *Globe and Mail* of 8 May 1990, noted that missing from the emergency fisheries aid package was any response to a provincial proposal that the current fisheries crisis be used to permanently reduce the size of the fishery by the joint funding of ten to fifteen projects each year to provide alternative employment for fishermen and fish plant workers. The provincial plan required $97.5M for fishery diversification and revitalization and $250M to be spent in Newfoundland over five years for economic diversification.[56] The federal program avoided the primary issues; the provincial plan is reminiscent of Smallwood's failed industrialization program, but at least it faces up to the requirement that the fishery be permanently downsized.

The issue of permanently downsizing the Newfoundland fishery was about to finally become joined, despite the resistance of some. Shortly after the announcement of the emergency fisheries aid program, the *Evening Telegram* returned to the question of whether there are too many Newfoundland fishermen. "Are there too many Newfoundland inshore fishermen and fisherwomen," they asked. "We would like to see a full discussion of this matter by economists and other observers, before giving our assent to the proposition"; the "human factor" cannot be overlooked "by policymakers ... those who are anxious to 'diversify' the rural economy (which for hundreds of years has resisted such diversification) or 'retrain' workers. ..." They continued to argue that:

> bona fide fishermen must make a living like the rest of us, and that the immediate prospects in many parts of the province are bleak. Thus we see some need for some (even if temporary) restrictions on moonlighters who are already earning incomes from other jobs. But the opportunity should not be denied to young Newfoundlanders — and not just the offspring of existing fishermen — to get into the fishery ... As we recall, it was a similar unexamined notion [too many fishermen...], widely accepted by government bureaucrats and others, that led to the resettlement program of the 1960s. We all thought that isolation was a bad thing. ... There was something to these ideas, but the effects on many communities were disastrous, as we all now realize.[57]

This is a good summary of the traditional attitude that the fishery must be maintained — at roughly its existing size — regardless of the cost. It is interesting to note that the editorial, which is wary of downsizing, says nothing of the subsidies required to maintain the fishery as it is.

The provincial government was recognizing the difficulty. By September 1990, the provincial minister of Fisheries was quoted as stating that "the downsizing of the industry is a difficult task, but that most involved agree that it is the only solution because of the simple fact that there are too many fishermen chasing too few fish."[58] The 4 February 1991 issue of the *Sunday Express* quoted the provincial deputy minister of fisheries as saying:

> The fact of the matter is the market will not sustain all of the plants that are in the system. ... We just won't be able to keep them operating. The forces in the marketplace are going to be helpful here, in that they are going to force a long-term solution on the industry.

Finally, on 7 June 1991, Fisheries and Oceans Canada explicitly introduced downsizing into the policy arena by announcing a program to aid older workers (those over 50) who are displaced by plant closings or trawler cutbacks. The program would require government payments to displaced workers, payments that would continue until the person is 65, as long as the individual stays out of the fishery, regardless of whether or not the individual obtains alternative employment *outside* the fishing sector. Between the restrictions on licensing which might limit entry at the lower age end which had been announced earlier, and this new program to permanently displace workers in the fishing industry at the upper age end, we may be starting to see programs leading to a permanent reduction in employment in the fishing sector. Of course, as currently structured, the new program for older workers will not directly affect the inshore sector.

A final theme that appeared in the press during this period was essentially a counterattack by the inshore sector, blaming the problems on the offshore sector of the industry. At a conference "Cooperation 1990: Planning for Survival" sponsored by the Newfoundland and Labrador Rural Development Council, the vice-president of the Newfoundland Inshore Fisheries Association was quoted as saying that "the biggest problem in the fishery has been caused by trawler technology."[59] This theme was elaborated upon in the summer 1991 issue of *The Rounder*, a magazine published by the Council. There, the author states that "prior to the introduction of trawlers, vast standing stocks of fish provided a sustainable surplus that endured for four and one-half centuries. ... [Therefore] a realistic program to save the fishery would see the trawler fishery phased out over a five year period."

Adoption of such a program implies the rejection of technological efficiencies developed over the past fifty years, and any attempt to suppress such efficiencies cannot survive in the long term. Among other things, it would mean that a fishermen's population of twenty thousand or more would be employed to catch the same volume of fish that could be caught by only several thousand trawlermen. It also assumes that the fish can be caught inshore when in fact one of the gaps in the biologists' knowledge of the fishery is the percentage of offshore fish which migrates inshore during the fishing season. This gap in knowledge was pointed out by Munro in his study for the Economic Council of Canada; ten years later, Harris again recommended biological research into this question. It is not at all clear what percentage of the existing fish stock could be caught inshore, even with maximum effort, since the answer to this question depends on knowledge of the percentage of the stock that moves inshore, and this is unknown.

Having said this, we note that ten years ago, we published a study in which we computed the relative cost effectiveness of alternative fishing techniques used in the Newfoundland groundfishery.[60] We found that, applying the best available inshore and offshore technology in use at that time, the unit cost of catching fish was the same regardless of whether inshore or offshore technology were used. An important element of the inshore cost was omitted however, the cost of the necessary social overhead capital — such as wharves and breakwaters required in nearly every Newfoundland outport. Further doubt on this balance of inshore and offshore costs arises from speculation that there have been greater productivity increases in the offshore sector than in the inshore sector over the past decade. While we believe such an imbalance in technological progress probably exists, the cost effectiveness study has not been repeated.

We also note that our 1980 study also showed that, while the efficient inshore and offshore techniques were equally cost effective, both required, at then current costs and revenues, a subsidy equal to the value of the fish landed. Abandoning the offshore sector does not seem to us to be a reasonable approach to rendering the Newfoundland fishery economically viable.

THE OPTIONS

Despite the hesitancy on the part of all sectors of Newfoundland society to recognize the fact that the fundamental problem of the Newfoundland fishery is the excessive number of fishermen, the issue of diminishing the size of the inshore fishery is finally being faced, probably for the first time. For twenty-five years or more the inshore fishery of Newfoundland has been a troubled industry. There are periods of "good times" but these are interspersed and all but overwhelmed by the "bad times" caused by marketing or supply problems. There is little reason to hope that the industry, as currently structured, can ever become self-sustaining on a commercially viable basis. As long as the present structure remains, the high subsidies and constant worry over the future of the fishermen, and of the industry itself, will continue.

The essential problem is that there are too many fishermen. However they are counted, there are ten or twenty thousand inshore fishermen when a viable industry would include a much smaller number. An individual's ties to the industry are great; there are important historical and social factors to be considered in the search for policy. These relate to the actual fish harvesters; the same cannot be said for the fish plant workers. Their jobs are not traditional and are equivalent to any semi-skilled factory jobs that might be obtainable locally. The great problem in reducing the size of the fishery, of course, is that the Newfoundland economy does not generate a suitable number of alternative jobs. Relevant policies must account for the double problem of an uneconomical inshore fishery and no alternative employment. What, then, is to be done?

We see three options. The first is to let things drift as they are. If this option were adopted, probably by default, then the repeating crises will continue as will the high subsidies. This situation has existed for a long time and could continue for a longer time; but one foreseeable event that might create the conditions for stopping the subsidies would be a change in the formal political structure of Newfoundland. During the 1960s, according to a study done by Copes, about 40 percent of the electoral districts fell into two classes: one with an extreme (20 percent or more) representation of fishermen on the electoral role, and one with a strong (12.5 percent - 19.9 percent) representation of fishermen. These districts, therefore, were effectively controlled by fishermen and those identified with their interests. In addition, with respect to a third class moderately populated by fishermen (7.5 percent - 12.4 percent), he noted that "as the largest voting bloc in the 'moderate' constituencies, fishermen and their allies would often cast the deciding ballots also in these latter districts" and concluded that

> altogether the fishermen's vote, as described, should be considered the dominant industrially defined electoral interest in a good majority of Newfoundland's constituencies. The electoral power of Newfoundland's fishermen obviously rests on the strategic distribution of their numbers over a relatively large number of constituencies with relatively small electoral rolls. Only in this way can the comparatively small number of fishermen (13 to 15 percent of the labour force) be so placed as to constitute the dominant influence in a majority of electoral districts.[61]

In the 1960s, then, it appeared that the power of the fishery in Newfoundland politics rested upon an outdated and demographically inequitable distribution of provincial electoral districts. The Newfoundland Statistics Agency has mapped the 1986 census enumeration areas onto the provincial electoral districts. We arranged for the results of this mapping to be sent to Statistics Canada to have demographic data from the 1986 census superimposed on the map. The result is that for each of the fifty-two provincial electoral districts (PEDs), we know the voting age population, and the occupational affiliation, if any, of each individual of voting age. The elections with which Copes was concerned were sufficiently long ago that there was virtually no fish processing (i.e., freezing) sector and relatively few plant workers, so the political influence of the fishing industry could be measured by looking at the fishermen's vote (remembering, of course, that this measure understates the influence of fishermen by neglecting their natural allies). By 1986, however, there was a very substantial fish processing sector in Newfoundland, and the importance of fish plant workers could no longer be neglected.

Our definition of a potential voter with an interest in the fishery, therefore, is an individual who declares himself (or herself) to be a fisherman, a fish plant worker, or to be in a related occupation (e.g., a fisheries inspector, employee of a bait centre, etc.). The results, using Copes's classifications, are shown in Table 3. Our measure of the strength of the "fishermen's" vote is the percentage of individuals of voting age in a PED who declare themselves to be in a fishery-related occupation. Our figures for the voting population and fishery related occupations other than fishermen are based upon the 20 percent sample of census respondents who complete the "long form" that includes the occupational data. Fishermen are defined as individuals holding full-time or part-time fishermen's licenses for the Newfoundland and Gulf regions of Fisheries and Oceans Canada in 1988. We recognize the traditional difficulties in using census data and the insensitivity of our techniques. We believe, however, that the results presented here are at least indicative of the true situation.

Table 3
Strength of the Fishermen's Vote

Strength Class	Full-time Fishermen Plus Other Fishery Related Occupations		Full- and Part-time Fishermen Plus Other Fishery Related Occupations	
	# of PEDs	% of PEDs	# of PEDs	% of PEDs
Nil	4	7.7	4	7.7
Light (0.1-7.4%)	22	42.5	20	38.5
Moderate (7.5-12.4%)	7	13.5	3	5.8
Strong (12.5-19.9%)	4	7.7	8	15.4
Extreme (>20%)	15	28.8	17	32.7

While Copes found that approximately 40 percent of the districts fell into the strong and extreme classes, we find that this figure is now more, at a substantial 48 percent for full- and part-time fishermen. On the basis of these data, it is reasonable to conclude that almost one-half of Newfoundland electoral districts are dominated by the fishery, the figure rising to nearly 54 percent if the moderate category is included. The critical comparison is that, while one-half of the PEDs are controlled by the fishery, the same census figures show that only 14 percent of the voting age population of Newfoundland is engaged in the fishery or fishery-related industries. Copes's conclusion remains valid — Newfoundland's electoral map is disproportionately weighted towards fishermen and their natural political allies.

There are substantial disparities in the voting age population of PEDs in Newfoundland, although these disparities are not extreme, ranging from approximately 5,300 to 11,400 (except for Labrador, where one district has a population of less than two thousand). Nevertheless, the fishing population of the province is concentrated in the smaller districts. To take an arbitrary cutoff, eleven of the fifteen island districts with populations of 6,500 or less fall into our moderate to extreme classes while only four of the eighteen districts with populations of 8,000 or more fall into these classes.

The Canadian federal standard permits deviations of plus or minus 25 percent from the equal population norm, and this is becoming the norm for the provinces as well. Other jurisdictions allow narrower ranges, for instance 10 percent in Australia and virtually none in the United States. It is clear that those disparities that exist in Newfoundland increase the effectiveness of the fishermen's vote.

Were these disparities to come under pressure, then the voting map of New-foundland could change dramatically, making the argument for reducing subsidies politically tenable.[62]

There is also a natural solution to the problem that will take effect within a generation, even if no specific policy is adopted to reduce the size of the inshore sector. Traditionally, there has been substantial emigration from Newfoundland, as members of large families seek better economic opportunities elsewhere. There is a tendency for a reverse migration during periods of recession in Canada, but the net emigration from Newfoundland to other parts of Canada has been consistently large over the years. What has changed is that the large families are fast disappearing but, with limited economic opportunity in the province, outmigration continues. The birth rate in Newfoundland has fallen from 34.1 births per 1,000 population in 1961 to only 13.0 in 1990, the lowest of any province in Canada. The drop has been fairly steady, and the death rate has been constant for thirty years. Continued emigration, combined with a low birth rate, can be expected to ease the population pressure that to some extent fuels support for the inshore fishery. Tables 4 and 5 show selected migration and birth and death rate figures.

Table 4
Net Population Outflow from Newfoundland to Other Provinces

1961-1966	15,213
1966-1971	19,344
1971-1976	1,857
1976-1981	18,983
1981-1986	14,715
1986-1990	12,342

Source: Statistics Canada 91.210.

Over the next generation, the total population will stagnate or even decline and new economic opportunities outside the fishery will be created (even if they are rather limited in scope and number). Thus, even if society continues to pay the necessary subsidies, ultimately the inshore population will decline simply for demographic reasons. Economic parts of the inshore fishery will continue to exist without subsidies. The uneconomic aspects will dissolve in one or both of two ways: the few remaining required subsidies will be withdrawn and few, politically impotent, individuals will be affected by the withdrawal; or, in an economic "boom" period in Newfoundland, the remaining uneconomic inshore fishermen will finally give up fishing in favor of better paying jobs.

Such are the implications of a "muddling through" policy, essentially a con-tinuation of the present approach.

An alternative option is that subsidies simply be withdrawn as implied in the Nielsen Task Force report. The results would be severe economic dislocation, with the "horrendous implications" that so disturbed Harris in 1974. It is not even clear that government would save money in the short-run because, in the absence of alternative employment — and none is foreseen, the welfare system would have to provide support. We doubt if anyone would want to repeat the resettlement experiment with its history of unsuccessful "regional growth centres." It is also difficult to conceive of this option being politically viable.

Finally, there is the third option — implementing policies

> that will not cause the present number employed in the fishery to drop rapidly, but allow it to decline slowly over time, thus helping to ensure reasonable incomes for those who remain and giving adequate time for other employment opportunities to be found for those who choose to leave.[63]

In other words, adopt one of a range of policies that lie between maintenance of the present system on the one hand, and suddenly cutting off subsidies on the other. It is difficult in the Canadian political world for a government (or in this case two governments — the federal government of Canada and the provincial government of Newfoundland and Labrador) to enunciate a long-term policy and then see it carried through. Governments are changed by the electoral process, or even when they are not, political pressures and government's susceptibility to such pressures change over time. Nonetheless, what is required is a gradual, planned, process for reducing the size of the inshore fishery.

Table 5
Newfoundland: Births and Deaths Per 1,000 Population

Year	Births	Deaths
1951	32.5	8.3
1961	34.1	6.6
1967	25.7	6.2
1970	24.3	6.4
1973	22.0	6.3
1976	20.0	6.0
1979	18.0	5.6
1982	16.1	6.0
1985	14.6	6.1
1988	13.2	6.3
1990	13.0	—

Source: Statistics Canada 91.210, 91.508; *Historical Statistics of Newfoundland and Labrador*, 1990, Table A-2.

The current action being taken towards reducing part-time fishing licenses is a step in the right direction. But it is likely to reduce primarily the number of licenses held by individuals with little serious interest in the fishery — weekend fishermen. What it might do that is more important, is act to keep new entrants out of the fishery. Of greater long-term interest is the recent policy innovation described above whereby older fishermen and fish plant workers who leave the fishery receive monthly cash payments until they reach normal retirement age. A similar scheme could be devised for the inshore fishermen — but the number of people displaced from the inshore would be substantially larger than the number covered by the present scheme and the required payments would be proportionately more.

When one explains the problems of subsidies to someone sympathetic to the problems of the fishery, the reaction tends to be "what about farming, is the situation any different?" In fact there are strong similarities. Both industries are heavily subsidized. While we found[64] that the value of "subsidies" (actually, total government expenditures) was about equal to the value of the landed catch in Newfoundland, such subsidies were equal to only one-third of the output of the fish products industry in Newfoundland. In a study of farm subsidization, Arcus[65] found that the value of provincial and federal financial assistance to the industry was 24 percent of gross farm production in 1982-83. While the two studies use different definitions, the results of both are similar enough to support the view that subsidization in fishery, at least in the early 1980s, was not out of line with that in the larger farming sector of the Canadian economy. The question of farm subsidies is now in the world's centre stage. The recent "Uruguay Round" of the GATT tariff reduction talks were stalemated by international disputes over farm subsidization. A recent OECD study[66] using the concept of "producer subsidy equivalents" found that 41 percent of agricultural incomes in Canada in 1990 were provided by government — compared to 30 percent in the United States and 48 percent in the EEC. The degree of agricultural subsidization in Canada grew substantially during the past decade. We can safely assume that the degree of subsidization of the Newfoundland fishery is approximately equal to that of Canadian agriculture.

An analogy, useful for policy purposes, was drawn by the head of economic research for Fisheries and Oceans Canada shortly after the Kirby report appeared.[67] He noted that during the 1960s there were too many people on marginal prairie farms, just as there were too many people in marginal fishing operations, both groups being heavily subsidized. Farmers left the land, occasionally having lost their farms in bankruptcy. But more frequently, farmers had an equity in their farm which was realized when they left farming, so that they either could retire on the proceeds or, if they were younger, could use the money for a "down payment" elsewhere. The first critical point for policy is that they generally left the farm with some cash. The second critical point is that having sold their farm, they could not return to it — entry was limited by the excessive cost of entry, i.e., the cost of purchasing a new farm.

The Newfoundland resettlement program was vaguely analogous to some of the "resettlement" schemes in farming areas. However, the Newfoundlander did not leave the fishery with cash in his pocket — there were no fishing rights to sell — and fishermen were not barred from re-entering the fishery elsewhere in the province. As Wise implied in his analogy to farming, fishermen leaving the industry must have cash for retirement, retraining, or migration. Buy-back programs whereby the government purchases a specified number of licenses each year for substantial sums is one way of doing it, although there is always a danger that the policy of this year will change by next, or that in either an economic downturn or fisheries upturn the government will start to reissue licenses. For the proposed type of policy to work, it must be understood that the policy will be in effect for, say, five to ten years, and that there will be no going back. Perhaps the only new licenses issued will be to the children of those fishermen who remain in the industry after the buy-back program is complete. We have referred earlier to the *Evening Telegram*'s opposition to such programs;[68] implementing them will not be easy.

Alternatively, the buy-back scheme might involve the fish processors purchasing the individual fishermen's rights to a quota, perhaps the cost matched by government, with the processing company being permitted to use the quotas for its offshore catch. This process would amount essentially to the scheme proposed by the Economic Council of Canada but without their proposed "protection" of the inshore sector. The advantage of such a scheme would be that the repurchase of a specified number of licenses could be planned for each year of the program, so that the dislocation in any year is kept to a minimum. It is very likely that migration out of the outports would be required unless transfer payments to unemployed former fishermen were to replace the "subsidies" to active fishermen in which case the potential benefits of the plan would be lost.

We do not propose details of such a plan; such details would be premature. The government and the society must decide which of the three general approaches listed here is to be adopted; the default is "muddling through" and waiting for electoral redistricting, demographic change, or House's "revitalization" to bring about the inexorable adjustments. The other options are to suddenly cut the subsidies or to plan a scaled cut in the size of the inshore fishery.

The Newfoundland inshore fishery is in deep trouble. While during the past quarter century the fishing industry has had a few periods of heady optimism, it has been dominated by recurring crises, crises which have been growing worse over time and each of which is caused by one or both of a shortage of supply of fish to catch and problems of marketing the fish that are caught. The quarter century started with a fish population crisis caused by foreign overfishing; it is now suffering another population crisis with the added twist that the biologists' methods for estimating populations have been thrown into serious doubt. Highly sensitive to economic conditions in the specialized United States market for its products, the Newfoundland fishery is devastated with each American recession. The world market tends to volatility, with prices of cod, for instance, doubling in 1986-87, then falling, and quantities caught in locations such as Newfoundland varying widely from year to year as well. This volatility leads penultimate consumers, often large fast-food chains with tremendous market power, to seek alternative products and more stable sources of supply, factors which damage Newfoundland's prospects. Geirsson and Trondsen[69] discuss the substitution of cheaper pollock for cod during the 1986-87 cod price rise. This experiment failed for a number of reasons they describe and with the subsequent drop in the price of cod the "normal" market was restored. But cod prices have again been high and McDonald's is experimenting with a catfish product which could replace cod as its fish staple and Burger King is substituting pollock for cod.[70] Newfoundland faces very uncertain markets. On top of all this, the Newfoundland fishery is heavily subsidized; it is an expensive proposition to keep it functioning.

Implicit in the argument of this paper is the question of for how long the federal government will be willing to subsidize this industry. We remain agnostic on the question of "how long" but the weight of our argument is that it cannot last forever. Financial pressures are growing to reduce the subsidies and these pressures must ultimately succeed. Nevertheless, the agony of the "death" of the industry as we know it is likely to continue to be dragged out. Newfoundland simply cannot afford to effectively liquidate the inshore fishery — for economic, political, and social reasons. It is likely, however, that the legal challenges to the electoral system will succeed, and these will hasten the end of subsidization by removing some of the political pressure on the provincial government. With careful planning, policies can be put into place for the gradual reduction of the industry. With such policies, ultimately the number of inshore fishermen will decrease to the point where they can be displaced without major economic or political repercussions. In the absence of such policies, demographic changes can be expected to reduce the size of the inshore fishery to the point where subsidies can be removed without excessive reaction, and this could happen within a generation. We do not predict the complete end of the inshore fishery. A fishery specializing in profitable areas of endeavor will continue, but this fishery will be quite small and will no longer be a major social and economic factor in Newfoundland.

Notes

The authors wish to thank G.S. Kealey for helpful comments on an earlier draft, P.O. Parsons for research assistance, and H. Ridler of the Newfoundland Statistics Agency and D. Wrighte of Statistics Canada for help with provincial electoral district mapping. Financial assistance from the Institute of Economic and Social Research of Memorial University is gratefully acknowledged.

1.   D. Alexander, "Newfoundland's Traditional Economy and Development to 1934," in J. Hiller and P. Neary, eds., *Newfoundland in the Nineteeth and Twentieth Centuries: Essays in Interpretation* (Toronto: University of Toronto Press, 1980), 22-23; orginally published in *Acadiensis* 5 (1976): 56-78.

2.   R.E. Ommer, "What's Wrong with Canadian Fish?" *Journal of Canadian Studies* 20 (1985): 122-40.

3.   E.E.D. Day, "The Fishing Industry in Newfoundland and Labrador," in G.F. Pushie (chairman), *Report of the Royal Commission on the Economic Prospects of Newfoundland and Labrador* (St. John's: Queen's Printer, 1967), 185.

4.   H.A. Innis, *The Cod Fisheries: The History of an International Economy* (Toronto: University of Toronto Press, 1940).

5.   R.G. Lounsbury, *The British Fishery of Newfoundland, 1634-1763* (New Haven, CT: Yale University Press, 1934).

6.   Alexander, "Newfoundland's Traditional Economy," 23.

7.   W. M. Mackenzie (chairman), *Report of the Amulree Royal Commission* (London: HMSO, 1933); Ommer, "What's Wrong with Canadian Fish?"

8.   Newfoundland and Labrador, *Historical Statistics of Newfoundland and Labrador* (St. John's: Newfoundland Statistics Agency, 1990), Volume 2 (6), Table K-6.

9.   Day, "Fishing Industry," 183-84.

10.   *Historical Statistics*, 1990, Volume 2(6), Table K-1; W.E. Shrank, E. Tsoa and N. Roy, *The Relative Productivity and Cost-Effectiveness of Various Fishing Techniques in the Newfoundland Groundfishery* (Ottawa: Economic Council of Canada, 1980), Discussion Paper # 180, 98; *Newfoundland Flashsheet*, 22 February 1991.

11.   Fisheries and Oceans Canada worksheets.

12.   R. Wells and C.A. Bishop, *Some Recent Changes in Cod Stock in Divisions 2J and 3KL* (Dartmouth, NS: NAFO, 1980), Research Document 8/VI/101, #156, Table 1.

13.   M.J.L. Kirby (chairman), *Navigating Troubled Waters: A New Policy for the Atlantic Fisheries, Report of the Task Force on Atlantic Fisheries* (Ottawa: Supply and Services Canada, 1982), 17.

14.   United Nations, *The Law of the Sea: United Nations Convention on the Law of the Sea* (NewYork: United Nations, 1983)

15.   E. Tsoa, W.E. Schrank and N. Roy, "U.S. Demand for Selected Groundfish Products, 1967-80," *American Journal of Agricultural Economics* 64 (1982): 483-9.

16.   L. Harris (chairman), *Report of the Conciliation Board Appointed in the Matter of the Fishing Industry (Collective Bargaining) Act and in the Matter of a Dispute Between Newfoundland Fishermen Food and Allied Workers, Local 465 and B.C. Packers Limited,* Atlantic Fish Division of Atlantic Consolidated Foods Limited, National Sea Products Limited, Fishery Products Limited, and Booth Fisheries (St. John's Government of Newfoundland and Labrador, 1974), 77.

17.   United States Internation Trade Commission, *Certain Fish From Canada* (Washington, DC: USITC, 1978), Publication #919.

18.   *Historical Statistics*, 1990 Volume 2(6) Table K-1.

19.   For further details, see W.E. Schrank, B. Skoda, N. Roy and E. Tsoa, "Canadian Government Financial Intervention in a Marine Fishery: The Case of Newfoundland, 1972/73 - 1980/81," *Ocean Development and International Law* 17 (1987): 533-84 and W.E. Schrank, N. Roy and E. Tsoa, "Government Expenditures in the Newfoundland Fishery: Some Policy Questions," in Groupe d'Etude des ressources maritimes (ed.),

Proceedings of the Third Biennial Conference of the International Institute of Fisheries Economics and Trade (Rimouski, Quebec: University of Quebec at Rimouski, 1986), 39-44. The "fever" of the time for domestic expansion of the fishery is described by Kirby, *Navigating Troubled Waters*, 20-21.

20. Kirby, *Navigating Troubled Waters*, 21-23.

21. *The Top 1000 Companies: The Globe and Mail Report on Business*, July 1991, 94; *Financial Times Investors 500*, 17 June 1991, A22.

22. For further details see W.E. Schrank, E. Tsoa and N. Roy, "Optimism and the New-foundland Fishery," *Newfoundland Lifestyle* 5(1987): 13-21; and the prospectus, *Initial Public Offering, FPI Limited, the Holding Company of Fishery Products International Limited* (New York: Dominion Securities Inc., 24 March 1987).

23. *The Top 1000 Companies: The Globe and Mail Report on Business*, July 1990, 124.

24. Canada, *Resource Prospects for Canada's Atlantic Fisheries: 1980-1985* (Ottawa: Fisheries and Oceans Canada, 1980)), 46. The previous year's government forecast of the 1985 catch of northern cod was considerably higher at 402,000 metric tons, see Canada, *Resource Prospects for Canada's Atlantic Fisheries: 1979-1985* (Ottawa: Fisheries and Oceans Canada, 1978), 43.

25. G.R. Munro, *A Promise of Abundance: Extended Fisheries Jurisdiction and the Newfoundland Economy* (Ottawa: Economic Council of Canada, 1980), 26.

26. P.A. Larkin, "An Epitaph for the Concept of Maximum Sustainable Yield," *Transactions of the American Fisheries Society* 106 (1977): 1-11; M.P. Sissenwine, "Is MSY an Adequate Foundation for Optimum Yield?" *Fisheries* 3 (1986): 22-24.

27. A.T. Pinhorn, *Living Marine Resources of Newfoundland and Labrador: Status and Potential* (Ottawa: Fisheries Research Board of Canada, 1976), Bulletin #194.

28. D.L. Alverson (chairman), *A Study of Trends of Cod Stocks Off Newfoundland and Factors Influencing Their Abundance and Availabilty to the Inshore Fishery: A Report Submitted by the Task Group on Newfoundland Inshore Fisheries to the Honorable Tom Siddon, Minister of Fisheries* (Ottawa: Fisheries and Oceans Canada, 1987), Table 1.

29. L. Harris, *Independent Review of the State of the Northern Cod Stock* (Ottawa: Fisheries and Oceans Canada, 1989), 34-35.

30. Canada, *1989 Atlantic Groundfish Management Plan* (Ottawa: Fisheries and Oceans Canada, 1988).

31. Harris, *Independent Review*, 38.

32. L. Harris, *Independent Review of the State of the Northern Cod Stock: Final Report* (Ottawa: Fisheries and Oceans Canada, 1990), 110, 134, 136.

33. Canada, *1991 Atlantic Groundfish Management Plan* (Ottawa: Fisheries and Oceans Canada, 1990), 16-17.

34. St. John's *Evening Telegram*, 27 July 1991.

35. Schrank, "Canadian Government Financial Intervention," Table A.1.

36. W.E. Schrank, N. Roy and E. Tsoa, "Employment Prospects in a Commercially

Viable Newfoundland Fishery: An Application of 'An Econometric Model of the New-foundland Groundfishery'," *Marine Resource Economics* 3 (1986): 253.

37. *Historical Statistics*, 1990 Volume 2(6), Table A-1; *Historical Statistics*, 1970 Volume 1(1), Table C-1; Statistics Canada 17.201.

38. Economic Council of Canada, *Newfoundland: From Dependency to Self-Reliance* (Ottawa: Supply and Services Canada, 1980), 22.

39. *Response of the Government of Newfoundland and Labrador to the Recommendations of the Economic Council of Canada Study: "Newfoundland — From Dependency to Self-Reliance,"* St. John's: Text of Address by Hon. Brian Peckford, Premier of New-foundland and Labrador, 16 June 1981.

40. Pushie, *Report of the Royal Commission*, 179; and for instance, Economic Council of Canada, *Newfoundland*, 95.

41. Economic Council of Canada, *Newfoundland*, 101.

42. Kirby, *Navigating Troubled Waters*, vii.

43. Canada, *Natural Resources Program: From Crisis to Opportunity — A Study Team Report to the Task Force on Program Review* (Ottawa: Supply and Services Canada, 1986), 27, 31, 32, 94.

44. Newfoundland and Labrador, *Building on Our Strengths: Report of the Royal Commission on Employment and Unemployment* (St. John's: Queen's Printer, 1986), 446.

45. J.D. House, M. Hanrahan and D. Simms, *Fisheries Policies and Community Development: Proposal for a Revised Approach to Managing the Inshore Fisheries in Newfoundland — Background Report to the Royal Commission on Employment and Unemployment* (St. John's: Royal Commission on Employment and Unemployment, 1986), 151.

46. Ibid., 93.

47. Kirby, *Navigating Troubled Waters*, 48.

48. Canada, *Commercial Fisheries Licensing Policy for Eastern Canada* (Ottawa: Fisheries and Oceans Canada, 1989), 6-7.

49. House, *Fisheries Policies*, 33-36.

50. *Evening Telegram*, 28 April 1990.

51. St. John's *Sunday Express*, 17 February 1991.

52. Canada, *Report of the Implementation Task Force on Northern Cod* (Ottawa: Fisheries and Oceans Canada, 1990).

53. *Fisheries News*, April 1991.

54. Canada, *Atlantic Fisheries Adjustment Plan — New Initiatives* (Ottawa: Fisheries and Oceans Canada, 1990).

55. Canada, *Atlantic Fisheries Adjustment Plan — Existing Initiatives* (Ottawa: Fisheries and Oceans Canada, 1990).

56. *Evening Telegram*, 8 May 1990.

57. Ibid., 22 May 1990.

58. *Newfoundland and Labrador Business Journal*, September 1990.

59. *Evening Telegram*, 27 March 1991.

60. Schrank, *The Relative Productivity*.

61. P.Copes, "The Fisherman's Vote in Newfoundland," *Canadian Journal of Political Science* 3 (1970): 592-3.

62. See the decision of Chief Justice Mclachlin, then of the Supreme Court of British Columbia, in the case of *Dixon v the Attorney General of British Columbia*, 18 April 1989, for a discussion of these issues. See also the Supreme Court of Canada decision in *The Attorney General for Saskatchewan v Roger Carter*, 6 June 1991.

63. Kirby, *Navigating Troubled Waters*, 354.

64. Schrank, "Canadian Government Financial Intervention," 546.

65. Arcus Consulting Limited, *Government Assistance to Agriculture in Canada, by Province: A Report for the Office of the Deputy Minister, Ministry of Agriculture and Food, Province of British Columbia* (Victoria, B.C.: Arcus Consulting Limited, 1985), 35.

66. *Globe and Mail*, 15 August 1991.

67. T.F. Wise, *Fishermen and Prairie Wheat Farmers: A Model of the Effects of Technical Change* (Ottawa: Fisheries and Oceans Canada, n.d.).

68. Editorial, *Evening Telegram*, 22 May 1990.

69. M. Geirsson and T. Trondsen, "Frozen Fish Products in the U.S. Market," in W.E. Schrank and N. Roy, eds., *Econometric Modelling of the World Trade in Groundfish* (Dordecht: Kluwer Academic Publishers, 1991), 194-7.

70. *Sunday Express*, 17 February, 14 July 1991.

9

A Constitutional Commitment to Survival on the Margins

Wade MacLauchlan

Canada's constitutional discourse has become encoded into a whole series of mini-debates about identity, institutions, amending formulae, rights, distinct societies, self-government and the division of powers. However, from the perspective of the four Atlantic provinces and the Prairies, this discourse fails to squarely address the most basic issue of Confederation — how are we to survive?

In this constitutional round, the issue of marginal survival must be brought to the centre of the debate. Atlantic and prairie Canadians, as well as people in the North and potentially in other remote and comparative "have-not" areas of the country, must develop a new advocacy, one that goes beyond despondency and dependency. We must come away with a constitutional commitment to survival on the margins. We must design political institutions that have the capacity to act on that commitment. And we must begin to think about how we should organize our public and private lives on the margins.

1991-92 is a time for imagination about Canada, and about its future. It is a time for people and governments in "the regions" to ask about our place in a world dominated by fiscal retrenchment, constitutional decentralization, competitiveness and globalization. It is time to ask some hard questions about economic union. Is this ostensible union limited to bringing down barriers to interprovincial trade? If so, does it offer anything more to Atlantic Canadians than an opportunity to "go down the road?"

Putting the question of survival on the constitutional table means that we must reflect on traditional political strategies. Can we continue to place our best hopes in strong central government, national standards, and *ad hoc* federal assistance? Are we not destined to fall ever further behind, to see our best and brightest leave for better opportunities? Is there any alternative to the conservative and demeaning politics of postponed military base closures, farm bailouts and inflated fishing quotas? Is our political discourse stalled forever in protests against "beating up on the baby of Confederation" and cyncism about lost defense contracts?

Some will object that adding marginal survival to the constitutional order

152

paper at this stage is impertinent, that we should concentrate first on "saving Canada." There is the Quebec question, and this may be our *dernière chance*. There is the issue of justice for aboriginal peoples, which might be taken seriously for the first time in five centuries. There is the challenge to "bring the West in" through long-overdue Senate reform. Is there a place in all of this to deal with concerns about regional disparities?

From the perspective of Atlantic and prairie Canadians, it may well be a question of now or never. It is clear that the provinces and the regions are being left increasingly on their own. The federal government is "off-loading" the fiscal burden for the most expensive areas of shared social jurisdiction: health, education and social assistance. It is cutting back or "clawing" back direct payments to individuals, such as unemployment insurance or pensions. The GNP-CAP and the downturn in the economy have combined to reduce equalization payments. Regional development monies go increasingly to Ontario and Quebec projects.

1991-92 is the time for the "regions" to make a new bargain, while they still have something to bargain with. We ought to understand the scenario, by now. It is all about making a deal before things deteriorate to the point where you no longer have anything to trade. One is inclined to think of metaphors like closing the barn door before the horse gets out; but it may be more a case of reinforcing the structure of the barn before it falls down on top of you *and* the horse.

We should recognize the strategic crossroads, for we have been here before. For example, there is the process by which we either bargained away or simply lost the railways. Newfoundland made a deal for better highways when it "gave up" the railroad. Other provinces opted for more piecemeal deterioration (e.g., Prince Edward Island now has no railroad, and little to show by way of a *quid pro quo*). Prince Edward Island cried loud and hard over the closure of CFB Summerside, and obtained a substantial "compensation" package; those who have been fortunate enough to hang on to their military bases for a few more years may find that they have a lot of long-faced company and little in the way of federal sympathy when the next round of closures arrives. We have seen the same thing in the context of fish plant closures — the bargaining power for new economic development is lost if the people in the communities have already moved "away." So we have to think about a new bargain before the old one is completely discredited.

If 1991-92 is the time to make a new constitutional bargain, and if that bargain is to include a commitment to survival on the margins, three "analyses" are required. First, we must develop a discourse that attracts the support of other constitutional players, and that is, moreover, convincing to ourselves. Second, we must devise an institutional mechanism that will be effective in advancing the commitment, and in enforcing it. Third, we must imagine the general outlines of public policies that will be appropriate for an evolving Canada, and for a regional existence that is more than bare survival.

ADVOCATING FOR OUR SURVIVAL

If there is to be a new commitment to survival on the margins, it cannot be presented as a bare grab by the have-nots from the haves. And it must be more than a payoff for going along with other constitutional reforms and not exercising the effective veto that any four provinces have under the 7/50 amending formula. While the small provinces should not be embarassed to have a potentially preponderant voice at the constitutional table, our stance this time should be proactive and positive if we are to put in place a commitment that can be relied upon into the future.

Since we are looking for something positive, the case must be put in terms that will draw the support of other constitutional actors, particularly the bigger provinces and the federal government. The need for consensus, in the most instrumentalist terms, is imposed by the 7/50 formula, and must include at least two of Ontario, Alberta and British Columbia. If Quebec is not onside, then all three of Ontario, Alberta and British Columbia, as well as the federal government, must be.

It is particularly important in the 1991-92 round that there be a strong provincial consensus. While the federal government must be a party to any new constitutional commitment, it has lost its standing as the bully and the banker, or the maestro, of the Canadian social contract. The heady post-World War II days when new social programs were swept through on the say-so of the federal government, or on the promise of fifty-cent dollars, are long past. The federal government has reached its fiscal limit; and its credibility in this area has been seriously undermined by its backtracking on CAP and EPF, as well as on pensions and unemployment insurance.

We not only have to develop an advocacy that convinces others; we have to persuade *ourselves* that our survival is as important as other items on the constitutional short list. In the recent past Atlantic and prairie political leaders and opinion makers have focussed primarily on the constitutional concerns of others, and have tended to see regional disparities and social programs as belonging to the domain of rough and tumble politics. There has also been a tendency to see survival as something that we ask as a favour, or as a *quid pro quo* around election time. There has even been a tendency to see federal assistance as a zero-sum game among the provinces. If we are to advance the constitutional case for survival it must be stated as a matter of entitlement.

For too long we have thought of interregional sharing in Canada as a form of charity. The wealthy provinces consider themselves to be the milk cows of Confederation, and the poor provinces think of themselves as the free riders. This demeaning discourse must be set aside. We should understand that there are important, quintessentially Canadian, values that underlie the commitment to horizontal rebalancing. These values include portability, mobility, democracy, equity and survival.

Survival

The idea of survival begins with a sense of place. It involves the knowledge that you are connected to a locality, to its geography, its people, its customs and its culture. And it involves the quiet knowledge that leaving means surrender, even suicide; and the recognition that if enough of us leave suicide becomes genocide.

It is difficult to explain the importance of survival in abstract terms. So I will personalize it. All sixteen of my great-great grandparents landed in Prince Edward Island in the first half of the nineteenth century. One was born on board ship while crossing the Atlantic. That does not make me an indigenous person; but it does mean that I have a place called home. That sense of home now extends to the Maritimes as a region, as I have developed substantial connections to New Brunswick and Nova Scotia as well as to Prince Edward Island. I can move from one part of the region to another without feeling a sense of *dépaysement*. For me the future and the well-being of the Atlantic region have become a question of personal survival, and a question of keeping faith with my grandparents and all of the others who have struggled to survive in and to make something of the region for generations.

What is so important about staying, or at least having the option to stay? It comes out of an identity that is itself a product of survival on the margins. Atlantic Canadians share a knowledge of our marginality, in relation to the rest of Canada and in relation to the rest of the world. We gain this knowledge from generations of grim partnership with the ocean, and from endless seasons of working with and against the elements. In terms of political economy, we have (from the time of European settlement) never had our own metropolis. Our economies have been constructed on the export of primary products and the import of value-added goods. Our political landmarks have been located in London and Ottawa, always with an undercurrent of inferiority and syncophancy, if not total powerlessness.

The most constant reminder of our marginality has been migration, most notably the out-migration of the talented and the restless. The notion of going "away" has for years been a significant aspect of our social and cultural discourse, and of our daily self-identification. Out-migration has been an enormous drag on our capacity to develop, socially, politically and economically. We all have family and friends who have moved to "the Boston states," or to "T.O.," or to "the oilpatch," following economic opportunities and/or family and friends. A reverse aspect of our "home-and-away" consciousness is the "C.F.A." treatment accorded those who dare to migrate *to* the region. Perhaps the most poignant underscoring of our sense of home and away is the story of the Acadians, who returned to the region after years, and even generations, in exile, following deportation in the mid-eighteenth century. Antonine Maillet captures the sense of *dépaysement* and the sense of the *retour* in her novel *Pélagie-la-charrette*, the romantic account of Acadians making their way back in a metaphorical ox-drawn cart. The hardship of the century in exile "was as if the gods had resolved not to give the Acadians back their land until they had been forced to empty the cup to the dregs."[1] The return itself is evoked in this passage:

> Maine! Maine at last, the last lap. A state with ill-defined and disputed boundaries. Where did Maine end and Acadie begin?
>
> "Acadie? Never heard of it."
>
> And Pélagie realized that their homeland would have to be rebuilt.
>
> "Reposessed, acre by acre."
>
> But the others weren't in the least upset by the sombre thought of having to reconquer their own front yards. The autumn was too beautiful and the yellows and reds of the Maine woods melted without boundaries into the ochres of the Acadian forest. How did you go about dividing that up? Where was the median line between red ochre and flame red? None of these homebound exiles could have told you by what channel they were entering the country or when, precisely, they had crossed the border. Between the stormy autumn sea, the brilliant forests with their complete palette from yellows to flaming reds, between the warm singing inland winds and the smell and the rustle of dead leaves beneath their feet, somewhere in the midst of all that, Acadie lay concealed, every son of a son of this land could recognize that.[2]

In 1991-92, Atlantic Canadians are more reminded than ever of our marginality, and of the challenge to our survival. The fishery is menaced by a generation of excess. The forest-based industries are caught in a worldwide downturn, mostly due to surplus capacity. Some agricultural sectors (e.g., dairy, poultry and eggs) are threatened by free trade, while the potato industry has been temporarily ravaged by the *PVYn* virus. We have serious deficits in infrastructure development, such as highways or sewage treatment facilities. All aspects of the public sector are menaced by reductions in funding, notably through federal funds and transfer payments. The extraregional public sector contribution to the economy has been constantly reduced over the past decade and the pattern promises to continue, perhaps more dramatically. Proposed further cuts in federal and interprovincial transfers are the most serious menace to the continued viability of the region.

The bottom line in our advocacy for survival on the margins goes beyond a claim that we ought to continue to receive all of the funding that we have become accustomed to receiving in all of the familiar packages. The claim has a genuine ideological core — if we cannot survive in the places we call home, then Canada itself cannot survive. It has to be understood that Canada itself is about survival on the margins. The relationship to the elements, the sense of connection to a physical place, and the struggle to build up communities and economies against the odds have been the dominant themes in the story of Canada as a whole. If there is an identity that binds us together, it is that we have survived in what is now the world's largest country, and that we have constructed networks of transportation, communications, social programs, health care, education and culture that tie us together and that make us Canadians. Most of this has not been easy. But it is the struggle itself that provides the sense of accomplishment, and the sense of attachment.

I recently heard an economist say that the problem with Canada is that it is too big. This is another, currently very powerful, way of saying that we cannot afford marginal survival. Indeed, it is a way of saying that we cannot afford Canada. It suggests that we ought to all huddle together in southwestern Ontario, metropolitan Montreal, the lower mainland of British Columbia, and perhaps a few other centres like Calgary and Edmonton and do our very best to get along in a new competitive global environment. The problem with such a scenario is that we would not only have surrendered on the margins, but we would have committed national suicide. It is in this sense that Canadians, wherever they live, have to understand the importance of survival on the margins as a national good that we ought to translate into a constitutional value.

Portability and Mobility

The values of portability and mobility are important to the survival of Canada. We cannot pretend to be a single nation if an Albertan or an Ontarian is reluctant to accept an otherwise attractive opportunity to move to Atlantic Canada because the move would mean substantially inferior health care or education. We have a serious problem if universities in Atlantic Canada cannot hold our own best students or attract good students from elsewhere.

Portability does not require that Mount Pearl have the same transit service as Scarborough, or that Charlottetown have the same urban amenities as Ottawa. Nor does it require that each province have a denticare or pharmacare or daycare program. But there is a problem if the disparities are so systemic that there is only one-way traffic out of Newfoundland or Prince Edward Island. There is a problem if parents of children with special educational needs feel obliged to move to or stay in Edmonton or Toronto or Vancouver. And there is a problem if businesses stay away from the Atlantic region because we have a higher rate of illiteracy, or an underskilled labour force.

Canada cannot be complete if social assistance arrangements are so superior in Calgary that Maritimers move West to go on "the dole." Hordes of "eastern welfare bums" are hardly an appealing prospect for municipal officials in Calgary, or for the long-term dignity of the Maritimes. Neither is it desirable for Atlantic Canadians to routinely go down the road to be the housekeepers and gardeners and nannies for the middle and upper classes of wealthier provinces.

So mobility cannot be a one-way street. There must be adequate economic opportunities and public services on the margins so that we are not assigned the sole choice of going down the road. The pattern of out-migration must be resisted, and in-migration must be an option. This hardly seems like too much to ask in a Canada committed to survival on the margins.

Democracy

In Canada we work to systematically undermine democratic values in marginal communities. One way or another, federal spending in Atlantic Canada and in other regions gets packaged as a form of largesse. In the 1950s and 1960s Newfoundland and the federal government teamed up to represent every family allowance cheque, every post office, and every mile of paved road as an act of patronage rather than of responsible governance. Premier Devine's much publicized flight to Ottawa to secure another $800 million in *ad hoc* grain subsidies during the 1991 Saskatchewan election proves that the tradition is alive and well in Saskatchewan politics (although, to their credit, Saskatchewan voters proved that their is a limit to their gullibility for such ploys). How many times has Prince Edward Island been promised the causeway (now fixed link)? The Halifax harbour cleanup seems to be shaping up along the same lines. Cape Bretoners have learned to live by "announcements." The challenge these days is for the spin doctors to manage the bad news so that there is still a positive announcement to be made close to election time.

The game of playing one marginal region against another is becoming increasingly common. We saw it in the case of the Lytton plant, which eventually went to metro Halifax, after the local government made enormous tax concessions. We are into a fresh round with the scramble to hang on to military bases. The same phenomenon shows up when it comes time to grant fishing licenses, to build new ships, or to create a waste disposal facility. We play out a reverse version of the NIMBY syndrome — we clamour over each other to get any project into our backyards.

There are few positive, and many negative, consequences to this patronage-ridden game that pretends to do marginal communities a favour. First, the practice does not achieve its ostensible main objective of making the electorate happy and submissive. There is invariably a greater measure of negative feeling on the part of those passed over than there is gratitude on the part of the "beneficiaries." For example, few federal decisions have had such a negative impact as the awarding of the CF-18 maintenance contract to a Quebec company over a Manitoba firm.

As for making the population submissive, the opposite seems to have occurred to the point that people are highly unlikely to believe, let alone be grateful to, their politicians. Perhaps the most discouraging evidence of just how cynical we have all become is the fact that many serious political observers believed Frank McKenna opposed Meech Lake initially in the hope that New Brunswick could bargain for a four-lane highway (or a second nuclear reactor) and that Clyde Wells was really after a renegotiation of the Churchill Falls power contract.

In substantive terms, the linking of federal funding to patronage politics has backfired on the ostensible beneficiaries in the "have-not" regions. It is no coincidence that the majority of regional development money now goes to Ontario and Quebec, and that the election time announcements are no longer focussed on Cape Breton but on metro Toronto. It is inevitable, once political mileage becomes the primary criterion for making spending decisions, that the marginal areas will lose out to those with more voting power.

It is critical, from the perspective of Atlantic and prairie Canada, that there be a more explicit constitutional commitment to marginal survival and that there be new institutions to imagine and to monitor fiscal federalism. In the interest of democratic values, there must be a long-term commitment that we will be able to survive, and that we can have effective control over what is done with the available resources.

Equity

The arguments for marginal survival as a matter of equity are well understood by Atlantic and prairie Canadians, but they are frequently forgotten, particularly in a world dominated by a discourse of economic efficiency and political expediency.

The equity argument is simple. We are citizens of the same nation as Albertans and British Columbians and Ontarians. There are minimum standards of living for communities and individuals. These standards need not be uniform. They ought to be sensitive to local conditions, including available resources. However, it is not equitable for one region to consistently have a higher rate of illiteracy, infant mortality, and morbidity. It is not equitable for one region to have chronic out-migration of its best young talent. It is not equitable for there to be first- and second-class regions of Canada, nor is it in the long-run interest of any part of the country for there to be the kind of imbalances that we are moving toward as the federal government scales back its support of provincial social programs and infrastructure.

The equity argument could be protracted, but it need not be. Atlantic Canadians are not free riders on the train of Confederation. We have made our contribution as citizens. And, as a region, we have played our role in the building up of a national economy in substantial measure that has meant surrendering indigenous industry and capital, especially human capital, to the cause of "developing" Canada. We still have vital communities, and we want to develop them. At this point, we are entitled to ask for a commitment that the disparities between rich and poor regions will not become so great as to undermine our integrity and our sense of equality as citizens of Canada.

So that is the rhetorical case for a constitutional commitment to survival on the margins. The question now is whether it is possible to reduce it to constitutional language.

CONSTITUTIONALIZING MARGINAL SURVIVAL

The 1982 entrenchment of the principle of equalization was taken by many to be a significant achievement in guaranteeing fiscal federalism. Section 36(1) of the Constitution Act promises equal opportunities to individual Canadians, and Sec. 36(2) commits the federal government to the principle of making equalization payments to ensure that provincial governments have sufficient resources to provide reasonably comparable levels of public services at reasonably comparable levels of taxation.

In fact, the key programs that make up fiscal federalism have fared worse in the ten years since 1982 than they did in the previous ten years. And they fared worse in the 1972-82 period than they did in the previous ten years. So the constitutional promise of comparable levels of public service with comparable levels of taxation has hardly turned out to be a major turning point for the better for "have-not" provinces. Indeed, it is difficult to point to any tangible difference that has resulted from the inclusion of Sec. 36 in the Constitution Act.

The decade since the entrenchment of the equalization clause in the constitution has been the worst of the three decades since 1960, and the coming decade promises to be bleaker still. Payments under the EPF scheme are forecast to run down to zero early in the twenty-first century. Equalization has been subjected to a GNP cap. Federal support for *ad hoc* programs has been cut back in all sectors. CAP continues to favour the richer provinces with fifty-cent dollars. Across the board, the federal administration is concerned with three priorities: reducing spending, encouraging competetiveness, and continentalism. Together these three priorities offer little room for encouragement to those concerned with marginal survival.

The federal government's 1991 constitutional proposals promise to make "economic union" a priority. In fact those proposals focus primarily on the free flow of people, goods, services and capital, and on the harmonization of economic policies. The proposals do reiterate a commitment to continue making transfer payments to individual Canadians and to individual provinces, in the context of a discussion of the federal spending power. As well, the federal government "affirms its intention to continue making grants to provincial governments on the basis of bilateral negotiations, especially in the field of regional development."[3] And there is a commitment that all Canadians continue to receive the benefits of Canadian citizenship, regardless of where they live or what they do. The document observes that: "We are bound together as a society by our belief in the fundamental obligation to share our wealth with our fellow Canadians." It is, however, somewhat worrying that the federal proposal goes on to claim that "[t]he federal government will continue to support this principle in the future, as it does today."

The clear overall objective of the federal proposals is a well-coordinated, or at least a well-oiled, free market. For Atlantic Canadians this may not amount to more than a constitutionalized invitation to go down the road. We should bear in mind Charles McMillan's observation that "Central Canada, in the name of national policy, has shaped a deeply ingrained industrial structure that seems to favour Central Canada but without the negative connotations of 'regional development' with all of its attendant welfare trappings."

What Atlantic and prairie Canadians do not need in the current round of reforms is another piece of literature for the constitutional coffee table. We need a reliable and enforceable commitment to our survival. It is striking that the promise of "equality of opportunity" adverted to in the general proposals is not returned to in the federal government's discussion paper on economic union. *Canadian Federalism and Economic Union: Partnership for Prosperity* is about enhancing mobility of people, goods, services and capital, and about coordinating economic policies. There is absolutely no recognition that for some parts of Canada mobility, i.e., *out-migration* of people and capital, is the problem, not the solution.

What Atlantic and prairie Canadians need in the current round is a set of commitments and a set of institutions that work. And we need to come at this with a sense of "realpolitik." The following is an attempt to sketch some of the realities that we ought to bear in mind as we develop our 1991 constitutional position. Specifically, there are six premises about national institutions and their effectiveness; and there are six premises that come out of our experience with federal provincial fiscal arrangements. These twelve pieces of observation and conjecture lead to a proposed strategy for the coming constitutional round.

National Institutions

We cannot rely on parliamentary institutions to ensure our survival. The votes belong to the more populated and more prosperous centres.

We cannot even rely on elected politicians who come from the margins to be effective advocates for regional survival. The party system and the power of the prime minister are so overwhelming that elected members of Parliament face great sanctions for not falling in with the party line; there is little reason to believe that elected senators who rely on parliamentary political parties for their electoral machine will act differently.

We ought not to exaggerate the role of parliamentary institutions in any event. The real power is in the prime minister's office and in the Department of Finance. The politicians, the advisors, the senior public servants, and the prime political supporters have their principal reference points in Montreal, Toronto and Ottawa, if not in Washington or New York. It is highly unlikely that this Toronto/Montreal preoccupation can be displaced in favour of a more self-consciously regionalist view. We simply do not constitute a national elite.

The federal public service, even in those parts that happen to be located outside of Ottawa, is not regionally oriented. The career paths and social class identity of federal public servants are incompatible with a commitment to survival on the margins. As well, the current federal public service is, for a variety of reasons — related to poor management and fiscal paralysis — beyond revitalization.

Major social programs in areas of continuing provincial responsibility cannot be administered, or even monitored, by federal public servants. There must be provincial, or regional, control. We need a revitalized and more contextually-sensitive public service.

The most effective advocates for marginal survival are the provincial or territorial governments, although the tendency to province building ought to be resisted and the door should be left open to more integrated or coordinated regional approaches.

Financial Arrangements

A primary technique adopted by the federal government in its bully/banker role has been the shared-cost program. Such programs (the Canada Assistance Plan being the most significant today) discriminate against have-not provinces as they ensure that those on the margins fall even further behind. This is especially true of programs based on fifty-cent dollars.

Any commitment to marginal survival must include the "have" provinces. The federal government is no longer able to play an effective solo role as the bully and the banker. Indeed we do not collectively have the capacity to maintain the apparatus of fiscal federalism as it now exists.

There will be no major new pool of tax revenue. We have to manage with current, or even reduced, public resources. And we have to be internationally and interprovincially competitive. An unelaborated call for more funds is not realistic or responsible.

There are limits to the principle of national standards. If major urban centres adopt the view that high quality health care requires multiple cardiac by-passes and elaborate neonatal care, we should not assume that Prince Edward Island is inferior if it establishes different priorities. The same applies to income-support policies and, in a lesser measure, to education.

The preferred form of fiscal transfer is block funding. Bilateral agreements or discretionary federal spending ought to be avoided. This will ensure that accountability matches up with spending decisions, while at the same time avoiding the temptation to *ad hocery* and paternalism inherent in many current federal-provincial arrangements. In effect, this suggests an expansion of equalization or comparable vehicles and a cutting back on cost-shared and wholly federal programs.

New fiscal arrangements necessary to ensure marginal survival, as well as changes to existing programs, ought to be agreed to by the federal government and a majority of the provinces and territories.

What this suggests is a radical rethinking of the institutions and the instruments of fiscal federalism. It may even be compatible with economic union, although it would be a union that cares at least as much about staying as it does about moving. It suggests new institutions, and it suggests a radical decentralization of the administration and policy making for the Canadian social contract. It also suggests a recommitted centralization of the fiscal arrangements that make the social contract possible. In the end, what we need are new institutions at the centre that fully reflect the interests of provincial and regional constituencies.

Before laying out a prescription for such constitutional changes, it is appropriate to signal three caveats or reservations. The kind of fiscal federalism that flows from these twelve observations, a centralized revenue source with decentralized responsibility for policy making and administration, has several critical downside risks. They can be briefly identified as follows:

> That the "have" provinces will not participate in fiscal federalism unless they too are "takers." The key to selling Alberta, British Columbia and Ontario on a more explicit commitment to marginal survival is that the overall tax burden will be reduced, thereby leaving them more room to develop intelligent social programs and public services in their own jurisdictions. From the beginning of the second National Policy, in the response to the conditions of the 1930s, the have provinces have been persuaded only in terms of their own material interest, and that discourse is unlikely to change this time around.

> That we will have more explicit disparities between have and have-nots than we now have. We probably will have greater diversity. But these need not be disparities. Some of the differences may even be more appropriate for local circumstances, cultural and economic, than would be policies derived from what is perceived to be most important in Toronto from time to time. What is more, we have to balance concerns about diversity against the spectre of utter collapse that attends our present charade of national standards. Education and health care in Prince Edward Island and Newfoundland are not presently equal to that of Ontario, and if we insist on pursuing national standards for their own sake we face a continual deterioration of all public services and programs.

> That at some point the consensus will come undone. That is a risk in any event. Indeed, it seems to be a pretty good description of present reality.

An Emergent Constitutional Commitment

So what kind of constitutional arrangement flows from these premises, and from these nascent reservations? The best way to guarantee marginal survival is to move dramatically to a super-added equalization, and to get away from conditional funding and cost-shared programs. Instead of the vague commitment of Sec. 36, there should be a formula guaranteeing unconditional block funding to bring the public-sector resources in each province to a stipulated percentage of a national norm. It could be the current equalization formula, although there seems to be little justification for leaving Alberta out of the four-province standard. There would need to be a factor to average out abrupt changes in economic cycles, and to keep the process from being inherently retrospective. And there would need to be an incentive for both "have" and "have-not" provinces to do better, particularly in public finance management, from year to year.

As for an institutional format for developing and monitoring such a constitutional guarantee, it is clearly not a matter for judicial enforcement. And there is little reason to think that a reimagined Senate could be effective. The policy initiative, and the capacity to crack the whip over the federal "caucus," would still belong to the prime minister.

An institution with considerable potential is the proposed "council of the federation." While the council was initially conceived by the federal government as a body with a veto power over new federal initiatives under its extended economic powers, its general mandate is to decide on issues of intergovernmental coordination and collaboration. The council could be a monitoring body for equalization, and for coordinating policy development and administration in significant policy fields such as education, income assistance and health care. The council would also be responsible for taking the initiative to modify the equalization formula as needed.

A VISION OF MARGINAL SURVIVAL

The question of how we should survive is a big one to open up at the tail end of a paper that is a self-confessed think piece. However I will attempt to touch on some key points.

The most important goal should be to get ourselves out of a downward psychological and material spiral. We have to regain our sense of dignity. We cannot do that through the "national standards" route; neither can we do it through the mechanisms of the federal public service or Parliament. There must be indigenous and contextually-sensitive solutions.

Second, we need to break up our entrenched institutions. We have to fight province building and encourage cooperative and regional solutions. We also have to get away from too many local governments, and from too many hospitals and universities and various other sites of entrenched lack of imagination. We have to encourage people to have more than one career, and to be entrepreneurial. One of our major problems (and we on the margins are not alone in this) is that we are too bureaucratized, in both the private and the public sectors. Too many people are doing the same thing they were doing ten years ago, especially those who have the advantage of higher education. Along with this bureaucratization has come a stratification of social classes. Too many people, especially young people, are down and out before they ever gain a sense that they could have useful lives, while many others, especially in white collar positions in the public service, universities, health care and education sectors, as well as in "private" enterprise, are settled into comfortable patterns of consumption and self-indulgence. If we are entitled to be supported in our commitment to survive on the margins, we have to regain the sense of struggle and enterprise and responsiveness to changing circumstances that give us our claim on the margins in the first place. We are not entitled to be supported as some kind of folksy or over-bureaucratized backwater.

Third, we have to avoid creating new margins within the region. If there is to be a constitutional commitment to survival on the margins, it would be hypocritical to take those resources and turn Halifax or Winnipeg into bigger metropolises than they already are, while draining the best people away from smaller centres. Of course there will be a limit to what can be done in the context of a market economy, but it would be wholly cynical to take funds devoted to the principle of marginal survival and turn them to creating more white-collar jobs in a few big centres.

Fourth, we have to develop infrastructure. Highways are a better investment than most things we have spent public resources on in Atlantic Canada, and they are generally in need of major upgrading. We must, in any event, develop our infrastructure of transportation and communication. In electrical generation there must be a more integrated regional approach. The transmission of Labrador hydro power to Newfoundland and to the "mainland" should be reinvestigated.

Fifth, we have to make a more effective commitment to the environment. If our claim to marginal survival is based on an inate bonding to the land and the sea, then we have to start treating our sewage and being more responsible in our "use" of forests, and water, and soil and fish.

Sixth, we have to struggle for a more inclusive public life. One of the major arguments for national standards has been that we cannot trust local majorities. That has been particularly true in the area of language. One of the major arguments against central national institutions is that it excludes those on the margins. If our essential claim to indigenous solutions is our desire for a more effective democracy, then we have to practice what we preach. We have to take advantage of our relative small size and our sense of civic connection that is an ostensible basis for our claim to survive on the margins and we must develop truly open and inclusive processes. The status quo is hardly acceptable as a standard. We must work to eliminate conditions of patriarchy and racism and class bias and other practices of exclusion.

Seventh, we have to learn to look out for each other, in greater measure than we might do if we lived in Toronto or Montreal or Vancouver. We ought not to assume that every problem we identify in the public domain has to be responded to with high technology or with big bureaucracy. Take the example of health care, our most significant public-sector expense. Atlantic and prairie Canadians just cannot afford high-tech immortality. Nor can we afford to run to the emergency ward or the pharmacy with every small ailment. But we might still be able to have a superior standard of health if we define health in a way that is appropriate for our marginal context.

CONCLUSION

These seven elements do not represent a manifesto for survival on the margins. They are specifically identified because they derive from the overriding claim that we have a right, even an obligation, to stay. And they are identified because they demonstrate that we might even have a better life if we gave up some of the highly bureaucratized "national" solutions that we have come to accept as essential for our survival.

In the end we have to recognize that the constitution plays only a small role in our struggle to survive on the margins. The first challenge is almost ideological — do we want to stay? Do we believe we can have useful personal lives and public lives that are appropriate for our marginal contexts? Once we decide that we are commited to stay, and that we want to have a national community that includes us, we can work out constitutional terms and institutions to achieve those goals.

Notes

1. Antonine Maillet, *Pélagie-la-charrette*, trans. Philip Stratford (Toronto: Doubleday, 1982), 148.

2. Ibid., 215.

3. Canada, *Shaping Canada's Future Together: Proposals* (Ottawa: Supply and Services Canada, 1991), 40.

10

Social Programs, the West and the Constitution

Alvin Finkel

Many scholars, echoing provincial politicians, attribute the growth in federal involvement in social policy since World War II as much to Ottawa's ambitions for centralized power as to altruism.[1] This skeptical interpretation of the growth of social programs with substantial federal government finances and control parallels the critical literature on the growth of the "welfare state" generally.[2] In this literature, social control over the population on the part of governmental and business elites is stressed as a motivator for introducing social programs in capitalist societies. A growing body of feminist literature meanwhile argues effectively that welfare programs have sought to intensify patriarchal social relations by using the male-dominated state to regulate the private lives of women. Though the availability of social assistance may free low-income women from the control of an individual man, its provision is conditional upon following rules that limit women's choices as workers, mothers and lovers.[3] Indeed the jurisdiction establishing programs is of minor interest here because it is argued that bureaucrats rather than prospective recipients call all the shots at all levels of the state.

While there is much to be said for the argument that the "welfare state" controls the poor, particularly poor women, more than poverty and that federal programs subjugate provinces as much as distress, there is also much to be said for the opposite point of view. The welfare state does alleviate poverty and distress and the federal government has, whatever its motives, introduced important programs in areas such as unemployment, health and old-age insurance where most provinces showed no willingness to legislate before the federal government cajoled them to either surrender an unused power or to participate in a shared-cost federal-provincial program.[4] While limiting the rights of women, particularly low-income women, is an implicit goal of many social welfare programs, the impact of the women's movement on the state has produced changes both in legislation and implementation that have benefitted women.[5] The "welfare state" then is best understood as an arena of class, race and gender struggle rather than as an unequivocal achievement or detriment.

This paper explores the possibilities of creating social programs that can access the revenues available to the senior government of the country and yet be characterized by a high degree of grassroots control. The history of western Canadian social policy is assessed to indicate the importance both of federal monies, on the one hand, and local experimentation that points the way to more democratic management of social policy, on the other. The provinces within this perspective are as much problematic entities as the federal government — easily captured by business and bureaucratic interests, they are often suspicious of any attempts from below to implement reforms. Nonetheless, because the provincial politicians and civil servants are, at least in theory, closer to the grassroots than the federal bureaucracy, it will be argued here that their role in administration of social programs ought to be strengthened. I will begin, however, with a defense of federal government economic involvement in social programs and a strong assertion, provincial rights advocates notwithstanding, that such involvement was puny even before the cutbacks of the Mulroney era.

CANADA'S WELFARE STATE

Studies comparing Canadian spending on social programs before cutbacks started in earnest in the mid-1980s demonstrated the feebleness with which Canada has attempted either to emphasize social policy or to use state expenditures to alleviate poverty. In 1981, Canada ranked twelfth among sixteen OECD countries in the percentage of its gross domestic product (GDP) devoted to social expenditure. While Canada spent 21 percent of GDP on publicly funded education, health care, pensions, unemployment insurance, social housing and income maintenance, Belgium spent 38 percent, the Netherlands 36.1, Sweden 33.5, and Germany 31.5.[6] Canada's performance in the areas of health care and education was respectable; but its public spending on pensions and social assistance, two areas where federal programs were visible and the subject of long controversy in federal-provincial relations, was relatively small. "Austria, the Netherlands and Belgium devote twice as much of their GDP to income maintenance as Canada or the United States,"[7] wrote political scientist Keith Banting in 1982. The record on public pensions was even worse, with nations such as Germany, Italy, France and Sweden putting between 2.5 and three times as much of their GDP as Canada in this area.[8] It was a particularly appalling performance for a country whose private pensions covered a smaller percentage of the working population than any other western democracy except the United States.[9]

Keith Banting has argued that unitary states and states with federal systems where the central government's constitutional powers over social policy are unambiguous have done better in the provision of social programs than federal states with powerful regional governments.[10] OECD figures bear this observation out, but skeptics would correctly note that the relative strength of progressive forces (particularly the labour movement and social democratic parties) and conservative forces (particularly big capital) explain more about the reform process than constitutional arrangements.[11] There is a great deal of historical evidence however that the Canadian provinces, the American states, and the Australian states have played important roles in retarding social-policy development.[12] What must be emphasized here is that the junior levels of government, while on the surface merely defending their turf, have, on many occasions, acted as political agents for reactionary forces within their provinces. In other words, while the public debate has suggested that at issue was which level of government would introduce a specific program, in practice conservative provincial governments have attempted to reject the proposed program(s) altogether.

This was the case, for example, when the provinces scuttled the King government's Green Book proposals of 1945 that would have introduced several universal social insurance schemes and committed the federal government to Keynesian fiscal policies, particularly to planning a sufficient body of public works so that their timing would coincide with recessions and have a noticeable influence on the business cycle.[13] While Ontario's George Drew and Quebec's Maurice Duplessis howled about federal interference in matters properly left to the provinces, privately they believed that the federal proposals amounted to a prescription for state socialism.[14] After killing the Green Book plans, neither premier went home to introduce provincial versions of the same proposals. Indeed, only Saskatchewan and British Columbia introduced universal hospital insurance before the federal government entered the arena and only Saskatchewan introduced a medicare scheme.[15]

Provincial pressures to limit federal creation of universal social insurance programs did not end in 1945. When the federal Liberals announced plans in the early 1960s to introduce a public pension scheme for workers, Ontario's Conservative government, prodded by the province's life insurance industry, worked diligently to insure that the resulting scheme would be too modest to cut seriously into the business of that industry.[16] Several provincial governments rejected a federal universal medicare program though private insurance programs within their jurisdiction left large sections of the population without coverage.[17] Would it not be more useful to attribute this inaction to the reactionary character of the particular provincial administrations rather than to resort to theories of inevitable conservatism on the part of junior governments in a federal system? After all, Saskatchewan did pioneer both hospital insurance and medicare and NDP administrations in Manitoba, Saskatchewan and British Columbia in the 1970s and 1980s as well as the first Péquiste administration in Quebec could boast of significant improvements in the social policy area. But an examination of the structural limitations affecting reform-minded governments in western Canada suggests that a purely provincially funded welfare state could have only a modest reach, whatever the good intentions of social democratic officials.

LIMITS ON EXCLUSIVELY PROVINCIAL SOCIAL POLICY INITIATIVES

The argument for transfers of wealth within a federal system where per capita provincial incomes differ significantly was well made by the Macdonald Commission, a commission which otherwise appeared happy to allow those in control of the marketplace to make major economic decisions for Canadians. If transfers disappeared, argued the commissioners:

> Canada could eventually find itself with a completely disharmonized tax system in which taxation rates and even definitions of taxable income vary greatly across provinces. This state is the "tax jungle" which so concerned Canadians in the 1980s. Similarly, the nation could produce a completely disharmonized service-delivery system which lacked any portability of benefits and which made widely different services available from one jurisdiction to the next. In either situation, the principle of horizontal equity as applied to federalism would be eroded: that is, individual Canadians who are identical in every respect except in their province of residence and who should be treated equally by the government sector, would, in fact, be treated quite differently.[18]

Certainly, the importance of federal transfers to the various western provinces has varied over time. In 1980-81, for example, transfers accounted for five times as much of the Manitoba budget as the Alberta budget. (See Table 1) Since that time, cuts in federal transfers and the end of Alberta's oil boom have narrowed that figure to less than two to one, but the fact remains that transfers help poorer provinces to afford services that they would otherwise be unable to afford. This argument is particularly persuasive for the maritime region since, arguably, within the western provinces, a transfer arrangement among the four provinces would produce much the same result as a national transfer system.[19] The structure of the western Canadian economies however would tend to continue to mitigate against new social programs even if the region, rather than the province, provided the jurisdiction within which funds for these programs would have to be found.

Table 1
Federal Transfers as a Percentage of Gross General Provincial Revenues

	1980-81	1984-85	1987-88
Manitoba	37.6	30.3	22.1
Saskatchewan	16.9	14.9	19.3
Alberta	7.7	9.2	13.5
British Columbia	16.1	16.9	13.7

Sources: *Report of the Royal Commission on the Economic Union and Development Prospects for Canada*, Volume 3 (Ottawa: Department of Supply and Services, 1985), p. 229; Canadian Tax Foundation, *Provincial and Municipal Finances, 1989* (Toronto: Canadian Tax Foundation, 1990).

This is because the continued dependence of the western Canadian economies on world markets for their natural products sets the major limit on provincial governments eager to insure a guaranteed decent income and a generous set of universal social programs for their citizens. Long-term planning of social spending appears difficult within a context of abnormal income fluctuations from year to year and dramatic shifts in population via migration and outmigration sparked by changing provincial economic fortunes. No wonder then that Saskatchewan, as it pioneered public medical insurance, never regarded a purely provincial scheme as desirable. Saskatchewan, from the time it implemented hospital insurance campaigned loudly for federal financing or at least shared-costing of universal health programs.[20] Premier T.C. Douglas was not keen to shoulder a program whose costs might appear unbearable during a severe downturn in resource prices and therefore provincial revenues. Indeed the Saskatchewan NDP, as it faced defeat as a government in 1982, and the Manitoba party as it was trounced in 1988, had disillusioned supporters because of a fiscal conservatism that stemmed from pessimism about deficit spending. Keynesian notions seemed inappropriate to many in provinces where a large part of consumer purchases consisted of goods manufactured elsewhere. So the Saskatchewan NDP boasted about its budget surplus when citizens anticipated help in coping with stagflation and the Manitoba NDP maintained its social programs by dramatically hiking taxes on average people.[21]

Cy Gonick argues that the preservation of social programs, while praiseworthy, constitutes no more than a "stalling action" at a time when global restructuring of capital and the Canadian-American free trade agreement threaten to further weaken the economies of resource-dependent provinces like Manitoba. He maintains that greater economic interventionism by provincial governments than NDP governments in the west have so far proved willing to undertake will be necessary to turn the economic tide and create the wealth required to enrich social programming. "Unless Manitoba finds a place in the global restructuring," he warns, "it will be unable to maintain present living standards without massive transfers from the rest of the country. This altruism it cannot presume."[22]

But the potential for the western provinces to become winners in a global restructuring dominated by multinational corporations,[23] even if aggressive provincial regimes are determined to achieve diversification via public investment, is difficult to demonstrate. The "New Right" alternative, by contrast, in which social spending, union rights and the like are attacked within an overall program emphasizing the market's ability to reduce regional disparities given a fair chance (and cartloads of public dollars to selected "free enterprises"), has proven a catastrophe. The Lyon government in Manitoba (1977-81) and the Devine government in Saskatchewan (1982-91) imposed incredible hardships on the poorest sections of their provincial populations to produce the belt-tightening that supposedly would demonstrate that their provinces were, in Devine's words "open for business."[24] But few legitimate businesses were listening.

Alberta's failed attempts to diversify its economic base away from the energy industry have been well documented. That province, while its governments since the 1940s have been hostile to universal social programs and to federal involvement in shared-cost programs, could use energy revenues to fund an array of social services while keeping provincial taxes low. A sharp decline in energy revenues — from 55.4 percent of provincial revenues in 1979-80 to 24 percent in 1989-90 — caused the Alberta Conservative government to join the cutback crew and to espouse "New Right" sentiments. A government statement of social policy in 1988 noted in its preamble that: "Albertans have tended to regard social policy as being separate from economic policy. There must be a consistency between social and economic policies. Social policy — to be effective — should not be developed independently of the economic environment."[26] Older notions that social programs, by boosting consumer spending, help to create the economic environment, are ignored in the social policy statement. Again, "New Right" philosophy on this subject differs only in degree from the NDP view that provincial social spending, while it may stimulate the national economy, will not substantially boost the economy of a resource-sale-dependent province.

Debates in British Columbia differ little on this subject. Neither the Social Credit nor the NDP seriously regard consumer spending within the province as the key to economic development. The latter party however tends to regard social programs as no hindrance to development while the former tends not only philosophically to oppose universality and generous treatment of the poor but to regard social programs as obstacles to creating the low-tax environment that supposedly attracts businesses.[27] Within the four western provinces, in short, while social programs enjoy immense public support, the right and left share skepticism about the possibilities of extension of programs by provincial action alone, though only the left sees virtue in extending the scope of social programming at all. While one can expect a greater generosity from provincial NDP administrations than from their conservative counterparts, new universal programs or dramatic redistribution of income to the poor are not in the plans for any potential western Canadian provincial government. If past experience is a guide, however, there will be grassroots pressures in favour of such programs.

LOCAL CONTROL VERSUS GOVERNMENT CONTROL

In Saskatchewan, for example, while the provincial CCF-NDP government's establishment of medicare is rightly applauded, the role of the community clinic movement has received less attention. Involving 50,000 people or five percent of the provincial population, this grassroots movement established twenty-five clinics and created regional associations and a provincial organization to promote the cause of consumer-controlled medical services. Stan Rands, who worked for the provincial organization for three years, observes that the community clinic movement came about through "spontaneous and voluntary effort" and adds that it existed "outside of the official auspices of government or NDP party or the cooperative movement."[28]

The medical hierarchy of the province, however, rejected a movement that could limit physicians' absolute control over medical service delivery and won government over to its side. Successive government decisions undid the community clinic movement. The community health associations were made landlords rather than participants in clinic programs. Medical payments went directly to doctors rather than the health services associations. Meanwhile, the authority of the medical hierarchy to discipline members resulted in persecution of some doctors who practiced in community hospitals and denial of their public hospital privileges.[29]

As Stan Rand notes, "if the obstacles had been removed by government action, the basis would have been provided for community groups to take a more direct responsibility for health care programs."[30] He adds pessimistically however that "this kind of change will always be resisted by a ruling class, of which the medical profession is a part, and by social democratic governments committed to carrying out reforms without upsetting the class relations of capitalistic society."[31] Such resistance, arguably, would be even more effective on the federal level where organized vested interests have long felt they were better isolated from local plebeian pressures.[32]

Community control provides an alternative both to bureaucratic control and to privatization of social and health services. Throughout western Canada, conservative governments have promoted a gradual devolution of public programs to private companies. Ministers have argued that efficiencies can be effected via contracting out of delivery of services.[33] They have also argued that social service delivery could provide a boon to the small-business sector (though, in practice, big firms generally get the plum contracts). In Alberta, though social services delivery was the issue, it was the minister of Economic Development and Trade who took up the challenge from the opposition in 1988 to justify the government's increased reliance on the private sector for public service delivery:

> there are opportunities for individuals who are in business for themselves and are in business for profit to provide services to citizens. There are many professionals who do it now, so there is no reason why companies cannot in certain instances provide service. But it is not the intention of the government to sacrifice quality of service in favour of profit. Anyone who believes that the government is the only institution that can deliver social programs to people is stupid.[34]

This view obviously ignores that working people campaigned for public provision of services because the private sector, now seen by the new right as a saviour for social programs, provided inadequate and/or overly expensive protection for many, perhaps most, people. But the antigovernment sentiment that the "New Right" taps because of general disillusionment with bureaucracy can be countered by a militant defense of popular, democratic, as opposed to civil servant/professional, operation of programs.

CENTRAL FUNDING AND LOCAL CONTROL

So far, we have argued that both central funding and local control ought to be the cornerstones of social policy within Canada if the needs of the people of the western provinces are to be effectively met. There are several European examples that are instructive in this context. Thomas Hueglin, in an analysis of federal systems, observes:

> the spirit of federal mutualism would probably be better served if fiscal equalization were organized by means of direct transfers from richer to poorer regions, states, or provinces, according to a periodically renegotiated formula. This type of "brotherly" federalism is successfully practised in West Germany. It contradicts the commonly held view that a central enforcer is inevitably needed to harmonize the economic and fiscal disparities of a federal system.[35]

Even in several nonfederal states, particularly the Netherlands, central policy making and funding has been combined with a high level of decentralization of service delivery. Ramesh Mishra compares the experience of the Netherlands with that of the United States:

> In 1981 the Netherlands devoted 36.1% of its GDP to social welfare, compared with 20.8% in the United States ... the Netherlands had one of the most decentralized and plural systems of service delivery in the Western world, based historically on religious divisions within the nation ... Decentralization, pluralism and non-state forms of service delivery and administration nevertheless coexist with a high level of public expenditure and collective responsibility for maintaining a national minimum standard. ... The [American] government spends far less on social welfare and assumes far less responsibility for maintaining national minimum standards in respect of income, health, housing, education and personal social welfare ... the question of centralism versus pluralism in the organization and delivery of social services needs to be distinguished from greater or lesser collective responsibility for underwriting a national minimum. Neo-conservative countries have seen a shift on the policy dimension from institutional towards residual together with a shift away from centralized or statist towards decentralized and privatized service delivery systems. It is the former type of charge that the thesis of "welfare pluralism" or the "welfare society" argument tends to gloss over.[36]

What should the "national minimum" be and how can it be guaranteed to citizens? No doubt a constitutional provision that sets out a minimum income to be guaranteed to all citizens as well as guarantees of universal public provision of such basic services as medical care, education and daycare would be the best means for expressing a national commitment to a "welfare state."[37]

It would certainly place a long-term institutional commitment behind the cliché that Canada constitutes a more caring society than its southern neighbour. A modest proposal would be to guarantee all households an income no less than half the average gross Canadian household income, with size of household factored into the equation. The Senate task force on poverty, reporting in 1970, defined members of households with less income than that as too poor to afford more than the minimum necessities of life. According to Senator David Croll, the task force's chairman, five million of Canada's 25,625,000 people in 1987 or almost 20 percent of the population lived in poverty according to the Senate definition; and 1987 was a prosperous year.[38]

Apostles of the right will claim that a guarantee of this magnitude will inhibit the desire to work to earn income and even some left-wingers might believe that the taxation required to pay for a nonpoverty national minimum will scare away private investors. The experience of the European countries with well-developed welfare programs does not however reinforce such pessimism. In the early 1980s, the proportion of Sweden's low-income population, measured by numbers of people living in households with disposable income below half the median for all households, was only 40 percent of Canada's and 30 percent of that of the United States.[39] Yet that country as well as other countries that refused to make service cuts to social programming in the 1980s registered as good or better an economic performance in that decade than the United States, Britain and Canada which cut back on already relatively weak programs.[40]

Clearly, the commitment to social services in these countries, apart from serving the interests of equity, kept consumer spending high enough to balance losses from potential investors seeking cheap-labour, low-tax environments for investment.

A commitment to full employment in several of the European countries, notably Austria and Sweden,[41] has also been an important factor in alleviating poverty. Arguably, a constitutional commitment to providing state funds to those who fall below an agreed poverty line would provide an inducement to governments to favour full-employment policies so as to avoid having to make huge public outlays to people who are poor only because they are unemployed and unable to find work. Control over the minimum wage, logically, would then have to be given to the federal government since it would be reasonable to expect that the government responsible for topping up poverty incomes should have the power to prevent employers from keeping wages artificially low.

Of course, the economic elite would not welcome full employment. As Michael Kalecki, the Polish economist, noted in a famous essay first published in 1943:

> The *maintenance* of full employment would cause social and political changes which would give a new impetus to the opposition of the business leaders. Under a regime of permanent full employment, "the sack" would cease to play its role as a disciplinary measure ... "discipline in the factories" and "political stability" are more appreciated by business leaders

than profits. Their class instinct tells them that lasting full employment is unsound from their point of view and that unemployment is an integral part of the normal capitalist system.[42]

Strong welfare states, as mentioned earlier, depend upon the strength of the working class and other nonelite forces in the politics and general life of the country. No real progress in areas such as income maintenance, daycare, social housing and the like is possible without strong people's movements pressing for their extension. In this equation, provincial governments calling for local control for the sake of local control ought to be regarded suspiciously since, as Ramesh Mishra notes, democratic control and decentralization are not synonymous. Indeed, while provinces should play a key role in service delivery, real decentralization of service delivery requires that control over delivery be democratized further than a handing down of authority from federal to provincial officials. Only a genuine institutionalized control by recipients of services themselves deserves the name democracy. Well-funded community clinics, parent-controlled daycares, and a variety of mutual-aid services run by Native peoples and by single mothers for their own communities offer a real opportunity for ordinary people to have some control over their lives while squabbles between bureaucrats for control over these people offer nothing.[43]

CONCLUSION

The vulnerable character of the western Canadian economies suggests the suitability of a national umbrella for the programs meant to protect citizens against poverty and aid the sick, old, out-of-work and out-of-luck. Western Canadians ought, indeed, to question why such programs are so feeble in Canada relative to other capitalist democracies and to demand that they both be enriched and constitutionally entrenched. They ought, however, to insist that centralized funding and minimum national standards not become an excuse for federal control or arbitrariness. But provincial control, in turn, should not become an excuse for programs being elite-administered. While capitalist and patriarchal relations may continue to dominate the marketplace for some time, progressive movements should regard the removal of such relations from social service provision as an obtainable goal. Whether or not it becomes a first step towards a replacement of the systems of ownership and control that exist within the so-called "productive sphere," the "reproductive sphere" should be characterized by democratic and egalitarian values. Within this context, the bitterness among regions and provinces regarding past wrongs and present entitlements could certainly be alleviated, if not eliminated.

Notes

1.   See, for example David Milne, *Tug of War: Ottawa and the Provinces Under Trudeau and Mulroney* (Toronto: James Lorimer, 1986). Milne, like many critics of federal behaviour, points out its hypocrisy. Though health costs were rising, the federal

government passed the Canada Health Act in 1984 to prohibit user fees but failed to provide the provinces offsetting income: "the provinces were expected to cope with rising costs with inadequate federal grants and reduced access to other financial sources." (p. 184).

2. The classic text on welfare as social control is Frances Fox Piven and Richard A. Cloward, *Regulating the Poor: The Functions of Public Welfare* (New York: Pantheon, 1971).

3. Among feminist works on the welfare state adopting a social control model are Elizabeth Wilson, *Women and the Welfare State* (London: Tavistock, 1977); Anne Showstack Sassoon, *Women and the State: The Shifting Boundaries of Public and Private* (London: Hutchinson, 1987); and Jane Ursel, "The Maintenance of Patriarchy: A Case Study of Family, Labour and Welfare Legislation in Canada," in James Dickinson and Bob Russell, eds., *Family, Economy and State: The Social Reproduction Process Under Capitalism* (Toronto: Garamond, 1986), 150-91.

4. The contradictory character of the welfare state is discussed in a variety of works, of which the classic is Ian Gough, *The Political Economy of the Welfare State* (London: Macmillan, 1979).

5. The contradictory character of the welfare state in its dealings with women is examined in Linda Gordon, "The Welfare State: Towards a Socialist-Feminist Perspective," in Ralph Miliband and Leo Panitch, ed., *Socialist Register 1990* (London: Merlin, 1990), 171-200.

6. Andrew Armitage, *Social Welfare in Canada: Ideals, Realities and Future Paths*, 2nd ed. (Toronto: McClelland and Stewart, 1988), 22.

7. Keith G. Banting, *The Welfare State and Canadian Federalism* (Montreal/Kingston: McGill-Queen's University Press, 1982), 34.

8. Keith G. Banting, "Institutional Conservatism: Federalism and Pension Reform," in Jacqueline S. Ismael, ed., *Canadian Social Welfare Policy: Federal and Provincial Dimensions* (Montreal/Kingston: McGill-Queen's University Press, 1985), 51.

9. Ibid., 52-53.

10. Banting, *The Welfare State*, 41.

11. Among important works on social struggles and their impact on welfare developments are: J.D. Stephens, *The Transition from Capitalism to Socialism* (London: Macmillan, 1979); Walter Korpi, *The Democratic Class Struggle* (London: Routledge, 1983); Gosta Esping-Andersen and Walter Korpi, "Social Policy as Class Politics in Post-war Capitalism: Scandinavia, Austria and Germany," in John H. Goldthorpe, ed., *Order and Conflict in Contemporary Capitalism* (New York: Oxford University Press, 1984), 179-208; and John Saville, "The Origins of the Welfare State," in Martin Loney, David Boswell and John Clarke, eds., *Social Policy and Social Welfare* (Milton Keynes: Open University Press, 1983), 8-17.

12. On the egregious role of the states, particularly the racist southern states, in retarding and limiting welfare developments in the United States, see the essays in Margaret Weir, Ann Shola Arloff and Theda Skocpol, *The Politics of Social Policy in the United States* (Princeton: Princeton University Press, 1988). On the reactionary role of the 'states'

rights' movement in Australia, see Ronald Norris, "Federal Politics and Social Policies," in Bruce W. Hodgins, Don Wright and W.H. Heick, eds., *Federalism in Canada and Australia: The Early Years* (Waterloo: Wilfrid Laurier University Press, 1978), 267-76. Larger issues of why Australia has been a laggard in social policy development are explored in the Australia portion of James Struthers and Ronald Mendelsohn, "Federalism and the Evolution of Social Policy and the Welfare State," in Bruce W. Hodgins, John J. Eddy, Shelagh D. Grant and James Struthers, eds., *Federalism in Canada and Australia: Historical Perspectives 1920-88* (Peterborough: Frost Centre for Canadian Heritage and Development Studies, Trent University, 1989), 228-60.

13. Marc J. Gottlieb, "George Drew and the Dominion-Provincial Conference on Reconstruction of 1945-6," *Canadian Historical Review* 66, no. 1 (March 1985): 27-28; Paul Martin, *A Very Public Life, Volume One: Far From Home* (Ottawa: Deneau, 1983), 386-88.

14. Robert Bothwell, Ian Drummond, John English, *Canada Since 1945: Power, Politics and Provincialism* (Toronto: University of Toronto Press, 1981), 96.

15. On the evolution of health policy in the Canadian provinces, see Malcolm G. Taylor, *Health Insurance and Canadian Public Policy: The Seven Decisions That Created the Canadian Health Insurance System* (Montreal/Kingston: McGill-Queen's University Press, 1978).

16. Banting, "Institutional Conservatism," 64.

17. Taylor, *Health Insurance*, 366-68.

18. *Report of the Royal Commission on the Economic Union and Development Prospects for Canada*, Volume 3 (Ottawa: Department of Supply and Services, 1985), 231.

19. According to the Canadian Tax Foundation, total transfer payments in Canada in 1987-88 were $24,267 million or about $1,000 per Canadian. The four western provinces received together $6,823,000, also approximately $1,000 per resident. Federal expenditures in the region likewise call into question views common, particularly in Alberta, that federal spending discriminates against western Canada in favour of Quebec. In fact, federal expenditures in the region are slightly greater than federal revenues derived from individuals and corporations in the four western provinces. But there was a net revenue over expenditure of $2,454 million from Alberta in 1987 and $727 million from British Columbia. By contrast, spending in Saskatchewan exceeded federal revenues by $2,043 million and spending in Manitoba was $1,398 million over revenues. In a sense, as with transfer payments, the effect of federal policy is to redistribute wealth slightly within the region rather than to redistribute wealth from the region to other areas of the country. Canadian Tax Foundation, *Provincial and Municipal Finances, 1989* (Toronto: Canadian Tax Foundation, 1990), pp. 3:5, 3:10.

20. Taylor, *Health Insurance*, 184-85.

21. James A. Pitsula and Kenneth A. Rasmussen, *Privatizing a Province: The New Right in Saskatchewan* (Vancouver: New Star Books, 1990), chapter 2; Cy Gonick, "The Manitoba Economy Since World War II," in Jim Silver and Jeremy Hull, eds., *The Political Economy of Manitoba* (Regina: Canadian Plains Research Center, 1990), 39-40.

22. Gonick, "The Manitoba Economy," 47.

23. On global economic restructuring, see Stephen Gill and David Law, *The Global Political Economy: Perspectives, Problems and Policies* (Baltimore: John Hopkins University Press, 1988); Robert Gilpin, *The Political Economy of International Relations* (Princeton: Princeton University Press, 1987); and Swasti Mitter, *Common Fate, Common Bond: Women in the Global Economy* (London: Pluto Press, 1986).

24. On the Devine years, see Pitsula and Rasmussen, *Privatizing a Province*; on the Lyon regime, see Harold Chorney and Phillip Hansen, "Neo-Conservatism, Social Democracy and 'Province Building': The Experience of Manitoba," *Canadian Review of Sociology and Anthropology* 22, no. 1 (February 1985): 1-29.

25. Ed Shaffer, "Oil and Class in Alberta," *Canadian Dimension* 13, no. 8 (June 1979): 42-45; John Richards and Larry Pratt, *Prairie Capitalism: Power and Influence in the New West* (Toronto: McClelland and Stewart, 1979).

26. Alberta, *Caring and Responsibility: A Statement of Social Policy for Alberta* (Edmonton: Executive Council, 1988), 2.

27. On British Columbia Politics in the 1980s, see Stan Persky, *Fantasy Government: Bill Vander Zalm and the Future of Social Credit* (Vancouver: New Star Books, 1989); and David J. Mitchell, *Succession: The Political Reshaping of British Columbia* (Vancouver: Douglas and McIntyre, 1987).

28. Stan Rands, "Recollections," in Donald C. Kerr, ed., *Western Canadian Politics: The Radical Tradition* (Edmonton: Newest Institute for Western Canadian Studies, 1981), 63.

29. Ibid., 63-64.

30. Ibid., 64.

31. Ibid.

32. On attitudes in the 1930s see Alvin Finkel, *Business and Social Reform in the Thirties* (Toronto: Lorimer, 1979), chapters 6 and 9.

33. Health Minister Nancy Betkowski, though one of the more liberal members of the Alberta government, argued in 1989: "There may be ways ... to effect efficiencies in our health system through the private delivery of nonmedical services such as dietary, maintenance, laundry services, waste disposal, and other examples ... there are two facilities in Alberta that have employed private management groups to advise the board. In these cases the funding of this service comes from within that hospital's global budget, and in both cases the boards are very pleased with the approach." *Alberta Hansard*, 27 July 1989, 1093.

34. Ibid., 22 April 1988, 601.

35. Thomas O. Hueglin, "Legitimacy, Democracy and Federalism," in Herman Bakvis and William M. Chandler, eds., *Federalism and the Role of the State* (Toronto: University of Toronto Press, 1987), 49.

36. Ramesh Mishra, *The Welfare State in Capitalist Society: Policies of Retrenchment and Maintenance in Europe, North America and Australia* (Toronto: University of Toronto Press, 1990), 113-14.

37. It should be noted that notions of a guaranteed annual income have received support from disparate groups both of the Left and the Right. The Macdonald Commission and various business groups have seen the G.A.I. as a potential substitute for a variety of existing social programs which, as long as it keeps recipients well below the poverty line, poses no disincentive to workers to accept low-wage jobs on offer.

A review and critique of various income maintenance proposals is found in: Mario Iacobacci and Mario Seccareccia, "Full Employment Versus Income Maintenance: Some Reflections on the Macroeconomic and Structural Implications of a Guaranteed Income Program for Canada," *Studies in Political Economy* 28 (Spring 1989): 137-73.

38. *Globe and Mail*, 5 January 1989.

39. Mishra, *The Welfare Sate in Capitalist Society*, 133.

40. Ibid., 125-27.

41. Ibid., 48.

42. Michael Kalecki, *Essays on the Dynamics of the Capitalist Economics* (Cambridge: Cambridge University Press, 1971), 140-41.

While some critics of income maintenance programs regard them as system-supporting substitutes for the allegedly more radical goal of full employment, other commentators see nothing particularly radical in the latter goal. William A. Robson comments:

> full employment is essentially a negative concept aimed at preventing heavy unemployment. It lacks any sense of purpose or direction. Its object is to insure that all the workers will be busy all the time, making goods and providing services. It does not inquire what kinds of goods and services, or for what ends they are produced. William A. Robson, *Welfare State and Welfare Society: Illusions and Reality* (London: George Allen and Unwin, 1976), 85.

43. British feminist social worker and scholar Elizabeth Wilson presents the following as goals for a welfare state that serves the needs of all citizens. "The feminist message to the policy makers is that diverse and varied forms of household — which do actually exist — require diverse and flexible forms of provision of all kinds. It reminds them that the care of all dependants should be the responsibility of society as a whole, not simply of individual fragile households. It is a call for preventative medicine, for local provision, for flexible working hours and genuinely shared care." Elizabeth Wilson, "Feminism and Social Policy," in Martin Loney, David Boswell and John Clarke, eds., *Social Policy and Social Welfare* (Milton Keynes: Open University Press, 1983), 44.

11

The Struggle for Regional Integration:
Atlantic-Maritime Canada

Stephen G. Tomblin

Over the past three decades, the idea of maritime/Atlantic economic or political union has been discussed and debated as conditions have changed in the larger Canadian federal system. With the failure of the Meech Lake Accord, reduction of federal transfer payments for various programs, and the rest of the country seeking new solutions to its economic problems, it is not surprising that the Atlantic premiers again see the need to reconsider an old idea. It is certainly not by chronological coincidence that the issue of regional integration has resurfaced at a period in Canadian history when there is a lot of concern with over-government and the need to reduce trade barriers. The present attack on existing federal policies and the call to drastically decentralize the country, based on the needs of economic efficiency, have raised many new challenges for the Atlantic premiers. On the other hand, as illustrated by Alan Cairns's depiction of "governmental societies,"[1] we should never underestimate the capacity of provincial governments to survive, despite changes within the larger society. It needs to be stressed that governments in Atlantic Canada have the power and capacity to gain control over any new experiment in regional integration and will likely respond by defending their territorial and jurisdictional interests.

From an institutional perspective, it is an opportune time for re-examining the historical role of government competition in connection with the problem of regional underdevelopment in Atlantic Canada. The contention of this paper is that a common approach to institutional and economic change did not take place in the region because our federal system of territorial specialization, bureaucratic duplication, and self-defeating competition simply created too many obstacles for the governments involved, and the premiers were unable to reach a consensus. In a sense, the failure of the Atlantic premiers to agree on a common economic development strategy tells us a great deal about the declining capacity of the federal system to meet the challenges of socioeconomic change. Our present constitutional system tends to promote political deadlocks and, at best, can only offer an incremental and conservative approach to socioeconomic and institutional change.

Indeed, it is often recognized that the expansion of government in Canada has seriously eroded our capacity to meet the challenges of industrial development in a new age of global competition. Yet, despite this recognition, many scholars tend to be more critical of government competition and duplication in Atlantic Canada. To the distress of many in the region, there is a tendency to impose different standards of conduct on the politicians who compete for power and operate in a political system where there is little incentive for developing an integrated approach to economic development. Rather than blaming the system as a whole, there is a proclivity in Canada to focus too much negative attention on the Atlantic provinces and their governments. One purpose of this paper is to challenge some of these old stereotypes and images which exist in the literature and to refocus our attention on the fact that the actions of the Atlantic premiers are a natural product of a highly competitive and divided political system.[2]

Particularly relevant to this discussion is Alan Cairns's state-centred approach to Canadian federalism which clearly identifies province building as a product of the institutional structure.[3] State-centred theory stresses that provincialism is a consequence of provincial elites pursuing goals where the primary aim is to increase their power and to regulate economic and political development within their respective boundaries. This paper adopts a state-centred view of province building to explain the significance of territorial and jurisdictional considerations in the ongoing battle to restructure the economies and societies of Atlantic Canada. By examining the history of resistance to institutional reform in the Atlantic region and the fears and concerns of the premiers involved, this paper offers a fresh perspective in which to interpret past failures to promote a common approach to institutional and economic reform in the region.

As noted by Cairns, there is a need to carefully examine some of the underlying assumptions which have fuelled the debate over whether province building is a product of state initiative or changing societal conditions.[4] There are a couple of issues that have been highlighted by Cairns which are relevant to our discussion here. First, state-centred explanations of province building and the problems associated with economic planning in Canada stress that we cannot ignore the fact that our federal system naturally reinforces competition between governments and a paternalistic view of politics at the provincial level. There have been a number of ambitious political leaders at the provincial level who have resisted centralization and have been characterized as conservative or reactionary. We need to recognize that federal-provincial conflicts over opposed plans for societies and economies have reinforced a pattern of governmental conservatism and executive dominance at the provincial level in every region of the country.

Cairns's work also focussed on the tendency of scholars to adopt the view that "technological interdependence and the evolution of a national market made centralized leadership necessary for planning purposes and destroyed the sociological basis for the vitality and meaningful survival of the provinces."[5] Yet to the disappointment of a whole generation of scholars, provincial status and power has expanded over time, despite changes within society and the rise of a more rational approach to planning at the centre. Cairns's argues that scholars were wrong in their assessment because they paid inadequate attention to the possibility that province building was a product of the political system itself and was not greatly influenced by changes within the larger society.

In describing the impact of the federal system on the expansion of government in Canada, Cairns argues that,

> These pyramids of bureaucratic power and ambition are capped by political authorities also possessed of protectionist and expansionist tendencies. The eleven governments of the federal system endow the incumbents of political office with the primary task of defending and advancing the basic interests of crucial sectors of the provincial or national economy and society. Each political office, particularly those of prime ministers and premiers, has a history that influences and constrains the succession of incumbents who briefly possess it.[6]

Hence, when we assess the recent history of economic and institutional reform in Atlantic Canada it is imperative that we do not impose different standards of conduct on the region. After all, the Atlantic premiers operate within a political system where the players are naturally suspicious of outside interference and there is a natural tendency to defend provincial plans and priorities against outsiders. Separated by political systems where different leaders compete for power at different times and under very different circumstances, it is not surprising that provincialism has survived and flourished in Atlantic Canada. Nor is it surprising that economic planning has been difficult under these conditions.

The rest of the paper will be devoted to examining the issue of region building in Atlantic Canada from a comparative and historical perspective. The paper offers a comparative study on recent province-building and region-building trends within Atlantic Canada in an effort to identify many of the constitutional and political issues which need to be addressed before change is possible. The paper is informed by Alan Cairns's province-building approach to state expansion and pays considerable attention to the significance of institutional and territorial factors to explain the distinctive styles of province building in Atlantic Canada.[7] From this perspective, province building and the history of resistance to region building can be seen as an assertion of territoriality in a competitive federal structure that guarantees that premiers are naturally sensitive about attacks on their territorial integrity or jurisdictional interests. The politics of self-interest and survival have remained a driving force in Canadian federalism and there seems little doubt that any premier in the country would be sensitive about potential attacks on their powers and influence. By examining recent trends in province building and region building in Atlantic Canada, the study seeks to expand our understanding on how territorial conflicts and considerations influenced the way the four governments have responded to previous calls for economic and political reform.

PROVINCE BUILDING, STATE IMPOTENCE,
AND THE CONCEPT OF THE "EMBEDDED STATE"

There is a growing literature that seeks to explain the expansion and growth of the provincial state in Canada and the impact on industrial expansion and economic performance.[8] Important to this discussion is Alan Cairns's thesis that the inability of the various competing governments in Canada to agree on a common approach for resolving many of the problems now facing the country really comes down to the experience of state growth and increasing government-societal interdependence.[9] For Cairns, the ongoing competition between governments in Canada to integrate societies and economies based on different plans or visions has seriously undermined efforts to develop common solutions to common problems. Within our highly competitive federal and parliamentary structure, a primary task performed by any provincial government is the need to defend the territorial integrity and jurisdictional powers of the provincial community against outsiders.

According to Cairns,

> New governments inherit massive program commitments put in place by their predecessors. These programs are enmeshed in bureaucracies; they are supported by clientele expectations; they are protected by the incremental processes of policy making and budget decisions; their sanctity is preserved by their number and the crowded agenda of cabinets of legislatures that can only focus their attention on the minuscule proportion of ongoing state activity; except in revolutionary times, their existence is usually equivalent to their survival. To turn around a huge loaded oil tanker steaming full speed ahead is child's play when contrasted with the difficulty of engineering a significant change of direction for the great ship of state. The latter task is beyond the capacity of particular governments between elections. It is a task for decades of clear-sighted leadership possessed of a vision of an alternative relationship between state and society. Competitive democratic politics, the short-run perspective of most politicians concerned with the next election, and the sheer difficulty of visualizing such an alternative in the face of the intimidating complexity and interdependence of what exists, foster a pragmatic conservatism over major innovations.[10]

The following analysis while informed by state-centred theory, fully recognizes as Cairns does that, "State power in Canada is so widely dispersed and its applications so fragmented that the state is incapable of achieving anything approximating total control of the citizenry. It can scarcely keep its own house in order."[11]

Whether it is province building in Atlantic Canada or elsewhere, once transportation infrastructure has been built or other policies introduced, these commitments become embedded within society, and new governments inherit

old structures, policies, and ways of thinking. In many ways the problems facing
governments in Canada today are not new. What is new is that we are beginning
to question whether such an approach to problem-solving and conflict management can continue in these times of economic change and fiscal crisis.

THE POLITICAL SETTING

The history of Canadian federalism and the struggle for control by provincial
governments in Atlantic Canada over the timing and pace of economic development, cannot be fully appreciated unless we first take into account historical patterns of similarity and dissimilarity in socioeconomic and political experience in
the region. After all, the four Atlantic provinces approach the issue of restructuring with very different experiences and expectations.

Newfoundland is generally recognized as the most unique of the four Atlantic
provinces. When the province joined the federal system in 1949, Newfoundland
had many internal communication and transportation problems and the relative
isolation of many fishing and other resource-based communities not only
hampered industrial growth, but made it difficult for many provincial residents to
share common frustrations, interests, and fears. Hence, the differentiated
economic base, the isolation, and the historical dominance of the periphery by
the merchants of St. John's helped to reinforce major economic and political
divisions within the province. Within an economic and political climate, where
one urban centre has always dominated the periphery, finding a consensus on
economic development strategy has never been easy. To make matters worse,
bad past experiences with planning and industrial policy have made the selling of
the industrial model even more difficult.

While transportation infrastructure and the industrial sectors of the economy
are not as well developed as the Maritimes, at the same time, people within the
province are proud of their non-industrial rural-based economy and the tradition
of community-based self-reliance and independence. No premier could last very
long in this setting if he ignored the lessons of the more recent past, particularly
the problems associated with industrialization and resettlement.

Much of the distinctiveness of Newfoundland comes from its relative isolation from the other maritime provinces and its long history as a separate
economic and political entity. Newfoundland is different from the maritime
provinces in several respects, and any plan to restructure the regional economy
based on the needs of industrial capitalism must take into account these differences. Newfoundland has had a lot of experience being a peripheral and dependent
society and any new economic development plan must take into account the historical record of the last few decades.

As indicated by Doug House, the former chairman of the Royal Commission
on Employment and Unemployment, and who now heads the Economic
Recovery Commission in Newfoundland, many Newfoundlanders believe that

the process of industrialization may have actually weakened Newfoundland's economy. According to House,

> The failure of Newfoundland's first development plan in the 1890s holds some lessons for Newfoundland in the 1980s, because it points to some basic misperceptions of our potential for development that remain with us to the present day. With the benefit of hindsight, we can see that what was tried focused more on Newfoundland's weaknesses than its strengths.[12]

Viewed within the Newfoundland context, the commissioned study argued that the province's development problems were created by those who were determined that they could push the economy forward by building industrial infrastructure and by imposing the industrial model on the predominantly rural-based economy. While the report suggests that there were some benefits, overall it concluded that the policy "in many ways [was] inappropriate for a small, peripherally located society distant from marketplaces of the world."[13] The fact that many Newfoundlanders feel this way about industrialization is certainly going to make it more difficult to develop a common industrial plan for the region.

To conclude, Newfoundland is a unique society and should not be characterized simply as an appendage of the other maritime provinces. Geographically isolated, internally divided, and with its own economic and political history it is unlikely that Newfoundland will respond in a predictable way to external pressure for change. When we take into account the reliance on the inshore fishery, past experience with other industrial schemes and rational planning under the commission government, it will not be easy convincing Newfoundlanders about the merits of redrawing boundaries and restructuring societies and economies based on the industrial model.

The socioeconomic and political setting in New Brunswick is very different from the one described above. Not surprisingly, these differences in socioeconomic experience help to explain why the province of New Brunswick has consistently been more open to the idea of restructuring the regional economy and society based on the industrial model. New Brunswick's most distinctive characteristic has to do with its ethnic make-up. The Acadian population makes up about one-third of the New Brunswick population, and there is little question that especially since the 1960s that ethnicity has been an important force in New Brunswick politics.[14] The French factor has been further solidified by the concentration of the Acadian population in the northern regions of the province, and by the close proximity to the province of Quebec.

While New Brunswick is highly dependent on forestry, agriculture, mining, electricity, and other primary resource industries, there does not appear to be the same fear of industrialization or centralization found in the other three provinces. There are a couple of factors which help to explain this difference in approach. First, New Brunswick with its close proximity to Quebec was greatly influenced by the experience of the Quiet Revolution. The vision of building a new industrial economy and society and the need to centralize planning struck a responsive chord within the community, particularly in the 1960s when the province was experiencing its own economic crisis. Rather than promoting further divisions, the new approach to industrialization had broad support. There is little question that the demand to balance the needs of the English- and French-speaking populations and to share resources in a fair and equitable way also contributed to the centralized approach to economic problem solving.[15]

Another factor important for understanding New Brunswick's more general openness to industrialization and the need for economic planning has to do with the number of urban centres in the province. In a province not historically dominated by one industrial centre, there is little doubt that there would be less fear of industrialization and centralized decision making in the province. In the end, it is hard not to conclude that New Brunswick is unique and approaches economic issues with a very different set of expectations.

Province-building traditions in Nova Scotia are also unique. While many people believe that common patterns of economic and political activity naturally flow across provincial boundaries in Atlantic Canada, it is not clear that conditions are identical in the four provinces. While a number of scholars argue that, "Nova Scotia has usually regarded itself, and it has been seen by outsiders, as the most prosperous and progressive of the Atlantic provinces,"[16] it is unclear whether Nova Scotia really is the most progressive and prosperous province in the region.

To understand fully the recent history of failed attempts to develop an integrated approach to industrial development in the region, it is important to understand fully the many differences in governing philosophy in Nova Scotia. It is important to keep in mind that Nova Scotia is not the most progressive thinking province in the region and the refusal of various premiers in the province to give up power over decision making to experts has certainly contributed to the failure of past efforts to integrate the region.

As illustrated by Paul Brown, in his assessment of the political culture of Nova Scotia, the provincial society is characterized by a long history of cultural insularity, a sense of regional distinctiveness, and economic independence. With "small patch mentalities in some areas"[17] and established patterns of segmentation, along with strong independent political traditions, many observers have concluded that the decentralized features of Nova Scotia politics have placed the political leadership in a more precarious position there than in New Brunswick.

There is not much evidence to support the claim that there are many similarities between the politics of Nova Scotia and New Brunswick. While both provinces are highly reliant on primary industries and federal transfers, it would be misleading to conclude on this basis alone that conditions are identical in the two provinces. In a province historically dominated by one industrial centre, it is natural that there would be greater fear of industrialization and centralization in many regions of Nova Scotia.

It is ironic that Nova Scotia's reputation as the most progressive and prosperous province in the region may have contributed significantly to the problems associated with earlier experiments in interprovincial cooperation. According to Drummie, the former director of the maritime union study and the person most responsible for implementing the Equal Opportunity Program in New Brunswick, a major reason why Nova Scotia refused to accept the need for change had to do with this false pride which he characterized as "an arrogance born of insecurity" and a tendency to be more inward looking than New Brunswick.[18] But it makes sense that in a province that has never really faced the same economic and institutional problems that have plagued both Newfoundland and New Brunswick that there would be a different attitude about the need for change. In many ways, Nova Scotia is a unique society and has not responded to the call for reform in the same way as New Brunswick did.

As an island, Prince Edward Island shares much in common with Newfoundland, since both societies are geographically isolated and both economies are rural-based. Because of its small size and proud rural traditions, it is not surprising that many islanders have had concerns about any economic development strategy which ignores small scale development and the needs of local people and rural communities. Comparable to the history of Newfoundland, the citizens of PEI have not found it easy agreeing on the costs and benefits of stimulating industrial development and increasing external dependency. While PEI is not divided on the basis of region or ethnicity, seeking a common consensus on development strategy has never been easy since few people agree on the costs and benefits of modernization and on opening up the economy to outside industrial interests.

PATTERNS OF STATE BUILDING AND DEMANDS FOR REFORM

Of course, even if one were to accept the argument that the four Atlantic provinces are distinctive and this is based on a sociological fact, it would be a mistake if we were to end our investigation here. After all, with all of the changes in communication and transportation technology and the world economy, not to mention the tendency to eliminate political boundaries in Europe and elsewhere, it is clear that recent proposals to consolidate the four Atlantic provinces is not based solely on sociological criteria. There is no doubt that the current campaign to redraw boundaries in the region is based strictly on economic considerations. Yet, on the other hand, while the cultural significance of political boundaries should not be ignored, nor can the fact that province building has survived despite overwhelmingly powerful changes in the socioeconomic environment in the past. It would be a mistake to again underestimate the capacity of governments to survive, despite the changes taking place in the environment.

A major obstacle to region building is the fact that the institutional structure is organized on the basis of provincial units, and any attempt to restructure the region on a regional basis must deal with the fact that the current constitutional system is naturally resistant to change. As stated by Cairns, "We have long known that institutions represent a mobilization of bias, that states are historical products whose evolution is subtly channelled by the incentives and disincentives of their institutional arrangements, arrangements that are usually peculiarly resistant to change."[19] Provincialism has survived simply because the premiers have always been in a position to defend their interests. In a federal system which features separate policy traditions, and executive-dominated parliamentary institutions, it is natural that the various competing state elite in Atlantic Canada are more concerned with provincial concerns than regional ones. When we take into account the high level of interdependence between the state and society at the provincial level, and how past commitments have become embedded within society, it is unclear how this institutionally entrenched system of provincial isolation and competition is going to suddenly change. After all, each of the premiers is a major participant within a federal structure which has always been structured based on the philosophy that the name of the game is to defend your own interests against outside threats to your territory or autonomy.

NEW ERA IN FEDERAL REGIONAL POLICY
AND THE FIRST PUSH FOR INTEGRATION

While the quest to consolidate New Brunswick, Prince Edward Island, Nova Scotia and perhaps Newfoundland into one province did not really become a political issue until 1963, the idea of the four Atlantic provinces working closely together to deal with their common economic problems can be traced as far back as 1951, when the Maritime Board of Trade first launched a series of discussions on the need for an integrated approach to regional economic management. Such a voluntary approach to problem solving was generally well received as evidenced by the fact that in 1953, a round-table discussion was organized around the theme of economic change and participants included the four Atlantic premiers as well as business leaders in the region. Among the topics discussed was the need to erect new regional institutions that would help to facilitate regional cooperation in a number of policy areas.[20]

However, perhaps the most significant development to come out of these meetings was the commitment to establish the Atlantic Provinces Economic Council as a nongovernment research body in 1954.[21] If nothing else, such an initiative guaranteed that economists in the region would have an opportunity to push their ideas onto the public agenda. Suddenly, as indicated by Brodie, the supporters of the growth-pole approach to industrial strategy had an opportunity to criticize "the federal government's welfare approach to uneven development" and to come up with a new integrated industrial plan for the region.[22] Whether the premiers liked it or not, the needs of rural communities and nonindustrial sectors of the regional economy were about to become a target of criticism. It was the beginning of a new era in regional development policy and a time in Canadian history when reformers, Ottawa, and the Atlantic premiers were beginning to square off in a major battle over the territorial boundaries in the region.

There is little doubt that a significant event which influenced the original drive for an integrated approach to industrial development was the change in direction in the federal government's regional development policy. In 1956, Prime Minister St. Laurent started the ball rolling by announcing that Ottawa was concerned about Atlantic Canada's poor economic record and proposed that the Atlantic premiers should work together in solving common problems. As indicated in a recent Council of Maritime Premiers' publication, this call for a regional approach to problem solving resulted in the first regular meeting of the Atlantic premiers in July 1956.[23] Responding to the prime minister's challenge, the four premiers began meeting on a regular basis.

As argued by Careless, the year 1957 was a significant watershed in regional development policy in Canada.[24] For the first time Ottawa recognized the special problems of Atlantic Canada and began pushing for a more integrated approach to economic development. While the Atlantic premiers naturally welcomed the federal support, there were concerns that Ottawa was about to interfere in areas of provincial jurisdiction.[25] As pointed out by Careless, these concerns were justified. As the federal government became more involved in trying to resolve the problems of Atlantic Canada, it went out of its way to substantially enlarge its influence over regional development policy.[26]

Suddenly, the premiers faced a policy dilemma. While they welcomed Ottawa's new support, there was growing fear that they were about to lose control over regional development policy to Ottawa and a group of reformers who did not understand or appreciate the special needs of rural development in the region.[27] It was natural that government officials in the Maritimes were suspicious that Ottawa's endorsement and active participation in Smallwood's centralization and resettlement policies in the mid-1950s were linked to this sudden commitment to regional development policy in 1957. As indicated by Copes, from the beginning the resettlement program "had the purpose and effect of reinforcing a pattern of population movement that followed the rational and natural pressures of social and economic change."[28] Of course, not everyone agreed that such movement of population to industrial areas was rational or natural and, as a consequence, the premiers responded to Ottawa's new interest in regional development policy with caution and with different expectations.

BYRNE COMMISSION AND THE PUSH FOR INTEGRATION

The concept of an integrated Atlantic region was first pushed onto the public agenda in 1963 by the Byrne Commission on local government reform in New Brunswick.[29] With the sudden rise of the Liberal government in New Brunswick in 1960 and Premier Robichaud's determination to build a more rational industrial economy and society, it was not surprising that the concept emerged first in New Brunswick. Louis Robichaud, with the strong support of Prime Minister

Pearson, offered a plan for reforming the economies and societies of the region but it was not well received by the other premiers.[30] Despite the opposition, Robichaud adopted the view that the premiers had little choice but to modernize their bureaucracies and to work closely with Ottawa in designing a common industrial plan for the entire region.[31]

The Byrne Commission was launched at a time when the Quiet Revolution was gaining momentum in Quebec and when many governments across the country were trying to build more systematic and comprehensive planning systems hoping that this would stimulate new industrial activity. There is little question that these changes in philosophy influenced political events in New Brunswick as well as in the region.

The Byrne study concluded that existing bureaucratic and political structures were undermining industrial expansion and that the province needed to work more closely with Ottawa in developing a more integrated approach to industrial development. The study concluded that there was a need to abolish rural governments, to centralize general services, and to create a more modern bureaucracy. To the surprise of many, the report went beyond its original mandate and concluded by committing itself to the idea of full Atlantic political union.[32]

There is little doubt that the Equal Opportunity Program that was put in place in New Brunswick, based on the recommendations of the Byrne report, influenced the decision to further study the option of political union. With his commitment to change and endorsement of the Equal Opportunity Program, few people were surprised when, in 1964, Premier Robichaud first raised the idea of sponsoring a study on amalgamating the four provinces. On the other hand, given past differences, it was not surprising that the other premiers were less enthusiastic about the need to restructure boundaries and reform institutions in the region based on the needs of industrial capitalism.

In 1965, the Smallwood government responded by announcing that the province was no longer interested in meeting with the other premiers to discuss common problems. The Newfoundland premier also declined the offer to participate in a study on political union. When Premier Shaw of Prince Edward Island also declined, for awhile it looked like only premiers Robichaud and Stanfield were open to the idea of establishing a commission. However, with the change of government in PEI, there was also a change in policy. On 26 March 1968 all three Maritime governments agreed to endorse a study on maritime union.[33]

Given the difference in governing philosophy, and past experience with state-directed industrial programs, it was not really surprising that the Newfoundland premier declined the offer. In stark contrast to the commitment by New Brunswick to abolish rural governments, and to work cooperatively with the other premiers in pushing economic and political reform in the region, the Newfoundland government showed little interest in the project. Near the end of Smallwood's years as premier, it was becoming increasingly clear that there was less concern about restructuring government based upon the principles of centralized control and enlightened management.

Unlike Robichaud, Smallwood was not committed to reorganizing provincial-municipal structures or building a modern bureaucracy based on the desire to stimulate new industrial opportunities in the province. Yet, the proposition advocating a more industrial and centralized approach to government planning was by no means new in Newfoundland. General services such as health, social services, and justice were already centralized. Moreover, the idea that there was a need to reform the economy based on the industrial model was certainly not novel to Newfoundlanders, and given the many problems associated with the government's previous attempts to foster industrial growth it was unlikely that the premier would consider adopting such a strategy. To have done so would have been political suicide. Within this context, it was not surprising that Smallwood refused to endorse the call for an integrated approach to economic and political reform.

In a federal system which guaranteed unilateral decision making at the provincial level, the premier was provided with the option of choosing a separate course for Newfoundland. Rather than endorsing a common approach to economic problem solving, the Smallwood government, in an effort to defend its own interests and in the process of carrying out its constitutional responsibilities, clearly rejected a common industrial plan for the region.

While Smallwood continued to work with Ottawa on resettling rural communities, building physical infrastructure, and sponsoring megaprojects in selected locations in the province, the premier showed little interest in restructuring his bureaucracy and system of local government based on the industrial model. In fact, a major problem with Smallwood's personalized approach to political decision making and his determination not to give up power to experts in the bureaucracy was that decisions were often based on political consideration and not on any comprehensive plan. As a consequence, many of the policies sponsored by Smallwood worked at cross-purposes with Ottawa's plan to restructure the region based on a common industrial plan. As indicated by the Economic Council of Canada, while Smallwood's transportation and resettlement policies promoted the growth of industrial centres, "Other government policies on taxation, and transfer payments tend to have the opposite effect by restraining the migration of people from the outports to the urban system."[34]

There is little question that Smallwood's approach to province building created a number of obstacles for those committed to the idea of coming up with a common industrial plan for the region. In a society that was originally suspicious of local government and had only twenty organized municipalities when it entered the federal system in 1949, it saw the rise of 290 municipalities by the early 1970s.[35] What is even more remarkable is that the number of municipal units doubled after 1966, at the same time that New Brunswick was abolishing its rural local governments.

As clearly demonstrated by the Whalen Commission, what was perhaps more disturbing was the fact that the system of local government sponsored by the Smallwood government was not based on any rational plan, industrial or otherwise. The study concluded that decisions were often based more on the political whims of the government than any clearly defined set of objectives. As a consequence, there was little effort placed ensuring that money was spent in communities based on a clearly defined economic philosophy. Rather than targetting funds for communities where there were special economic needs or industrial potential, funds were usually distributed based solely on the political needs of the provincial government. Many of these programs and contradictions in policy were financed by Ottawa.[36]

What is ironic about all of this is that in a province that was supposedly committed to reforming its economy and society based on the industrial model, Smallwood was not, at the same time, against using federal monies to defend and promote the needs of rural Newfoundland. In fact, entire new programs and structures were built which guaranteed that small communities would survive the onslaught of state-directed industrialization. In a federal structure characterized by fragmentation and diffusion of power, the policy-making system in Ottawa was not particularly well equipped to deal effectively with these contradictions in policy. In many ways the growth of government at the federal level contributed to the problem. Perhaps the greatest irony of all of this was that the push for rationalization and expansion of government activity which characterized the times, in many ways contributed to the problem. In the end, there is little question these mixed signals from Ottawa influenced the way the Atlantic premiers responded to the call for reform.

With Smallwood's refusal to participate in designing a common industrial strategy for the region, Byrne's call for Atlantic union remained but a dream. Yet there was still hope for maritime integration. Several factors contributed to the decision on the part of the maritime premiers to support the maritime union project. As mentioned, these included: Ottawa's new commitment to dealing with the special needs of the region; the threat of Quebec separatism; the new era in government planning; the prosperity of the time; and the fact that the idea of maritime union was not new. Under the circumstances, there was great pressure to support the new initiative. On the other hand, the premiers knew that even if they sponsored a study on union, in the end, nothing could be changed unless they all agreed. As a consequence, the project went ahead as planned, but the premiers remained in control.

MARITIME UNION

There is little doubt that the maritime union study was inspired by the Equal Opportunity Program in New Brunswick and was informed by the same assumptions as the Byrne Commission. Both studies were committed to centralizing power, redrawing political and economic boundaries based on the needs of industrialization, and increasing the role of planning. Part of the reason for this had to do with the fact that some of the key people involved in designing and implementing a new system in New Brunswick worked on the maritime project.[37] With the rise in demands for change by Ottawa and planners within the bureaucracy, it was not surprising that the report pushed for reform and called for a new approach to addressing economic problems in the region. To the surprise of no one, the experts challenged the traditional powers of the premiers and the way decisions had been made in the past.

As a consequence, the maritime union study that was released in 1970 was highly critical of the government planning in the region, rural traditions, and the barriers to industrial development that had been created by politicians and provincial bureaucrats.[38] The authors adopted the view that reform was inevitable and that unless the premiers took the initiative themselves, it was likely that Ottawa would either impose its own solutions, or lose interest in reversing the history of underdevelopment in the region. The report concluded that the premiers had little choice but to accept full economic and political union. The study recommended that three political structures be built in order to facilitate region building. First, it proposed that the premiers should establish a Council of Maritime Premiers and a small secretariat to oversee the experiment in region building. Second, it proposed that a maritime provinces commission be created to ensure that there was nonpolitical means for resolving disputes. In the view of the authors, fundamental change would not likely occur if the premiers made all the critical decisions alone. Third, it was recommended that a joint legislative assembly be established to ensure that the public was well informed, and to ensure that any decisions reached were endorsed by the general population.

When the union study was first released, given the economic and political environment, it would not have been easy for the premiers to simply ignore the recommendations. However, on the other hand, it is perhaps not surprising that, in the end, the premiers responded to these threats to their autonomy and territorial integrity by ensuring that their interests were well defended. Ironically, the premiers used their power and influence to seize control over the experiment in interprovincial cooperation to ensure that any new regional institutions built reinforced existing boundaries and defended province-building tendencies in the region.

The supporters of reform put forward ideas that directly challenged the rural traditions of the region and the decision-making powers of the premiers, at the same time, the study failed to prove its case that economic and political reform would produce the many economic benefits promised.[39] Much of the analysis was based on an emerging orthodox economic theory and the premiers were not willing to sacrifice past traditions or their ability to regulate the forces of economic and political change based simply on faith. As noted by Cameron in his analysis of the report, ''the problem in attempting to evaluate these arguments is simply that we have no basis for comparison, and must accept or reject them essentially on the basis of belief, rather than knowledge."[40] The premiers were naturally concerned about endorsing a new development plan for the region, particularly when no guarantees were provided that the experiment would or could work.[41]

The premiers responded to the challenge and pressure for reform by gaining control of the project. This was done by deliberately ignoring the recommendations of the union report and choosing to implement a new experiment in interprovincial cooperation based on the existing confederal system of power sharing. In 1971, the premiers committed themselves only to establishing the Council of Maritime Premiers (CMP) and a small secretariat. There were several advantages in responding this way. First, the premiers met the challenge posed by Ottawa and the planners by guaranteeing that their powers to defend their political and territorial interests were not to be sacrificed during the experiment. Nothing would happen unless all three premiers agreed. In this way, the final decision-making and initiating powers remained with the premiers.

While originally the province of New Brunswick supported the idea of establishing a commission, the other two premiers were not willing to give up power. Nova Scotia, in particular, was against the idea, and has over time been less supportive of maritime cooperation. As a consequence, early on in the game, the premiers seized control of the project and played according to the rules set out by Nova Scotia.

Another advantage was it offered an opportunity to increase federal spending in the region. The premiers were well aware of the interest that Ottawa had in the project, and there is little doubt the promise of new federal money provided extra motivation. Finally, the CMP offered an opportunity to meet regularly to discuss common problems. The premiers saw the benefits of working together on common projects, but only if they remained in control.

While the regional confederacy has established a number of innovative programs, there is little question that the ideas outlined in the Maritime union study have been reshaped to fit closely with the province-building aspirations of the maritime premiers. Regional offices have been deliberately built to defend provincial boundaries, meetings are held in many of the small communities that were supposed to be resettled, and a municipal training program has been established to ensure that municipal leaders in small communities are in a better position to defend their interests against outsiders.[42] The idea was to guarantee that province building and rural traditions in the region were well defended against outside attacks.

The CMP throughout its history has been more concerned with defending the territorial and political interests of the three maritime premiers than it has with developing a common industrial plan for the region. Consequently, little interest has been shown for sacrificing provincial powers and the interests of rural communities with the hope that this would stimulate industrial growth. Rather, the premiers have always defended the view that cooperative efforts between the provinces must properly "reflect and represent the integrity of the respective provinces."[43]

In the end, the propensity for pursuing provincial initiatives, with the intention of defending existing economic and political boundaries in the region, ensured that the drive for full integration was undermined. The premiers met the challenge posed by Ottawa and a group of reformers by seizing control of all programs and structures and ensuring these did not threaten the territorial interests of the three provinces. Regional cooperation would continue but only if province building was not threatened. To the surprise of no one, Ottawa lost interest in the project and decided in 1979 to pull out all federal funding. While the premiers were naturally disappointed, they had succeeded in gaining full control of the project.

OTHER CHALLENGES IN THE REGION

The 1970s was a decade which featured ongoing competition and conflict between the governments of Canada. This decade was a period of province building as regional divisions over social policy, energy and the economy intensified. With changing economic and political conditions, and changing ideas about the political responsibilities of the federal government, the political initiative shifted back to the provinces. With these changes in prevailing conceptions of the role of the federal government in the larger federal system, coupled with the Trudeau government's determination to challenge provincial powers, the provinces responded by defending their control over their respective economies and societies.

With the changing economic and political conditions, it is really not surprising that the premiers responded the way they did to the call for region building. By the early 1970s, faith in state planning had declined. Furthermore, Canada's failure to reverse the history of regional disparity during the 1960s made it even more difficult to sell the ideas outlined in the union study. There is no doubt that the decline of the popularity of Keynesianism in the country, the changing international economy, the shift in national focus from regional development policy to the energy crisis all influenced political events in the region. It is also clear that the actions of the federal government contributed further to drive to preserve province-building traditions in the region.

The 1970s was a time when more and more people were beginning to question the benefits of centralization and were adopting a common industrial plan for the region. The momentum had shifted as relations between the national and provincial governments in the region soured. There are several examples which help illustrate this point. Perhaps the most important were the changes taking place in the province of Newfoundland. With the rise of first the Moores and then the Peckford government, new emphasis was being placed on increasing the power of the province to manage its own affairs, and to ensure that the government was in a position to defend the interests of rural Newfoundland against the threat of industrialization and centralism.

During the Moores and Peckford years much focus was placed on the need for decentralizing power, gaining control over resources, and ensuring that the province had more power to regulate patterns of economic development within the province.[44] With the new emphasis placed on rural development and the need to promote more provincial self-reliance, it was not surprising that this change in government created new obstacles for region building. In fact, the new political leadership deliberately went out of it way to restrict the influence of external economic and political forces. The key was refusing to operate within any framework designed by outsiders, and making sure that a new development plan was created based on the new philosophy.

Several significant changes were introduced. First, with the assistance of Ottawa, the status of rural Newfoundland was enhanced with the operation of the newly created Department of Rural Development, the emergence of the Newfoundland and Labrador Rural Development Council, and the organization of thousands of rural residents into regional development associations.[45] Second, in 1983, the province decided to withdraw entirely from the Atlantic Provinces Economic Council and set up its own body. The Peckford administration in doing so clearly indicated that it was not interested in restructuring the Newfoundland economy and society based on the models developed by orthodox economic thinkers. Moreover, the Peckford government, beginning in 1980, refused to acknowledge the existence of an Atlantic region.[46] It was felt that such an approach to regional development programming did not serve the interests of the province and an effort was made to reject any attempt on the part of Ottawa to make decisions based on the needs of the entire region. It is clear that these changes had a dramatic impact on the effort to develop a common industrial strategy for Atlantic Canada.

The 1970s were also unusual times in Nova Scotia politics. To the surprise of many, the province of Nova Scotia not only showed little interest in maritime cooperation, but failed to carry out the kind of changes implemented under the Equal Opportunity Program in New Brunswick a decade earlier. When Premier Regan in the early 1970s first hired John Graham, a well-known economist who had worked on both the Byrne and union studies to head up the commission on municipal reform, many people felt that the province would introduce new reforms, but this did not happen.[47] Rather than reforming the bureaucracy and the municipal structure, and centralizing general services as advised by Graham, Premier Regan chose a very different path for the province. With the exception of property assessment, the Nova Scotia government showed little interest in centralizing services or handing power over to a restructured bureaucracy. As a consequence of this refusal to establish a more centralized and integrated system of public policy, it became increasing difficult for Nova Scotia and New

Brunswick to work together solving common problems. These differences in governing philosophy created yet another barrier for region building.

The experience in Prince Edward Island was different again. As a result of its size and small population, PEI has always had a very rudimentary municipal system. Without any real municipal experience in rural communities, PEI has always had a highly centralized system of provincial-municipal relations. As a consequence, little emphasis has been placed on reforming the system.

On the other hand, the 1970s was a period of change for PEI. In the early 1970s, Ottawa and the province engaged in an active policy of social and economic change. In a highly controversial move, the two governments worked together to develop a comprehensive plan for restructuring the economy and society based on the need to rationalize the provincial economy. The decade was a highly controversial one as new malls were constructed, the agricultural sector was rationalized, industrial parks were built, and other changes introduced. Not surprisingly, for many voters these changes were seen as an attack on their traditional way of life.

The federal government contributed significantly to this problem by insisting that outside experts would be brought in to implement the policy. As suggested by Dyck, "Islanders had the feeling that a group of highly educated officials, ignorant of local circumstances, had moved in and taken over. Some doubted whether even the premier and cabinet continued to have any control."[48]

There were several consequences of such a policy. First, the controversy generated by the policy created an unstable political environment in PEI. The 1970s was a period which saw a rapid turnover of governments as more people in the province began to question the benefits of rationalization. Second, a major factor influencing the decision of the Nova Scotia government not to accept the recommendations of the Graham report and maritime union study was the problems created by the General Development Agreement (GDA) in PEI.[49] Third, the experience in PEI also helped to convince the Newfoundland government that there was a need to defend the territorial and political interests of the province against outsiders.[50] Finally, there is little question that the adoption of the GDA approach to regional development sent a message to the premiers that Ottawa was not completely committed to region building. The rise of GDAs helped to reinforce the view that provincial governments should be involved directly in designing regional development strategy. It is clear that this change or inconsistency in federal policy undermined further the drive for integration.

IMPACT OF FEDERAL POLICIES

Interprovincial relations in the region and the deliberate refusal of the premiers to adopt a common approach to economic problem solving were very much influenced by Ottawa's inconsistent policies. For example, in the area of regional economic development policy, Ottawa had changed directions so many times it was no wonder that the premiers were confused about the federal government's real intentions. In the early 1960s the accent had been on rural development and the need to resolve the needs of the most depressed regions. In the late 1960s, regional development policy suddenly shifted with Ottawa's new commitment to a growth-centred policy where emphasis was placed on strengthening industrial activity in urban areas and getting tough with the provinces. For a brief period of time, Ottawa even became directly involved in the area of municipal planning which was an area that normally was considered a provincial concern. However, the Ministry of State for Urban Affairs and the attempt to develop a coherent national urban policy quickly lost momentum and the experiment was terminated in 1979, primarily due to provincial pressure.[51]

The 1970s was a period of great confusion as federal policies appeared misdirected and were constantly changing. While Ottawa's new GDA approach and move away from the special areas concept was generally well received by the provinces, many people were concerned that the federal government was losing control over development policy to the provinces. As illustrated by Savoie, "From an Ottawa view, not one of the GDAs pointed to an overall development strategy. They supported rural development if a provincial government favoured it, or tourism projects, or highways construction. Simply put, no one could discern a central and coherent purpose in any of the GDA strategies."[52] The decision in the mid-1970s to provide new special unemployment benefits for fishermen and additional federal subsidies for equipment for the inshore fishery also indicated that Ottawa was backing down on the issue of reform.[53] Under these circumstances, it was not surprising that the Atlantic provinces showed little interest in creating a common industrial plan for the region.

DRIVE FOR INTEGRATION IN THE 1990S

The idea of maritime and/or Atlantic union has emerged under very different economic and political circumstances in the 1990s. With the accelerating federal debt, the push for a more competitive and efficient Canadian economy, and the decline in popularity of Keynsian economics, there is no doubt the premiers of Atlantic Canada face a different set of problems than those encountered two decades ago. One factor that has certainly changed is the federal government's interest in solving the economic problems of the region.

However, not everything has changed. Much of the pressure to redraw boundaries in the 1990s is again coming from the outside, and since the region continues to be highly dependent on federal transfers, the premiers again cannot afford to ignore these demands for change. Another factor which has remained constant over time is the influence of orthodox economic reformers and their determination to push their ideas onto the public agenda. The Byrne, maritime union, and the more recent McMillan reports are informed by common assumptions. It is truly remarkable how all three studies play upon the fears of the readers, and those most prominent in the region — a fear of continued slow economic growth coupled with the fear of a continued inferior status in the Canadian federal system.[54]

MCMILLAN REPORT ON INTEGRATION

In identifying the many challenges facing the premiers in these times of economic and political uncertainty, the McMillan report begins by arguing,

> Old attitudes die hard. Old institutions live on. Mythologies become perpetuated. In fact, Maritime cooperation is a fragile instrument. Maritime policy coordination, while real in a number of basic areas, remains a distant goal on the most important issue — industrial development. Parochialism, a short term horizon, lack of vision, institutional inadequacies and federal/provincial squabbling — all these factors and many others have played a role in reducing the potential for a visionary plan of action for the Maritime Provinces. Dependence on Ottawa, parochial rivalries and lack of coordinated leadership — these are the problems challenging the Maritime region in a tough new global environment. This new challenge is historic, nothing less than the long-term diversification of the Atlantic economy going into the next century.[55]

McMillan endorses fully the view that the premiers must put aside their differences, and work together solving common problems. Focussing attention on the changes taking place in the larger federal system, the McMillan report rejects the status quo as an option and warns that the region is going to have to get used to the fact that Ottawa can no longer afford to subsidize the extra costs associated with province building in the region. Playing upon the fears of the premiers, the McMillan report concludes that it is now time to overcome the long history of provincialism in the region and to work together constructing a more productive and competitive industrial economy.

To rally support for a new approach to industrial development in the region, McMillan points out that "there is not overwhelming evidence for a strong federal desire to make Atlantic Canada a focus of policy priorities."[56] McMillan concludes that whether the premiers like it or not, conditions have changed to such a degree that they no longer have the option of going it alone. It is argued in these times of economic and political uncertainty that there is much more at stake than just defending the territorial and political interests of the governments involved.

However, the McMillan report is unique in other ways. To begin, the study does not see political union as a viable option. There are a couple of factors that likely influenced this change. First, as a result of the experience of the 1970s and the past refusal of the premiers to endorse such a strategy, McMillan was in a better position to predict how the premiers would likely respond to the idea in the 1990s. As the author concluded, "Throughout the region, the Council has suffered from the complex that it was the bastard child of Maritime Unionists, those who aspired to a unitary vision of the Maritimes. Cursory examination of attitudes and government structures, both in the Maritimes and large jurisdictions like Ontario and Quebec, illustrates quite readily that such a unitary vision is totally unrealistic."[57]

A second factor that may have influenced this change in direction is the fact that while the 1970 union study was established to examine the general benefits of economic and political union, the task outlined for McMillan was much more specific. McMillan was hired by the premiers to focus specifically on the CMP and the challenges facing the region in the 1990s. Since the primary purpose of the report was to review the history of the CMP and to offer new insights and suggestions for improving the system of interprovincial cooperation, much of the information gathered came directly from the people who were or had worked with the CMP. As a consequence, it is likely that this information influenced both the assumptions and final recommendations of the report. As a result of past experience, it appears the maritime premiers in establishing the McMillan study deliberately went out of their way to ensure that political union was not the principal focus.[58] This was important because it provided an opportunity for the premiers to structure the debate based on their territorial and political interests.

McMillan's study was different in other ways. While McMillan begins by stating that for many Canadians "the Maritimes are a fractious, parochial economic backwater,"[59] he challenges the assumption that the premiers in the region are any more parochial or short-sighted than politicians elsewhere. Instead, the author concludes that, "These issues are not idle political concerns. They point to the historical basis of provincial equality, the legitimate suspicion of 'solutions' imposed from the outside, the understandable fear of creeping 'outsidism' that provinces will lose their capacity to guide their own future. The model of cooperation proposed in this study is not one of extremes. Maritime Union is a non-starter."[60]

For McMillan, it was natural that the premiers responded the way they did to the threat posed by outsiders and he goes out of his way to explain why the premiers felt they had the duty and obligation to resist changes which threatened existing social and economic institutions and their control over the development process. In line with his more pragmatic view of province building, McMillan fully recognizes and respects the political and territorial ambitions of the governments in the region. Rather than blaming the premiers for past failures, he encourages them to accept the need to work together building a more efficient industrial base. On the other hand, much like the maritime union study, McMillan sees the need to create a body of experts to "help the Premiers establish a collective strategic agenda ... particularly in the area of industrial development."[61] It is a remarkable coincidence that McMillan reintroduces the idea of establishing a regional commission or advisory board staffed by experts to oversee the project. Again, it appears that experts seek to take power away from politicians and hand it over to the unelected. But as before, it will be up to the premiers to determine whether such a policy is acceptable.

A major difference between the 1970 report and McMillan's study has to do with the recommendation to include Newfoundland in any new regional experiment. Acknowledging the fact that the four Atlantic provinces share many similarities and common economic problems, McMillan argues that a revamped council should include Newfoundland. With the new interest shown by Premier Clyde Wells in Atlantic cooperation, as evidenced in his participation in the fall 1989 meeting of the council and the decision to rejoin APEC, McMillan concludes it is time to seize the opportunity to eliminate trade barriers and to develop a more integrated approach to economic planning in Atlantic Canada. In the end, McMillan hopes that by fully recognizing the needs of the provincial governments to control the development process in the Atlantic region, the premiers will respond by working together to eliminate unproductive trade barriers and by erecting a more efficient and prosperous industrial-based economy in the region. Of course, whether this is possible or not under the current political system is still open to question.

THE RESPONSE OF THE PREMIERS

The premiers have responded to the call for a new vision for Atlantic Canada by again endorsing the need for regional cooperation. As if by instinct, the premiers have indicated that they are more determined than ever to the cause of eliminating unproductive trade barriers in the region and to working together on common economic problems. Acknowledging past failures, the premiers have adopted the view that "The forces and momentum of provincialism are formidable. Consensus comes slowly in the absence of a unifying crisis."[62]

At the same time, however, the premiers appear more determined than ever that provincialism must survive. Despite the times of great uncertainty and the commitment to change, the premiers have again clearly rejected the idea of political union. In fact, using the McMillan report to defend their political and territorial integrity, the premiers are more determined than ever that they themselves will be fully responsible for designing any new regional experiment in regional development. So far, there has been no endorsement of the idea of establishing a commission or advisory board to develop a common plan for the region. The premiers appear to have again seized control over the latest experiment in interprovincial cooperation.

While it is too early to predict whether the recent experiment will be more successful than the 1970 version, the premiers appear more committed than ever to at least eliminating interprovincial trade barriers in the region. Whether the premiers are fighting a determined holding action against further attacks on their territorial integrity is still uncertain, but there is much evidence to support the claim that the premiers are again attempting to seize control of the issue and they are more determined than ever that provincialism must survive in the region. The fact that the Newfoundland government has recently rejected a regional approach to fisheries management and are currently developing a provincial plan for the economy add credence to the thesis that region building will not come easy.[63]

On the other hand, several important initiatives have been introduced within the past year as the premiers attempt to provide a new vision for the region.[64] It is important to note that immediately following the release of the McMillan report, the maritime premiers decided that maritime economic union should be discussed first. Perhaps the most important development was the decision to sponsor a forum consisting of the maritime premiers and forty-six of their cabinet ministers on maritime economic union. The forum was organized in an attempt to ensure that the maritime governments had an opportunity to meet to discuss common economic problems and to come up with new ways for facilitating economic cooperation. The highlight of these meetings was an agreement on a common procurement policy for the Maritimes. The agreement provided that "any Maritime company can tender equally on government purchases of goods over $25,000, designated services over $50,000, and construction contracts over $100,000."[65] In addition, the maritime premiers agreed to work together in developing common policies in thirty other policy fields. While it is too early to know what the end result will be, the premiers have admitted that change will take time. But, of course, this holding action provides the premiers with much needed flexibility, and provides the opportunity to gain control over any new experiment in regional cooperation. While both the Newfoundland and federal governments were granted observer status at these early meetings, initially the primary focus was maritime economic union.

However, with the recent announcement that the Wells government now supports the idea of eliminating local preference policy and has endorsed the 1989 maritime procurement agreement, it appears that the premiers are now more committed than ever to eliminating trade barriers within the entire Atlantic region. The new agreement will be phased in over a three-year period, and will eliminate local preference tendering for government services and goods by December 1993.

With opposition from both labour and business groups, it was certainly not an easy decision for the Newfoundland government to make.[66] On the other hand, Premier Wells appears to be confident that the idea can be sold to the voters. Focussing on the Canada-US Free Trade Agreement, the recent federal constitutional proposals and the need to lower government expenditures, the premier has gone out of his way to defend the new policy. Given the pressure to eliminate interprovincial trade barriers in the country, it is unlikely this decision will be reversed. After all, it appears the whole country is moving in this direction anyway. In fact, when we consider the changes taking place in the global economy, and in North America generally, it would be difficult to view the commitment to reducing interprovincial trade barriers in the Atlantic region as a radical move.

There is little question that while Atlantic premiers are motivated by a common desire to improve economic conditions in the region, they are also naturally suspicious of any threat to their territorial jurisdictional powers. In the end, the final decision on region building in Atlantic Canada will likely be determined in the next round of constitutional talks. If the current system survives, and the principle of provincial equality remains, it is likely that province building will survive in the region.

Already there are signs that the Atlantic premiers disagree on the benefits of adopting a regional approach to solving the economic and constitutional problems of the country. Premier Wells, in particular, has indicated that, "I am not sure that achieving a common constitutional position for the Atlantic provinces is in itself necessarily a desirable end. We ought to be focussing on a national consensus in a national forum — always thinking in a national context rather than a provincial or even a regional context like the Atlantic provinces."[67] The premier of Newfoundland remains a strong proponent of an integrated national economy and for the need to strengthen the role of the national government in the area of economic development.

Of particular concern to Premier Wells is the fear that regional solutions may actually create further barriers to trade. He suggests his biggest concern is not the idea of dismantling trade barriers. Quite the contrary, he fully endorses the need for economic reform. However, he is concerned that Atlantic economic union might restrict trade within the larger federal system and send out the wrong kind of message to other regions. As a consequence, Premier Wells wants to ensure that the concept of Atlantic economic union does not in any way threaten effective economic decision making at the national level.[68] Premier Wells is a strong proponent of the need for national rather than regional or provincial solutions for the problem of regional disparity. This is an issue which needs to be investigated further, and this helps to explain why Premier Wells has concerns about moving too quickly in the direction of regional integration.

CONCLUSION

Whether or not economic and/or full political integration would create new industrial opportunities in Atlantic Canada remains a mystery, and few people, let alone scholars, would agree on the potential benefits of Atlantic union. Yet it is clear that there are a couple of conclusions that can be drawn by examining past efforts to redraw boundaries in the region. First, the concept of Atlantic integration poses a threat to province-building traditions in the region, and as a consequence, has naturally been viewed by many provincial government elites in the region as a threat to their territorial and jurisdictional powers. The past history of conflict over Atlantic/maritime union has featured an ongoing power struggle between Ottawa, the Atlantic premiers, and a group of planners over the need to redraw boundaries. Basic questions about territorial integrity and state initiative have been raised by Cairns and other state-centred theorists, and the history of struggle over Atlantic/maritime union provides clear evidence that institutional and territorial factors are important for explaining the survival of provincial governments in Atlantic Canada over time. The premiers have consistently refused to establish any structures which would limit their ability to control the public agenda, and they have always responded to the threat posed by Ottawa and a group of orthodox thinkers by exploiting their constitutional powers to the fullest in order to gain control over any new experiment in intergovernmental cooperation. Unless the constitutional system is changed, it is likely any new experiment in interprovincial cooperation will be shaped to reflect the territorial and jurisdictional needs of the Atlantic premiers.

Second, the history of struggle over region building and the goal of establishing a common industrial strategy for Atlantic Canada challenges the thesis that the region is a conservative monolith and that patterns of economic and political experience are common in the region. Given the many differences in governing philosophy, institutional and economic experience, and the fact that these differences have become embedded within society, the idea of developing a common approach to region building faces a number of obstacles. Certainly it is possible that the premiers themselves could play a crucial role in pushing the region in a common direction, but for this to occur they would have to ignore the pressures inherent in a highly competitive federal system. Given these pressures, it is clear that developing a common vision for the region will not be easy. But this is also true for all provinces in the country since province-building structures naturally inhibit region building. In the final analysis, region building will not likely occur in Atlantic Canada or elsewhere unless the entire constitutional system is restructured. The propensity to pursue provincial initiatives and to defend provincial powers will remain as long as province-building structures and traditions survive.

Notes

The research for this paper was made possible by financial assistance from the Institute of Social Research, Memorial University of Newfoundland.

1. Alan Cairns, *Constitution, Government, and Society in Canada* (Toronto: McClelland and Stewart, 1986), especially chapters 4, 5, 6.

2. For details and examples see P.A. Buckner (ed.), *Teaching Maritime Politics* (Fredericton: Acadiensis Press, 1986); Peter Boswell, "The Atlantic Provinces," in M. Whittington and Glen Williams, eds., *Canadian Politics in the 1990s* (Scarborough, Ontario: Nelson Canada, 1990); and E. Forbes, *Challenging the Regional Stereotypes* (Fredericton, New Brunswick: Acadiensis Press, 1989).

3. Cairns, *Constitution, Government, and Society in Canada.*

4. See Alan Cairns, "The Governments and Societies of Canadian Federalism," in Cairns, *Constitution, Government and Society in Canada*, 141-70.

5. Ibid., 143.

6. Ibid., 150.

7. For details on such an approach to state-expansion see ibid., particularly chapters 4, 5 and 6.

8. For examples see Keith Banting, *The State and Economic Interests* (Toronto: University of Toronto Press, 1986); and Michael M. Atkinson and William D. Coleman, *The State, Business, and Industrial Change in Canada* (Toronto: University of Toronto Press, 1989).

9. See Alan Cairns, "The Embedded State: State-Society Relations in Canada," in Keith Banting, *State and Society: Canada in Comparative Perspective* (Toronto: University of Toronto Press, 1986), 53-83.

10. Ibid., 57.

11. Ibid., 83.

12. Newfoundland and Labrador. *Report of the Royal Commission on Employment and Unemployment* (St. John's: Queen's Printer, 1986), 42.

13. Ibid., 40.

14. See Boswell, "The Atlantic Provinces," 120.

15. Much of the information in this paragraph came from interviews conducted by the author.

16. Rand Dyck, *Provincial Politics in Canada* (Scarborough, Ontario: Prentice Hall Canada, 1986), 103.

17. Paul Brown, "The Political Culture of Nova Scotia: An Historical-Cultural Analysis," paper presented at the annual meetings of the Canadian Political Science Association, Halifax, Nova Scotia, May 1981, 11.

18. Provincial Archives, University of New Brunswick (PAUNB), Janet Toole, Interview with Fred Drummie, February 1987, pp. 63, 67.

19. Cairns, "The Embedded State," 81.

20. For a more complete discussion on these experiments in regional cooperation see Council of Maritime Premiers, *Twenty Years of Partnership* (Halifax: Council of Maritime Premiers, November 1989), 9-11.

21. For details on APEC see Anthony Careless, *Initiative and Response* (Montreal/Kingston: McGill-Queen's University Press, 1977), 30-31, 37, 111, 117-18.

22. Janine Brodie, *The Political Economy of Canadian Regionalism* (Toronto: Harcourt Brace Jovanovich, 1990), 169.

23. *Twenty Years of Partnership*, 9.

24. Careless, *Initiative and Response*, 33.

25. Based on interviews conducted by the author.

26. See Careless, *Initiative and Response*, 187.

27. Based on interviews conducted by the author.

28. Parizival Copes, *The Resettlement of Fishing Communities in Newfoundland* (Ottawa: Canadian Council on Rural Development, 1972), 25.

29. New Brunswick, *Royal Commission on Finance and Municipal Taxation in New Brunswick* (Fredericton: Queen's Printer, 1963).

30. For an assessment of these differences see PAUNB, Janet Toole, Interview with Louis Robichaud, 7 June 1988.

31. For details see Della Stanley, *Louis Robichaud: A Decade of Power* (Halifax: Nimbus Publishing, 1984), 124.

32. *Royal Commission on Finance and Municipal Taxation in New Brunswick*, x.

33. See *Twenty Years of Partnership*, 10.

34. See *Newfoundland: From Dependency to Self-Reliance* (Ottawa: Economic Council of Canada, 1980), 20.

35. Newfoundland and Labrador, *Royal Commission on Municipal Government in Newfoundland and Labrador* (St. John's: Queen's Printer, 1974), 2.

36. Ibid., 138.

37. Fred Drummie, John Deutsch, John Graham, and J.F. O'Sullivan participated in both projects.

38. For further details see Stephen Tomblin, "The Council of Maritime Premiers and the Battle for Territorial Integrity," *Journal of Canadian Studies* 26, no. 1. (Spring 1991): 105-7.

39. For details see PAUNB, Janet Toole, Interview with Robert Stanfield, January 1988.

40. David Cameron, "The Report on Maritime Union," *Canadian Public Administration* 15, no. 1 (Spring 1972), 172.

41. See Alexander B. Campbell, Gerald A. Regan, and Richard B. Hatfield, "The Move Toward Maritime Integration and the Role of the Council of Maritime Premiers," *Canadian Public Administration* 15, no. 4 (Winter 1972): 592.

42. For further details see Tomblin, "The Council of Maritime Premiers and the Battle for Territorial Integrity."

43. Press Release, 22nd Session of the Council of Maritime Premiers, Charlottetown, PEI, 25-26 May 1976.

44. For details see J.D. House, *The Challenge of Oil* (St. John's: Institute of Social and Economic Research, Memorial University of Newfoundland, 1985); and J.D. House "The Mouse that Roars: New Directions in Canadian Political Economy — the Case of Newfoundland," in R.J. Brym, *Regionalism in Canada* (Toronto: Irwin, 1986).

45. For further information see Newfoundland and Labrador, *The Social and Economic Development of Rural Newfoundland and Labrador, 1971 to 1981* (St. John's: Department of Rural, Agricultural and Northern Development, 1983).

46. Based on interviews.

47. See Nova Scotia, *Royal Commission on Education, Public Services and Provincial Municipal Relations* (Halifax: Queen's Printer, 1974).

48. Dyck, *Provincial Politics in Canada*, 106.

49. Based on interviews with several officials in the Nova Scotia government.

50. Based on interviews.

51. For further details see Elliot Feldman and Jerome Milch, "Coordination or Control?" in Lionel D. Feldman, ed., *Politics and Governments of Urban Canada: Selected Readings*, Fourth Edition (Toronto: Methuen, 1981); J. Atcheson, D. Cameron, D. Vardy, *Regional and Urban Policy in Canada* (Ottawa: Economic Council of Canada, 1974); and Lloyd Axworthy, "The Housing Task Force: A Case Study," in G. Bruce Doern and Peter Aucoin, eds., *The Structures of Policy-Making in Canada* (Toronto: Macmillan, 1974).

52. Donald Savoie, *Regional Economic Development* (Toronto: University of Toronto Press, 1986), 55.

53. See *Newfoundland: From Dependency to Self-Reliance*, 20.

54. See *Standing Up To The Future: The Maritimes in the 1990s* (Halifax: Council of Maritime Premiers, 1989).

55. Ibid., 1.

56. Ibid., 3.

57. Ibid., 6.

58. Based on interviews.

59. *Standing Up To The Future*, 1.

60. Ibid., 16.

61. Ibid., 13.

62. *Twenty Years of Partnership*, 5.

63. For details see *St. John's Evening Telegram*, 1, 2, 3 December 1991.

64. For highlights see Press Release, 81st Session of the Council of Maritime Premiers, Moncton, New Brunswick, 17-18 June 1991.

65. Ibid., 2.

66. For further discussion see *St. John's Evening Telegram*, 30, 31 October and 2 November 1991.

67. Press Release, The Conference of the Atlantic Premiers, Sydney, Nova Scotia, 31 May 1991.

68. Based on interviews.

12

Regionalism and the Acadian Community: Problems and Prospects

Léon Thériault

INTRODUCTION

The Acadians of the maritime provinces are much involved in regional and constitutional issues. They constitute about 29 percent of the francophone population outside Quebec. Distinct not only from Quebecers but also from other French-Canadians, the Acadians consider themselves a "people," though of course with a smaller constitutional agenda than the Quebecers.

This paper aims at explaining the specificity of the Acadians, at least insofar as they see it themselves. It also intends to show why and how the Acadians of New Brunswick view themselves as somewhat different even from other Acadians. Finally, since constitutional questions and regional issues such as maritime union are frequently debated among Acadians, this paper will try to explain the Acadian points of view.

French Canada is far from being one unit, and that diversity will be apparent throughout this paper: "Acadians," "Quebecers," "French-Canadians outside Quebec," these names are not mere expressions of the same thing; on the contrary, that terminology bears witness to basic differences. How reconcilable these differences are, only the future will tell.

THE ACADIANS: A DISTINCT PEOPLE

Though it is not my purpose here to present an historical account of the Acadians of the Maritimes, it is important first to draw upon history in order to better understand their specificity, because the Acadians, like Quebecers, for example, have developed an "historical conscience" which is an integral part of their identity. I admit it is difficult to define what an historical conscience is, but by and large it is an awareness that certain major events and situations have, over the years, shaped one's society and rendered it distinct from other communities. What is certain, is that the Acadians do refer to what they consider their particular historical experience. And though one could question the relevance of the historical facts supporting such a vision, it could be argued that more important than the facts and the situations themselves, is the *perception* a given community has of its past.

The first historical point the Acadians like to stress is that their community was the first permanent European settlement in North America — it was founded three years before Jamestown, Virginia, and four years before Quebec. Indeed, the Acadian settlement goes back to 1604.

A second point of historical reference is that the Acadian population draws its origin from men and women who arrived in the maritime provinces well before the mid-1700s. There were newcomers, of course, after the 1760s, but far less numerous than the first settlers.

Thirdly, these French immigrants came primarily from central-western France, in what was formerly the Poitou province, whereas the Quebec population draws its origin from all over France, particularly the regions north of the Loire valley. This accounts for the differences in vocabulary, grammar and folklore, when comparing Acadian and Quebec heritages. Acadians have more words relating to the sea, for example. They will say *amarrer* [a marine term] *ses souliers* ["to tie one's shoes"] instead of *attacher ses souliers*. Cut off from the evolution of French to a certain degree, their language has also kept old grammatical expressions. They still say *si que* ["if"] instead of *si*; *ils travaillont* [they work], instead of *ils travaillent*, like it was spoken in the Poitou region three hundred years ago.

A fourth element would be that the Acadians have had to rely upon themselves for a long time, even when France controlled the Maritimes. From 1608 on, France was more interested in its colony of the Saint Lawrence than in Acadia. New villages were founded solely through the initiative of the Acadians; they developed ways to survive even though it meant illegal trading with the American colonies to the south, for example.

Finally, the Acadians have struggled through major crises. In 1713, mainland Nova Scotia became British and by the Treaty of Paris of 1763, the rest of the Maritimes became British. But before that, Acadia had been attacked nine times and changed hands four times. In the process, some parts of it had been under British control for several years at a time. Acadia, being adjacent to the New England colonies, always suffered the full effects of war and peace. And especially, it must be remembered that the Maritimes did not become "British" until the Acadians were deported from the region between 1755 and 1762.

In a sense, their society was decapitated in the 1750s. Out of the approximately 15,000 Acadians in 1755, about one-third escaped and remained hidden in the woods; one-third fled to what is now Quebec, and one-third were captured and sent either to the American colonies, to Britain, to France or kept in local jails.

From this checkered historical experience, especially the long history of their settlement in the Maritimes, the Acadians generally draw the conclusion that the term "immigrants" does not quite apply to them in the same fashion as it applies to other groups that followed. More precisely, the Acadians consider themselves as "founders."

After the 1760s, a new Acadia was refounded. Some of the Acadians came back, others came out of the woods. Now though, their situation was entirely different. They were on their own, as they did not have the support of a friendly government for the preservation of their culture. They were, suddenly, a minority. The official language was English everywhere. And they had had to settle far away from their original villages which, in the mean time, had been occupied by British immigrants.

For English-speaking Maritimers, on the contrary, the period between 1763 and 1867 is the era which forged their identity. It is during that time, more than in any other period, that the distinctive character of Nova Scotia took shape, for example.

The historical experience of the Acadians, after the British conquest, is also very different from Quebec's — when Quebec was conquered by the British, its citizens were allowed to remain in the province and their institutions and language were guaranteed. Up to the 1960s, the Acadians progressed largely through their own endeavours. Since they considered themselves a people, distinct even from the "Québécois," they adopted their own national symbols: a distinct flag, a distinct national holiday, a distinct national anthem, and a distinct national motto, all of which were adopted in the 1880s. They founded academies, universities, newspapers, hospitals, and a host of cultural organizations, most of the time without much government support. Even a pressure group, the National Society of the Acadians, was formed in 1881. Just the field of literature provides a fine argument for the specificity of the Acadians — forty years ago, for example, it was a matter of debate as to whether or not there was such a thing as an "Acadian" literature; not now.

The Acadians of New Brunswick: Somewhat Distinct from Other Acadians

There are, of course, Acadians in all four Atlantic provinces; but the Acadians of New Brunswick stand out as the most dynamic and the best equipped francophone community outside Quebec. The law of numbers, primarily, explains that. New Brunswick is 33 percent French, while Prince Edward Island, Nova Scotia and Newfoundland are respectively 5 percent, 4 percent and 0.5 percent French. Furthermore, the Acadians of New Brunswick represent about 85 percent of all francophones within the Atlantic provinces. Consequently, the Acadians of New Brunswick tend to view themselves not only as different from French-Canadians in Ontario and western Canada, but different also from Acadians in the other Atlantic provinces. It is interesting to note, too, that Franco-Ontarians and New Brunswick's Acadians account for 75 percent of all French-Canadians outside Quebec.

Because of their demographic strength, the Acadians of New Brunswick enjoy unique cultural guarantees and they have built French institutions, the scope of which exist nowhere else in French Canada outside Quebec.

New Brunswick is the only real bilingual province in Canada, having become officially bilingual in 1969. Though the Acadians are not necessarily happy with the day-to-day application of the Official Languages Act, they do have that legal protection which they successfuly invoke on certain occasions. Furthermore, in 1981, New Brunswick passed a law proclaiming the equality of status for the two linguistic communities within New Brunswick ("Bill 88"). That is also unique in Canada.

At the federal level, the Acadians of New Brunswick, like all Canadians, enjoy the linguistic guarantees contained both in the federal Official Languages Act and in the Charter of Rights and Freedoms. Here again, there is an important distinction regarding the Acadian community of New Brunswick — the major clauses of the provincial law on official languages have been enshrined in the charter, hence an additional guarantee. As for the equality provisions contained in Bill 88, the Acadians would like to enshrine them into the charter and they are now engaged in that political process.

"Equality" is more and more being translated into "administrative duality" and the latter has become a household expression within the Acadian community of New Brunswick. The best example is the Department of Education which has two completely separate administrations for francophones and anglophones, under a single minister. That means that there are two school maps in New Brunswick: one for the anglophones, one for the francophones. There are no bilingual schools nor bilingual school districts in the province; only unilingual French schools and districts, alongside unilingual English schools and districts. In Moncton, for example, there are two school districts, one for the French, one for the English-speaking. Voters have to decide for which school board they wish to vote and they cast their ballots for the candidates of only one board. That system, which goes back to the 1970s, works very well. It means that each group controls its school matters.

The association of New Brunswick teachers itself is a federation: one fran- cophone branch, one anglophone branch, each with its separate buildings and staff. Of course, New Brunswick has its unilingual community colleges (French and English), its unilingual universities (one French and three English-speaking). Nowhere else in Canada does one find such a duality in public schools.

The Society of New Brunswick Acadians would like to further extend the concept of administrative duality to other fields. Already, the Acadians enjoy, for example, their own credit union federation, their own association of municipalities, their own association of farmers, and their own association of school commissioners. Even one francophone region of northeast New Brunswick has lately been asking for the official status of "administrative region" within the province.

In the three other Atlantic provinces, there is no such talk of duality, the law of numbers being what it is; instead, those francophones must still work to obtain their French schools.

The Challenge of the Last Three Decades

One must admit that the situation has evolved dramatically in the last thirty years or so, not only in Canada as a whole but in New Brunswick in particular.

From the 1960s on, the government of New Brunswick, like all governments in Canada, has been intervening more and more in the daily lives of people. It could be argued that most of that intervention has been for the well-being of the citizens. For example, in New Brunswick, it has meant the control, by the government, of Acadian colleges and universities which were, before then, privately administered, and without much government support. It has also meant government control of private French hospitals, centralization of matters related to schools as well as a better and more equitable funding of these schools.

That fundamental reorientation of the role of the provincial government then brought about two dramatic changes, as far as the Acadians are concerned — the power shifted to Fredericton and their society became more secularized, as the clergy lost its control over a vast array of institutions. In other words, a new dimension manifested itself, and it is the *political* dimension of the struggle of the Acadians, of their "existence." At least the Acadians of New Brunswick see it that way. Before the 1960s, the Acadians interpreted their society primarily in terms of cultural and language rights. Now, they wanted to share power; they wanted to establish a new partnership, a new "social contract," with the anglophone community. It is in that context, for example, that the Acadians asked for duality within the Department of Education. Elsewhere outside Quebec, French-Canadians still tend to view their problems largely in terms of culture and language. It is not so in Acadian New Brunswick.

Another important factor in the recent evolution of Acadia, especially concerning French New Brunswick, has been an increased awareness that there is such a thing as the *francophonie*. There are about thirty countries around the world that officially use French at some level or another. These countries have formed various associations and the Acadians have asked for a representation, which they have obtained, primarily through the government of New Brunswick. That opening to the francophone world at large is actually further promoted through a host of private associations. That, of course, further sets apart The Acadian community from the other francophone communities outside Quebec.

ACADIANS *VIS-À-VIS* ATLANTIC CANADA, QUEBECERS AND FRANCOPHONES OUTSIDE QUEBEC: SOME REGIONAL AND CONSTITUTIONAL ISSUES

Since this conference addresses the issue of regions within the Canadian constitutional framework, I would like now to turn my attention to that fundamental aspect of the question.

There are four Atlantic provinces, three maritime provinces. They belong in fact to two relatively different concepts and it is only recently that New-foundland and the rest of the Atlantic provinces have started to cooperate at the provincial level. Although the first Atlantic Premiers Conference was held in 1956 and they met at least once a year until 1970, that kind of cooperation then decreased, only to resume in the last two years.

It is a somewhat different story for the three maritime provinces themselves. The extent and the limitations of their cooperation, starting especially in 1971, with the creation of the Council of Maritime Premiers has been outlined by other speakers. It remains to be seen whether or not the three maritime provinces have now forged a solidarity strong enough to create a common maritime identity. All Maritimers, French- and English-speaking, have provincial loyalties that are still very strong and valued as such. I would venture to say that most of the efforts aimed at greater cooperation have probably had more to do with economic problems than with a sentiment of common belonging. But then again, I may be wrong, because it could be argued that shared problems aptly constitute major elements of a common identity.

Be it as it may, the three maritime provinces, joined to a certain degree by Newfoundland, are now involved in a process that points towards greater economic integration and greater political cooperation. It is still doubtful, though, that they will present a common front in constitutional debates.

In the context of maritime union, or simply in the context of greater coopera-tion between the three provinces, would the Acadians of the Maritimes not con-stitute an ingredient favourable to new directions? After all, are there not Acadians in all three provinces? Would they not wish, then, more formal links, since they consider themselves a same people? Would they not value, at the very least, the idea of "region" and be sympathetic to a common approach to the redefinition of Canada?

The answers to these questions are not evident. The problem with maritime union, as far as the Acadians of New Brunswick are concerned, lies in the fact that while they represent 33 percent in that province, they would be a mere 16 percent in the new greater province. Also, the rate of assimilation is running very high in Prince Edward Island and Nova Scotia. Would the Acadians be able to conserve and develop their collective tools in a greater province, given the dif-ficulties they encounter periodically in New Brunswick where they represent one-third of the population? It is not surprising, then, that the Acadians of New Brunswick tend to be negative towards maritime union, while the Acadians of the two other provinces, on the contrary, tend to support the idea. It is almost certain though, that if Quebec seceded from Canada, this could create compell-ing circumstances in favour of the union. At the moment, the question is — would the maritime provinces be stronger speaking with one voice in a group of eight provinces or speaking with three voices in a group of ten?

An important factor here is that the Acadians of New Brunswick have begun to consider themselves a majority within New Brunswick, not in numbers, but in a sociological sense. They argue that there are two "majorities" in New Brunswick, the Acadians and the anglophones. And some would say that Bill 88 adds credibility to that interpretation. It would certainly be difficult for Acadians to argue along that same line in the eventuality of maritime union.

The Acadians of New Brunswick are among those, within French Canada, who best understand Quebec. Their proximity to the province of Quebec, the fact they share the same language, and the fact that Quebecers have been at the origin of many Acadian institutions (colleges, newspapers, hospitals, etc.) all contribute to a certain sympathy towards Quebec. Thousands of Quebecers are of Acadian origin and quite a few Acadian families from the Maritimes have settled in Quebec since the 1950s and even before. Quebecers though, control their own government, and the Acadians of New Brunswick do not, and that accounts for a big difference in the way they perceive one another.

What about the French-Canadians outside Quebec, including the Acadians from the Maritimes? Do they speak with one voice? Sometimes yes, sometimes no. True, the "Federation of Francophone and Acadian Communities in Canada" is there to look after questions shared by all French-Canadians outside Quebec. It is important to note that the Acadians of New Brunswick especially, are rather jealous of their own prerogatives. It can be said that, generally, they rely more on their own provincial government than do other French-Canadians; they are rather inclined to knock at Ottawa's door for help and understanding. In the spring of 1991, the Acadians of New Brunswick even succeeded in having the words "Acadian communities" included in the official name of their pan-Canadian federation.

The name change is more than symbolic. For the Acadians, it means the recognition of two major ideas. First, the idea that the Acadians constitute a distinct people, distinct even from French-Quebecers and French-Canadians elsewhere. Second, the idea that the Acadians of New Brunswick have greater human and material resources at their disposal, hence, greater possibilities of development. One group (French-Canadians outside Quebec) speaks in terms of language and culture, the other (New Brunswick Acadians) in terms of shared power within their own province. To sum it up, it means that the Acadians are indeed "distinct."

That being said, the future of French-Canadians outside Quebec, even of New Brunswick Acadians, is quite uncertain. Only 60 percent of the francophone population outside Quebec speaks French at home as their sole language: 58 percent in Nova Scotia, 48 percent in Prince Edward Island, 58 percent in Newfoundland; but 88 percent French New Brunswickers still speak French only at home. For the other provinces, the figures are: 58 percent in Ontario, 37 percent in the prairie provinces and 23 percent in British Columbia. (Of course, those percentages would be higher if one was to take into account figures relating to francophones using French and another language.) So, as some have said, the possibility is that, eventually, the problem of bilingualism wil resolve itself naturally, there being no francophones to request it. These are times of uncertainty for the French culture outside Quebec. How many of our grandchildren will still be able to speak French? Some problems are indeed difficult, if not impossible, to solve. I will mention only two:

> 1. Exogamy — marriages outside one's linguistic cultural group now account for about one-third of francophone marriages outside Quebec. In those marriages, 88 percent of the male spouses and 82 percent of the female spouses assimilate to the English-speaking community. Is it an element of consolation that in French New Brunswick, these marriages account for only 10 percent of marriages and that the French spouses assimilate to a lesser degree?

> 2. Aging affects much of the francophone population. Outside Quebec, the francophones in the 0-20 years bracket represent only 23 percent of the francophone population, while that age group accounts for 32 percent of the English-speaking population. Only in New Brunswick and in Quebec is there an age structure comparable to that of English Canada. Lower birth rates, but especially linguistic transfers, explain that phenomenon.

Regarding Quebec's requests for a redefined federalism, French-Canadians outside Quebec are rather ambivalent. On the one hand, they generally agree that the only francophone government in North America should have all the tools it needs to further its development in French. They believe in a "distinct society" clause for Quebec. On the other hand, they are concerned that such a federalism invites a decentralization of powers. Since it is Ottawa, rather than the provinces, that has been sympathetic to them in the past, the French-Canadian community outside Quebec has reason to look at the Quebec proposals with a certain apprehension. Here again, the Acadian community of New Brunswick would be less fearful.

One way to tackle the issue and allay those fears, would be for the provinces themselves to guarantee certain fundamental linguistic and cultural rights. The range of those rights could vary, of course, from province to province, given the numerical importance of the francophone community in question.

For the Acadians of New Brunswick, the situation is of course markedly different — there are already provincial laws that guarantee fundamental rights. Consequently, the Acadians of New Brunswick would probably be more inclined to accept a degree of decentralization that would be unthinkable to other French-Canadians outside Quebec. What is certain is that Acadians of New Brunswick and other French-Canadians outside Quebec have disagreed more than once in the recent past.

CONCLUSION

What, then, of the so-called "maritime identity," from an Acadian point of view? To a certain degree, such an identity exists, and it is founded on similarities in our economies, in our natural resources, in our history, even in our traditions. As I mentioned earlier, all three provinces have a francophone community, the vast majority of which comes from the same Acadian stock. To a degree, there is even an Atlantic regional identity which rests on the same elements mentioned above, but Maritimers have a lot more in common among themselves than they have with Newfoundland. Maritimers seldom visit Newfoundland, they seldom work there, while we can find more New Brunswickers, Nova Scotians and Islanders working and visiting in all three maritime provinces. Speaking of regional identity, Newfoundland could probably be best compared to British Columbia: the latter province is part of the "western Canada" concept, like Newfoundland is part of Atlantic Canada. But then the "prairie region" concept excludes British Columbia — likewise, the concept of "maritime provinces" excludes Newfoundland. Maritimers, at least, would not confuse these two regional concepts.

It is possible, also, that the prairie provinces have more in common than Atlantic Canada does. Manitoba, Saskatchewan and Alberta were all formed from the Canadian North-West Territories, and are relatively recent communities, whereas the Atlantic provinces were once distinct French or British colonies, each with its own particular history, its own colonial government and institutions.

In any case, as far as the Acadians of the maritime provinces are concerned, they strive to reconcile very different aspects of the same question. They first have to address the problems of the francophone communities in Canada, and these, in turn, constitute at least three different groups: 1) the Acadians, who themselves form, as I mentioned, three distinct communities: one rather strong, in New Brunswick, the two others weaker; 2) the other francophones outside Quebec, whose strength also varies from province to province but is everywhere weaker than in New Brunswick; 3) then the Quebec francophones. The Acadians then turn their attention to Canada as a whole and they try to understand how constitutional arrangements may affect their own situation as well as the situation of others, irrespective of language issues. Like all Maritimers, for example, they remain committed to the preservation of the constitutional guarantees regarding equalization grants. Furthermore, there is always on the horizon the idea of maritime union that is being debated in one form or another. We can readily say that the Acadians are much involved in the constitutional process. However, we do know that nothing is engraved in stone and nothing should be. Even in New Brunswick, nothing much is considered sacred. Last September's provincial election brought to the fore the Confederation of Regions party (CoR). Opposed to legislated bilingualism, CoR is now the official opposition in Fredericton. It is estimated that about 30 percent of the anglophone vote went to CoR candidates. CoR and its policies will have to be reckoned with in the next four years and Premier McKenna's government will have to address the concerns of these dissatisfied New Brunswickers.

13

Balance of Power: Provincial vs. Regional Equality

J. Peter Meekison

One of the most important statements in the federal government's document, *Shaping Canada's Future Together*, is the following comment:

> Although the original distribution of Senate seats was based on the equal representation of the three *regions* of Canada at the time of Confederation — the Maritimes, Quebec and Ontario — the reality of contemporary Canadian politics is that *provinces and territories, and not regions,* are basic to our sense of community and identity.[1]

This comment, made in the context of the section on Senate reform, speaks directly to the question of provincial equality. While recognizing that regional equality was the original basis of representation in the Senate, circumstances have changed since 1867. It is argued in this paper that provincial equality is now — and should continue to be — one of the cornerstones of any new constitutional arrangement.

DEFINING EQUALITY

One of the most difficult tasks is to secure agreement on what provincial equality means in terms of the constitution. Reduced to its basic elements it means that provinces are treated alike and that the constitution recognizes their similarities or sameness. This is made very clear in Sec. 92 which opens with the following words: "In each province the legislature may exclusively make laws." There are no exceptions or differences amongst the provinces.

In addition, since the 1982 Constitution Act, provinces have had an equal say in constitutional amendments. Since federal systems are predicated on differences, the question logically arises — does similar mean identical or can there be mutually agreed differences amongst provinces? If one uses the Canadian experience as an example, there can be differences although they are not major. The constitution is filled with examples from the regulation of oleomargerine by

Newfoundland, to the language provisions of Sec. 133, to the provisions governing the division of debt and assets in 1867. What must be recognized is that every exception or deviation was negotiated and agreed to either at Confederation or when a province was admitted to Canada. In other words, similar treatment could have been sought or some other form of protection established for an individual province at the same time. It should also be acknowledged that the negotiated differences or exceptions reflected circumstances already in existence at Confederation. To this extent, maintaining or recognizing the status quo was used to establish either a level playing field or one that was seen to disadvantage another province or the federation.

There is one notable exception to the foregoing and that is the case of natural resources for the three prairie provinces. They neither owned or controlled their public domain or natural resources when they entered Confederation. The public domain, including its natural resources, was owned and controlled "by the Government of Canada for the purposes of Canada."[2] While this fact can be used to demonstrate asymmetry, I would argue that it is negative asymmetry, i.e., the differences were not mutually agreeable but unilaterally established and were seen to be a disadvantage. This reality is clearly demonstrated in the Natural Resources Transfer Agreement of 1930 with the following quotation from the agreement:

> And whereas it is desirable that Alberta should be placed in a *position of equality* with the other provinces of Confederation with respect to the control of its natural resources as from its entrance into Confederation in 1905.[3]

In short, for twenty-five years Alberta and Saskatchewan (longer for Manitoba) fought to be treated equally — not better than, but the same as, the original provinces. Paradoxically the transfer agreement did establish differences between the prairie provinces and the others simply in terms of the language of the constitutional amendment but not to the point of giving the former preferred status.

Before leaving this section I would be remiss in not stating the obvious. While provinces are more or less equal constitutionally in terms of responsibilities and authority, they are not equal in other ways. They are not equal in terms of size, population, climate, natural resources, wealth or political clout. But these differences are a result of geography and history and therefore not subject to control. They are not a result of constitutional fiats.

In summary, provincial equality has been a constitutional premise from Confederation to today. Under the constitution the provinces are treated equally.

REGIONALISM AND THE CONSTITUTION

The only reference to regionalism in the constitution is found in the provisions governing representation in the Senate. Up to 1949 the regions were balanced in the constitution. With the admission of Newfoundland the principle was modified but by no means abandoned. Moreover, I would argue that the deviation itself was relatively insignificant because the Senate by then was of little consequence politically.

While of importance in terms of balancing representation in the Senate the principle of regionalism within the constitutional framework had not been given too much attention in Canada until the Victoria amending formula surfaced in the early 1970s. From that point through to today there has been a conflict between the principles of regional and provincial equality. Closer examination would suggest that the two uses of regional representation, i.e., the one in the Senate and the other in the Victoria amending formula, are predicated on very different assumptions and have very different constitutional consequences.

Looking at representation in the Senate in 1867, Quebec, Ontario and the Maritimes each had one-third of the seats. No region dominated the others in terms of representation nor could any region veto a position advanced by the other two. Senators from each region were not expected to vote as a group in any event unless they were from the same political party:

> The principle of equality in the Senate for the three sections laid down at Quebec in 1864 simply recognized the ugly fact that there were two great gulfs which must be bridged before the provinces could be forged into a national entity. These were created, the one by the racial and religious differences which separated Quebec from its neighbours and the other by the peculiar economic interests of the Maritime provinces.[4]

What is critical here is the symbolism of regional equality, but that symbolism did not convey any special privilege to any one of the regions. That symbolism was reinforced in 1915 when the four western provinces were identified as a senate region. Equality was observed but it was regional equality. What needs to be recognized is that the principle of region and province overlapped in two instances, i.e., in Ontario and Quebec, but not in the West and in the Maritimes. Even then the two peripheral regions were equal only in terms of their aggregate representation in the Senate. There was no requirement that any region act within the Senate as a single unit under any set of circumstances. Factors other than region, such as their political party, governed their behaviour once they were appointed.

While the principle of regional representation in the Senate in 1867 originated with the recognition of the three sections, that principle was not reflected in other parts of the constitution. The House of Commons was based on representation by population. Other national institutions such as the cabinet and Supreme Court reflected regions but regional equality was not a requirement of the constitution. In the case of the cabinet, representation ultimately depended upon the number of members elected in a province as was demonstrated in both the 1979 and 1980 federal elections.[5] As far as the Supreme Court is concerned, the principle of regional equality has not been followed. There are obvious reasons for not doing so. What needs to be emphasized is that only in the composition of the Senate is there a constitutional recognition of the regional principle. This concept was extended in 1971 with the Victoria amending formula.

THE VICTORIA AMENDING FORMULA

The structure of the Victoria amending formula is fundamentally different than what one finds for the Senate. While masked in the pretext of regional equality its true purpose was to assure Quebec a veto over constitutional amendments. The wording of the formula clearly illustrates this point:

> Amendments to the Constitution of Canada may from time to time be made by Proclamation issued by the Governor General under the Great Seal of Canada when so authorized by resolutions of the Senate and House of Commons and of the Legislative Assemblies of at least a majority of the Provinces that includes:

> 1) every Province that at any time before the issue of such Proclamation had, according to any previous general census, a population of at least twenty-five per cent of the population of Canada;

> 2) at least two of the Atlantic Provinces;

> 3) at least two of the Western Provinces that have, according to the then latest general census, combined populations of at least fifty per cent of the population of all the Western Provinces.[6]

While the western and Atlantic provinces are identified, Ontario and Quebec are not specifically referred to. They fall under the category of any province which has or had 25 percent of the population. While that description applies only to the two largest provinces, the design of the formula does not reflect a regional perspective. If it had, the regions of Ontario and Quebec would (or should) have been singled out. The regional justification came afterwards. It was more a matter of *post hoc* justification. Perhaps what is most telling is the safety net, i.e., once a province achieves a 25 percent threshold it keeps a veto regardless of future demographics, a point worth noting given the fact that Quebec's population is currently only 25.4 percent of the Canadian total. The wording makes it clear that the formula was designed to accommodate Quebec, give Ontario similar treatment, and was not based on the regional premise since both a population floor and region are used in the formula. Unlike the regional requirement in the provisions governing representation in the Senate, the regional requirement in the amending formula confers specific authority on each region. Moreover, by doing so, it assumes a degree of homogeneity in both the West and Atlantic Canada that does not exist other than in geography.

Perhaps what is even more telling is the special rule for the four western provinces which required the assenting provinces to represent 50 percent of their population. Why the anomaly? Put simply, from 1969 onwards British Columbia argued it was a fifth region. Premier W.A.C. Bennett based his case on the fact that the Government of Canada recognized five economic divisions in terms of reporting statistical data.[7] Once again province and region coincided.

At the 1976 premiers' conference both British Columbia and Alberta formally indicated they could no longer support the 1971 Victoria amending formula.[8] It should be recalled that in 1971 the then governments of Alberta and British Columbia supported the Victoria amending formula. With changes in government that support disappeared. British Columbia continued to advocate a five-region approach. Alberta pursued provincial equality — no first and second class provinces, i.e., no one province regardless of size or special circumstance should have a veto which was the underlying premise of the Victoria formula.

In the ensuing negotiations on the amending formula it was the latter principle — provincial equality — which was accepted and entrenched in the amending formula adopted in 1982. Ontario and Quebec were not given preferential treatment. Under Sec. 41 of the amending formula, the unanimity section, all provinces were treated alike and received a veto for a limited number of matters. No one province was given a veto over any item whereas under the Victoria formula two provinces had vetoes over any amendment.

Regional equality first emerged in terms of balancing representation in the Senate. Later the concept was transferred to the search for an amending formula. The latter assumes a degree of homogeneity in terms of decision making at the subnational level whereas the former allocates a proportion of voting rights which are not linked to region when the votes are counted, i.e., senators are not required to vote as a regional bloc or as a provincial bloc. Applying the voting principles of the Victoria amending formula to passage of legislation in the Senate would make for interesting results.

THE TWO AMENDING FORMULAE COMPARED

Table 1 demonstrates the population distribution in Canada in 1991. Table 2 shows the combination of provinces necessary to secure an amendment under the

Table 1
Population Distribution

	Population	% Nat. Pop.
Ontario	9.8 million	36.6
Quebec	6.8 million	25.4
British Columbia	3.2 million	11.9
Alberta	2.5 million	9.3
Manitoba	1.1 million	4.1
Saskatchewan	995,000	3.7
Nova Scotia	898,000	3.4
New Brunswick	726,000	2.7
Newfoundland	572,000	2.1
Prince Edward Island	130,000	0.5
Total	26.8 million	

Victoria amending formula. It should be realized that the table shows the minimum number of provinces necessary to secure approval.

Table 2
The Victoria Formula

West		Ontario		Quebec		Atlantic		Total
BC + 1	+	1	+	1	+	2	=	6
				or				
Man., Sask., Alberta	+	1	+	1	+	2	=	7

Depending upon which combination of provinces one chooses the highest percentage of population represented is 89.3 while the lowest represents 80.2 percent.[9] In terms of reflecting the Canadian population there is no doubt that the Victoria formula is very demanding from a majoritarian perspective but the formula works only if both Ontario and Quebec agree and therein lies the problem. A hierarchy of provinces was established which undermined the principle of provincial equality and which offended Alberta among others. When a limited number of actors have a veto, as opposed to nobody or everybody the dynamics of the negotiations change dramatically regardless of the deceptively low threshhold for approval.

THE 1982 AMENDING FORMULA

Under the 1982 amending formula the number of combinations of provinces required to forge a consensus is considerably greater. There are two requirements which must be met — two-thirds of the provinces must agree and together they must represent 50 percent of the population. At the moment, this means at least

Table 3
Possible Combinations of Provinces

Case	West	Ontario	Quebec	Atlantic	Total	L (%)	H (%)
1	1	1	1	4	7	74.4	82.6
2	2	1	1	3	7	74.0	89.3
3	3	1	1	2	7	84.4	95.5
4	4	1	1	1	7	91.5	94.4
5	4	1	—	2	7	68.2	71.7
6	4	—	1	2	7	57.0	61.1
7	3	1	—	3	7	59.0	70.1
8	3	—	1	3	7	47.8	59.9
9	2	1	—	4	7	53.1	66.5
10	2	—	1	4	7	41.9	55.3

seven provinces must agree and at least either Quebec or Ontario must be amongst the seven. If either of them dissents then the role of both Alberta and British Columbia becomes far more crucial in determining the outcome.

What are the possible combinations? Table 3 outlines the ten possible mixtures of provinces. The actual number of combinations is greater as the individual provinces in each of western and Atlantic Canada columns are varied.

Approval of seven provinces is required as a minimum. In each instance a minimum of five western and Atlantic provinces combined is required. When either Quebec or Ontario is removed the number of western and Atlantic provinces climbs to six and under certain circumstances the number is increased to seven. When the two amending formulas are compared the impact of western and Atlantic Canada on securing amendments is far greater under the existing formula and the impact of Ontario and Quebec is significantly reduced.

SENATE REFORM

When the principle of provincial equality is applied to Senate reform the significance of the principle is much greater. Western and Atlantic influence increases from roughly 50 percent of the votes to 80 percent.[10] Leaving aside the question of provincial equality being accepted by Ontario or Quebec, the fact remains that the principle of provincial equality in the Senate is a powerful argument for the two outer regions to advance to redress the population imbalance or the hegemony of the two central provinces in the House of Commons.

Skeptics argue that neither Ontario nor Quebec will agree to the principle of equality when applied to the Senate. That may very well prove to be the case but it is they who should advance that argument not the other eight provinces. Either the principle is defensible on its merits as a manifestation of the federal system or it is not. When compared to the United States the spread between the largest (Ontario) and smallest (PEI) province is 75:1 (1991 data), whereas in the United States it is 61:1 (1989 data) — California to Wyoming. It is this gap which is usually presented to defend a concept other than equal. If in Canada one applies the same principles as found in the equalization formula of dropping the two extremes (Ontario and Prince Edward Island) the ratio is considerably less and is in the order of 12:1 (Quebec and Newfoundland). The danger of using extremes is that they often tend to obscure the real issue which in this instance is provincial equality.

Securing provincial equality in a reformed senate is by no means a *fait accompli*. While the idea of provincial equality has gained it is by no means automatic when it comes to restructuring our political institutions. In the federal paper and the recently released Manitoba report on the constitution the term "equitable" is used.[11] While this represents a step towards equal it is by no means the same. The concept of "equitable" is based on fairness. If one adheres to principles of federalism then fairness means one house should reflect the provinces or the land base and the other population. The counterargument is that population may need to be taken into consideration in both houses. Just as there are minimum guarantees through the Senate floor for the less populous provinces, a similar case can be made for representation in the Senate. One can only conclude that some change in Senate representation will be forthcoming with increased representation from both the West and Atlantic Canada (or parts of it). It is conceivable that something similar to what one finds in Germany will be considered as "equitable" where representation in the Bundesrat reflects both population differences and geography.

THE ASCENDENCY OF EQUALITY

The push for provincial equality began with the search for an acceptable amending formula and is reflected throughout the various discussions on the amending formula commencing in 1927 and continuing through to today. With the emergence of the Victoria formula in 1971 an alternative model based on region was the preferred approach of the federal government.[12] During the 1981 negotiations the model based on provincial equality finally won the upper hand. As a result, both principles — regional and provincial equality — were entrenched, the former in 1867 with respect to Senate representation and the latter in 1982 with respect to constitutional amendments.

With Meech Lake the principle of provincial equality once again was debated but this time in the context of a Quebec veto. When Gil Remillard outlined Quebec's five principles for constitutional reform in 1986, one of them was for a Quebec veto on constitutional amendments. Without rehashing the Meech Lake debate, the compromise eventually reached was to give *all* provinces a veto over certain amendments, a principle already found in Sec. 41 of the amending formula. My purpose here is not to defend the position but to point out that provincial equality continued to be the preferred principle rather than one which would give Quebec special privileges under the amending formula.

What is perhaps of even greater significance is the statement in the recitals preceding the Meech Lake amendments which read: "And whereas the amendment proposed in the schedule hereto also recognizes the principle of the equality of all the provinces."[13] This reference is significant because it was approved during what was known as the Quebec round of constitutional change. In the final analysis the principle of special treatment for Quebec became subordinate to the idea of provincial equality.

The Allaire report released in January 1991 contains a brief mention of a new amending formula. It says:

> The new agreement will include a new amending formula that will stipulate that any constitutional change will require the approval of a substantial majority of provinces representing at least 50 per cent of the population of Canada, Quebec necessarily being included.[14]

The Allaire proposal is similar in its design to the existing amending formula with one notable difference — Quebec has a veto over *any* constitutional amendment. This recommendation captures the central dilemma of the amending process in Canada — the Quebec veto. Throughout the long search for an amending formula, protecting Quebec's interests was of major concern. Once this reality has been identified then a second dimension very quickly materializes, namely the question of provincial equality. If Quebec or any province has a veto, then, within a federal system all constituent units, regardless of their population or needs, should be treated alike. Combining the principle of provincial equality and the principle of a Quebec protective veto inevitably leads to a requirement for unanimity. It is the only way that both principles can be fully satisfied. A classic example of this approach is the 1964 Fulton-Favreau formula where amendments to the division of powers was subject to provincial unanimity. Another is the Meech Lake Accord which expanded the short list of items already subject to unanimity under Sec. 41 of the amending formula to encompass those matters outlined in Sec. 42 of the amending formula.

The main criticism of the unanimity principle is its rigidity and the argument that it places the constitution into a straight jacket which presents an obstacle which some believe to be insurmountable. Despite the failure of Meech Lake, an omnibus amendment, unanimity has been achieved on other occasions on specific amendments, e.g. unemployment insurance (1940), and old age pension (1951). Thus, while difficult to achieve, it is by no means impossible. Nevertheless, the collapse of the consensus in favour of Meech Lake highlighted the obstacles to change under the unanimity rule. What then was the alternative? It should be noted, however, that those instances where unanimity was achieved were single issue amendments whereas Meech Lake was an omnibus amendment whose parts were not related to each other.

The parliamentary committee (the Beaudoin-Edwards Committee), assigned the task of coming up with an acceptable alternative proposal found refuge in the 1971 Victoria formula.[15] What is perhaps most surprising is that there is little justification given by the committee for this recommendation. There was no weighing of the pros and cons of a formula based on a regional approach which established first- and second-class provinces and one based on provincial equality.

The main rationale for the recommendation, which is the principal recommendation in the report, is the apparent clash between equality of the provinces and equality of persons. The latter concept is rooted in the idea of one person, one vote. My reading of the report is that the committee translated "equality of the provinces" into meaning a unanimity rule for constitutional amendments. Whereas a more realistic interpretation is that the weight of the provinces is equal in that no single province has a greater say than any other. To quote the committee,

> Our view is that a balance between the equalities of province and person
> can be achieved in a regionally-based amending formula, along the lines of
> the Victoria formula, which recognizes the Atlantic provinces, Quebec,

> Ontario, and the West as regions and gives each a veto over constitutional amendments. In addition to balancing the equalities, this formula largely avoids the combination of too much protection (unanimity) and too little protection (two-thirds and 50 per cent) contained in our present formula. It thus strikes a more consistent balance between resistance to change and receptivity to change even while, as we propose, preserving the unanimity requirement for certain essential matters.[16]

One must conclude that the committee, in the time available, could not endorse the position taken by the Allaire Committee, found unanimity in light of the Meech experience too rigid, had to protect Quebec interests and therefore retreated to familiar territory.

The strongest reaction to the report came from Alberta. The response was predicated on the principle of upholding provincial equality. On 20 June 1991 Alberta's minister of Federal and Intergovernmental Affairs, Hon. Jim Horsman, summarily rejected the recommendation and said, "I can assure the Assembly, the people of Alberta, and our fellow Canadians that the Alberta Government will not agree to any change that would make Albertans second-class Canadians."[17]

Primarily as a result of this reaction the federal government ignored the Beaudoin-Edwards recommendation in developing the most recent constitutional proposal. Instead they indicated they were prepared to resurrect the Meech Lake provisions (with the exception of the admission of new provinces) if anybody was interested in so doing.[18]

The apparent unwillingness to embrace (or for that matter even to acknowledge) the Beaudoin-Edwards recommendation coupled with the reference to the position of provinces found in *Shaping the Future Together*, leads me to conclude that provincial equality has successfully replaced regional equality as the dominant constitutional principle. By doing so, the position of the four Atlantic and the four western provinces is greatly enhanced in terms of constitutional change.

EQUAL BUT NOT IDENTICAL

At the beginning of the paper the premise was advanced that under the constitution the provinces are equal and this reality is reflected in Sec. 92 of the Constitution Act. Two questions arise. Is equality forever and can there be exceptions? It was mentioned that while there were differences amongst the provinces these were relatively minor and/or were the result of the Confederation agreement either in 1867 or when a province joined.

The answer to both questions is a qualified yes. To unravel this conundrum one must first recall that provincial equality is already part of the constitution and was intended to be one of its characteristics. The challenge to equality arises when the issue of constitutional change is addressed. The Canadian genius for compromise is found in Sec. 94A, the 1951 constitutional amendment on old age pensions. The clause reads as follows:

> The Parliament of Canada may make laws in relation to old age pensions and supplementary benefits, including survivors, and disability benefits irrespective of age, but no such law shall affect the operation of any law present or future of a provincial legislature in relation to any such matter.

While the amendment applies to all provinces (indeed all ten agreed to it) individual provinces obtained the right to exercise their jurisdiction in the future if necessary. The amendment provides flexibility to the constitution, treats provinces equally, but provides for future differences to occur. The clearest manifestation of this flexibility is found in the development of the Canada and Quebec pension plans. Obviously all provinces have the constitutional authority identical to that exercised by Quebec but have chosen not to exercise it.

The approach to flexible amendments is found elsewhere in the constitution, in particular Sec. 33 of the charter which allows a province to use the notwithstanding clause with respect to certain parts of the charter. Another example is found in the amending formula where a province can opt out of amendments which derogate from existing provincial legislative powers, proprietary rights or any other rights. In essence, an individual province can elect to keep the status quo for itself should others choose to transfer certain responsibilities to the federal parliament. Provincial equality is preserved but provinces can by choice be different. Again equality does not lead to identical behaviour.

Similar efforts at achieving flexibility are found in the recently released federal document and include the provisions on delegation of legislative authority and on federal-provincial agreements. While provinces can expect equal treatment there is no requirement for them to exercise this authority as long as the opportunity is there for them to do so.

Critics can argue that any of the above illustrations of flexible amendments may lead to checkerboard federalism. That is possible, but is it bad? In my view, no, because it permits individual provinces to pursue their own policies without restriction. Without flexibility, in all probability, amendments desired by many would not secure the necessary provincial approvals. On balance this approach has proven to be successful in Canada. The Spicer Commission said

> Given that provinces have entered Confederation on different terms and operate under different provisions, we believe that special arrangements in provinces based on special needs are a fundamental principle of Canadian federalism. This principle would apply where needed to all provinces.[19]

EQUAL AROUND THE TABLE

The 1982 amending formula has had another important effect on the federal system. Since it is predicated on the basis of provincial equality, this principle has been reflected in the evolving processes of executive federalism. Although executive federalism was severely criticized during the Meech Lake round, the reality thus far of the Canadian federal system is that intergovernmental negotiations are very much part of the political landscape.

In the federal government's paper on Canada's constitutional future one finds a proposal to establish a "council of the federation." This suggestion is similar to entrenching a First Ministers Conference or a body equivalent in composition in the constitution. Perhaps what is more important is that the council, if approved, would be given specific constitutional responsibilities ranging from approval of the exercise of the federal spending power to the proposed federal power over the economic union.

To achieve a consensus the same formula as for amending the constitution is used, i.e., two-thirds of the provinces representing 50 percent of the population. No single province can determine the outcome. Instead each has an equal voice around the table. Again, what is critical here is that support for a particular decision is based on provincial and not regional equality.

Does it make for better decisions? In my view, yes, because any decision will need to reflect the distribution of provincial support outlined in Table 3. To achieve this degree of support requires a clear intergovernmental consensus. It is far more readily attainable if individual provinces do not believe they have been either co-opted or forced into the decision. When all are treated equally there is a greater tendency to seek a consensus because the necessity of support has not been predetermined, or put another way, the playing field is level.

CONCLUSION

While the principles of regional and provincial equality were established in the Constitution Act 1867, with the acceptance of the 1982 amending formula, the former principle has gradually given way to one of provincial equality. While the idea has gained favour it has not been embraced in the composition of central institutions. Rather than equal, the idea of equitable has been introduced into the debate with respect to Senate reform. How this new principle will evolve remains to be seen.

By any measure, however, provincial equality enhances the political clout of the western and Atlantic provinces when it comes to constitutional change. As this idea has evolved it has also been recognized that provinces cannot be forced into identical molds so measures assuring equal treatment have been developed making the constitution flexible. This has the double advantage of preserving the idea of provincial equality and allowing provinces the opportunity to be different under certain circumstances.

Notes

1.   Canada, *Shaping Canada's Future Together: Proposals* (Ottawa: Minister of Supply and Services Canada, September 1991), 18.

2.   See Alberta Act 1905.

3.   See Alberta Natural Resources Transfer Act, 1930, emphasis added.

4. Robert A. MacKay, *The Unreformed Senate of Canada* (London: Oxford University Press, 1926), 206-7.

5. In 1979 the Conservatives managed to elect only one M.P. from Quebec while in 1980 the Liberals did not elect a single member in Saskatchewan, Alberta or British Columbia. In both instances prime ministers Clark and Trudeau appointed members of the Senate to the Cabinet to represent provincial interests.

6. See Canadian Intergovernment Conference Secretariat, *The Constitutional Review, 1968-71* (Ottawa: Information Canada, 1974). The Victoria Charter is found at pp. 376-396 and the amending formula at pp. 389-391.

7. See comments at the February 1969 Constitutional Conference, *Constitutional Conference, Proceedings, Second Meeting, Ottawa, February 10-12, 1969* (Ottawa: Queen's Printer, 1969), 84.

8. See correspondence dated 14 October 1976 between Premier P. Lougheed of Alberta and Prime Minister P.E. Trudeau. At that time Premier Lougheed was chairman of the premiers' conference and was writing on behalf of all ten provinces. Alberta, Department of Federal and Intergovernmental Affairs, *Fourth Annual Report to March 31, 1977* (Edmonton: n.p., 1978), 63-64 and 75-77.

9. The highest is achieved by combining B.C., Alberta, Ontario, Quebec, Nova Scotia and New Brunswick. The lowest is achieved by combining B.C., Saskatchewan, Ontario, Quebec, Newfoundland and P.E.I.

10. This figure is just an approximation and does not take into consideration representation from the Yukon or Northwest Territories and any future representation from aboriginal peoples as suggested in the federal paper, *Shaping the Future Together*, 8-9.

11. See *Shaping the Future Together*, 18-19 and Manitoba Constitutional Task Force, *Report* (Winnipeg:1991), 31-32. There is virtually no comment on seat distribution in the Manitoba report.

12. See correspondence from Prime Minister Trudeau to Premier Lougheed dated 31 March 1976 in Alberta, Department of Federal and Intergovernmental Affairs, *Fourth Annual Report to March 31, 1977*, 56.

13. See Canada, *A Guide To The Meech Lake Accord* (Ottawa: n.p., 1987), 13.

14. Constitutional Committee of the Quebec Liberal Party, *A Quebec Free to Choose: Report of the Constitutional Committee* (Montreal: Quebec Liberal Party, 1991). The report has been named for the chairman of the committee, Jean Allaire.

15. See Special Joint Committee of the Senate and House of Commons, *The Process for Amending the Constitution of Canada*, 20 June 1991.

16. Ibid., 26.

17. Alberta Legislative Assembly, *Debates*, 20 June 1991, p. 1848.

18. *Shaping Canada's Future Together*, 25.

19. Citizen's Forum on Canada's Future, *Report to the People and Government of Canada* (Ottawa: n.p., 1991), 124. (Emphasis in original.) Acceptance of this principle is also found in Beaudoin-Edwards report, see p. 26.

14

Constitutional Change, Ideological Conflict and the Redistributive State

Jim Silver

At stake in Canada's current multifaceted constitutional debate is, among other things, the future shape of fiscal federalism and the redistributive state which it supports. Around this issue an ideological struggle is being waged. The neoconservative objective is to limit the capacities, particularly the redistributive capacities, of the state in order to derive greater advantage from the forces of the market and the free flow of capital. This is a process already well underway. It includes a series of reductions in the rate of increase in federal transfer payments, and the effects of the Canada-US Free Trade Agreement (FTA), and is a central element in post-Meech constitutional proposals. The precise manner in which the Canadian federation ends up being restructured will be a function, in part, of ideological and political conflict. Its outcome will have significant regional and class implications. Yet many of those who might be expected to defend the redistributive state, given the regional and class implications of its erosion, are not doing so, or are not doing so effectively. The neoconservative vision is being clearly articulated and aggressively promoted by powerful forces; an alternative vision that includes a redistributive federal state is not. At the very moment that increased competitive pressures arising from globalization and trade liberalization have placed the redistributive state most at risk, there has been a failure at the level of ideas — a failure to fashion an alternative intellectual road map by which to make possible a retention and enhancement of the redistributive state.

THE EROSION OF THE TRANSFER PAYMENT SYSTEM

The redistributive capacity of the Canadian state is being gradually unravelled, the result of the cumulative impact of a series of measures since the mid-late 1970s, and especially since the early 1980s. Expenditures for health, education and social services grew from $11.4 billion in 1960 to $120 billion in 1980 according to one calculation,[1] financed in large part by transfer payments of various kinds from the federal to provincial governments, the latter of which bore the bulk of the constitutional responsibility for these services. This growth came to an end when, starting in the mid-late 1970s and continuing through the 1980s, expenditures on these programs were limited and even eroded in various ways. In the early 1990s, the size and configuration of Canada's "welfare state" is hotly contested terrain. It is the crucial site of an ideological struggle, the outcome of which will shape Canada's future.

Though elements of Canada's welfare state had been put in place earlier — unemployment insurance in 1940, family allowances in 1945, universal Old Age Security pensions in 1952 — it was in the late 1950s and 1960s that the social expenditure boom began. The main elements included the 1958 Hospital Insurance and Diagnostic Services Act, the 1966 Medical Care Act, the 1966 consolidation of various social assistance programs into the Canada Assistance Plan (CAP) — the federal government picking up approximately half of the costs of each of these programs — and increased federal expenditures for education, primarily university education, approximately 50 percent of the costs of which the federal government met from 1967.[2] To these and various other shared-cost programs was added the formalization, and increased amounts, of equalization payments from the federal government to provinces with relatively weak fiscal capacity under the 1957 Tax Sharing Arrangements Act.[3] The result of all these measures was a very dramatic increase in total federal government expenditures, and in the proportion of those expenditures consisting of shared-cost and equalization payments,[4] all of which were paid out of the "growth dividend" or "fiscal dividend" arising from the long postwar economic boom.

When the boom ended in the early to mid-1970s, to be replaced by declining growth together with chronically high levels of unemployment and inflation[5] and growing federal deficits, the whole edifice of the welfare state began to be called into question. Various reviews of Canada's social security system were quietly undertaken in the early 1970s.[6] By the second half of the decade the federal government was seriously concerned, largely because of the rapid rise in the size of the federal deficit:

> Where deficits in previous years had seldom exceeded one percent of GNP, those of 1977, 1978, 1979 and 1980 were respectively 2.5 percent, 4.6 percent, 3.5 percent and 3.7 percent.[7]

The economic downturn of the early mid-1970s eroded the growth dividend which had made possible the transfer payment expansion of the late 1950s and 1960s, and these ever growing payments[8] came to be seen by many as "the cause" of the rising deficits. Thus steps were taken to limit the growth of federal transfer payments.

As an interim measure the federal government announced in its 1975 budget that the increase in the federal per capita contribution to medicare costs would be limited to 13 percent in 1976, 10.5 percent in 1977, and 8.5 percent in subsequent years.[9] The limits in subsequent years were replaced by the Federal-Provincial Fiscal Arrangements and Established Programs Financing Act, 1977, as a result of which the federal government withdrew its open-ended commitment to pay 50 percent of hospital and medical insurance and postsecondary education costs, and replaced this arrangement with a new system of block cash grants and tax points. Federal contributions were now determined independently of provincially administered program costs; they were tied instead to the growth in per capita GNP.[10] A part of the rationale was that: "(s)ince the provinces must now bear the full cost of any marginal expenditures on these programs, a sizeable incentive to increase expenditures is removed."[11] This move to control federal spending on health and postsecondary education was consistent with the establishment two years earlier of the Anti-Inflation Board as a means of attempting to contain soaring price and wage increases.[12] It was also consistent with provincial desires to gain greater control over spending decisions in these areas.[13]

Since 1977, and especially since the early 1980s, the federal government has repeatedly placed further limits on its commitments to the costs of health, education and social services. In 1978 the federal government threatened to shave two points off the GNP escalator. When the provinces refused, other transfer payments were cut.[14] In 1980 federal Finance Minister Allan MacEachen announced that he would be looking for "significant savings" in federal-provincial transfers. In 1982 the federal government unilaterally eliminated the revenue guarantee component of Established Programs Financing (EPF), which had been added in 1972 to assure the provinces that they would not suffer financially as a result of that year's tax reforms.[15] This measure reduced transfer payments by just under $1 billion in 1982-83, and ever rising amounts thereafter. In 1983-84 and 1984-85, following the introduction of the federal government's "6 + 5" restraint program, increases in the postsecondary education component of EPF were limited to 6 percent and 5 percent respectively (although in 1985 additional federal payments made up the shortfall).[16] This was after the federal government had split the EPF block grant, contrary to the intended purpose of a "block" grant, and arbitrarily designated the postsecondary education component as 32.1 percent of the total, even though in most provinces the real proportion was closer to 25 percent. The federal government then accused the provinces of diverting block funds from postsecondary education to health, and used this as a justification for cutting health payments.[17]

After the Conservative government's election to office in 1984, the cuts deepened, largely as a result of reductions in the GNP escalator. Ottawa's contribution to EPF was limited to an annual growth rate of 2 percent below the rate of GNP growth in 1985-86, then 3 percent below the rate of GNP growth in 1989, and then zero in 1990 and again in the 1991 budget, through to 1995.[18] These cuts removed a very substantial amount of money from provincial treasuries:

> because of the ·continually dropping base upon which provincial

calculations are made, ... the initial 1985/86 cut (2 percent below the
growth of the economy), because it runs the longest, will save the federal
government slightly over $100 billion over 15 years. The further 1 percent
reduction increased this figure to $130 billion, and the first and second
freezes on EPF yielded another $12 billion and $7 billion respectively.
Therefore, this apparently "incremental" process will save the federal
government [and take from the provinces] about $150 billion over the next
15 years.[19]

The provinces had long since expressed concerns about the inadequacy of EPF
payments when they increased *at the same rate* as GNP, because the costs of
health and postsecondary education were rising *faster* than GNP, so that the
federal contribution to EPF was already falling ever further behind the old 50/50
formula.[20] The passage in 1991 of Bill C-69, entitled An Act to Amend Certain
Statutes to Ensure Restraint of Government Expenditures, combines with the earlier federal limits on EPF contributions to eliminate entirely the cash portion of
Ottawa's contribution before 2010.[21]

Bill C-69 also places a 5 percent cap on federal contributions to Ontario,
Alberta and British Columbia under the CAP. The danger is not only that these
three wealthiest provinces will experience a shortfall relative to demand — it is
estimated that payouts by these three provinces under CAP will rise by an
average 7 percent in 1991-92 — but also that the 5 percent cap could be extended to other provinces, and/or rolled back from 5 percent to 4 percent or 3
percent or lower.[22] Already Ontario estimates that CAP will cost it $310 million
in 1990-91 and an additional $510 million in 1991-92, while British Columbia
estimates the cost to it at $45 million in 1990-91 and increasing thereafter.[23]

The cumulative impact of this long series of cutbacks to the rate of growth of
federal transfer payments will be a dramatic impairment of the provinces'
capacity to meet their constitutional obligations with respect to the provision of
health, education and social services.

Changes in the equalization formula have also resulted in payments smaller
than the provinces would otherwise have received. Equalization payments from
the federal government to designated provinces are designed to ensure that all
provinces, no matter what their fiscal capacity, are able to spend reasonably
comparable per capita amounts on public services, without having to raise taxes
to unduly high levels.

The Fiscal Equalization Program provides for annual, unconditional payments to provinces which have a below-average capacity to derive tax revenues,
and consequently, below-average capacity to finance public services for their
residents. The purpose of equalization is to make it possible for these provinces
to provide reasonable levels of public services without having to resort to levels
of taxation which are unduly high.[24]

Early versions of equalization payments have been made since Confederation, but "the philosophical underpinnings of Canada's present equalization

programs are really to be found in the Rowell-Sirois Commission.'' The current equalization program was formally adopted in 1957. As of 1957 equalization recipients received an amount sufficient ''to bring per capita yields from the three standard taxes [personal and corporate income taxes and succession duties] up to the average yield in the two wealthiest provinces.''[25] In 1962 the equalization standard was reduced from the two wealthiest provinces, to an all-province average, and the revenue sources included in the formula began to move beyond the three standard taxes. In 1967, sixteen separate provincial revenue sources, excluding energy, were included in the equalization formula, and ''Canada's equalization program became the most comprehensive and most generous in the world.''[26] In 1982 the federal government unilaterally abandoned the all-province national average standard and replaced it with a five-province representative average standard. Because Alberta is excluded from the representative average standard, the new formula removed the bulk of the oil and gas revenue from the standard base. Provinces complained because ''[t]he current five province 'representative average' formula provides equalization support some $1.8 billion below the total of full equalization under a national average standard.''[27] Thus, despite equalization being enshrined in the Constitution Act, 1982 — ''Parliament and the Government of Canada are committed to the principle of making equalization payments to ensure that provincial governments have sufficient revenues to provide reasonably comparable levels of public services at reasonably comparable levels of taxation'' — the formula changes of that year, together with the requirement that as of 1983-84 equalization payments could not grow faster than the rate of GNP growth,[28] reduced equalization payments at the same time that EPF payments were being reduced. Further, the constitutional requirement to enable provincial governments to provide ''reasonably comparable levels of public services'' loses some of its strength as EPF and CAP cuts erode the quality of those services in all, even the most wealthy, provinces.

It is possible to overlook the importance of federal transfer payments to the provinces, especially EPF and equalization payments, and in doing so to miss their philosophical significance. It has been said recently that equalization

> was a revolutionary step, and for the weaker provinces yielded funds far beyond those obtainable from their own resources. This is particularly true of the personal income tax, where provincial levels are most disparate. Today the equalization payments represent the largest source of revenue in several provinces.''[29]

Whether equalization and the more specifically targetted transfer payments now embodied in EPF and CAP[30] were revolutionary may be a definitional matter. They are certainly of profound ideological importance. They represent a massive reallocation of resources on the basis of political, rather than market, considerations. As such they are a direct affront to the neoconservative vision of Canada's future, and it is for this reason that they are being so seriously eroded. The conflict over the redistributive state and the social programs it supports is an ideological conflict — a struggle over competing visions of Canada's future.

THE NEOCONSERVATIVE AGENDA AND THE REDISTRIBUTIVE STATE

The cuts to transfer payments already documented are but part of a larger federal government strategy aimed, in part, at eroding the capacity of the central government to redistribute wealth. This objective was identified by the Conservative government immediately upon their taking office in 1984. The government has been flexible and pragmatic in seeking means by which to achieve this objective — partly of necessity, since so much of what they have done has been contested — but a common characteristic of many of their initiatives has been that they would have the effect of limiting existing, and preventing future, redistributive social programs. The purpose is to erode the capacity of the state to redistributive wealth and to make the allocation of resources within Canada more strictly market-based.

The Conservative government set out their vision in *A New Direction for Canada: An Agenda for Economic Survival*.[31] In his first budget speech six months later, Finance Minister Michael Wilson emphasized the importance of *A New Direction*, saying that it "set out our guiding principles and new policy directions."[32] Perry has referred to the document as "this Conservative Magna Carta."[33]

A New Direction identified deficit reduction as the government's first priority for securing economic renewal:

> First, we must put our own fiscal house in order so that we can limit, and ultimately reverse, the massive build-up in public debt and the damaging impact this has on confidence and growth.[34]

Repeated references to the primacy of deficit reduction are to be found throughout *A New Direction* and other Conservative economic and fiscal documents.

Second, the deficit is to be reduced more by changes on the expenditure than the revenue side of the budget: "[o]ur immediate goal is to reduce the deficit through expenditure reduction and not through tax increases."[35]

Third, a major target on the expenditure side was to be transfer payments for social programs, the reductions thereof to be effected through greater "targeting," or "selectivity" of payments, i.e., through a breach of universality:

> there is considerable scope for improving and redesigning social programs based on the twin tests of social and fiscal responsibility. Social responsibility dictates that wherever possible, and to a greater extent than is the case today, scarce resources should be diverted first to those in greatest need.[36]

An attempt to effect this "guiding principle" of the Conservative economic and fiscal agenda was part of Finance Minister Wilson's first budget speech in May

1985. Stating that "we cannot make significant savings without examining transfer programs," Wilson announced that old age security and family allowance payments would be indexed "only for the annual increase in the consumer price index greater than 3 per cent."[37] The result was a storm of protest: "never has the unwritten covenant of the welfare state been so starkly revealed."[38] Wilson was forced to back off. It had been made clear that cutting the deficit by cutting transfer payments — a "guiding principle" of the Conservative "Agenda for Economic Renewal" — was contested terrain. This did not mean that this approach was to be abandoned — it is a linchpin of the Conservative ideology — but rather that it was to be pursued in a variety of different ways.

The government's major thrust in cutting transfer payments has been to reduce the rate at which they increase, as already shown, until the cash portion of federal EPF contributions is completely eliminated. Without funds to withhold, the federal government will lose the leverage needed to enforce national standards. Canada will consequently be left with a much more fragmented, and given varying provincial fiscal capacities, less effective social system, as individual provinces each respond differently and with varying degrees of effectiveness to the added financial strain created by the erosion of federal funding.

The FTA is likely to have similar effects, i.e., reduced expenditures on existing social programs, and strict limits on future social programs. The removal of tariff and nontariff barriers will intensify the competitive pressures faced by Canadian businesses to reduce taxes, and the government programs, especially social programs, that these taxes support, to the lower levels applicable in the United States.[39] The pressures created by this process of "harmonization" are consistent with the strategy, set out in *A New Direction for Canada*, of bringing the deficit under control by cutting government expenditures.

Future social services which may be most effectively delivered as universal public programs will be made close to impossible by Articles 2010, 2011, and 1605 of the FTA.[40] Before introducing any such program, Canada would have to notify and, if it were requested, consult with the United States — Article 2010.2(a). If after such notification and consultation Canada still was able to proceed, the program would have to be operated in such a way as to minimize the costs to American companies — Article 2010.2(b). And under Article 2011 American companies could take Canada to dispute settlement if they believed our universal social programs deprived them of benefits they would have earned had Canada not chosen to introduce such a measure. This is so "whether or not such measure conflicts with the provisions of this Agreement" — Article 2011.1. Further, any American company already delivering such services in Canada would have to be paid "prompt, adequate and effective compensation at fair market value" — Article 1605(d). The added costs necessitated by the provisions of the FTA could be sufficient to prevent Canada from introducing any more universal social programs.

It is likely that the Meech Lake Accord would have added to the difficulty in introducing new universal social programs. Sec. 106A(1) stated that provinces choosing not to participate in future national shared-cost programs in areas of exclusive provincial jurisdiction would be compensated "if the province carries on a program or initiative that is compatible with the national objectives." The terms "compatible with" and "objectives" are nebulous, and "objectives" are much looser than "standards." Though this section was much contested,[42] a strong case can be made that its effect would have been that in future, rather than new nationwide programs with common standards, Canada would have been restricted to a patchwork quilt of social programs differing by province. Universality would have been extremely difficult in these circumstances, despite the very considerable sense of national community that has been created by national shared-cost programs.[42] When taken in conjunction with the increased provincial powers related to Senate and Supreme Court appointments, the increased veto powers over constitutional amendments given to individual provinces, and the constitutional requirement for annual First Ministers' Conferences on the constitution and on the economy, the result of the Meech Lake Accord would have been a substantial devolution of powers to the provinces. The resulting balkanization of the country would have had effects consistent with the Conservative government's desire to limit public expenditures and erode universality.

The failure of the Meech Lake amendment has led to the current round of constitutional problems, a central aspect of which has been the renewed fear that Canada will be held together only at the expense of a dramatic devolution of powers to the provinces, one of the results of which would be a more fragmented and less effective social safety net. Both the Allaire report and the Bélanger-Campeau report have called for dramatically increased powers to Quebec. The Allaire report calls for Quebec to exercise full sovereignty in twenty-two areas in which it would have exclusive jurisdiction, and adds that: "[t]he federal government's spending power in Quebec's areas of exclusive authority will be eliminated."[43] In a restructured Canada each province could, like Quebec, exercise exclusive jurisdiction in all twenty-two areas, or alternatively, could redelegate whatever powers it chose to the central government.[44] Since health, education, income security and social affairs are among the twenty-two areas of exclusive provincial jurisdiction, this proposal would mean the end of such shared-cost programs as EPF and CAP, and the end of universality more generally. This is an intended consequence. The report refers to the central government's "obstinate determination to maintain, at any cost, much too restrictive national standards," argues that "the policy of national standards and other initiatives poorly targetted at the provinces have led the country to a perilous financial situation," and adds that:

> the Canadian federal state is based on centralizing practices based on an inflexible will to standardize public services to the utmost and the pursuit of grand, so-called 'national' policies. But these federal concerns are poorly

suited to the real needs of the provinces, businesses and people. In addition, the federal state no longer has the financial means to carry out its policies.[45]

The Bélanger-Campeau report also refers to the federal government's imposition of national standards which are "rigid and clearly oriented towards the quest for uniformity and the negation of differences," and refers to the problems created by overlapping jurisdictions, which have resulted "from the increasingly extensive use of the federal spending power."[46] The Allaire report continues with repeated references to the high cost of overlapping jurisdictions and duplication of services, and the need to create a state system which is more flexible and efficient, and better able to respond to market globalization and increased international competitiveness. Consistent with this purpose, "one of the objectives will be to reduce substantially the size of the central government," and to reduce the size of the deficit:

> Specific targets will be set to severely limit the power of central institutions to contract debts. Institutional constraints will be imposed to curb the possibility of developing deficits at the central level.[47]

At the same time, and also in response to the competitive pressures of globalization, the Allaire report calls for "eliminating all obstacles to trade" between Canada's regions.[48] The causal sequence — the need to cut state expenditures and the deficit, and more generally to reduce the size and role of the state while making it more decentralized and more flexible, all in the interests of improving the capacity to respond to increased international competitiveness — is the same as that set out in *A New Direction for Canada*.

Prime Minister Mulroney has repeatedly made clear his desire to restructure the federal-provincial distribution of powers in search of greater "efficiency." In a speech in Buckingham, Quebec, in December 1990 he said:

> I believe in a modern and flexible federalism. ... I have absolutely no doubt that we can achieve substantial savings — to pass on to taxpayers — by eliminating the waste and inefficiency resulting from the duplication and overlapping of federal and provincial programs. Nor do I doubt that significant changes in the division of powers could accommodate the legitimate aspirations of the provinces, make our system more efficient and move decision-making closer to the people.[49]

In a February 1991 speech to the Quebec City Chamber of Commerce the prime minister reiterated this theme:

> the federal government is prepared to discuss a rational, dynamic and profound redistribution of powers between Ottawa and the provinces. ... The Canadian Constitution obviously needs a major overhaul — one I am prepared to undertake.[50]

Another part of such an overhaul, also related to reductions in federal spending in areas of provincial jurisdiction, is a decentralization of taxing powers. The Allaire report states that increased powers for Quebec "assumes a complete reevaluation of the distribution of taxation powers."[51] The power to tax must be located at the same jurisdictional level as the power to spend, and both powers must be moved closer to those who use and pay for government services. The Bélanger-Campeau report makes the same case, calling for "the transfer of tax and financial resources related to the powers and responsibilities which Québec exercises."[52]

This aspect of a renewed federalism has been seized upon by the western finance ministers. They have argued, in a manner echoing the Allaire and Bélanger-Campeau reports and *A New Direction for Canada*, that high deficits are the primary problem, that deficits are best reduced by spending cuts, and that government deficits and spending are out of control because of the character of Canadian fiscal federalism, by which they mean federal spending in areas of provincial jurisdiction via transfer payments:

> The separation of taxing and spending decisions has eroded constraints on government in meeting demands for publicly-provided goods or services. No one order of government remains clearly accountable to the taxpayer.[53]

The problem has worsened because of federal measures introduced since 1982-83, as a result of which "the four Western Provinces have experienced a combined fiscal impact from federal offloading of $2.2 billion in 1990/91, an amount which could grow by 24.3 per cent to $2.7 billion by 1991/92."[54] At the same time the federal government, through its introduction of the GST, has occupied tax room traditionally left to the provinces, while federal control of the income tax system, through the federal-provincial tax collection agreements, "has been exercised with less that appropriate flexibility for provinces."[55]

In response to the problems created by these developments, the western finance ministers propose options for "moving toward a renewal of fiscal federalism in Canada." These include: disentanglement, which would be "aimed at reducing federal spending in areas of provincial responsibility with accompanying transfer of adequate fully equalized tax room;" "an independent Western Canadian income tax administration to assume reasonable flexibility in provincial tax structures;" "and legislative and other means to control spending and taxing by all governments working towards elimination of deficits and a reversal of the escalating debt burden which is threatening our ability to maintain vital programs."[56] With respect to the latter option, "the overall objective is to restrict the size of government."[57] It is further recommended that changes be made "to facilitate effective provincial contribution to decision making in key national policy areas, including monetary policy and planning for fiscal policy."[58]

The demands by Quebec, and to a lesser extent the western premiers, for significantly enhanced spending and taxing powers in a much more decentralized federalism, mesh with the neoconservative ideological preferences of the federal and some provincial governments, and with the likely effects of the FTA, to create very substantial pressures for a much more fragmented, more market-oriented Canada, which is better able to compete in an increasingly global marketplace, and which is much less able to maintain national programs for the redistribution of wealth.

Numerous other reports have been produced in the post-Meech period, all of which have fed into the plethora of competing ideas and interests to which the federal government has had to respond in fashioning its constitutional proposals. While the particulars of these reports vary, most recommend that the constitutional restructuring process be responsive to the increased competitive pressures created by globalization, and that it do so by scaling back the role of the state in order to derive greater advantages from the forces of the market and the free flow of capital.[59]

It is precisely this which the September 1991 federal proposals do, though not in quite so decentralist a fashion as might have been expected given the very decentralist thrust of the Allaire, Bélanger-Campeau, and western finance ministers' reports. *Shaping Canada's Future Together* proposes an expansion of Sec. 121 of the Constitution Act, 1867, to create "an economic union within which persons, goods, services and capital may move freely without barriers or restrictions based on provincial or territorial boundaries."[60] Any barriers or restrictions to such mobility, whether in the form of laws, programs or government practices, are to be constitutionally prohibited. Thus the powers of the federal, and especially the provincial governments will be sharply limited. Many current provincial initiatives would be prohibited by this proposal. Others could be prohibited by the federal government's proposed power to "make laws in relation to any matter that it declares to be for the efficient functioning of the economic union."[61] While these proposals are interpreted by many as a centralization of powers, they can more accurately be described as a severe limitation on the powers of provincial governments, and as a corresponding expansion of the role of the market. In that respect they constitute a complement to the FTA. Corporations will be freed of impediments to their east-west movement, as they have already been freed of impediments to their north-south movement. This is likely to add to the process by which corporate activities are being concentrated and centralized — precisely the kind of restructuring being advocated in the interests of greater competitiveness. The proposal to commit the Bank of Canada strictly to the goal of price stability will add to the pressures forcing such restructuring.

After proposing what amounts to a dramatic reduction in the powers of provincial governments, *Shaping Canada's Future Together* proposes that the provinces be, in effect, handed back the specific power to block new shared-cost programs. This proposal is similar to, but even more restrictive than, Sec. 106A(1) of the Meech Lake Accord. The new federal proposal is as follows:

> The government of Canada commits itself not to introduce new Canada-wide shared-cost programs and conditional transfers in areas of exclusive

provincial jurisdiction without the approval of at least seven provinces representing 50 percent of the population. This undertaking would be
entrenched in the Constitution. The constitutional amendment would also
provide for reasonable compensation to non-participating provinces which
establish their own programs meeting the objectives of the new Canada-
wide program.[62]

This provision would make it as difficult to introduce new shared-cost programs
in areas of exclusive provincial jurisdiction as it is to amend the constitution, and
when considered together with the FTA, would make virtually impossible the introduction of new, universal shared-cost programs. This would achieve a major
neoconservative objective, and more generally would contribute to reducing further the powers of the state. The proposed addition of a "council of the federation" with decision-making powers respecting intergovernmental economic
matters would likely serve to limit further the capacity of the federal state to act.

   In addition to the new restrictive spending powers provision, it is proposed
that provincial powers be added to by affording the provinces exclusive jurisdiction with respect to labour-market training, housing, certain environment-related
matters, and other areas, and by shifting residual powers to the provinces. *Shaping Canada's Future Together* also notes, with respect to the proposal "to provide Parliament with a new power to make laws for the efficient functioning of
the economic union," that:

   Since this new power would provide a mechanism for shared management
   of the economic union by the federal and provincial governments, its
   entrenchment would allow for the transfer and/or decentralization of powers
   and responsibilities in a number of specific sectors to bring decision-making
   closer to the people."[63]

The result would be a substantial devolution of powers to the provinces. This
devolution is somewhat masked by the economic union proposal, and by the
widely-held expectation — following from the Allaire and Bélanger-Campeau
and other reports — of an even greater devolution.

   Also masked is the fact that the already well advanced erosion of transfer
payments for existing shared-cost programs will in no way be impeded by these
proposals. While attention is focussed on the many specific proposals
enumerated in *Shaping Canada's Future Together*, existing transfer payments go
without mention, silently being gutted, while new universal shared-cost
programs will be virtually prohibited. The redistributive state is being placed
well on the road to its demise. The "place prosperity" made possible by the
postwar redistributive state will be eroded, victim of the erosion of transfer payments, and the concentration and centralization of capital that follows from the
unimpeded forces of the market. The free flow of capital and people will decapi-
talize and depopulate the Canadian hinterland, as capital is more "efficiently"
allocated by market forces, and the whole process will be entrenched in the

constitution. The results will be detrimental to the interests of have-not provinces such as Manitoba.

MANITOBA AND THE CENTRALIZED, REDISTRIBUTIVE STATE

Manitoba governments have historically been centralists, and have been supportive of the redistributive mechanisms of the federal state. This position has been adopted out of financial necessity, flowing, at least partly, Manitoba governments have always argued, from the structural constraints imposed upon the province's fiscal capacity by the terms of Confederation.

These structural realities were described in 1938 by then Provincial Treasurer Stuart S. Garson, and his analysis at that time has formed the intellectual foundation for Manitoba's position on federal-provincial fiscal relations ever since. The structural constraints imposed upon Manitoba by the terms of Confederation were two: Manitoba's hinterland status *vis à vis* Ontario; and the imbalance between Manitoba's jurisdictional responsibilities and revenue-raising capacities. Because of these structural characteristics *all* Manitoba governments have seen redistribution and equalization, i.e., cash transfers from a strong central government, as an irreducible necessity for the province's financial well-being.

Manitoba governments have historically argued that such transfers were not gifts, but rights, because they represented a return of wealth initially produced here, and then transferred East. This is a standard, Manitoba-as-hinterland paradigm. Garson explained it as follows:

> Because the manufacturing industry, coupled with the Canadian protective tariff, the Canadian transportation system and the Canadian branch banking system tends to attract to and concentrate in Ontario and Quebec much of the wealth which is originally produced in Western Canada; because, therefore, provincial taxation in Ontario and Quebec is levied to a substantial extent upon wealth originally produced in Western Canada; because provincial taxation in Western Canada has to be levied not upon the wealth produced here, but only upon that portion of it which remains after the manufacturing and mercantile profits and the interest charges due to Eastern concerns have first been diverted to Ontario and Quebec; ... the present financial position of the Western Provinces of Canada could not be anything but critical.[64]

This analysis has led to Manitoba governments of all ideological stripes calling for a redistribution of wealth between regions, for reasons analytically similar to those used by social democrats and socialists who call for a redistribution between social classes.

The second structural problem is the mismatch between the rapidly escalating spending responsibilities of the provinces and their limited revenue-raising capacities:

> The financial plan of Confederation was based upon a social philosophy which did not recognize as a responsibility of the State the provision of

> social services as we have them today. ... The Fathers of Confederation
> either did not intend the Provinces to have any responsibility for these social
> services, or else failed in the financial plan of Confederation to provide the
> Provinces with adequate revenues to finance them.[65]

The consequence of these structural problems is that, without cash payments
from Ottawa, Manitoba governments are going to have fiscal problems no matter
how prudent and competent their financial management:

> After the passage of the BNA Act it was only a question of how soon and in
> what provinces these difficulties would develop. It is obvious that they
> would develop soonest in the Provinces which were financially the poorest.
> It is equally obvious that they would develop in those Provinces, not in
> times of prosperity, but in times of stress.[66]

It is not an historical accident that Manitoba played a key role in bringing into
existence the Rowell-Sirois Commission,[67] whose recommendations for the
federal collection of personal and corporate taxes and succession duties in return
for adjustment grants were supported strongly by the province.

Continuing throughout the postwar period, in times of prosperity as in times
of stress, and no matter the ideological orientation or fiscal philosophy of the
government in office, Manitoba has adhered to a centralist policy, in support of
the federal redistributive mechanism. As Murray Donnelly wrote in 1963:

> In Manitoba experience with financial independence on the basis of revenue
> and responsibility, as allocated by the British North America Act, was never
> a happy one and turned into near tragedy during the depression. The
> province has shown no desire to assume a proud but poor status ... the
> poverty of the past was scarcely compatible with dignity.[68]

The Campbell Governments

The postwar Campbell administrations were the epitome of fiscal conservatism, adopting a strict pay-as-you-go strategy. Rather than borrow relatively
low-cost capital to finance much needed economic and social development, they
paid down the province's accumulated debt. Spending was tightly controlled,
debt charges were low, taxes were low, and budget surpluses were the norm.[69]
Fiscal prudence, indeed extreme parsimony, was the hallmark of the farmer-
based provincial governments of this period.

Yet these fiscally prudent governments, contradictory though it may be, supported the federal transfer payment system. Premier Campbell demanded
equalization payments, based on the fiscally-strongest province, as a matter of
right: ''Manitoba has always argued and still claims that a significant portion of
the equalization payments represents merely a reimbursement of our own
money.''[70] When the federal government hinted in 1955 that certain taxing
powers might be devolved to the provinces, the Campbell administration reacted
with alarm, and expressed its opposition to:

> a return to the system of multiple taxation that our people found so unsatis-

> factory in the pre-war years. ... Having won our way to the simplicity, economy and efficiency of relatively uniform income taxation throughout the nation, let us not return to the tax jungles of the twenties and thirties.[71]

The farmer-based administrations that governed Manitoba from 1921 to 1958 were consistent in their inconsistency. The federal government should adopt an interventionist, redistributive role, no matter how inconsistent that might be with Manitoba's own parsimonious fiscal philosophy.

The Roblin Governments

The Roblin administration, elected in 1958, adopted a completely new fiscal philosophy. The tightly controlled public spending of which the Campbell governments had been so proud, and which had been the measure of their success, was to Roblin the source of the problem. The provincial government had to invest if Manitoba was to modernize:

> We have consistently maintained that inadequate capital investment in recent years has handicapped the growth of the Province. [It has created] a formidable accumulation of unfilled capital needs, inherited from a period of governmental inactivity and stringency.[72]

Roblin added: "Parsimony is rarely true economy. When such parsimony operates to inhibit normal growth, it can become the very opposite of true economy."[73]

Dramatic increases in public expenditures were investments, needed to create the conditions that would attract private capital and overcome the "underdevelopment in this province" that had been created by Campbell's ideologically inspired failure to invest. Roblin's free-spending fiscal philosophy — made possible by Canada's rapid economic growth and related increase in transfer payments — brought Manitoba into the modern era at the same time that the province accumulated very substantial surpluses.

Not surprisingly, therefore, the Roblin governments echoed their predecessors with respect to the redistributive role of the federal state. "It remains the contention of this Government that no single concept in the field of Federal-Provincial relations is as important as that of equalization. It is the embodiment of economic and fiscal justice which we in Manitoba, regardless of party, have demanded as a right — not as a concession."[74]

In commenting on the proposal by the federal government to allow provinces to "opt out" or "contract out" of shared-cost programs in return for additional tax points, Roblin reiterated Manitoba's traditional centralist position:

> The concept of 'contracting out' with tax abatement or cash compensation is a recent development with application so far in the field of university grants, in the Province of Quebec only. Manitoba views this new proposal with mixed feelings. We recognize particularly its threat to the continuing idea of a national standard of services. ... We shall probably not contract

out ourselves and do not recommend it as a general proposition to the people of this Province.[75]

The Schreyer Governments

The Schreyer years were, in fiscal terms, almost a replication of the Roblin years. Government spending continued to grow rapidly, the result of a Keynesian-inspired fiscal policy. In response to the beginnings of the slightly more tightened economic circumstances, Schreyer sought administrative savings in the delivery of essential programs. Yet attempts to innovate in program design were stymied by federal government rigidity. For example, Prairie Economic Council proposals made in 1971 for "more efficient alternative care services in their health programming," were rejected.[76] Manitoba responded with calls for more flexibility in federal health financing arrangements to enable program redirection, but insisted that, at least in the short run, this required more, not less federal funding.[77] Schreyer sought a system of fiscal federalism that was at once both centralized and flexible: flexible to make possible and indeed encourage provincial innovations tailored to regional and local needs; centralized to ensure availability of the funding to make these innovations possible, and to maintain national standards. Greater provincial flexibility, important though the Schreyer administration deemed it to be, could not be bought at the expense of federal spending powers and national standards. The possibility of federal withdrawal from shared-cost programs represented an even greater threat to Manitoba than federal inflexibility:

> The disengagement by Ottawa from consultation and direct partnership with the provinces through shared-cost programmes can only lead to the fragmentation of the nation; it will lead to inequalities and inefficiencies in programmes across the nation; it will confront all but the wealthiest provinces with the unacceptable prospect of reducing the standards of services provided to their people.[78]

The Schreyer government merely wanted more provincial flexibility in the design of major shared-cost programs; it did *not* want increased taxing powers, arguing that Manitoba — like most provinces — did not have the fiscal capacity to maintain standards in the absence of federally redistributed funds.[79]

Until 1975 the Schreyer governments, like their predecessors, were able to increase expenditures while running surpluses. In 1975 Schreyer budgeted for a small deficit; by 1977 the size of the deficit had increased substantially,[80] the result of the general economic crisis and of reductions in the rate of increase of transfer payments.[81] Manitoba estimated that as a result of the "systematic dismantling" of cost-shared programs, in 1975-76 the province would receive approximately $85 million less than would otherwise have been the case, with an estimated additional $100 million loss in 1976-77.[82] The Schreyer government responded to the fiscal squeeze by running up a substantial deficit.

The Lyon Government

The Conservative government of Sterling Lyon, elected in 1977, identified the deficit as the primary economic problem, and expenditure cuts as the solution. He called for a period of "acute, protracted restraint." Civil servants were laid off; public spending was slashed:

> The Lyon government declared war on the public sector in order to trim spending, cut the deficit and reduce taxes. Income taxes were lowered and succession duties abolished within weeks of the Tories' victory in late 1977. Over the first year, about 1000 civil service jobs were eliminated, programs were subjected to "acute, protracted restraint" and spending of the pump-priming variety was cancelled.[83]

In his first federal-provincial First Ministers Conference in February 1978, Premier Lyon set out the fundamental elements of his government's philosophical approach:

> The first must be a commitment to a private market economy system. ... private ownership, private initiative and the accumulation of private investment capital must continue to be the engines that drive our economy.
>
> And the second must be the redirection of government — including the imposition of real restraints on the growth of government's power and government's spending ... to make that commitment effective.[84]

When the Lyon government reported "zero growth" in its expenditures between 1977-78 and 1978-79 — "[t]he lowest of any senior government in Canada" — Finance Minister Donald Craik described it as "a remarkable achievement and an absolutely necessary one."[85] When, in the next budget, the Lyon administration was able to report that the deficit inherited from the Schreyer government had been cut by 76.5 percent, the finance minister revealed the Lyon government's fiscal philosophy by boasting that:

> The lifting of a burden of this magnitude from the shoulders of the taxpayers of this Province may well be the single most important contribution any government could hope to make to the economic development of Manitoba, in this decade and beyond.[86]

Though doing so was completely inconsistent with his government's own fiscal philosophy, and completely inconsistent with his commitment to the free market, Lyon joined all previous Manitoba administrations in extolling the virtues of the nonmarket — indeed the antimarket — concept of equalization:

> Manitoba continues to believe that equalization is one of the most important ... if not the most important ... direct manifestations of what the country is all about ... ensuring provinces have the revenues necessary to provide reasonably comparable levels of service across the country.[87]

No matter how ideologically committed he was to rolling back the state and freeing up the market, Lyon could not help but recognize Manitoba's reliance upon the nonmarket, state-directed redistribution of wealth effected through the mechanisms of fiscal federalism.

The Pawley Governments

The erosion of the growth dividend, which had began to cause problems in the last few Schreyer budgets and continued to do so throughout the Lyon years, reached new and fiscally dangerous proportions during the Pawley years. The Pawley government assumed office when the country was suffering not only the effects of a severe recession, but also "a series of cutbacks in federal transfer payments which are unprecedented in scale."[88] The 1983 budget reported that "federal transfer payments will only account for about 35.5% of our revenues — a major drop off from the peak of nearly 43% five years ago."[89] The deficit in 1983 climbed to one-quarter billion dollars in 1982, and close to one-half billion dollars in 1983,[90] its rise being the price to be paid for protecting social services and employment levels. By 1986, transfer payment cuts had worsened substantially: "from $13 million this year to $86 million in 1990, for a five year total of $238 million."[91] The impact of such cuts on poorer provinces like Manitoba was dramatic, because there are strict limits to how high taxes can be raised to protect essential cost-shared services like medicare:

> the poorer provinces would soon find that the required tax levels were undercutting their competitive positions in relation to richer provinces. There would be irresistible pressure to lower program standards, comprehensiveness and accessibility. Universal and comprehensive Medicare would be threatened.[92]

Their lower fiscal capacity made it especially difficult for the poorer provinces to find their own solutions:

> For example, a basket of across-the-board tax increases in the equalization — recipient provinces would generate from 60% (in Newfoundland) to 80% (in Manitoba) of what they would raise nationally. Public debt is higher and credit ratings are lower in the equalization — recipient provinces, making further increases in deficit financing less attractive.[93]

And, "(t)he Equalization Program already leaves the recipient provinces with a fiscal capacity which is $217 per capita below the all-province average."[94]

It is remarkable, under these circumstances, that the Manitoba economy performed even as well as it did throughout the 1980s. While deficits were allowed to run up, and new taxes were imposed,[95] private capital continued to be attracted to the province, and levels of unemployment remained relatively low. By comparison with the results of the neoconservative strategy imposed during the Lyon years — when cuts to federal transfer payments were not yet as severe as they were to become later in the 1980s — the Manitoba economy performed relatively well, to the considerable benefit of Manitobans.[96] Nevertheless there are strict limits to provincial Keynesianism, especially given the constraints imposed by capital mobility and by the continued erosion of federal transfer payments.

The Filmon Governments

The fiscal philosophy and strategy of the Filmon governments are a replication of the Lyon government. Budget speeches make reference to the "fiscal excesses of the past," leading to an "unsustainable level of public sector spending which has left a legacy of high debt, high taxes and a growing burden of debt service costs."[97]

> We must pay for past choices which ignored reality, which deferred again and again the necessary decisions, and refused to tailor spending to fit the Province's income. The accumulating debt load and rising interest costs threaten to cripple our Province's capacity to meet the real needs of Manitobans, and to contain taxes to competitive levels.[98]

The result has been budget cuts, some of which have been enumerated in *The 1991 Manitoba Budget of Choice,* which notes that:

> Many of these cuts are aimed directly at the most vulnerable members of our society. ... many of these cuts directly affect women and children especially poorer ones; they affect aboriginal people, recent immigrants, youth, and those with physical or mental disabilities.[99]

While all previous provincial governments, no matter their fiscal philosophy or ideological orientation, have been unequivocal in their support of the centralized redistributive capacity of the federal state, the Filmon governments have been less so. They appear torn between Manitoba's economic reality — reliance upon a nonmarket, central government-directed reallocation of resources — and their own neoconservative, market-driven ideological orientation. The Filmon government reportedly approved of the Meech Lake amendment's potentially decentralist spending power provision, refused to agree to provincial Liberal and NDP recommendations to improve the clause, and in the end agreed to a compromise position which called for deletion of the clause.[100] The Filmon government has been supportive of the Mulroney administration despite increasingly severe federal cuts to transfer payments. Premier Filmon went so far as to applaud the prime minister's "consultative style" at a November 1989 First Ministers Conference, even though Finance Minister Manness had confirmed that the impact upon Manitoba of the 1989 federal budget would be a reduction of $108 million in federal transfer payments over five years. Only with the 1990 federal budget did the Filmon government adopt a more traditional Manitoba posture. In 1990 Finance Minister Manness reported that:

> I have written the Federal Finance Minister to underscore the important role of equalization in strengthening our nation. ... equalization is the glue which holds our country together. The integrity of the equalization program must be protected.[101]

By 1991 his anger at continued cutbacks had risen:

> We reject the dishonesty inherent in the federal approach to health and
> higher education financing — repeated, unilateral reduction to transfers,
> with federal cash payments virtually eliminated by the end of the decade,
> accompanied by loud proclamations of a federal commitment to postsecon-
> dary education and to national standards for medicare.[102]

Yet at the same time the Filmon government has endorsed the 1990 report of the
Western Premiers Conference, which calls for a massive devolution of spending
and taxing powers to the western provinces — a position diametrically opposed
to Manitoba's centralist redistributive position, and contrary to Manitoba's real
economic interests.

Throughout most of the twentieth century Manitoba governments have, as a
result of self-interest, been advocates of a centralized, redistributive federal state.
Since the end of the postwar boom and the onset of crisis in the mid-late 1970s,
however, the province has been torn in two contradictory directions — by strong
global and national socioeconomic and ideological forces for decentralization
and fragmentation, on the one hand, and by its continued and obvious self-
interest in centralized redistribution, on the other. This contradictory pull is
reflected in the current party alignment in Manitoba, with the provincial New
Democratic and Liberal parties promoting a strong, centralist position,[103] and the
Conservative Party visibly torn between the need to promote the province's real
interests in a redistributive federal state, and the party's ideological commitment
to a neoconservativism which vigorously opposes a redistributive federal state
and promotes the unfettered forces of the market. Right up until the release of the
Report of the Manitoba Constitutional Task Force, there was uncertainty about
whether the increasingly neoconservative Filmon government had broken with
Manitoba's traditional centralist redistributive position, or not. Jim Eldridge,
secretary to cabinet for intergovernmental relations, insisted that it had not.[104]
The evidence, he argued, would be found in the *Report of the Manitoba
Constitutional Task Force*.

The *Report of the Manitoba Constitutional Task Force*, three of whose six
members were Conservative MLA's, forcefully reasserted the traditional
Manitoba position. Citing the frequent references by Manitobans in the public
hearings to the need for a strongly redistributive state, the task force reported
that:

> Manitobans believe that all Canadians should be able to share equitably in
> the resources and benefits of the nation as a whole. A strong central govern-
> ment is required for such programs as equalization, Established Programs
> Financing (EPF) and the Canada Assistance Plan (CAP). We are concerned,
> therefore, by federal government cutbacks to such programs. While means
> can be found to ensure that these national programs better reflect the
> regions, they are essentially national in scope and play a crucial role in
> preserving national unity.[105]

The task force reiterated its concern "that national programs in areas of provincial jurisdiction do not stifle creativity at the community level and that national programs should be adaptable to the specific needs of a region," and therefore provincial governments should be able to opt out if the national and provincial programs are "sufficiently parallel," but it quickly added:

> Of course this must be balanced by a recognition of the danger to Canada's social security system if the criteria for compensating 'opting out' provinces is made too lenient. This was a central concern of Manitoba during the debate over the Meech Lake Accord.[106]

The *Report of the Manitoba Constitutional Task Force* ended up supporting "the maintenance of a strong central government," with "the capacity to respond to the needs of the less advantaged citizens and regions of the nation," and more specifically recommended:

- the strengthening of the constitutional provisions regarding equalization by including guidelines to establish a process for changing the formula.

- the constitutional entrenchment of a federal government obligation to fund the Established Programs Financing program.[107]

The Filmon government's support of these recommendations is clear evidence of the overwhelming importance to Manitoba of the redistributive state.

Nevertheless, the Filmon government's position is contradictory, the result of a clash between the province's economic needs, as expressed so clearly in the *Report of the Manitoba Constitutional Task Force*, and the provincial government's ideology. The obvious contradiction in the Filmon government's advancing the traditional Manitoba position is that it means they oppose at the federal level the very policies they simultaneously espouse at the provincial level. This contradiction represents but one example of the confused, hesitant, and relatively ineffective ideological positions of those who might be expected to defend the redistributive state. At the level of ideas, those who seek to promote a neoconservative solution have been very effective, while those who have reason to oppose such a solution — have-not provinces, the New Democratic Party, the Left more generally, for example — have been relatively ineffective. They have failed at the level of ideas, and at precisely the moment when ideas have been especially significant in shaping political outcomes.

CRISES AND IDEAS

At times of systemic crisis — such as occurred when the long postwar boom gave way to stagflation and economic decline in the 1970s, and such as is occurring now, as Canada struggles to find a way to respond to the increased competitive pressures arising from globalization and trade liberalization while also responding to a wide variety of domestic problems — there emerge differing interpretations or definitions of the causes of the crisis. Struggles develop around such interpretations and their related solutions. Ideological differences become especially sharp. Mishra describes this process as follows:

> It is at such a point in the crisis of a social system that different definitions of the situation in the form of theories, ideologies and interpretations move to centre-stage. These definitions include an analysis of the nature of the crisis, its causes and possible solutions. Such theories and ideologies compete in the marketplace of ideas seeking to persuade both elites and the masses as to their "correctness" in terms of the diagnosis and proposed remedies.[108]

It follows that "how problems are perceived and prioritized, which issues are seen as the 'problem' and which as 'solution,' is the result of defining the situation in a particular way — in short, a matter of ideology."[109]

Similarly Jenson argues that no outcome is preordained in the wake of a crisis. While it is true that since the end of the postwar boom there have been very considerable forces — particularly the heightened competitive pressures unleashed in large part by globalization and trade liberalization — which have been pushing for neoconservative solutions, such outcomes need not have occurred. A neoconservative constitutional proposal, for example, cannot be explained simply as a function of capital's need for greater flexibility. Simply to read off state responses from capital's needs is an inadequate, overly determinist form of explanation. Powerful forces may be pushing in a particular direction, making some outcomes more likely than others. Yet the state can make choices; alternatives are possible; politics is significant. As Jenson puts it: "a solution to any crisis is not predictable in advance; it is a product of politics, a solution constructed out of social conflict and conflict resolution."[110]

Central to this conflict is the role of ideas: "[c]rises ... are times of political agitation, of competition among world views, and of uncertainly about the meaning of things."[111] Political conflict, including and perhaps especially conflict at the level of ideas, of ideologies, is an important variable in shaping the outcome of crises.[112]

Similarly, in the United States Blumenthal has argued that "ideas and ideology are now central to American politics." Moreover, their production and dissemination require institutions developed specifically for that purpose.[113] Neoconservatives have grasped this, he argues. Their "factories of ideology" — think tanks, institutes, journals — have been resolutely policy-oriented, and have been committed not just to the production, but also to the implementation, of ideas. The American Enterprise Institute, for example, pays "as much attention to dissemination of product as to the content," aiming its efforts at "the policy-makers and the opinion making elite."[114] As a consequence, Blumenthal argues, much of the policy-making function in American politics has been taken over by these institutions.[115] Neoconservatives, intent upon producing ideas and selling them to policy makers, have been successful in turning ideology into power.

A similar process has taken place in Canada. Neoconservative "factories of ideology'' have contributed significantly to setting the terms of public debate, and to shaping the policy initiatives of the Mulroney government.[116] Their task has been made easier by the confusion of the Liberal and New Democratic parties throughout the 1980s at the level of ideas. Neither party has been able to articulate a coherent economic strategy; neither party has an adequate alternative to the Conservatives' constitutional strategy, a central thrust of which is the erosion of the redistributive state. The Conservatives have been the beneficiaries of clearly articulated ideas, energetically promoted by neoconservative "factories of ideology;'' the opposition parties, by contrast, have been confused at the level of ideas, unable to articulate a clear and coherent alternative, either economically or constitutionally.

The BCNI and CDHI

For the Mulroney government, the Business Council on National Issues (BCNI) and the C.D. Howe Institute (CDHI) have been among the most important of the neoconservative "factories of ideology," contributing significantly to setting the terms of public debate, and to shaping government policy initiatives. They have provided the Conservative government with a clear sense of direction, a well-defined road map, in the constitutional negotiations, as the following summary of their work on the constitution reveals.

For both, the need to reduce the deficit and accumulated debt is the conceptual starting point. This is to be achieved by the reduction of expenditures, not the generation of revenues.[117] Social programs are a major target for expenditure cuts, both because they constitute a substantial portion of total federal expenditures,[118] and because they are inconsistent with neoconservative market-centred ideology. For the BCNI, social policy reforms:

> should increase the selectivity of social programs, improve the labour market incentives facing individuals, and curtail the growth of costs which is keeping the deficit at record levels after four years of recovery. These social and economic challenges are interdependent and inseparable, and meeting them must be recognized and pursued as a national priority.[119]

The CDHI takes the same position. The welfare system:

> is too expensive and too counter-productive in the sense that it neither facilitates economic adjustment nor provides adequate social and economic support for those most in need. ... the task of the 1990's will be to rationalize this network — to reintegrate social and economic policies so that they contribute to, rather than inhibit, adjustment and competitiveness.[120]

In pursuit of these objectives, both the CDHI and the BCNI are promoting the restructuring of Canadian federalism. They argue that the current allocation of powers results in excessive duplication, and is therefore costly. The BCNI advocates:

> a re-ordering of federal and provincial powers. The re-ordering would result

in some shift of responsibility to the provincial and the local level from the federal government, to be sure. But in some cases, it also would mean that certain responsibilities would be transferred from the provinces to the federal government.[121]

Along with this realignment of spending powers would go a realignment of taxing powers:

the level of government responsible for making spending decisions should also be the one publicly responsible for raising the necessary taxes. This simple linkage would go a long way to addressing some basic inefficiencies in the current incentive structure of intergovernmental fiscal transfers. ... For example, the tax room to finance health and welfare might be transferred to the provinces.[122]

This is a process which might require a constitutional amendment, or might take place independently of the constitutional process:

we cannot make our way to the millennium if all of our challenges are approached via formal constitutional amendments. We must fall back on our tradition of resorting to all manner of creative instruments (tax-point transfers, opting out, altering intergovernmental transfers, ordinary legislation, bilateral agreements).[123]

Such a massive restructuring, i.e., an attempt to undo the postwar welfare state, is justified by its advocates on the grounds that Canada needs to be more competitive, and that a "more flexible federalism" will make this possible:

Competitiveness is the foundation upon which an improved social, economic and environmental order will be built. In the quest for competitiveness, the Canadian political system must be an ally and not an impediment.[124]

Consistent with this objective, the removal of trade barriers between Canada and the United States by means of the FTA must be complemented by the removal of interprovincial trade barriers, in order to maximize factor mobility:

First and foremost, the reforms to our federal system must ensure that the Canadian common market is established in fact and that the Canadian economic union is strengthened. The free movement of labour, capital, goods, and services must be guaranteed under any new constitutional arrangement, and in this area, we see the federal government having a strengthened role.[125]

The general thrust of the analysis and recommendations offered by the BCNI and the CDHI is consistent with the objectives being pursued by the federal government. The failure of the Meech Lake amendment has created a crisis in Canada. The BCNI and CDHI have seized the opportunity created by this crisis to advance their ideological objectives. Courchene states this explicitly: "For Canadians generally, this movement represents an enormous opportunity. Quebec has alerted us to the need to restructure on the economic front in order to regain

Canada's former competitive edge in the global economy."[126] In this drive to become more competitive in response to global economic pressures, government "must be an ally and not an impediment," ie., the state must be restructured, and the redistributive capacities of the state reduced, in order to derive greater advantage from the forces of the market and the free flow of capital.

Part of this process involves the elimination of "place prosperity," and the transfer-payments system which makes it possible. Courchene, for example, has argued that:

> [t]he current definition of Canada as a *transfer economy* needs to be put to bed ... the future of the transfer system must be one where Ottawa treats individual Canadians as equals wherever they reside; and backs away from policies that go well beyond this and have tended to bestow privilege on place at the expense of people.[127]

Jenson explains the emergence of this neoconservative emphasis upon the need to eliminate place prosperity and the transfer payments which support it by arguing that the collapse of Canada's "permeable fordism" — a differentiating characteristic of which the representation of interests and collective identities and the development of a political discourse was based less on class than on region, or "place" — has found expression not so much in direct ideological attacks on labour and the welfare state, as in an erosion of fiscal federalism, and of the "place sensitivity" or place prosperity which Canada's postwar form of federalism has facilitated.[128] The erosion of "place prosperity" is precisely what is being advocated by neoconservatives who, in search of greater flexibility and competitiveness, seek to dissolve the redistributive capacity of the federal state.[129]

Neoconservative ideologists have provided a clear and detailed road map for the restructuring of Canada and the erosion of the redistributive state, while the Conservative government has demonstrated the political will to pursue these objectives. By contrast, the voices speaking for the maintenance and enhancement of the redistributive state have been few, and relatively ineffective. Neither the NDP nor the Liberal Party has succeeded in articulating a constitutional strategy which might preserve the redistributive state; neither party has succeeded in articulating an economic strategy which might make the retention of the redistributive state possible. If the redistributive state is to be saved and improved — i.e., if resources are to be allocated at least partly on the basis of political considerations, rather than solely on the basis of market signals — then an economic and constitutional strategy is needed. Brodie and Jenson's observation that "[e]very party of the Left, if it proposes a fundamental transformation of society, needs a roadmap,"[130] has a more general applicability to this case, i.e., to the need to fashion a strategy, economic and constitutional, by which the redistributive state might be retained and enhanced. Yet the very forces which have placed the redistributive state at risk — especially the intensified competitive pressures arising from globalization and trade liberalization — are making it particularly difficult to fashion an economic and constitutional strategy, a road map, that would guide the attempt to retain and enhance the redistributive state. The crisis of post-Keynesianism and the dramatic global and national changes associated with it have been responded to, at the level of ideas, extremely effectively by those who would erode or eliminate the redistributive state, and by comparison, extremely ineffectively by those who might be expected to attempt to maintain and enhance or improve it. The latter have failed at the level of ideas.

The Liberal Party

For the Liberal Party, this is not surprising. It has always been a brokerage party, never a party of ideas. Tom Kent argues that contrary to popular belief, even the famous 1960 Kingston Conference produced no new ideas:

> If a party needed such a gathering to give it ideas, it would be broken down beyond any hope of rebuilding. Access to ideas is the least of the problems of politicians of any competence at all. The real problem is to identify the ideas that are right for the times and the party's role in those times.[131]

Thus the postwar Liberal Party seized upon the Keynesianism in which the Ottawa mandarinate were steeped,[132] and used the growth dividend created by the postwar boom to become at once both social reformers and the representatives of big business.

The fiscal dividend is now gone, the easy, positive-sum politics of the middle ground is no longer possible, and the Liberal Party alternative is not clear. A brief fling at what Smiley called the "third National Policy"[133] collapsed along with falling oil prices, leaving the Liberal government without a sense of direction: "[t]he government had run out of ideas and options to cope with the growing economic crisis."[134] Without the support of big business, now firmly committed to the neoconservatism expressed by the Conservative Party, or failing them the Reform Party, and without the fiscal dividend to support social reform, the Liberal Party has lost its moorings, and is adrift. The party's position on the FTA is confused; its position on the constitution and a renewed federalism is confused. Historically supporters of the centralized redistributive state, the party may have difficulty opposing *Shaping Canada's Future Together*, given the document's centralist elements and the absence of a direct attack on existing social programs. The constitutional resolution unanimously adopted at the Liberal Party of Canada (Quebec) Biennial Convention in Sherbrooke, Quebec, 25-26 May 1991, for example, includes a spending powers provision similar to that included in the Meech Lake amendment, and is peppered with references to the need for flexibility, the reapportionment of powers to eliminate the overlapping of programs, and the necessity to make changes to the federal structure in the interests of Canada's competitiveness. This is the language of neoconservatism, and is not inconsistent with the objectives of the federal government as set out in *Shaping Canada's Future Together*.

The Left and the NDP

The NDP's historical commitment to the centralized redistributive state has also been eroded, the result of a centralization/decentralization split within the party, and more generally, of the rethinking of socialism and social democracy inspired by the developments — the problems of Keynesianism, the globalization of capital, the collapse of Eastern European and Soviet Communist regimes, for example — of the 1980s.

The social democratic Left built a postwar politics around the parliamentary struggle for the Keynesian welfare state. But as has been the case for the Liberal Party of Canada, the end of the long boom and the elimination of the fiscal dividend, and the increased competitive pressures arising from globalization have combined to erode the basis for a positive-sum politics of redistribution. No coherent strategy has emerged in its place. There has been a failure at the level of ideas, a loss of a sense of intellectual direction.

This has been the case not just for social democracy, but for Marxism as well.[135] While Marxist analyses of capitalism reach ever-growing levels of sophistication — much of it inaccessible to non-academics[136] — confusion reigns as regards a politics of socialism or social democracy. Kitching quite rightly argues that Left intellectuals tend to "know what they are against but are much less clear what they are for."[137] Thomas Hueglin concurs: "The radical Left ... appears to be much better equipped for providing such an analysis [i.e., of the causes of the current crisis] but fails to give precise directions as to where late capitalist societies might move from here"[138] The rise of a host of new demands — for example, environmentalism, feminism, a deepening of democracy — has added to the complexity, and at least in the short run, the intellectual incoherence, of a politics of the Left. So too has the globalization of capitalism and the limits it places on the sovereignty of the nation-state, and the collapse of Eastern European and Soviet Communist regimes. The net result has been a necessary rethinking of socialism, and of a socialist politics. Traditional socialist instruments, including and perhaps especially the centralized, bureaucratic welfare state, have consequently been subject to even more criticism than had hitherto been the case. The welfare state, for all its benefits, is seen by many, including its users, as distant, alienating, nonempowering. Those who might otherwise have been its defenders have quite rightly criticized its flaws. Important though such criticisms are, much less effort has been devoted to finding the means by which to transform the welfare state into an institution which empowers people.

Panitch has recently discussed this problem, arguing in favour of a radical democratization of the state and empowerment of users of state services. Yet he makes clear that the means by which this might be done is not yet known. The result is that while its advocates begin to puzzle out the problem of how to democratize the state, the federal state's redistributive capacity is being steadily eroded. The Right has a clear idea of where to go and how to get there; the Left as yet does not. Worse, there is in Panitch a trivialization of the question of the federal-provincial distribution of powers which appears to be consistent with an intellectual abandonment of the redistributive state.[139] A more useful formulation would be one in which a radical democratization of the state is seen as consistent with, rather than as a substitute for, a federal state with a redistributive capacity. The state should be brought closer to the users of state services, as the Right often argues, but the means by which to do so is not devolution, but democratization.

The Left, it might be hypothesized, has sadly underestimated the importance of fiscal federalism and the redistributive capacity of the federal state, having either ignored issues like the constitution and federalism,[140] or simply condemned what is seen as the overly centralized and bureaucratized federal state through which this redistribution is effected. Simple defense of the welfare state is not an adequate Left position, but neither is an abandonment of the welfare state.[141] The Left, it seems, is at an impasse, a paradigmatic impasse, with respect to the role of the redistributive state at a time of rapid economic restructuring:

> What is clearly required is a new paradigm to take us forward. So what is the new paradigm? The answer is that we do not know.[142]

This paradigmatic impasse finds expression in the position of the federal NDP in the post-Meech restructuring process. There is tension within the party over the centralized, redistributive state. And an economic strategy that would make possible the maintenance and enhancement of the redistributive state — a paradigmatic alternative to the neoconservative vision of Canada — has not yet been developed. The NDP, like the Left more generally, appears still to be in the midst of a necessary rethinking. This is evident in their specific position on the post-Meech constitutional process, as shown in their *Canadian Constitution Discussion Paper* of March 1991, and in their broader economic strategy, as revealed in *Putting People First: Towards a Fair, Environmentally Sustainable and Democratic Economy* of June 1991.

These documents reflect the confusion and the internal conflicts that have riven the NDP throughout the 1980s. The Laxer report criticized the party's emphasis on redistribution, and even adopted some of the language of neoconservatism,[143] while from the party's western-Canadian base has come a call for a break with the NDP's traditional centralism, and a greater emphasis on decentralization and provincial rights. The decentralist theme present in their 1985 report, *Canada Unlimited*, is plainly evident in Richards's most recent publication,[144] and is at least implicit in the ideas being advanced by many of the popular movements.[145] The resultant confusion and conflict has meant that, throughout the 1980s, "the NDP presented no coherent response to economic restructuring and the changing circumstances of the Canadian economy."[146] This confusion is reflected in their current constitutional position.

The party has historically been weak on constitutional issues. Cairns notes that "[t]he New Democratic Party initially saw the constitutional issue as a distraction and a smokescreen to veil the leadership failures of the government in other areas," and cites Bob Rae's 1979 comment that "[t]alking about the constitution makes us uncomfortable."[147] The same appears to be the case today. Their 1991 *Canadian Constitution Discussion Paper* places primary importance upon the need to make the process of constitutional renewal more democratic. The principles and values expressed in the paper are consistent with the defense of a centralized, redistributive state, and along with the questions which comprise the last part of the paper lay the basis for a fruitful debate. Yet the tentativeness and lack of specifics as regards options for the post-Meech restructuring of the federal state suggest that the party's legacy of neglect of, and differences over, such matters now weighs heavily upon its ability to provide intellectual leadership. Audrey McLaughlin's insistence that party members listen to what other Canadians have to say,[148] while consistent with the party's primary emphasis upon process and democracy, adds to the uncertainty about the substantive issues.[149] This uncertainty contrasts sharply with the clear sense of direction provided by the federal Conservative Party and its "factories of ideology."

Putting People First reinforces the sense of uncertainty, of rethinking, as regards broader economic strategy. The document expresses a commitment to a centralized, redistributive state and to national standards, albeit with greater provincial input into the design and delivery of shared-cost programs.[150] More generally, there is a continued commitment to traditional objectives, somewhat reconceptualized in response to new societal demands and realities, but without clarity as to how these reconceptualized objectives can be achieved. For example, the document places primacy upon low levels of (not the elimination of) unemployment, as opposed to the neoconservative primacy upon deficit reduction. Yet the means is fuzzy:

> The experience of other countries demonstrates that what is needed to achieve low levels of unemployment is political will. What is required is that this objective be made a central objective of economic policy. There is no single prescription to achieve this end. ... But fiscal and monetary policy are central, as are policies to improve the long term potential of the economy for growth.[151]

These latter appear to include a greater emphasis upon human skills development, research and development, further processing of natural resources, tax reform, all of which are familiar, but which do not in their totality constitute a coherent alternative economic strategy. There is, as is the case in the constitutional document, an emphasis upon a broadening and deepening of democracy — more democratic control of the economy, a greater use of cooperatives, of community-based planning, of democratic control of investment capital — but again, the overall vision is unclear, the impression created is of a work in process, a rethinking, a time "in which the familiar is dying ... but not yet dead

... while the new struggles to be born.''[152] And again, the contrast with the clarity and decisiveness of the neoconservative project for the restructuring of the Canadian economy is striking.

Ideas and the Redistributive State

Neoconservatives have been very effective in advancing their ideological project, while those who might have been expected to defend the redistributive state have been relatively ineffective. This failure of ideas is especially evident on the Left, which has been unable to fashion a viable vision of Canada's future in which political, as opposed to market, allocations of resources would play a significant role. Neoconservatives have seized upon the opportunities created by crises as a means of advancing their ideological project; the same crises have elicited only ideological confusion from the political and intellectual Left.

The confusion has followed the disappearance of the easy middle ground of Canadian politics, long occupied by the Liberal Party and long aspired to by the NDP. This political space, like the fiscal dividend of the postwar boom that made it possible, is now gone. In its stead has emerged the politics of neoconservatism, the ideological expression of the "increasingly globalized capitalism," the success of which is at least partly attributable to the skill and energy with which neoconservative factories of ideology have produced and marketed their products, their ideas. Alternative ideas are much less clear. The Liberals and NDP, their traditional postwar politics eroded, are without a sense of direction, unable to articulate a new politics suitable for a more globally-competitive world. The intellectual Left, at least with respect to the way forward, is equally confused. The competitive pressures that have placed the redistributive state at risk, also make it especially difficult to articulate an alternative economic strategy that would make possible the retention and enhancement of the redistributive state.

And yet, there is strong public support for the social programs funded by the redistributive state. As Banting puts it:

> public support for social programs remains strong ... indeed the depth of concern over the future of these social programs under a free trade regime with the U.S. demonstrates that they are deeply embedded in Canadian culture.[153]

And Canadians have increasingly become politically involved — indeed, have insisted upon being involved — in matters of constitutional change, as was made evident during the patriation of the constitution, and again at the time of Meech Lake.[154] One might reasonably hypothesize that this constitutes the social basis for a determined effort to defend the redistributive capacity of the federal state, and to build a strategy of economic reform that would make this possible. These forces may yet prevail — recent events caution against underestimating the power of a people aroused, and it is always inappropriate to read off the results of social change directly from the needs of capital. As Houle puts it: "In addition to the logic of accumulation, other factors are at work determining the future of social programs: the multiple compromises that result from different power relations and the diverse claims recognizing social rights and entitlements."[155]

But a defense of the redistributive capacity of the state is extremely difficult in the face of the powerful forces unleashed by the restructuring of capital and the liberalization of trade. And the political and intellectual leadership that is required to mount an effective political campaign for an alternative vision of Canada that includes the maintenance and enhancement of the redistributive capacity of the federal state is not up to the task. Those who oppose this neoconservative vision of Canada are mounting a struggle which is largely defensive, without a clear and compelling vision of an alternative. Thus even though NDP governments are now in office in Ontario, Saskatchewan and British Columbia, giving the NDP the provincial numbers to block the current federal government initiative, the party is without a coherent alternative to put in the place of *Shaping Canada's Future Together*, beyond the insertion of a social charter. A social charter may well be an appropriate means by which to express broadly shared values and aspirations, and by which, in general terms, to guide national policy. But to determine which social and economic rights and what kinds of standards and monitoring mechanisms might be included in a social charter would require a lengthy process characterized by substantial public involvement. The social charter proposals that have come forward from the government of Ontario, for example, are vague, have been presented only very recently, are of a preliminary character, and would require a great deal of public discussion before being entrenched, in some form, in the constitution. The Ontario government's discussion paper, *A Canadian Social Charter*, acknowledges this: "As this discussion paper shows, much thinking and many decisions will be needed before a social charter can be entrenched in the constitution."[156] Even once finally agreed upon, such social and economic rights, important though they might be, would not likely be enforceable in the courts, and would be a very poor trade-off for the parallel entrenchment in the constitution of the various neoconservative economic policies that are currently included in the constitutional proposals. After all, the constitutions of over half the world's countries currently include some such rights, in the majority of cases without discernible benefit to their citizens.[157] For the purposes of the current round of constitutional negotiations, the greater likelihood is that the idea of a social charter will be traded, in effect, for the removal of some or all of the neoconservative economic policy proposals now included in the constitutional package. In either case, i.e., with or without the recently proposed and still vaguely formulated social charter proposal, the steady erosion of the redistributive state, already well underway, is likely to continue, because although there is public support for an alternative economic and constitutional strategy in which the redistributive state would play a crucial role, such a strategy is, as yet, ill-formed. At the level of ideas, the struggle for the realization of different visions of Canada's future, which lies at the heart of the Constitutional conflict, is an unequal struggle. The result of the ensuing conflict, at least in the immediate future, is likely to be a continued erosion of the redistributive state, much to the detriment of provinces like Manitoba.

If the redistributive state and the transfer-payment system upon which Manitoba is so reliant are to remain in place in the absence of the postwar fiscal dividend, structural change is necessary. Neoconservatives have seized upon the need for structural change. They have fashioned the ideas and mustered the political will needed to make such change possible. Saving and enhancing, rather than eroding, the redistributive state would require an alternative form of restructuring which might include, *inter alia*, significant tax reform, more effective delivery of social programs, and a democratization — rather than a devolution — of the powers of the state. It is likely that such initiatives would inspire broadly based popular support. But how these objectives might be achieved is not clear. There is confusion at the level of ideas. Without a clearly expressed alternative around which public opinion might be mobilized, the forces of globalization will continue to push relentlessly for fragmentation, flexibility, and the erosion of the redistributive state.

CONCLUSION

A crucial aspect of the current multi-faceted constitutional process is the future of the redistributive state and the social programs it supports. Numerous forces — among the most important being the increased competitive pressures created by globalization and trade liberalization, and the effectiveness of neoconservatives in promoting their market-based ideological project — are combining to erode the redistributive capacity of the federal state. This erosion is already well underway as the result of cuts in the rate of growth of transfer payments. The post-Meech constitutional negotiations currently underway threaten to further the process. The adverse consequences are especially severe for relative have-not provinces like Manitoba. Manitoba has always been heavily reliant upon federal transfer payments, and Manitoba governments, no matter their ideological stripe, have historically been supportive of the centralized, redistributive state. The latter's erosion, and the related erosion of "place prosperity," will adversely affect Manitoba, and more specifically those Manitobans least able to defend themselves.

Yet, defense of the redistributive state has been largely ineffective. The explanation, this paper has argued, lies at least partly in the realm of ideas. In the wake of the crisis occasioned by the collapse of the long postwar boom, neoconservatives have very successfully defined and promoted their ideological project, while those who might be expected to defend the redistributive state have not, or have not done so effectively. To the extent that the struggle over the redistributive state is being fought out at the level of ideas, it is thus far, an unequal conflict. The political and ideological Left in particular is undergoing an historic rethinking, necessitated primarily by developments in the 1980s. The basic tenets of its beliefs, including and especially the bureaucratic welfare state, are the subject of intense, but as yet inconclusive debate. At the very moment that the postwar gains of working people as embodied in the redistributive capacity of the state are most at risk, in large part as a result of the immense competitive pressures created by globalization and trade liberalization, confusion reigns at the level of ideas about whether and how to retain and enhance the redistributive capacities of the state. The easy politics of the postwar period, made possible by the existence of the fiscal dividend, are gone. The politics of the middle ground are impossible. Retaining and enhancing the welfare state requires restructuring. Yet how this might be done is not clear. There is no longer an intellectual road map. There is no paradigm. This failure at the level of ideas compounds the pressures created by globalization and trade liberalization, placing the future of the redistributive state, and therefore of provinces like Manitoba, at grave risk.

Notes

1.   J. Harvey Perry, *Background to Current Fiscal Problems: Canadian Tax Paper No. 68* (Toronto: Canadian Tax Foundation, 1982), 26-27.

2.   Ibid., 31-34.

3.   Robin W. Boadway, *Intergovernmental Transfers in Canada* (Toronto: Canadian Tax Foundation, 1980), 1; Thomas J. Courchene, *The Evolution of Equalization Payments: The BNA Act to the Constitution Act, 1982* (Kingston: Institute for Economic Research, Queen's University, 1983), 24-25.

4.   The proportion of federal government expenditures consisting of transfers to other governments rose from 9.5 percent in 1947 to a high of 22.8 percent in 1977, then declined to 18.2 percent in 1986. See J. Harvey Perry, *A Fiscal History of Canada: The Postwar Years* (Toronto: Canadian Tax Foundation, 1989), 132 - Table A.10.

5.   Average GDP growth: 1960-73, 5.6 percent; 1973-79, 3.4 percent; 1980-84, 2.0 percent. Average unemployment: 1960-68, 4.8 percent, 1969-73, 5.4 percent; 1974-79, 7.2 percent; 1980-84, 9.9 percent. Average inflation: 1960-68, 2.4 percent, 1969-73, 4.6 percent; 1974-79, 9.2 percent; 1980-82, 11.2 percent. See Richard Simeon and Ian Robinson, *State, Society and the Development of Canadian Federation* (Toronto: University of Toronto Press, 1990), 217.

6.   Perry, *Background to Current Fiscal Problems*, 35.

7.   Ibid., 50.

8.   The cost of medicare, for example, increased by 100 percent between 1967 and 1971, and by another 100 percent plus between 1971 and 1975. See Perry, *A Fiscal History of Canada*, 650.

9.   Ibid., 650-51.

10.   See Boadway, *Intergovernmental Transfers*, 23-27; Thomas J. Courchene, *Refinancing the Canadian Federation: A Survey of the 1977 Fiscal Arrangements Act* (Toronto: C.D. Howe Institute, 1979).

11. Boadway, *Intergovernmental Transfers*, 83.

12. "In 1974 and 1975 cost and wage increases were in the 15-20 percent range. Wage contract increases in the private sector were: 1974, 16.8 percent and 1975, 17.8 percent; in the public sector: 1974, 14.0 percent and 1975, 19.6 percent. The implicit price index for GNP rose 15.3 percent in 1974 and 10.8 percent in 1975. The increase in the Consumer Price Index was a relatively modest 5.5 percent in 1974, but soared to 12.0 percent in 1975." Perry, *A Fiscal History of Canada*, 79.

13. See Courchene, *Refinancing the Canadian Federation*, 11-12; Allan J. MacEachen, "Federal-Provincial Fiscal Arrangements in the Eighties: A Submission to the Parliamentary Task Force on the Federal-Provincial Fiscal Arrangements," 23 April 1981.

14. Statement by provincial ministers of finance and treasurers, April 1983, p. 2.

15. Canada, Department of Finance, *Fiscal Arrangements in the Eighties: Proposals of the Government of Canada*. Presented by the Honourable Allan J. MacEachen, minister of Finance, 8 November 1981.

16. The removal of the revenue guarantee and the capping of postsecondary education payments had a cumulative effect because they "reduced the size of the block (grant) and therefore, as the escalator is applied to the new reduced base, the cutback is magnified annually." Manitoba, Department of Finance, *Background Information on Equalization*, December 1984, p. 26.

17. Assuming this artificial allocation of the block grant into a health and a PSE component, "the federal share of health spending has dropped from 46.7 percent in the first year of the Established Programs Financing arrangements (1977/78) to 43.9 percent in 1981 and 40.4 percent in 1984/85." Manitoba, Department of Finance, *Background on the Federal-Provincial Arrangement for Financing Health and Post-Secondary Education*, November 1985, p. 6.

18. See National Council of Welfare, *Funding Health and Higher Education: Danger Looming* (Ottawa: Minister of Supply and Services Canada, 1991), 16-17.

19. Hilary Grammer, "Social Policy by Stealth," *Canadian Dimension* 25, no. 4 (1991): 23.

20. Manitoba, Department of Finance, *Background on the Federal-Provincial Arrangement*, 3.

21. National Council of Welfare, *Funding Health and Higher Education*, 21.

22. See Canadian Council on Social Development, *Canada's Social Programs Are in Trouble* (Ottawa: Canadian Council on Social Development, 1990).

23. Grammer, "Social Policy by Stealth," 20.

24. See MacEachen, "Federal-Provincial Fiscal Arrangement in the Eighties," 5-6.

25. Courchene, *The Evolution of Equalization Payments*, 59.

26. Thomas J. Courchene, "Equalization Payments," *The Canadian Encyclopedia*, 2nd ed., vol. 2 (Edmonton: Hurtig Publishers, 1988), 716.

27. Howard Pawley, "Manitoba's Position on Federal Provincial Arrangements.

Equalization: Evaluating the Commitment.'' Annual Conference of First Ministers, Vancouver, 20-21 November 1986, p. 8.

This change has had a particularly adverse impact on Manitoba. (For estimates of the loss in revenue that Manitoba would suffer as a consequence of this change see Manitoba, Department of Finance, *Background Information on Equalization*, especially pp. 3, 27-30; and Howard Pawley, *Notes for a Statement on Federal-Provincial Fiscal Relations*, Premiers' Conference, St. John's, Newfoundland, 20-22 August 1985, p. 6. Premier Pawley claimed that Manitoba's share of equalization payments had dropped from 9.1 percent under the old formula in 1981-82, to 7.0 percent under the new formula. And: ''The current five-province standard means that the revenue available to recipient provinces including equalization falls $250 per capita short of the all province national average.''

28. In 1990, for the first time this cap on the rate of increase of equalization payments reduced the amount that Manitoba would otherwise have received. See Tim Sale, ''Federal Surgeons Cut the Heart Out of Medicare: Accident or Design.'' Unpublished paper, June 1991.

29. Perry, *A Fiscal History of Canada*, 476.

30. Elsewhere Boadway notes: ''the Equalization commitment involves more than the equalization system per se. Other programs must be seen as contributing to the equalization objective. The EPF program does so directly and in a way which is complementary with Equalization.'' Robin W. Boadway, ''Federal-Provincial Fiscal Relations,'' in Ronald L. Watts and Douglas Brown, eds., *Canada: The State of the Nation 1989* (Kingston: Institute of Intergovernmental Relations, 1989), 125.

31. Canada, Department of Finance, *A New Direction for Canada: An Agenda for Economic Renewal*. Presented by the Honourable Michael H. Wilson, minister of Finance, 8 November 1984.

32. Canada, Department of Finance, ''Securing Economic Renewal: The Budget Speech.'' Delivered in the House of Commons by the Honourable Michael H. Wilson, minister of Finance, 23 May 1985, p. 1.

33. Perry, *A Fiscal History of Canada*, 192.

34. Canada, *A New Direction for Canada*, 2. See also Canada, Department of Finance, ''Economic and Fiscal Statement.'' Delivered in the House of Commons by the Honourable Michael H. Wilson, minister of Finance, 8 November 1984, p. 2.

35. Canada, ''Economic and Fiscal Statement,'' 6.

36. Canada, *A New Direction for Canada*, 71.

37. Canada, ''Securing Economic Renewal,'' 17.

38. Perry, *A Fiscal History of Canada*, 108.

39. Laurent Thibault, then president of the Canadian Manufacturers' Association, is reported as having said, a mere three months after the signing of the FTA, that the FTA makes it more urgent for Canada to become competitive, that this requires reducing the deficit, and that deficit reduction necessitates significant cuts in social spending. ''CMA'S

Thibault Seeking Cuts in Spending on Social Programs," *Globe and Mail*, 1 March 1989, p. B13.

40. Canada, Department of External Affairs, *The Canada-US Free Trade Agreement* (Ottawa: Minister of Supply and Services, 1988).

41. See K.E. Swinton and C.J. Rogerson, eds., *Competing Constitutional Visions: The Meech Lake Accord* (Toronto: Carswell, 1988), especially part 2; and Michael D. Behiels, ed., *The Meech Lake Primer: Conflicting Views of the 1987 Constitutional Accord* (Ottawa: University of Ottawa Press, 1989), especially chapter 6.

42. Deborah Coyne, "The Meech Lake Accord and the Spending Power Proposals: Fundamentally Flawed," in Behiels, *The Meech Lake Primer*, 247, 249.

43. Constitutional Committee of the Quebec Liberal Party, *A Quebec Free to Choose: Report of the Constitutional Committee* (Montreal: Quebec Liberal Party, 1991), 37-38, 60-61.

44. Ibid., 41.

45. Ibid., 4, 19 and 55.

46. Quebec, Commission on the Political and Constitutional Future of Quebec, *Report of the Commission on the Political and Constitutional Future of Quebec*, 27 March 1991, pp. 4 and 47.

47. Constitutional Committee, *A Quebec Free to Choose*, 39, 41.

48. Ibid., 29-30.

49. Canada, Office of the Prime Minister, "Notes for an Address by Prime Minister Brian Mulroney," Buckingham, Quebec, 16 December 1990, p. 3.

50. Canada, Office of the Prime Minister, "Speaking Notes for Prime Minister Brian Mulroney," Chamber of Commerce, Quebec City, 13 February 1991, pp. 6 and 7.

This language, like so much else — the need to eliminate "a duplication of services" and "overlapping jurisdictions," the need for flexibility" in order to improve "competitiveness" — is consistent with that in the Allaire report, which asserts that: "the federal system needs more than a tune-up. It needs to be radically overhauled." Constitutional Committee, *A Quebec Free to Choose*, 25.

51. Constitutional Committee, *A Quebec Free to Choose*, 2.

52. Quebec, *Report of the Commission on the Political and Constitutional Future*, 48.

53. *Economic and Fiscal Developments and Federal Provincial Fiscal Relations in Canada*. Report of the western finance ministers submitted to the Western Premiers' Conference, Lloydminster, Saskatchewan, 26-27 July 1990, p. 8.

54. Ibid., p. 14.

55. Ibid., p. 177.

56. Ibid., p. 25.

57. Report of the western finance ministers, *Supplement*, August 1990, p. 10.

58. *Economic and Fiscal Development*, p. 25.

59. For a useful summary see *The Network: Newsletter of the Network on the Constitution* 1, no. 4 (September 1991).

60. Canada, *Shaping Canada's Future Together: Proposals* (Ottawa: Minister of Supply and Services Canada, 1991), 43.

61. Ibid.

62. Ibid., 46.

63. Ibid., 31.

64. Manitoba, Department of Finance, *Budget Speech*, 7 February 1938, pp. 28-29.

65. Ibid., 30-31.

66. Ibid., 30.

67. "In the winter of 1937 there was not enough money in the provincial account to pay civil servants. In fact Premier John Bracken's statement that the province was about to default set in motion an inquiry by the Bank of Canada which resulted in the Royal Commission on Dominion-Provincial Relations." M.S. Donnelly, *The Government of Manitoba* (Toronto: University of Toronto Press, 1963), 163.

68. Ibid., 170; see also Paul G. Thomas, "Manitoba: Stuck in the Middle," in Watts and Brown, *Canada: The State of the Nation*, 80.

69. Manitoba, Department of Finance, *Budget Speech*, 23 March 1955.

70. Manitoba, Department of Finance, *Budget Speech*, 26 March 1958, p.71.

71. Manitoba, Department of Finance, *Budget Speech*, 28 March 1956, p. 91.

72. Manitoba, Department of Finance, *Budget Speech*, 1960, p. 28.

73. Ibid., 31.

74. Manitoba, Department of Finance, *Budget Speech*, 1961, p. 27.

75. Manitoba, Department of Finance, *Budget Speech*, 1965, pp. 24-25.

76. Manitoba, Department of Finance, *Budget Speech*, 1972, p. 79.

77. Ibid., 102.

78. Manitoba, Department of Finance, *Budget Speech*, 1970, p. 12, quoting Premier Schreyer's introductory remarks to the Third Constitutional Conference, Ottawa, 8 December 1969.

79. Manitoba, *Budget Speech, 1970*.

80. Neil Tudiver, "Constraints and Opportunities with Provincial Budgets," in Jim Silver and Jeremy Hull, eds., *The Political Economy of Manitoba* (Regina: Canadian Plains Research Center, 1990), 301.

81. For details see Manitoba, Department of Finance, *Budget Speech*, 1976, pp. 9-11.

82. Ibid., 138 and 140.

83. Frances Russell, "Lyon Government Record Wasn't Very Impressive," *Winnipeg Free Press*, 6 April 1988, p. 7.

84. Manitoba, Department of Finance, *Budget Speech*, 1978, p. 54.

85. Manitoba, Department of Finance, *Budget Speech*, 1979, p. 16.

86. Manitoba, Department of Finance, *Budget Speech*, 1980, p. 19.

87. Sterling Lyon, "Statement on Equalization," presented at First Ministers' Conference on the Constitution, September 1980, in Manitoba, Department of Finance, *Budget Speech*, 1981, p. 200.

88. Manitoba, Department of Finance, *Budget Address*, 1982, p. 2.

89. Manitoba, Department of Finance, *Budget Address*, 1983, p. 12. The 1991 Manitoba budget estimates that federal transfers will account for 34.8 percent of Manitoba's revenue in the 1991-92 fiscal year — the *1991 Manitoba Budget*, Budget Paper B, p. 13.

90. Tudiver, "Constraints and Opportunities," 301.

91. Manitoba Department of Finance, *Budget Address*, 1986, pp. 14-15.

92. Howard Pawley, "Notes for a Statement on Federal-Provincial Fiscal Arrangements," presented to the Conference of First Ministers, 28-29 November 1985 and in Manitoba, *Budget Address*, 1986, p. E6.

93. Ibid.

94. Ibid., D11

95. See, for example, "The Manitoba Levy for Health and Post-Secondary Education," Manitoba, *Budget Address*, 1982, Appendix IIIB, pp. 87-89.

96. See, for example, Russell, "Lyon Government Record," and Cy Gonick, "The Manitoba Economy Since World War II," in Silver and Hull, *Political Economy of Manitoba*, 25-48.

97. Manitoba, Department of Finance, *The 1988 Manitoba Budget*, 8 August 1988, pp. 1-2.

98. Manitoba, Department of Finance, *The 1991 Manitoba Budget*, 16 April 1991, p. 5.

99. Choices: A Coalition for Social Justice, *The 1991 Manitoba Budget of Choice*, 15 April 1991, p. 6. This comprehensive, alternative provincial budget was prepared by a team of economists from the University of Manitoba.

100. Interview with Gary Doer, 19 August 1991.

101. Manitoba, Department of Finance, *The 1990 Manitoba Budget*, 1990, p. 5.

102. Manitoba, *The 1991 Manitoba Budget*, p. 7.

103. Personal interviews with Jim Carr, 21 August 1991; Sharon Carstairs, 27 August 1991; Gary Doer, 19 August 1991.

104. Personal interview with Jim Eldridge, 5 September 1991.

105. Manitoba, Department of Finance, *Report of the Manitoba Constitutional Task Force*, 28 October 1991, p. 41.

106. Ibid., 44-45. The report of the Meech Lake Task Force concluded, referring specifically to the proposed Sec. 106A(1), that: "The Task Force cannot endorse an amendment

to the constitution which is so controversial and which many presenters believe might undermine our sense of national community by limiting the ability of the federal government to respond to the universal need of Canadians'' — Manitoba Task Force on Meech Lake, *Report on the 1987 Constitutional Accord*, 1989, p. 55.

107. Manitoba, *Report of the Manitoba Constitutional Task Force*, 1991, pp. 56 and 67.

108. Ramesh Mishra, *The Welfare State in Capitalist Society: Policies of Retrenchment and Maintenance in Europe, North America and Australia* (Toronto; University of Toronto Press, 1990), 12.

109. Ibid., 15.

110. Jane Jenson, "'Different' But Not 'Exceptional': Canada's Permeable Fordism,'' *The Canadian Review of Sociology and Anthropology* 26, no. 1 (February 1989): 73.

111. Gilles Breton and Jane Jenson, "After Free Trade and Meech Lake: Quoi de Neuf?'' *Studies in Political Economy* 34 (Spring 1991): 202.

112. See also Glen Williams, *Not for Export: Towards a Political Economy of Canada's Arrested Industrialization* (Toronto: McClelland and Stewart, 1986), 5-6.

113. Sidney Blumenthal, *The Rise of the Counter-Establishment: From Conservative Ideology to Political Power* (New York: Harper and Row, 1988), 10-11.

114. Ibid., 43 and 49.

115. Ibid., 3.

116. See, for example, David Langille, ''The Business Council on National Issues and the Canadian State,'' *Studies in Political Economy* 24 (1987): 41-85.

117. See Byrne Purchase, *The Innovative Society: Competitiveness in the 1990's, Policy Review and Outlook, 1991* (Toronto and Calgary: C.D. Howe Institute, 1991), 72-73; and Boadway, ''Federal-Provincial Fiscal Relations,'' 134.

118. Business Council on National Issues (BCNI), *Social Policy Reform and the National Agenda* (Ottawa: BCNI, 1986), 2.

119. Ibid., viii. There is evidence that it is *not* escalating social program costs that are driving up the deficit. See, for example, H. Mimoto and P. Cross, ''The Growth of the Federal Debt,'' *Canadian Economic Observer*, June 1991, pp. 3.1 - 3.18.

120. Thomas J. Courchene, ''Social Policy,'' in Thomas E. Kiernans (ed.), *Getting it Right: Policy Review and Outlook, 1990* (Ottawa: C.D. Howe Institute, 1990), 67-68. See also *Ottawa's Next Agenda: Policy Review and Outlook, 1989* (Ottawa: C.D. Howe Institute, 1989), 122; Maureen Farrow and William B.P. Robson, ''The Long Road Back to Balance: Federal Fiscal Policy Following the April 1989 Budget,'' *Fiscal Policy Monitor* 2 (July 1989); Edward A. Carmichael, *Tackling the Federal Deficit, Observation 26* (Ottawa: C.D. Howe Institute, 1984), esp. pp. 39 and 41.

This latter argument is used frequently as the rationale for eliminating universality. The BCNI, commenting on the universality of the Old Age Security Program, said: ''Some cheques will go to retired executives, while others will go to poor citizens. Is this sensible or socially and fiscally responsible? We think not.'' BCNI, *Social Policy Reform*, 47.

121. BCNI, "Canada and the 21st Century: Towards a More Effective Federalism and a Stronger Economy" (a statement of the members of the BCNI), 26 April 1991, p. 5.

122. Purchase, *The Innovative Society*, 75-76; see also Simeon and Janigan, *Toolkits and Building Blocks*, esp. pp. 23-24, 38, 41-42 and 121.

123. Thomas J. Courchene and John N. McDougall, Summary of "The Context for Future Constitutional Reform," in *Canada's Constitutional Options*, summaries and papers prepared for the BCNI Symposium on Canada's Constitutional Options, Toronto, 16 January 1991.

124. BCNI, "Canada and the 21st Century," p. 8.

125. Ibid.,

126. Thomas J. Courchene, *In Praise of Renewed Federalism* (Toronto and Calgary: C.D. Howe Institute, 1991), 93.

127. *Globe and Mail*, 26 June 1991.

128. See Jenson, "'Different' But Not 'Exceptional'," and Jane Jenson, "Representations in Crisis: The Roots of Canada's Permeable Fordism," *Canadian Journal of Political Science* 23, no. 4 (December 1990): 653-83.

129. See Canadian Broadcasting Corporation, interview with Thomas J. Courchene, *Sunday Morning*, 23 March 1991; Courchene, *In Praise of Renewed Federalism*; Purchase, *The Innovative Society*. Also see Canada, *Report of the Royal Commission on the Economic Union and Development Prospects for Canada* (Ottawa: Minister of Supply and Services, 1985), part II, pp. 613, 773 and 802.

130. Janine Brodie and Jane Jenson, *Crisis, Challenge and Change: Party and Class in Canada Revisited* (Ottawa: Carleton University Press, 1988), 233.

131. Tom Kent, *A Public Purpose* (Montreal/Kingston: McGill-Queens's University Press, 1988), 79, 85.

132. See J. L. Granatstein, *The Ottawa Men: The Civil Service Mandarins, 1935-1957* (Toronto: Oxford University Press, 1982); Douglas Owran, *The Government Generation: Canadian Intellectuals and the State, 1900-1945* (Toronto: University of Toronto Press, 1986).

133. Donald Smiley, *The Federal Condition in Canada* (Toronto: McGraw-Hill Ryerson, 1987), 179.

134. Brodie and Jenson, *Crisis, Challenge and Change*, 318.

135. See, among many examples, Stuart Hall, *The Hard Road to Renewal* (London: Verso, 1988); Gavin Kitching, *Rethinking Socialism* (London: Methuen, 1983); Michael Rustin, *For a Pluralist Socialism* (London: Verso, 1988); Anthony Wright, *Socialism: Theories and Practices* (Oxford: Oxford University Press, 1986).

136. Wright, for example, laments that "so much contemporary socialist argument seems to consist of socialists talking to, and writing for, each other in a private language, and so little of it to be an exercise in public persuasion." Wright, *Socialism: Theories and Practices*, 126. Kitching adds: "The intellectual left's current style of writing and speaking is part of its problem, not part of its solution." Kitching, *Rethinking Socialism*, xii.

137. Kitching, *Rethinking Socialism*, 73.

138. Thomas O. Hueglin, "The Politics of Fragmentation in An Age of Scarcity: A Synthetic View and Critical Analysis of Welfare State Crisis," *Canadian Journal of Political Science* 20, no.2 (June 1987): 246.

Even this is not entirely accurate. As Drache and Gertler note in their recent volume, the dramatic pace of change in the global economy has meant that "theoretical issues must now be rethought and the boundary lines of political economy redrawn." Daniel Drache and Meric S. Gertler, *The New Era of Global Competition* (Montreal/Kingston: McGill-Queen's University Press, 1991), xiii.

139. Leo Panitch, "How Our Democracy Could Work," *Canadian Forum* (June-July 1991): 5-8.

140. Thomas Hueglin, admitting to a professional interest in both federalism and political economy, notes wryly that: "When I talk to colleagues in the political economy community, even the mentioning of the word federalism is likely to provoke yawns of disinterest." Thomas O. Hueglin, *A Political Economy of Federalism* (Kingston: Institute of Intergovernmental Relations, 1990), 1.

141. Rather than ignore or condemn the welfare state, a more useful formulation is this observation by Robert Cairns: "The welfare state is one of the greatest accomplishments of post-war industrial society, but it cannot solve all problems, such as environmental degradation, or even eliminate all poverty. From exaggerated expectations in the welfare state many have succumbed to exaggerated skepticism." John Richards, Robert Cairns and Larry Pratt, eds., *Social Democracy Without Illusions: Renewal of the Canadian Left* (Toronto: McClelland and Stewart, 1991), 39.

142. John Myles, "Decline or Impasse: The Current State of the Welfare State," *Studies in Political Economy* 26 (1988): 84.

143. James Laxer, *Rethinking the Economy* (Toronto: New Canada Publications, 1983).

144. Not a single contribution to (Richards et al.,) *Social Democracy Without Illusions* is devoted to federalism or the constitution, nor to a defense of the redistributive state. On the contrary, the editors criticize social democrats' defense of the welfare state, arguing that while "the goals of the welfare state ... remain valid ... we have too often slipped from a defence of the goals into a defence of interest groups committed to particular means" (p. 8). Larry Pratt, a co-editor, argues vehemently in the same volume against what he considers to be the Canadian Left nationalists' unjustified defense of "the national welfare state in the face of an interdependent world economy..." (p. 151).

145. See Duncan Cameron and Daniel Drache, *The Other Macdonald Report* (Toronto: Lorimer, 1985); Duncan Cameron, "Beyond the Market and the State: How Can We Do Better?" in Daniel Drache and Meric S. Gertler, eds., *The New Era of Global Competition: State Policy and Market Power* (Montreal/Kingston: McGill-Queen's University Press, 1991).

146. Brodie and Jenson, *Crisis, Challenge and Change*, 310.

147. Alan Cairns, *Disruptions: Constitutional Struggles, From the Charter to Meech Lake* (Toronto: McClelland and Stewart, 1991), 86.

148. "I cannot emphasize enough how important listening is in this process. Listen to your neighbours. Listen to what is being said in Quebec and in the West. Hear what northerners and aboriginal people have to say. Pay attention to the women of Canada and to the minorities." New Democratic Party, *Canadian Constitution Discussion Paper*, March 1991.

149. See also Audrey McLaughlin, speaking notes, "A Canada for All Canadians," Kingston, 10 April 1991 and Winnipeg, 2 May 1991.

150. New Democratic Party, *Putting People First: Towards a Fair, Environmentally Sustainable and Democratic Economy*, a report prepared by the federal New Democratic Party Policy Review Committee, June 1991, esp. pp. 19-20.

151. Ibid., p. 8.

152. Breton and Jenson, "After Free Trade and Meech Lake," 202.

153. Keith G. Banting, "Social Policy in an Open Economy: Neoconservativism and the Canadian State," paper presented to the annual meeting of the American Political Science Association, San Francisco, 30 August - 2 September 1990, p. 10-11. See also François Houle, "Economic Renewal and Social Policy," in Alain Gagnon and James Bickerton, eds., *Canadian Politics: An Introduction to the Discipline* (Peterborough: Broadview Press, 1990), 440-41; Ramesh Mishra, "Public Policy and Social Welfare: The Ideology and Practice of Constraint in Ontario," in Jacqueline S. Ismael, ed., *The Canadian Welfare State* (Edmonton: University of Alberta Press, 1987), 330.

154. See Cairns, *Disruptions*.

155. Houle, "Economic Renewal and Social Policy," 440.

156. Ontario, Ministry of Intergovernmental Affairs, *A Canadian Social Charter: Making Our Shared Values Stronger* (a discussion paper), September 1991, p. 23. See also Ontario, Ministry of the Attorney General, Constitutional Law and Policy Division, *The Protection of Social and Economic Rights: A Comparative Study*, 19 September 1991; Institute of Intergovernmental Relations, *Approaches to National Standards in Federal Systems*, a research report prepared for the Government of Ontario, 19 September 1991.

157. Ontario, Ministry of the Attorney General, *The Protection of Social and Economic Rights*, pp. 6-9.

15

Alternative Futures: Region, Nation and Constitutional Change

James Bickerton

In the brief passage of time since the demise of the Meech Lake Accord in June 1990, constitutional commissions, committees, inquiries, forums, and other assorted vehicles for talking and writing about the constitution have spewed forth a veritable avalanche of commentary describing how Canadians got themselves into their current situation and how they might best set about getting themselves out of it. Atlantic Canadians were somewhat slow to acknowledge the latest constitutional crisis, or perhaps just loathe to plunge themselves yet again into Canada's tiresome national pastime, so soon after the wrenching experience of the Meech Lake debacle. Nonetheless, major constitutional changes are again being proposed, changes that if implemented will have important effects on the Canadian system of government and on the organization, delivery, scope and quality of public services.

This paper is concerned primarily with the interests of Atlantic Canadians in the process of constitutional change. Since the only outcome of the current crisis which seems unlikely is continuation of the constitutional *status quo*, the first task should be to identify the elements of this *status quo* that are central to the welfare of Atlantic Canadians. To do this one must first understand the place of Atlantic Canada within the Canadian federation, that is, the economic and political relationship of the region's people and provinces with the national government and with other Canadian regions.

On all of the key economic indices — income per capita, earned income per capita, gross provincial product per capita, rates of unemployment, work force participation rates — the provinces of the Atlantic region rank as the poorest in Canada. In fiscal terms, this produces corresponding dependency ratios which are the highest in Canada. This being the case, federal fiscal transfers make up a much higher proportion of provincial budgets in Atlantic Canada than is the case for other Canadian provinces. The most important of these intergovernmental transfers — equalization payments — make possible the provision of public services at a level comparable to that of other provinces, without the prohibitively high levels of taxation that would otherwise be necessary. And individual Atlantic Canadians rely more heavily on direct federal transfers such as unemployment insurance payments and other federal income support programs. As well, the federal role in funding regional economic development initiatives remains paramount in Atlantic Canada; as a rule, economic and industrial assistance programs in the region are either joint federal-provincial undertakings (wherein the federal contribution varies), or else exclusively federal, such as the Atlantic Canada Opportunities Agency (ACOA).

In sum, a complex web of fiscal relations tightly binds the people and governments of Atlantic Canada to the federal government. The character and content of these fiscal relations defines in part the place of Atlantic Canada within the Canadian federation and suggests certain imperatives for the region in constitutional affairs. In the first instance, the Atlantic provinces require a strong federal government in Canada with sufficient constitutional responsibilities and fiscal resources to continue to play a major role in interpersonal and interregional redistribution. Secondly, the national government must have a constitutionally assigned responsibility for regional equalization and development instructing it to pursue through its policies the goal of greater regional equality in Canada, both in terms of social conditions and economic opportunities.

Considering the interests of Atlantic Canadians in constitutional reform, however, requires more than simply looking at what the region gets out of Confederation in terms of. material resources, that is, its pecuniary stake in the federation. Money — and the goods and services money can buy — are obviously at stake here. But also at stake is the "Canadian" portion of Atlantic Canadian identities, whether Newfoundlander, Islander, Nova Scotian, or New Brunswicker. This is the part of their identity that they share with other Canadians and which is central to the legitimacy and support they accord to the political community and the political regime of which they are a part. Constitutional reform will have social and cultural implications that are inseparable from, yet go beyond, questions of fiscal and financial relations.

The arguments made in this paper are rooted in certain assumptions about state-society relations in Canada. These relations are understood to be interdependent and interpenetrative. This suggests a definite relationship between government 'outputs' — both substantive and symbolic — and political culture. Citizen political identity and attachment to both the community and the regime, and therefore the foundation for national political integration, is shaped and supported by state policies, programs and institutions. Canadian identity today, and popular support for continuance of the national political community and political regime, is bound up with a set of values and social entitlements embodied in a range of policies and programs that for the most part were designed and implemented only in the 1960s. Further, it is argued that dismantling control over this network of programs would be destructive of Canadian identity and national unity.

Beyond such substantive government outputs, Canadian identity and regime legitimacy also depend upon symbolic outputs and broad-based agreement upon a set of political principles and procedures, from which a shared Canadian identity can draw sustenance. The Charter of Rights and Freedoms has quickly become a statement of principles and values of great symbolic importance to Canadians; it also represents a significant procedural change in the process of defining and arbitrating citizen rights and citizen-state relations, one that appears to command wide public acceptance and respect. No other aspect of the present Canadian constitution has the unifying potential and effect of the charter, making it indispensible as a central feature of any future Canadian constitutional system.

Substantive and symbolic government outputs have ensured the integration of Atlantic Canada *as a region* into the Canadian federation; they have also been important in providing the basis for a common Canadian identity and political culture that is shared by individual Canadians. Changes to the Canadian constitution that substantially alter the substance of what the federal and provincial governments do, or the fundamental principles and symbols that govern the Canadian constitutional system and the degree of legitimacy citizens accord to that system, can also be expected to have social and cultural implications for Canadian society. The political, economic and cultural integration of Canadians into a single social formation or national entity has always been problematic, given its internal divide between English and French and the strong pull of the American hegemony to the south. The problem of maintaining an integrated nation is no less problematic now, and constitutional reform can either strengthen or dissipate the basis for an integrated Canadian nation. It is a consequence of institutional and constitutional design which Canadians in all regions would be wise not to ignore in the current negotiations.

REGIONAL EQUALITY AND ECONOMIC DEVELOPMENT

Equalization

The importance of federal equalization payments for Atlantic Canada cannot be overstated. In 1989-90, equalization payments alone made up between 21 percent and 30 percent of provincial budgetary revenues in the region. The corresponding figures for Manitoba and Quebec were 15 percent and 9 percent respectively.[1] This has enabled the provincial governments in the Atlantic region to provide a level of services to their residents far exceeding that which would be possible were they forced to rely exclusively on their own resources.

There has been a disturbing tendency of late to characterize equalization as a "hand-out" to the Atlantic region, and a fiscal burden that is becoming too heavy for the country to bear. There have even been arguments made which blame equalization payments for the continuing economic problems of the Atlantic region, or else downplay their importance to regional economic stability. All of these arguments about equalization have been made in the past and the same counterarguments that have always been used still apply. Equalization payments are made necessary in Canada because of our decentralized federal system; in other less decentralized countries the national government ensures a similar degree of interregional redistribution, and cross-regional equality in the level and quality of public services, through the direct provision of such services in all regions. Funds transferred to the the poorer provinces are used to build and maintain social and economic infrastructure and services that are necessary to the workings of a modern economy and marketplace. The beneficiaries of such public expenditure, of course, are not exclusively regional. The result of such expenditure is not just an extension of the national market, but a generally healthy and well-educated populace that provide a human resource that is utilized nationally within the private and public sectors, thereby making a substantial contribution to national output and productivity.

There are also sound efficiency arguments for equalization. The provision of a similar level of public services across the country without wildly varying levels of taxation permits businesses and individuals to make decisions on other market or efficiency-based criteria. In other words, equalization removes a distorting factor from the marketplace (i.e., the degree of variation between provinces in net fiscal benefits conferred upon provincial residents). Without this form of redistribution, the Canadian economy would be even more prone to agglomeration effects than it is already.

Finally, there can be no question of the importance of equalization payments and other federal transfers to the health and stability of the Atlantic economy. A great deal of the economic activity in the region is more or less directly dependent upon this flow of transfers. They provide a crucial element of economic stimulus and stability within the region without which there would be a sharp decline in living standards and regional economic performance. In an era when economic performance is increasingly dependent upon the quality of a region's work force and its social and economic infrastructure (as opposed to, for instance, lower wages), it would be senseless and counterproductive for any federal government to limit or arbitrarily cut equalization payments to the poorer provinces.

It is to be hoped, of course, that Atlantic Canada will not always require equalization payments, that one day the revenue-raising capacities of the provinces of the region will match or exceed national average capacities. There is virtually no possibility, however, that the regional economic disparities that underlie the need for equalization payments will quickly, if ever, disappear. In the interim, it is critical to the well-being of Atlantic Canadians and to the overall quality and stability of the Canadian community and Canadian economy that this fiscal arrangement continue, and that Sec. 36 of the Canadian Constitution (committing Canadian governments to the principle of regional equality and equalization payments) be protected, preserved and enhanced in any new round of negotiations.[2]

Regional Economic Development

The equalization burden shouldered by the federal government (and through it all Canadians) is a legacy of national policies that favoured the centre over the peripheries in Canada. A protected national market was created, but at a high cost for the Atlantic and western provinces. If this burden is to be eased over the long term, then the regional economies, particularly the Atlantic, will have to be strengthened and diversified. Federal assistance for this purpose began in the late 1950s, becoming significant in budgetary terms a decade later with the creation of the Department of Regional Economic Expansion (DREE). Over the past twenty years federal assistance to Atlantic Canada for economic development purposes has taken numerous forms, often under umbrella agreements with provincial governments in the region, such as the Fund for Rural Economic Development (FRED) plans of the 1960s, the General Development Agreements (GDAs) of the 1970s, or the Economic and Regional Development Agreements (ERDAs) of the 1980s. Currently, the ACOA administers federal economic development aid to the Atlantic region. Governmental approaches to the problem of regional economic development have also varied, progressing from an early rural development focus, through urban growth poles, to resource megaprojects, and most recently, nurturing local entrepreneurship. Through all these phases, federal monies for economic infrastructure in the region have been important, as have financial incentives of various sorts to encourage businesses to locate or expand there.[3]

The fact of the matter is that the autonomous capacity of individual Atlantic provinces to engage in discretionary economic development spending is sharply circumscribed. This is due in part to the priority provincial governments must give to maintaining social infrastructure and services (health care, education, social assistance), a priority necessitated by provincial participation in the national social programs that enormously benefit provincial residents; it is more directly a function of the fiscal limitations imposed by the relative impoverishment and indebtedness of the Atlantic provinces. There are no revenues for economic development initiatives available from a heritage fund made up of oil revenues, as in Alberta, or from a massive provincial pension fund, as in Quebec. If they want or need more revenue for economic development initiatives, the provincial governments in the Atlantic region are faced with limited options.

One way to alleviate their fiscal bind (and thereby free resources for more discretionary spending on economic development) is for governments in the region to sharply reduce the level of public services they provide to their residents. But not only would this be socially unhealthy, economically disastrous, politically suicidal, and for the moment at least, constitutionally difficult, it also would be corrosive ultimately of the citizen-state and citizen-citizen relations that help bind Canadians together. Alternatively, provincial governments in Atlantic Canada could increase the tax burden on their residents, a tax burden which is already the highest in Canada. However, if they did so, they would succeed only in further eroding their competitive position *vis-à-vis* other Canadian provinces and American states. If, on the other hand, they attempt to stimulate economic development through tax concessions to attract new investment, or other forms of tax expenditure or inducement such as changes to labour laws, they succeed only in alienating and disadvantaging established businesses not similarly subsidized, undermining their province's social arrangements, or engaging in expensive and regionally-destructive competition for investment with equally needy Atlantic neighbours.[4]

All of this suggests certain limitations on provincial governments in Atlantic Canada when it comes to the task of stimulating regional economic development. But there is another reason for federal involvement in this area, one which is especially pertinent to Atlantic Canada — there is no other single government that can act in the regional interest, only separate provincial governments acting for distinct and often competing provincial interests. This may not be particularly troubling to province-regions such as Quebec, but in the Atlantic region, the economic development efforts of each province have produced a plethora of instances where needless and wasteful duplication of effort has occurred or where directly competing or contradictory policies have nullified the effectiveness of all. Provincial governments have inherently limited visions that correspond to their limited constituencies; the temptation to adopt "beggar-thy-neighbour" policies is great.[5]

Efforts at regional cooperation, notably through the Council of Maritime Premiers, have been noninclusive and for the most part limited to peripheral matters with regard to provincial economies. Current circumstances have pushed the council beyond this limited range of cooperative activity, but it remains unclear whether an announced commitment to the pursuit of full maritime economic union can proceed beyond common government purchases of license plates or guardrails.[6] The process is fragile and acutely sensitive to ongoing political considerations and entrenched bureaucratic and group interests. While this could be overcome by the simple but effective solution of political union, all three maritime premiers have ruled this out categorically.[7] Moreover, Newfoundland has been excluded from even the limited initiatives at regional economic integration that have so far been launched.[8]

Of course, the mere presence of the federal government does not guarantee a fully regional approach to the economic development problem. Indeed, early in DREE's mandate, provincialism scuttled the agency's nascent regional strategy because it was arbitrarily "imposed from above" by federal technocrats. But the mere fact that the federal government's efforts are channelled through a single agency that has a *regional* mandate offers some hope of a regional approach, and federal-provincial economic development agreements during the 1970s and

1980s have at least ensured a certain degree of policy similarity and co-ordination.[9]

Nonetheless, the argument is made by some (especially in the current constitutional context) that a reduced federal role in regional economic development is both inevitable and desirable; that federal efforts in this direction have been abysmal failures; that in any event, deficit reduction, free trade and changing global patterns of production and competition have made the national government an inappropriate instrument for encouraging regional and local economic development.

The "new reality" of free trade and global competition, and the growing importance of the information economy and knowledge-based industries, does impose some new constraints as well as some new imperatives on the government role in the economy. At the same time, it presents an "opening" of sorts for the Atlantic provinces and other formerly peripheral regional economies. The world of protected national markets and mass production was not a particularly advantageous one for Atlantic Canadians. In the Canadian context, it necessarily privileged Ontario producers of consumer goods who were at the centre of the national market, both geographically and in population terms. Maritime industries became branch plants, then were shut down or phased out as ownership was consolidated and production centralized in an era of monopoly capitalism.

The economic parameters for maritime businesses have now been radically altered. And as always, the breakup of old economic structures presents both dangers and opportunities. There are fewer formal barriers now to economic success if governments and producer groups in the Atlantic region can seize the opportunity through strategies and policies that will enhance the region's competitiveness in the new global economy. Some approaches to fostering regional development — such as using large cash grants and like subsidies to entice industries into the region — may have to be shelved, given the stipulations of the Canada-US Free Trade Agreement (FTA). But this approach had already shown itself to be of dubious value in any event. Current wisdom and practice is based instead on an endogenous development model, emphasizing government support for small- and medium-sized local businesses attempting to occupy regional markets and/or export niches. Such ventures do not require the massive subsidies that multinational branch plants have bargained for themselves in the past, nor are they nearly as likely to be involved in trade disputes under the FTA. However, they do often require start-up, marketing, technological, managerial and training assistance. Cooperation is essential, and federal, provincial and local governments will have to be involved.

Indeed, the role that governments are called upon to play in the contemporary era is crucial, if national and regional economic performance and competitiveness is to be maintained and enhanced under conditions of increasing global economic integration. In this new era of heightened competition and more open trading arrangements, the Atlantic provinces are starting from a somewhat disadvantaged position relative to other Canadian regions. This is certainly no time to consider any scaling back or withdrawal of federal support for economic development initiatives within the region.

In addition to providing support to provincial and local efforts to promote economic development, the federal government remains a primary player in the region in its own right, especially with regard to the development and management of Atlantic Canada's resources, a federal role which flows from its *de jure* constitutional powers over the fishery, agriculture, offshore mineral development, shipping and navigation, the environment, and international trade. It also has important constitutional responsibilities in the area of transportation, a policy field of central importance to the Atlantic provinces. These responsibilities, combined with the power of the federal purse (relative to that of provinces in the Atlantic region), demand a significant if not leading federal role in the planning and financing of transportation infrastructure, including current proposals to twin the Trans-Canada highway through the Maritimes and build a PEI-New Brunswick "fixed link." Stripping the federal government of its constitutional responsibilities in these areas would serve no useful purpose for the Atlantic provinces; it would only weaken arguments for federal action in these areas and reduce the feasibility and probability of major new projects even further. If regional disparities in Canada are allowed to worsen, an increasingly embittered regional alienation will despoil any hope that constitutional reform can create the conditions for national unity and harmony. It is important, therefore, that the federal government not be excluded from this policy field juridically (through constitutional change in the division of powers) or practically (through the wholesale transfer of revenue-raising capacity to the provinces). Were it to be, the widely-varying capacities of provincial governments to engage in various forms of microeconomic intervention would augment the already distinct advantages some provinces have over others.

In the current negotiations, Atlantic Canadians and their political representatives should demand that the federal responsibility for regional equality that is already entrenched under Sec. 36 be further strengthened. One way this could be done is through reform of the Senate. An elected Senate truly representative of regional interests would provide greater assurance that such interests are given due consideration (and weight) in the deliberations of the national Parliament. Moreover, a reformed Senate should be given an explicit mandate to review the federal government's record of compliance with both the letter and the spirit of Sec. 36, and to force changes in federal programs and priorities if federal responsibilities under Sec. 36 are not being properly fulfilled.

NATIONAL SOCIAL PROGRAMS, THE CHARTER AND CANADIAN UNITY

Canadian unity has for some time been viewed by observers of the Canadian political scene as the central problem of Canadian politics. The problem has generally been seen to derive from the dual tensions produced by Quebec nationalism and by regionalism. The Canadian political discourse has been rooted in the politics of territory, its articulators heads of governments and their bureaucratic advisors, its main focus the conflicting claims and demands of federal and provincial governments over the distribution of revenues and powers. This has not been a debate, however, that has had great import and meaning for most individual Canadians, except when the wrangling could be related directly to their personal welfare and life prospects. In Quebec, however, the debate has been more consistently framed in just these terms. Nationalists and federalists in that province have appealed to their predominantly French-speaking populace to opt for one of two opposing visions of "the good life," a forced choice that the Québécois have until now persistently and astutely avoided. Anglophone Canadians, on the other hand, generally have been less moved by the unity question. For the most part, the bickering of their provincial and federal government has appeared to them as a pointless waste of time, or at least not a government activity deserving of their rapt attention.[10]

It is surely fair to say that for at least the last thirty years, Quebec has been at the centre of Canada's constitutional muddle, setting both the constitutional agenda for and the pace of federal-provincial negotiations. For a long time, other provincial governments either downplayed the need for dramatic constitutional reforms or opportunistically "piggy-backed" their own demands on those of Quebec. Generally speaking, however, individual anglophone Canadians have been willing to make some accommodation in order to placate a restive Quebec. New national symbols and official bilingualism were seen as appropriate by most. And if anglophone Canadians were only vaguely aware of *ad hoc* concessions made by their political elites to Quebec's "distinct status" within the federation (as with the Quebec pension plan or special provisions on immigration), at the time it did not cause a great deal of ire or political controversy.

This inattentive attitude toward constitutional affairs changed in the 1980s, first as a result of the political turmoil preceding and the negotiations leading to the 1982 Constitution Act, and secondly as the result of the 1987 Meech Lake Accord. The latter, by conferring upon Quebec "distinct society" status and granting to all provinces the additional rights, privileges and powers demanded by Quebec as the condition for its formal acceptance of Canadian constitutional arrangements, raised a political storm amongst Canadians. The prime minister and premiers were seen to be foisting changes upon anglophone Canadians that were neither requested nor desired. And when opponents of the accord made their arguments about some of the possible implications of the provisions contained in the accord — the discouraging effect they would have on any new national social programs, the decreased likelihood of comprehensive Senate reform, the greatly enhanced powers granted to one province by the distinct society clause, the potential threat to the supremecy and universality of the Charter of Rights — Canadians outside Quebec made clear their annoyance and objection to both the *process* and the *substance* of the accord.[11] For these reasons its demise in June 1990 was applauded by many anglophone Canadians, in sharp contrast to the public reaction in Quebec. There has doubtless never been a time since the conscription crisis of 1917 that francophone and anglophone opinion in Canada has been so diametrically opposed.

Also likely to be instructive for understanding the attitude of Canadians to currently proposed constitutional changes is the debate that occurred in Canada over the FTA and the 1988 election which secured its passage. The election was highly unusual in the degree to which it revolved around the single issue of the FTA. It was also unusual in its outcome. Though the Conservatives won a national majority, they secured a majority of seats in only two provinces — Quebec and Alberta. One of the main arguments made against the FTA by both the main opposition parties and anti-free trade interest groups was that over the long term Canada's social and regional development programs would be placed in jeopardy by the agreement because economic and political pressures would be exerted on Canadian governments to adopt social programs more akin to those of the United States. The validity of the argument is open to question, but it is difficult to deny the significance of the threat posited by the argument. It triggered a highly emotional debate of the sort that typifies only core issues of very high salience to the electorate. Suggesting that Canada's social programs would be undermined by the FTA was akin to impuning the patriotism of the FTA's supporters — it had to be refuted and refuted passionately. Canada's very sovereignty and identity were seen to be at issue.[12]

In Atlantic Canada, arguments suggesting that the passage of the FTA would lead to the demise of Canada's social and regional programs had a telling effect. By comparison, Conservative attempts to deflect Liberal and NDP arguments by appealing to traditional Atlantic regionalism — suggesting that the removal of tariffs would return the Maritimes to their nineteenth-century prosperity, or that opposition to free trade was nothing more than an Ontario conspiracy against the "regions" — seemed lame and outdated. In the election, the overwhelming majority that the Conservatives had secured in the region in 1984 was overturned. Given the centrality of Canada's national social and regional programs to the welfare of Atlantic Canadians, this electoral outcome should not be seen as a particularly surprising one. At the same time, it should also be expected that the strong attachment of Atlantic Canadians to and concern for the preservation of national social and regional programs will carry over into the current constitutional negotiations.

Following the failure of the Meech Lake Accord, the Quebec government demanded comprehensive constitutional change "or else." To back up its threat, a September 1992 deadline has been imposed, at which time a Quebec referendum on sovereignty will be held if an agreement between Quebec and Canada (represented by the federal government) cannot be consummated. At the centre of any new constitutional deal (from Quebec's point of view) there must be recognition and enhanced status in the constitution for Quebec's "distinct society" and there must be new powers for the province of Quebec. In the Meech Lake Accord, the new powers offered to Quebec (with the profoundly important exception of any new powers that might be associated with the undefined "distinct society" clause) were extended to all provinces in the federation. This "solution" to the constitutional crisis is also the recommendation of the Quebec Liberal Party in the Allaire report. A general decentralization of powers to the provinces is also advocated by others such as economist Thomas Courchene and the so-called "group of 22." The latter, made up of two ex-premiers, several retired politicians, as well as economists, businessmen and political operatives, would have Ottawa give up the spending power, and turn over to the provinces full and complete responsibility (along with the revenues) for pensions, family benefits, welfare and income supplements, and health care.[13] In such a regime, the provinces would have complete discretion to modify social programs without reference to the need to maintain any sort of national standards. This would quickly produce a patchwork quilt of social programs in Canada, with reduced scope and quality of services the most likely result, especially in the poorest provinces and in those with more ideologically-conservative governments.

In response to this threat (the dismantling of national social programs through provincialization of this responsibility), some constitutional experts are prone to refer to the original division of powers in the 1867 British North America Act, or else state the arguments for program diversity in a federal system, and/or defend the democratic right of provincial residents through provincial elections to decide on the level and quality of public services they will receive. But there would be a stiff price to be paid for such attitudes toward national social programs (and stiffer for some than others). The end result, however, would be both unfair and unwise — unfair in that principles of horizontal equity (between Canadians who live in different provinces) and vertical equity (between Canadians of different income levels) would be seriously compromised; unwise in that the foundations of Canadian identity and nationhood would be seriously weakened. This is because Canada's national social programs represent the embodiment of Canadian values and are therefore central to national identity — much more so than is the case for other oft-referred-to, nation-defining features such as "official bilingualism" or "multiculturalism."[14] For most Canadians, the latter remain purely symbolic as values and largely irrelevant as programs. National social programs, on the other hand, have come to constitute a *social contract* that binds Canadians in every region together and charges the federal government with a fundamental responsibility — to oversee these programs so as to preserve their national objectives and ensure their continued viability and effectiveness.

This characterization of national social programs implemented for the most part in the 1960s as central to Canadian national identity and political integration suggests that prior to the 1960s, the basis for a distinctive and common Canadian identity did not already exist, or at least was relatively weak, or else rested on a

set of values that were disappearing from society or for some other reason were
no longer viable as the basis for national political identity and attachment.

In fact, few would contest that one or more of the latter conditions were a feature of Canada in the 1960s. For most of Canada's history the country's two
main cultures had existed in relative isolation from one another, with English
Canadians clinging to their "Britishness" and French Canadians to their language, religion and rural "habitant" mythology. In the 1960s, both these bases of
identity were undergoing a process of disintegration due to their growing ir-
relevance and dissonance with social and cultural realities. Britain had long since
ceased being economically or culturally important to "English Canada," which in
any event, due to immigration, was becoming less and less British in its ethnic
composition. Herein lay the roots of English Canada's insecurity about its national identity. In Quebec, the Quiet Revolution was sweeping aside the old
defensive church-inspired nationalism based on *la survivance* and replacing it
with an expansive, secular, state-based nationalism promoting the need to
"catch-up" socially, economically, and technologically with anglo-North
America. "French Canada" was transformed into those francophones with their
own state (les Québécois) and others (les francophones hors Québec) who were
splintered into numerous and tiny (with the exception of New Brunswick)
provincial minorities.

The development of Canada's national social programs during this period
does not appear to have been done consciously as a way to enhance the processes
of national integration by providing Canadians with a substitute national identity
in which all could share (as was much more explicitly the case with the decision
to adopt a distinctively Canadian flag, or to adopt bilingualism and multiculturalism). Nonetheless, these programs did come to serve that purpose, amongst
others. Humane and fairly comprehensive social programs are one of the most
oft-cited distinguishing features that Canadians like to point to as setting their
country apart from the United States; it also has helped to foster social and
regional integration by compensating those left out of Canada's economic
prosperity and by offering universal access to a fairly high level of social and
health services.

Of course, it is not only the national identity of *Atlantic* Canadians that would
be affected by the dismantling of national social programs. But individual Atlantic Canadians do draw disproportionately upon such programs, while the
economies of the four Atlantic provinces are anchored by public-sector spending
that originates with the federal government to a much greater degree than are the
other Canadian provinces.[15] This provides Atlantic Canadians with an added incentive to oppose changes that would have the effect of undermining these
programs as they are presently constituted. Yet radical decentralization of the
Canadian federation would do exactly this since the current level of federal
transfer payments depends upon maintenance of the federal government's
revenue-raising and spending capacities and upon its continued "jurisdictional

entanglement" in the social policy field. Canadian national identity, then, is not only a matter of cultural expression through literature or popular culture (i.e., the usual cultural points of reference). It is also rooted in a system of *social entitlements* that have come to be highly valued as an integral part of what it is to be a Canadian. This demands that there continue to be not only strong and vibrant national cultural institutions (e.g., the CBC), but national social programs that help ensure the physical and social well-being of all Canadians, without discriminating on the basis of their province of residence.

In this connection, the idea of a social charter that would be entrenched in the constitution is a laudable one. As outlined in the Ontario government's discussion paper, "A Canadian Social Charter: Making Our Shared Values Stronger," entrenching a commitment on the part of Canadian governments to abide by basic national values and principles, and to finance the programs to implement them, is essential for reasons of social justice and individual freedom, for economic development reasons, and as a means of strengthening, "the bonds of citizenship which are anchored in the social contract."[16] The Ontario proposal envisages four elements to a Canadian social charter: an entrenched set of principles, institutions for implementation, public participation, and a commitment to national sharing. And it suggests a number of options for defining and including social principles in the constitution and identifying institutions for implementation of these principles. One suggestion is to expand and improve Sec. 36 of the constitution to include certain social rights or entitlements, and perhaps also Sec. 6 (mobility rights). The social rights entrenched could be implemented and monitored through a new federal-provincial institution that would review federal legislation in areas of exclusive provincial jurisdiction, or through a reformed Senate that could be given the power to act as a social charter watchdog by reviewing federal and provincial legislation, conducting regular assessments of federal-provincial agreements in the social policy field, holding hearings, proposing amendments, and if necessary, exercising a suspensive veto.[17] Given the importance of national social programs to Atlantic Canadians, the idea of a social charter deserves the attention and support of the region's governments.

The Charter of Rights

An even more recent development in Canadian identity formation than that of belief in a national system of social entitlements has been the widespread identification of Canadians (especially anglophone Canadians) with Canada's Charter of Rights and Freedoms, adopted as part of the 1982 constitution. The "psychological potency" of a "homogenizing Charter-derived rights-bearing Canadianism"[18] complicates French-English relations in Canada even more, since the rights entrenched as supreme constitutional law by the charter sometimes contradict and conflict with the particular *group* rights which the government of Quebec has sought to establish through provincial legislation.[19] So while it is true to say, I think, that the Charter of Rights has had a salutary effect on strengthening the Canadian *national* identity by providing each and every individual Canadian with a common frame of reference (in terms of identifying important national values), and subordinating both provincial and federal legislation to the Supreme Court's interpretation of the specific content and application of these values. For the Quebec government, charter supremacy is viewed as a threat to the province's power to preserve and promote the French language and culture. But for many if not most anglophone Canadians, charter supremacy renders as illegitimate certain Quebec legislation that appears to subordinate national values protected in the charter to the perceived needs of the numerically-dominant group within that province. And while strong arguments can be marshalled on the side of such legislation by its defenders, it remains both symbolically and substantively antagonistic to certain aspects of the newly formed national identity currently being embraced by most anglophone Canadians. This was especially apparent in the debate over ratification of the Meech Lake Accord.

The argument is repeatedly made that what Quebec francophones really want from constitutional reform, apart from enhanced provincial powers, is *symbolic* acknowledgement of their unique or special status as a distinct society or nation within the Canadian federation. It is seldom recognized, however, perhaps because it is a recent phenomenon, that anglophone Canadians also have become wedded to certain symbols that they demand be ensconced within the constitution, symbols that have come to define their *collective* nationhood. Symbols and "first principles" are intimately linked; together they constitute certain "national visions." When these are in conflict, the argument over which (or whose) vision shall take precedence in framing the fundamental and supreme law of the land is bound to be profound, emotional and perhaps irreconcilable. For this reason, achieving a compromise in the constitution between the need to preserve and promote Quebec's "distinct society" and upholding the individual rights of all Canadians as protected by the charter will be one of the key litmus tests of any new constitutional accord.

CONSTITUTIONAL OPTIONS

In a series of articles in the Halifax *Chronicle-Herald* in July 1991, the Nova Scotia Study Group (comprised of a number of prominent political scientists, economists, and lawyers) examined the current constitutional crisis with a view to the risks involved for Nova Scotians. The group looked at fiscal arrangements, social policies, Senate reform, the division of powers, and Canadian values. The Group warned of the potential economic costs to Nova Scotians (extremely severe) that would accompany either a "breakup" of Canada or a radical decentralization. Quebec separation, it was thought, would likely produce either one or the other of these worst case scenarios (breakup or a loose reconfederation), though they admit that it is not "inconceivable" that the rest of Canada might end up stronger without Quebec. The conclusion they draw from their analysis of the situation is that Canada must be kept together as *"one country, with Quebec firmly inside the tent, and with a strong and effective central government."*[20] The sentiment sounds suspiciously like that expressed by the renowned Quebec entertainer Yvon Deschamps' analysis that what his compatriots really wanted was "an independent Quebec within a strong and united Canada." The Nova Scotia Study Group also would like to have its cake and eat it too. The difference between the two is that the Quebec entertainer uttered his sentiment with the express intention of getting ironic laughs.

The technique that the study group advocates as the means for attaining its preferred constitutional outcome is that of *interdelegation* — each province would be given the right to interdelegate powers with the federal government. The idea is that this would "enable Canada to find a way to meet at least some of Quebec's objectives without implicating all of the provinces in the solution ... it would permit Quebec to negotiate with Ottawa for additional jurisdictional responsibilities, without requiring everyone else to do the same."[21] In other words, the group expects that only Quebec will make extensive use of this technique, thereby preserving a strong and effective federal government for the rest of Canada.

The Nova Scotia Study Group's constitutional proposals are one way of creating an *asymmetrical* federation in Canada, the only apparent solution to the problem of satisfying the demands and needs of both Quebec and the rest of the country within the confines of a single constitution. A similar, if more refined and flexible, constitutional model has been proposed by other constitutional experts in the academic community, utilizing other techniques to construct a constitutional basis for assymetrical federalism. David Milne advocates the technique of *concurrent powers with provincial paramountcy.*[22] Like interdelegation, the latter technique (as employed, for instance, with the Canada Pension Plan) would maintain the formal equality of provinces within the constitution, while giving to the only province that has consistently demanded more autonomy the means to obtain it. Concurrency, however, leaves open the possibility for both governments to continue to enact legislation and to develop various means of sharing the powers and responsibilities of governance.

As much as this solution has the merit of satisfying Quebec's demands without resorting to a formal "special status" for that province, it has its problems. There are no guarantees that federal powers will not be gradually eroded by the provinces under such constitutional arrangements, only the "hope" that this would not happen. Yet there are good reasons to think that it would happen. As argued by Albert Breton, intergovernmental relations in a federal system such as Canada's are just as often competitive as cooperative:

> To be re-elected, governments must meet the needs, interests and preferences of their constitutents. To that end, they will adopt policies that are attractive to skilled labour, to capital and to technology. If all governments do the same thing, they will inevitably be competing with each other.[23]

It is Breton's contention that Quebec and Ontario already have an enormous comparative advantage in the Canadian federation. Should Quebec's comparative advantage be further enhanced through constitutional means, the "playing field" for Canadian provinces will become even more distorted. Under such circumstances, other provinces would have to demand the same powers as Quebec in order to give them the necessary flexibility to respond to initiatives that may disadvantage other provinces in the area of economic competition. If small provinces now find that the federal government demonstrates a bias in its policies towards the larger provinces in the federation, the situation will not be improved by large provinces taking control of those federal powers. Will not other provinces (most probably, beginning with Ontario) be forced to follow Quebec's lead in order to maintain its competitive position? Would not the end result be greater competition between unequal provinces, with fewer restraints on the nature of this competition? In short, if Quebec is given the option of picking up extensive powers that the federal government now wields, it seems likely that sooner or later the other provinces will follow. Canada would have been reorganized to accommodate Quebec in a fashion that a clear majority of Canadians have expressed opposition to, and for which Atlantic Canadians, in particular, will pay a heavy price.

Should Canada escape a fatal weakening of its national government because the other nine provinces resist the urge to follow Quebec's lead in bringing federal powers and revenues under their own purview, the other half of the Nova Scotia Study Group's equation — keeping Quebec "firmly inside the tent" — is also problematic. This is because Quebec nationalists ultimately seek a situation in which all of the decisions that really count will be made for the Quebec people by their National Assembly in Quebec City. Yet Quebec would maintain seventy-five members in the House of Commons, twenty-four senators (one presumes), and a dozen or so ministers in the Canadian cabinet. What kind of a situation would this produce from the viewpoint of democracy and fairness in our system of government? As argued by the venerable Eugene Forsey, the ultimate result would be: "You stay out of our affairs; we stay very much in yours."[24] The wiser course to pursue in such circumstances may be, as Forsey recommended, "Get out of Canada if you want, we are ready to negotiate the terms on which you do. But independent within Canada you cannot be."[25]

Alan Cairns recognizes this problem in his own analysis of the asymmetrical model of federalism, arguing that major asymmetries in jurisdictional status

> lead inexorably to inequalities or to proportionate asymmetries in the role and responsibilities of Quebec MPs in the House of Commons, and probably of Senators as well. While minor anomalies are ubiquitous in a functioning constitutional order of some vintage, major anomalies that offend fundamental constitutional principles are unacceptable. The one in four members of the House of Commons from Quebec cannot be full participants when the House deals with matters that are in federal government

jurisdiction outside Quebec, but in provincial government jurisdiction in Quebec.[26]

According to Cairns, such a constitutional order would be "highly unstable":

> Within Quebec the attractions of nation-statehood are likely to be stimulated by the dynamics of nationalist competition. In the rest-of-Canada, the provincial equality imperative will be wielded by expansive provincial governments hoping to level-up and by others resistent to anomalies seeking to level down. ... [Within Quebec] the diminished pan-Canadianism that will flow from asymmetrical status with its relative enhancement of the status of Quebec politicians at home and the diminished status of Quebec politicians in Ottawa, along with the aggrandizement of Quebec citizenship at the expense of the Canadian, will be a weak counterfoil to Quebec nationalism. ... For Québécois, an asymmetrical federalism produces an asymmetrical psyche in which the balance of loyalties to and identifications with Quebec and Canada is strongly tilted to the former.[27]

As unpalatable and unstable as a truly asymmetrical federalism is likely to be in the long run, it may be necessary to negotiate some form of it, even if only as a transitional arrangement to Quebec independence. The objective under such circumstances would be to find ways to limit the extent of asymmetry to be incorporated within any new constitutional arrangement, while simultaneously reforming national political institutions in ways that will strengthen their representativeness and legitimacy.

Another possible outcome that is preferable from an Atlantic Canadian perspective would see Quebec accept what amounts to a limited rebalancing of powers within Canadian federalism, one that while enhancing provincial control over some areas, maintains a strong and effective national government. (In other words, no radical decentralization or asymmetrical federalism.) At the same time, there would have to be agreement on the part of all constitutional actors, including Quebec, to strengthen national political institutions (in particular, through Senate reform). In return for this "softening" of the Quebec position, there will have to be some agreement on constitutional recognition of Quebec's status as a "distinct society," though a form of recognition that falls short of conferring dramatic new powers on that province. This is the key trade off that will be necessary for any reasonable settlement. Such a settlement, however, would represent a considerable scaling down of previous Quebec demands, and seems likely only if popular support in Quebec for the idea of sovereignty (whether this is conceived in the form of outright independence or the protoindependence of dramatically enhanced provincial autonomy) abates.[28]

The other possibility is, of course, a rejection of Canada's proposals and an endorsement of Quebec sovereignty in a referendum, followed by negotiations on independence. This outcome is fraught with dangers. It could result in the dissolution of the rest of Canada. This scenario is referred to most often by those who feel that Canada means nothing without Quebec; that there is no Canadian identity or even *raison d'être* without Quebec. But this point of view gives little, if any, weight to the economic and social ties that presently bind Canadians together and it belittles the existence of a culture shared by anglophone Canadians that has existed and evolved throughout Canadian history, and which over the past few decades has flourished. It also refuses to acknowledge the recent rise of Canadian national feeling associated with institutions and values other than "mappism," bilingualism, or dualism. Finally, it ignores survey results which indicate that the clear preference of Canadians is to remain together as a country should Quebec separate.

It is conceivable that Quebec independence could entail some benefit for Atlantic Canada. The new Canada might be a more politically integrated and united country than is possible with a recalcitrant and nationalist Quebec. Its unity would be based on a strong national identity rooted in belief in and support for a system of social entitlements, the Canadian Charter of Rights and Freedoms, and national cultural institutions. If the economic implications of Quebec separation are worrisome, they are likely to be more severe for Quebec than for the rest of Canada, so long as the latter remain federated with a strong national government. Global economic pressures will remain important regardless what happens, of course, but a Canada without Quebec may be able to better agree upon appropriate responses to such pressures, such as an expanded role for the federal government in education and training or stronger powers allowing the federal government to manage the economic union. And it seems reasonable to assume that it would be easier to get agreement on the much needed reform of national institutions without Quebec, since that province has always been reluctant to see the role and legitimacy of the national government strengthened at the expense of Quebec City.

There could also be gains (of sorts) within the Atlantic region in terms of momentum for maritime union and closer Atlantic cooperation. This is because dramatic forward movement in the region toward economic and political union likely requires a genuine crisis in the current political economy and constitutional *status quo*, thus forcing otherwise reluctant regional politicians and social groups to champion integration as a survival strategy. Nothing less than Quebec separation or radical decentralization is likely to create the right political climate for such a development. While union still might not occur, the physical isolation of the region would have a dramatic effect upon regional consciousness and sharply raise general public awareness of the region's vulnerability. It is also possible that under these circumstances new political, entrepreneurial and cooperative energies would be unleashed. A decline in intraregional provincialism could be expected (at least with regard to the three maritime provinces) as the political agenda was focussed on the larger debate over strategies to ensure regional survival and prosperity. When one considers the highly parochial issues that often have dominated provincial agendas in the past, this would represent a welcome improvement in the level and content of public and political discourse.

CONCLUSION

The argument presented here is that the political and cultural identity of Atlantic Canadians as *Canadians* is at stake in the current constitutional negotiations, as well as their future social and economic welfare. The country "Canada" is not just a political entity that has been accorded nation-state status in the world; nor is it defined solely or additionally by its geography or its economy as a piece of territory marked by a notable division into several regions. It is above all a cultural and social space, one which has evolved over time and within which Canadians have developed a national identity as a people. Should the constitution of Canada be altered, it must be done with full cognizance of this reality, and the likely effects constitutional change will have upon it.

Regions are still salient in Canadian politics, but the content of Canadian regionalism has changed. Just as Atlantic regionalism has been transformed by the federal government's regional policies, so Canadian political culture has been transformed by national social programs and by the Charter of Rights and Freedoms. The provincialism of the 1970s has receded along with the energy crisis and the policy disputes it ignited; in the 1980s, "province building" based on natural resource wealth lost much of its appeal. And a crisis of confidence in political leadership and parliamentary institutions has led to demands for reforms to those institutions that would strengthen them by making them more responsive and regionally sensitive. The impact of these factors has been to undermine the legitimacy and appeal of political designs that derive from the notion that there are regional societies in Canada that take precedence over Canadian society. Outside of Quebec, there is no longer strong support anywhere for protecting regional interests by a massive transfer of powers to provincial governments.

From the perspective of Atlantic Canada, there should be several key objectives in the current round of constitutional negotiations. The first should be to protect federal constitutional responsibilities and national institutions that are essential to the region's economic well-being and that are germane to their political, social and cultural identity as Canadians. In particular, national social programs, equalization, and the federal role in regional development must be preserved. Jurisdictional entanglements and shared responsibilities are not something to be "cleared up" in order to make Canada function more efficiently or to eliminate intergovernmental friction; it is the inevitable and necessary outcome and condition of federal arrangements in a developed and integrated society. Secondly, the Charter of Rights and Freedoms has proven to be a powerful instrument of national integration; it should be buttressed by a social charter that recognizes a fundamental right to certain social entitlements for Canadians. Thirdly, the Atlantic region would benefit from Senate reform, especially if the mandate of a reformed Senate included overseeing the federal government's performance in meeting its regional and social policy commitments under an enhanced and expanded Sec. 36.

For some time, it seems, Canadians have been plagued by a persistent doubt and uncertainty about their own capacity and will to identify the national interest and act as a strong and united nation. Proposals aimed at resolving the present constitutional crisis must not undermine the capacity of Canadians to coalesce in order to address the nation's social and economic problems for the common good. Canadians desperately want to be part of a *nation*, not just a piece of territory or a convenient political arrangement. Atlantic Canadians, like other Canadians, should assess proposals for revamping the legal and working relations between Canada's various governments in order to ensure that they do not go so far as to destroy or erode the basis for this nation. They should resist proposed "solutions" to Canada's constitutional crisis that will ultimately strip the meaning from what it is to be a Canadian.

There are great risks involved when dramatic changes are proposed to the basic constitutional framework of any country. Potential losses as well as gains can be discerned in each of the various constitutional scenarios now facing Canada. It is important that all options be given as fair and complete a rendering as possible, if we are to envision the outlines of the alternative futures that await us.

Notes

1.   Canadian Tax Foundation, *Provincial Municipal Finances* (Toronto: Canadian Tax Foundation, 1990).

2.   Section 36, "Equalization and Regional Disparities", commits all of Canada's legislatures and governments to promoting equal opportunities, furthering economic development to reduce disparities in opportunities, and providing essential public services of reasonable quality to all Canadians; the Parliament and Government of Canada are further committed to the principle of making equalization payments to ensure that provincial governments have sufficient revenues to provide reasonably comparable levels of public services at reasonably comparable levels of taxation.

3.   Debates have raged within academic circles as well as in more popular forums about just how important regional development programs have been to the Atlantic region. Most analysts agree that some of the money that has been spent to enhance regional development has been wasted, but there is no agreement on just how much of this money has been misspent. Some observers have called for an end to regional development "subsidies," either because they think the problem so intractable that to attempt to address it is folly, or because they believe government intervention actually worsens the problem of dependency. For arguments of the latter position, see Thomas Courchene, "Avenues of Adjustment: The Transfer System and Regional Disparities," in M. Walker, ed., *Canadian Confederation at the Crossroads: The Search for a Federal-Provincial Balance* (Vancouver: Fraser Institute, 1978). For a more mainstream explanation and policy recommendation on improving the efficacy of regional development expenditures, see Donald Savoie, *Regional Economic Development: Canada's Search for Solutions* (Toronto: University of Toronto Press, 1986). For an accounting of the politics of regional development from an historical political economy perspective, see James Bickerton, *Nova Scotia, Ottawa and the Politics of Regional Development* (Toronto: University of Toronto Press, 1990).

4. At one time or another, every Atlantic province has resorted to such ultimately self-destructive policies in the name of economic development. See Bickerton, *Nova Scotia, Ottawa and the Politics of Regional Development*.

5. A regional veterinary college was delayed for years by the refusal of Nova Scotia to go along with the recommended PEI site; a regional energy corporation was proposed, only to sink on the shoals of competing provincial energy strategies and bureaucracies; interprovincial competition for investment had become so expensive that a newly elected P.E.I. premier was forced to renege on his predecessor's deal to create high-tech jobs on the Island by stuffing the purse of the Toronto-based corporation involved, only to have the Nova Scotia government steal the jobs and investment with its own lucrative offer. These are but a few of the many examples of how the political fragmentation of the region has worked against efficient and effective economic development policies.

6. Brian Ward, "Premiers lower barriers," *The Chronicle-Herald* (Halifax), 19 June 1991, p. A1.

7. Chris Morris, "McKenna nixes political union in Atlantic Canada," *The Chronicle-Herald*, 22 March 1991, p. C20.

8. Laurent Le Pierres and Roger Taylor, "Where does Newfoundland fit in?" *The Chronicle-Herald*, 23 May 1991, p. A1.

9. See Bickerton, *Nova Scotia, Ottawa and the Politics of Regional Development*, chapters 7 and 8.

10. There were exceptions to this general pattern, such as the passions raised by the conflict over energy policy in Canada that led some oil-producing westerners to sport bumper stickers that proclaimed a desire to let their oil-consuming eastern compatriots "freeze in the dark." Such rage was fed by the belief that westerners were being deprived of their rightful heritage (and billions of dollars in revenues) by federal energy policies more favourable to those Canadians in the more populous consuming provinces. This is one instance where the personal welfare and "life chances" of individuals appeared to be directly at stake in intergovernmental wrangling.

11. Any survey of media reports and voter survey results during 1989-90 suggests that the tide of sentiment and argument in English Canada was running against the accord. A good sample of such opinion can be gleaned from a reading of the proceedings of the public hearings on the accord held in Manitoba and New Brunswick. See in particular, Kathy Brock, *A Mandate Fulfilled: Constitutional Reform and the Manitoba Task Force on Meech Lake* (Winnipeg: University of Manitoba Outreach Fund, December 1990).

12. For an overview of the 1988 election on a constituency-by-constituency basis, and a good indication of the electoral importance in Atlantic Canada of the debate over the various threats posed by the Free Trade Agreement, see M. Eagles, J. Bickerton, A. Gagnon and P. Smith, *The Almanac of Canadian Politics* (Peterborough: Broadview Press, 1992).

13. John Dafoe, "Group of 22 may point way to future – at some social cost," *The Globe and Mail* (Toronto), 29 June 1991, p. D2.

14. To the extent that Quebec has departed from the rest of Canada in the design and administration of certain of its social programs (e.g., family allowance and pensions), the basis for a shared Canadian identity may be seen to have been weakened, while no doubt the basis for an explicitly Québécois identity has been correspondingly strengthened. It

seems quite logical to expect that the further *disentanglement* of social programs in this direction would be accompanied by a further *weakening* of a shared Canadian identity.

15. Federal transfers account for 47 percent of provincial revenues in Newfoundland, 45 percent in Prince Edward Island, 40 percent in New Brunswick, and 39 percent in Nova Scotia. The national average is 18 percent. Statistics Canada, 13-213.

16. Ontario, *A Canadian Social Charter: Making our Shared Values Stronger* (Toronto: Ministry of Intergovernmental Affairs, September 1991), 12.

17. Ibid., 18-25.

18. Alan Cairns, "Constitutional Change and the Three Equalities," in R.L. Watts and D. M. Brown, eds., *Options for a New Canada* (Toronto: University of Toronto Press, 1991), 80. Cairns cites the Manitoba and New Brunswick hearings on the Meech Lake Accord as evidence of the strength of this new Canadianism. Roger Gibbins makes a similar argument with regard to western Canadian attitudes based on his participation in some forty Alberta forums, panel discussions, and phone-in programs on the Meech Lake Accord. Roger Gibbins, "Another New West: Environmentalism and the New Policy Agenda," in Frances Abele, ed., *How Ottawa Spends: The Politics of Fragmentation 1991-92* (Ottawa: Carleton University Press, 1991), 114. Moreover, support for the inviolability of the charter seems to be one of the only common points of agreement for the left, centre and right in English Canada. Witness the position adopted on the charter by the Reform Party, Liberal Party, and New Democratic Party, or academics on the right such as David Bercuson and the left such as Reg Whitaker.

19. Part of the potency of the charter's appeal is that it is not just individual rights that it protects, but certain group rights as well. Women and aboriginals especially, but also other minority groups, view any perceived infringement of their charter rights by governments as a frontal assault on their hard-won constitutional status. They now have a vehicle and a venue to legally combat such perceived assaults, and a rights-based political discourse with which to make their claims in the court of public opinion.

20. Nova Scotia Study Group, "Confederation and the economic stakes for us," *The Chronicle-Herald*, 16 July 1991, p. A7.

21. Nova Scotia Study Group, "Dividing the powers," *The Chronicle-Herald*, 20 July 1991, p. A7.

22. For example, see the chapters by David Milne and Alan Cairns in Watts and Brown, eds., *Options for a New Canada*.

23. Albert Breton, "Endorsing an unsuitable model of federalism," *The Financial Post* (Toronto), 19 December 1989, p. 14.

24. Eugene Forsey, "Can Canada get by without Quebec? Absolutely," *The Globe and Mail* (Toronto), 21 September 1991, p. A19.

25. Ibid.

26. Alan Cairns, "Constitutional Change and the Three Equalities," 90.

27. Ibid., 91-92.

28. There are signs that this is occurring. Public opinion polls are recording reduced levels of support for independence in the province while the Quebec business community seems to be engaged in a sober rethinking of the issue. Clyde Farnsworth, "Separatist Fervor Fades in Quebec," *The New York Times*, 10 September 1991, p. D1.

16

Constitutional Negotiations in Canada:
A Progressive View from the West

Howard A. Leeson

The failure of the Meech Lake Accord in 1990 has again precipitated a constitutional crisis in Canada. Demands from Quebec for fundamental changes, and the threat to hold a referendum on sovereignty in that province before the Fall of 1992, have concentrated the attention of political leaders on questions like language rights, changes to the amending formula, and the role of a reformed Senate. Discontent in Quebec cannot be ignored, and debate about the future shape of Canada will undoubtedly reach a conclusion in the next months.

Echoes of discontent are also heard in other regions and groups in the country, including western Canada, where the Reform Party has gained strength. Drawing partly on traditional western alienation, and partly on a wave of cynicism about our political process, the Reform Party has managed to merchandize its views as the voice of the West. These views are generally decentralist, anti-Ottawa, pro-private enterprise, and continentalist in orientation. The major institutional demand of the Reform Party is for a revamped Senate, consistent with its view of the role of the present federal Parliament.

There is, however, another view from the West which should be considered. It is a view which is distrustful of proposals for decentralization, calls for greater federal government efforts to stabilize weaker economies in the region, demands greater provincial government control of resources instead of continental free trade, advocates new national mechanisms to facilitate international trade, is dismayed with the undemocratic nature of our national institutions and, above all, demands a process of renewal which is more attuned to the needs of all regions of Canada and not controlled by Ottawa. It is in short, a view which demands renewal of Canada, not just of the constitution.

This view has not been heard in recent discussions, in part because no western provincial governments have put it forward. However, it is a view which has deep roots in the Prairies, and can be counted upon to surface as we move into serious discussion. Both Quebec and the West have a stake in reforming the way Canada now works. The compromises that come from hard bargaining between the two regions can only result in a stronger and more durable union.

THE PROBLEM OF "TWO MANY NATIONS"

Part of the present impasse in the country results from a disjunction of views about what constitutes Canada. More precisely there is more than one premise about the nature and makeup of Canada. One view, rooted mainly in Quebec, perceives Canada to be a country of two founding nations, two founding equal peoples. It is a view with its origin in 1867, a view which Quebecers believe essential for the very survival of the French fact in North America. Outside of Quebec, and especially in the West, Canada is viewed as many nations, a mosaic of peoples with origins in the entire world, now bound together by an evolving Canadian identity. It is a view which suits the hopes and aspirations of many non-Anglo and non-Franco groups to become full partners in a future Canada. Finally, there is the view of the aboriginal peoples, a view of Canada which also perceives Canada as two nations, those who came lately to this part of North America, and those who were here originally. The clash of these views is at the root of present difficulties. Do we have two nations, or too many nations?

THE "WEST" AS A REGION

While western Canada has never accorded itself the status of a "nation," it has always regarded itself as a distinct region. This view is reinforced by institutions such as the Senate region, the Western Premiers Conference, and other agencies which use the western provinces as their basis of organization.

The concept of region is, however, an indistinct one. As Janine Brodie says:

> A variety of meanings and a great deal of confusion are associated with the spatial dimension of Canadian politics largely because ... social scientists often unconsciously interchange terms.[1]

She criticizes the traditional regional designations, of which the West is one:

> both subjective and objective measures suggest that geographic space is a relevant element in the Canadian political economy. These studies, however do not justify either the five-fold or the provincial demarcations of Canadian regions as an appropriate way of studying space.[2]

David Smith, a political scientist at the University of Saskatchewan argues that the four provinces do constitute a region:

> Thus, whether western Canada is one region or two depends on the context in which the question is asked. On balance, the geographical differences between British Columbia and the other three provinces are less important to understanding western Canada than the fact that all four provinces share a sense of isolation from central Canada.[3]

Professor Smith makes a case for considering all four provinces as the "West," based on similarity of grievance, but in doing so he ignores important dissimilarities which separate British Columbia from the rest. Chief amongst them is the role of agriculture on the Prairies. Students of prairie life from Seymour Lipset to John Richards have commented on agriculture and its role on the Prairies. The history of social and political action which has accompanied farming on the Prairies is not found in British Columbia, and despite its recent decline, the grain industry on the Prairies is still a major economic, social, and political force. One of the difficulties that accompanied the transformation of the Prairie Economic Council to the Western Premiers Conference in the 1970s was the obvious clash of interests that surrounded this industry. Eventually, the Western Premiers Conference was reduced to an anti-Ottawa coalition, precisely because there were several sharp economic cleavages which precluded collaborative regional action. It might be reasonable therefore, to divide the West into two regions, the Prairies and British Columbia.

Don Smiley noted this when he commented on the inapplicability of the dualistic notion of Canada in the West:

> To repeat, the cultural, linguistic and religious norms of central Canada are not congruent with the prairie experience, and for more than a century popular majorities and their governments from that area have struggled against the imposition of those norms by the elites of the central heartland.[4]

In particular, he concluded that the Quebec view of Canada which shapes political thought and action in Ottawa has "little resonance with the history and circumstances of the prairies."[5] By contrast, he asserts that the alienation of people in British Columbia is less decisive than on the Prairies:

> Although B.C. has chafed under various national economic policies, its resentment of the central heartland has been more subdued than in the Prairie and Atlantic provinces.[6]

Definitions of the "West" extend beyond this first dichotomy, however. There are those like Murray Beck and J.E. Hodges who argue that it is impossible to discuss regions in Canada, except as provinces. Don Smiley summarized their views by saying, "So far as effective political action is concerned the province rather than regions are the significant units."[7] This view is rejected by Janine Brodie.

The formal approach to defining regions as provinces also misrepresents and obstructs our vision of regional politics. While it is obvious that provincial governments have been very visible political actors in the past two decades, it is equally clear that the major conflicts over the past two decades reflect divisions between "groups" [emphasis in original] of provinces.[8]

The idea of groups of provinces suggests a division between the have and have-not provinces in western Canada. Both Saskatchewan and Manitoba are recipients of equalization payments, and depend more heavily on federal transfer payments for social programs.[9] Their view of decentralization, transfer of powers, and the role of the federal government is heavily conditioned by that dependence. This is especially true in Saskatchewan, where the grain industry is in severe decline.

This explains, in part, the concentration on certain issues and approaches by the different groups and parties in the West. Parties such as the Western Canada Concept, and now the Reform Party, have sought to aggregate support in the west by emphasizing changes which have appeal in all four provinces. For example, Senate reform is an issue which strikes a chord in all western Canadians, precisely because institutional reform cuts across other economic and social cleavages. It is the type of change which purports to increase influence for all western Canadians, regardless of economic or social circumstance. The same can be said of policies attacking "big government" in Ottawa, while supporting deregulation, and free trade. They are calculated to appeal primarily to business in all four provinces, but they also have support from other economic groups. By contrast, policies emphasizing a strong federal presence in agriculture, equalization payments, transfer payments, and the role of the federal government in setting national standards are given less prominence in the Reform Party agenda, in order to avoid clashes based on the "have" and "have-not" division of Alberta and British Columbia on one side, and Saskatchewan and Manitoba on the other.

Discussion of have and have-not provinces prompts one to examine the question of class cleavage in "western" concerns. Few will dispute that western alienation in Canada has a different class basis in the 1990s than it did in the 1930s. In the period prior to World War II alienation in the region was based on a significant component of class similarity, so much so that Seymour Lipset and others could assert a degree of homogeneity which, in retrospect, never existed. With the development of a vigorous natural resource industry in the period after 1948, a new group of entrepreneurs appeared on the western scene, a group which provided a significant new component to the class basis of western Canada.[10]

Both the older agricultural community and the new resource entrepreneurs continued to share a sense of isolation and alienation. As Doug Owram put it:

> The West's basic complaint concerns a hinterland status which seems to encompass everything from economics to culture and which leaves elsewhere the key powers of decision in these areas. The demand that this be changed underlies much of the region's quest for change.[11]

The result has often been political coalition between the Left and Right in the region, a coalition based in part on a confusion of status. While the political Right has been rigid in its demand for political autonomy, and access to the world market place, the political Left has demanded a combination of autonomy and national state policies designed to alleviate the boom and bust cycles. This has led to some curious alliances, such as between premiers Blakeney and Lougheed of Saskatchewan and Alberta respectively in the 1970s.

A closer examination of a class-based approach to regional alienation reveals that there is a conjunction between regional and personal economic status which is important to examine. While western entrepreneurs are economically subordinate to those in central Canada, they are dominant in their region, the West. Family farmers, together with service and production workers are, however, in a subordinate economic position both within the region, and between regions. The former group seeks to limit the role of the national state, over which it has little control, in order to support the local provincial state, over which it has more power. By contrast, the latter group has ambivalent feelings about both levels. Often, most particularly in the agricultural sector, it is the beneficiary of its relationship to the national state, and thus is less willing to shed that connection, while the local state, has been repressive and unresponsive to groups like organized labour. Regional alienation is present in this second group, but in a different form and to a lesser degree than in the entrepreneurial group.

The result is a wedding of the regional and class variables in the region, a wedding which cannot be adequately, or more precisely, completely, encompassed within the Reform Party agenda, which is largely directed toward the entrepreneurial class.

What this review suggests is that the West is not homogeneous, and that there is likely to be more than one western agenda. More importantly, while the Reform Party represents one view of the "West," there are other important views, particularly from the have-not provinces and from the have-not individuals in the West that need to be considered.

This brings us to the central point of this paper. While it is true that there are shared "western" concerns, it is important to recognize that there are differences. In part these differences can be identified on the basis of fiscal and economic capacity (have vs. have-not). Specific differences in types of industry (agriculture vs. mining and shipping as an example), urban-rural population distributions, and political attitudes toward the role of government in society, and in particular, the role of the federal government, are also important. As well, there is a class-based difference, linked to farmers, workers, Natives and small business people.

What would an agenda directed toward small farmers, workers, and other powerless groups in the West look like? What would be the principles upon which such an agenda would be based?

The first, and perhaps most important principle is that any new deal in Canada must ensure that the national government is capable of playing a significant role in aiding the economically subordinate regions of the country, and in particular the economically dispossessed within the regions themselves. Proposals which would transfer powers to provincial governments, or other groups, without taking account of this, are unacceptable.

The second principle is that the renewal process must be much more open than past processes in order that relatively powerless groups and individuals in the west have significant access to the negotiations and a real ability to influence the outcome.

The third principle is that whatever deal is struck, it must include significant guarantees that existing regional resources will be left under local control, and not bartered away in international agreements like the Free Trade Agreement (FTA).

The fourth principle is that a new deal should establish constitutional arrangements which will provide significant institutional reform, reform designed to ensure a more democratic society with greater regional sensitivity.

Finally, whatever the new Canada looks like, the West must be assured that the country is provided with a guarantee of future stability. New arrangements must be voted on and entrenched to the satisfaction of all regions and peoples. In particular, processes for future disassociation or separation by any group must be clearly spelled out in order that Canada not be left again in a state of uncertainty about its future.

With these principles in mind, what would some of the specifics of a progressive western agenda look like?

FISCAL TRANSFERS AND NATIONAL STANDARDS

In the first instance certain transfer functions of the federal government ought to be further constitutionalized in order to ensure greater regional equality.

> 1. The present equalization section (Part III, Sec. 36) should be rewritten to allow for greater flexibility to ensure payments continue to provinces which are subject to boom and bust cycles.
>
> 2. A provision similar to the equalization section regarding EPF transfers, levels, and standards, ought to be added.
>
> 3. Some constitutional provisions regarding a guarantee of vital public services in the areas of transportation, communication, postal, and other services should be inserted. Such a provision would provide some legal avenue of challenge in the case of arbitrary arrangements or changes by the federal government in these areas.

The thrust of these changes is obvious. Provinces like Saskatchewan, which may occasionally become classified as 'have' provinces are in reality "have-not" when considered over the long term. The equalization section must become more sensitive to this need. More importantly however, since 1976 federal governments have been reducing their transfers under EPF. The time has come to guarantee these transfers in order to guarantee adequate levels of education and health. Finally, certain services in the West, like rail service, post offices, communication, etc., have been significantly eroded in the past twenty years. These are vital to this region and ought to be restored and guaranteed.

NATURAL RESOURCES

The sections in the constitution dealing with natural resources now appear to be inadequate. Sec. 92A does not seem to provide sufficient protection for the provincial right to tax and control natural resources. The FTA has effectively removed 92A(4), the right to levy indirect taxes on energy resources exported to the United States, and circumscribed the power to control production and distribution. As well, provincial governments need a greater return for depleting natural resources, which requires a reexamination of federal revenues from resources. Accordingly:

1. There should be an amendment to Sec. 92A to reinforce provincial control over resources exported into international trade.

2. New revenue arrangements, especially with regard to oil and gas pricing, royalties, and taxation, need to be worked out, and possibly constitutionalized.

AGRICULTURE

It is now obvious that some aspects of national agriculture arrangements need to be constitutionalized. The removal of the Crow Rate, changes like the removal of the two-price system for wheat, alteration of the role of the Farm Credit Corporation, and continued pressure on the Canadian Wheat Board, provide ample evidence to support the contention that certain arrangements need constitutional guarantees. Like language rights in Quebec, certain agricultural policies are the cornerstone of social and economic life in prairie Canada. This requires that:

1. Renegotiated agricultural programs should be constitutionalized in principle, if not in detail.

2. The existing role of the Canadian Wheat Board, with producer control, should be constitutionally guaranteed.

3. There should be concurrent provincial power over patents in agricultural chemicals, and agricultural products, including organic plants.

4. Future international treaties which include agricultural objects require provincial involvement in negotiation, and provincial consent to agreement and implementation.

5. There should be a new section of the constitution added dealing with agricultural land, which creates a federal-provincial body with a mandate to plan, preserve, and properly develop agricultural land in Canada.

As well, there should be further discussion on some items which may or may not have constitutional implications. For example:

1. There should be implementation of a domestic price for grains, more reflective of actual costs of production and less related to artificial international prices created by the US and the EEC.

2. A federal-provincial trade body, with a mandate to aid in the marketing of agricultural products, should be created.

INSTITUTIONS

Certain institutional changes should also be included in a package of constitutional amendments:

1. The present Senate should be abolished immediately as a sign of serious intent. Governments should then proceed to implement a reformed upper house as soon as possible.

2. Aboriginal participation in appropriate institutions should be entrenched.

3. There should be more input into Supreme Court appointments. These appointments should be removed from the sole control of the prime minister.

4. There should be a provincial role in the Bank of Canada, through appointments to the board.

5. There should be provincial appointment or election of lieutenant governors, and we should constitutionalize certain aspects of their role. Abolish the powers of disallowance, reservation, and the declaratory power under Sec. 92(10)c.

6. Some element of proportional representation should be entrenched in national electoral arrangements.

7. The ability of federal regulatory agencies to control provincial crown corporations should be carefully reviewed and circumscribed.

The question of Senate reform has been considered at length. Certainly there are sufficient proposals in existence for consideration. What is needed now is political will. In order to catalyze the process the present Senate should be abolished immediately, forcing decision makers to implement reform.

Whatever the shape of a new Senate, or other institutions, we should consider carefully the question of aboriginal representation in these bodies. There are likely to be instances where there should be guaranteed aboriginal representation. This principle can be applied to the Supreme Court where it would be desirable to implement new appointment procedures which provide for provincial government input, and guaranteed representation for Quebec and aboriginals. The proposal on the Bank of Canada is similar in intent.

Recommendation five is designed to remove the last vestiges of colonial control. Lately the question of the powers and role of lieutenant governors has again arisen, and ought to be clarified.[12] Recommendation six speaks to a fundamental question of regional concerns, the tendency at times for our electoral system to deny regional representation in the governing party. Finally, the power of commissions like the CRTC needs to be clarified.

OTHER

Several other matters need to be addressed:

1. The *de jure* equality of the provinces in the amending formula should be maintained.

2. Appropriate aboriginal participation in the amending provisions should be entrenched.

3. A provision for national referenda should be included.

4. New provisions on control of environmental problems should be included.

5. There should be a section dealing with how and under what circumstance secession from Canada can be undertaken by any province.

One principle established in the amending formula of 1982, the *de jure* equality of the provinces, should not be abandoned. It provides smaller, have-not provinces, with a guarantee of legal equality. If a veto for Quebec is a necessary part of any agreement, it ought to be a *de facto* veto, through manipulation of the required population requirement. The requirement for aboriginal participation is self-evident, but the ambit of that involvement needs to be carefully considered. A provision for a national referendum to adopt the new constitution should also be included.

Two other items need to be considered. The first is an amendment which more carefully delineates control over environmental issues should be considered. It is unclear at the present how that would be drafted, but it is likely that this should be an area of concurrent jurisdiction.

Recommendation five is aimed at removing an ambiguity in the present arrangements. How does a partner in the federation terminate its relationship with Canada? More precisely, who can do so, under what conditions, and through what process, if at all. Unless this issue is addressed, there may be future uncertainty which is undesirable.

These proposals are not fully inclusive. A complete agenda would include other items important to other groups and governments. They do constitute the core of what could be considered a progressive western agenda, especially in the area of economic policy.

PROCESS

Perhaps as important as the substance of agreement is the process by which we achieve our goals. However desirable the proposals, Meech Lake tells us that they will fail without the general participation and agreement of the people of Canada. The process of reaching agreement must be carefully considered.

REPAIRING OR REBUILDING CANADA?

Before any process can be effective, there must be agreement on the task at hand. Are we attempting to repair problems with the 1867 agreement, or are we attempting to rebuild the country, to start anew. Prior to June 1990, there was general agreement that we were repairing Canada — modernizing it, accommodating changes thrust upon us by changing economic, social and political circumstances. Even the patriation exercise of 1981 could be included in that category. Now, with the deadline set in Quebec, and the increasing scope of the demand for change, it might be concluded that we are in a process of rebuilding the 1867 agreement. If so, it necessitates a different process than the one we have endured lately.

THE FAILURE OF EXECUTIVE FEDERALISM

The process of constitutional repair has largely occurred within a context most often referred to as "executive federalism." It has been a highly elitist, and secretive process, borne of the wedding of the federal and parliamentary systems. Whatever its virtues, it can be fairly concluded that in the area of constitutional change its record of success is spotty, to say the least. This can be claimed from the results of various attempts at constitutional change up to 1981, and from the reaction to the Meech Lake process in 1990. Executive federalism is most effective when the matters involved reflect fundamental agreement about basic views, that is, when matters are amenable to compromise. It is least effective when presented with problems which flow from distinctly differing premises about goals and objectives. As Donald Smiley said:

> Agreement between Ottawa and the provinces is more likely if their relations are 'factored' than if most of the important interactions occur at or near the summit. This factoring may involve interactions between Ottawa and individual provinces rather than all the provinces, or it may consist of intergovernmental relations among officials concerned with very specific programs as against broader aspects of public policy.[13]

Given the wide divergence of views in Canada today it is unlikely that the normal processes of executive federalism can be successful in breaking the present impasse.

THE ROLE OF THE FEDERAL GOVERNMENT

Critical to the success of any process is a correct assumption about the role of the federal government in the coming months. Its role has been generally perceived as that of leader, chair, arbiter, caretaker, and/or initiator. All of these roles have probably been appropriate to a process of repair, that is, a process of less than fundamental change. If however, we are set to rebuild Canada, to scrap the role of the 1867 bargain and build anew, the role of federal government must change.

Several observations support this conclusion. First, the present federal government itself is the creature of the previous agreement. It is the result of the coalition of several actors in 1867. Despite its role in Canada since 1867 it should not be a dominant partner to a new process. Indeed, it must be the outcome of a new "coming together" of the existing partners in the 1990s. If the existing state bargain dissolves, its creatures dissolve with it. By implication, any process seeking to fundamentally rebuild the state cannot be dominated by the creature of the previous bargain.

Second, and flowing from the above premise, the participation of the federal government may actually hinder the process of renewal. This is because the federal government has a vested interest in preserving its own position, powers, and role. It cannot be expected to approve a process and outcome inimical to its own future. Thus the federal government, by virtue of its national mandate, will attempt to dominate the process, speaking for "all Canadians," inhibiting the appropriate interplay of the various "parts" of Canada.

Third, the federal government will only be as strong as its perceived support in all of Canada. Unfortunately the present government is very weak, and this weakness will taint any process.

For these reasons, we must contemplate a process which is not dominated by federal government, *if* we believe that we are in the process of rebuilding Canada.

MORE PARTICIPATION

It is clear that the new process must be more participatory than the past. However, it is unlikely that it can stray too far from our present democratic processes and representatives. If it does, it will run the risk of becoming irrelevant. With that in mind, we can come to several conclusions.

The first is that the existing provinces and their governments must be participants in the rebuilding of the country. For good or ill, they are the major partners in any renewal. Together with them must be included the two territories. The second conclusion is that the three groups of aboriginal people must be at the table. How they select their representatives must be resolved by themselves internally. The third thing that is apparent is that delegations from each group must be selected in a manner which makes them highly representative especially in terms of gender and visible minorities. They cannot simply be selected as agents of any particular leader or party. Finally, the outcome of any process must be submitted to the people as a whole. Details of that submission need to be worked out.

QUEBEC PARTICIPATION

As we know, Quebec has chosen to absent itself from any future First Ministers Conferences. This is interpreted to mean from all of the processes of traditional executive federalism. However, if we are engaged in a different process, one in which there is an agreement to fundamentally rebuild Canada, Quebec should be able to participate. If it chooses not to, however, it should be invited to sit as as an observer in order to be fully informed of discussions and probable outcomes.

A PROVINCIAL PROCESS

What this concludes is that the present processes involving the federal government and Quebec are insufficient. If we are to renew Canada, we must broaden the base and keep it separate from the federal government. This means that the provincial governments through the premiers conference should undertake a process separate from that undertaken by Joe Clark, and the federal cabinet. If should be funded, and controlled by them, with representation selected as outlined above.

Such a process would be most valuable for western Canada. It would allow the West to put on the table a number of proposals which might otherwise be given short shrift if the federal government is involved in the initial phases. As well, given the large percentage of aboriginal people in the West, and the impact on western provinces of land settlements and resource transfers, it would allow for some face to face bargaining between the several groups of the west, *before* a meeting with federal representatives. It will also allow some governments to take strong pro-central government stands without risking the political liability of being associated with an unpopular federal government. Finally, such a process could also become the chief forum for the rest of Canada should Quebec carry through with its referendum next year. While such an outcome can be avoided through appropriate bargaining and good will, one should nevertheless be prepared for such an outcome if necessary.

CONCLUSION

This paper has attempted, in a very prescriptive way, to sketch out the major elements of a constitutional package for western Canada. It is a mixture which seeks to wed the best of decentralist and centralist proposals. It speaks consciously to a broader agenda, an agenda which is not limited to constitutional change as envisaged by the federal government and Quebec. As well, it tries to set out in detail changes which reflect the "have-not" view of the West, both in terms of provinces and individuals. It also encourages a process which is separate from the federal government, to allow the basic founding groups of Canada to refashion the federation free from the undue influence of the present federal government.

Quebec has set the wheels of change in motion. It is for us to be part of steering the federation to a new and better agreement.

Notes

1.   Janine Brodie, *The Political Economy of Canadian Regionalism* (Toronto: Harcourt Brace Jovanovich, 1990), 6.

2.   Ibid., 10.

3.   David E. Smith, "Western Canada," in Robert M. Krause and R.H. Wagenberg, eds., *Introductory Readings in Canadian Government* (Toronto: Copp Clark Pittman Ltd., 1991), 121.

4.   D.V. Smiley, *The Federal Condition in Canada* (Toronto: McGraw-Hill Ryerson, 1987), 164.

5.   Ibid.

6.   Ibid., 167.

7. D.V. Smiley, *Canada in Question: Federalism in the Eighties* (Toronto: McGraw-Hill Ryerson, 1980).

8. Brodie, *Political Economy of Canadian Regionalism*, 16.

9. Saskatchewan's situation is a bit ambiguous, since it was considered a "have" province from 1978 to 1984.

10. See John Richards and Larry Pratt, *Prairie Capitalism: Power and Wealth in the New West* (Toronto: McClelland and Stewart, 1979).

11. Doug Owram, "Reluctant Hinterland," in Larry Pratt and Garth Stevenson, eds., *Western Separatism: The Myths, Realities and Dangers* (Edmonton: Hurtig Publishers, 1981), 46.

12. In Saskatchewan in particular this has been a question.

13. Smiley, *The Federal Condition in Canada*, 98.

17

Challenging Constitutional Dependency:
A Revisionist View of Atlantic Canada

David Milne

The constitutional politics of Atlantic Canada is not well understood either by those living inside the region or outside it. Governments and practitioners of the art are not much inclined to develop a research inventory on the subject nor even to share their practical experience with others. On the academic side, to put the matter kindly, there has been little academic energy and even less light shed on the subject. This embarrassing neglect stands in marked contrast to the prominence given to constitutional politics in Quebec, the West, and recently even in the North. This apparent indifference calls out for explanation. It will be my contention that not many Canadians have had reason to suppose either from history or theory that the subject held much importance. Ever since the vain attempts of Maritimers to pull the region out of Confederation — a politics superciliously dismissed by national historians as parochial and paranoid — there has been little reason to take the constitutional politics of Atlantic Canadians seriously. After the prominence of two Atlantic provinces in holding up and blocking ratification of the Meech Lake Accord, however, such indifference may now be passing, together with the comfortable theory that had in effect justified this benign neglect.

We could, of course, proceed to label and discuss the various schools of dependency theory that have been advanced over the years to justify not taking Atlantic Canada's constitutional politics seriously.[1] Whether we find the roots of this lamentable condition in Atlantic underdevelopment, in an allegedly backward political culture, or merely in the simple welfare syndrome of dependence on federal financial transfers, the result is invariably said to be regimes of amiable docility.[2] If Ralph Winters is right that the Atlantic provinces are "mere satrapies of the federal government insofar as federal-provincial relations are concerned," there is indeed little reason to waste valuable intellectual energy on these.[3] This image of dependent compliance upon the federal paymaster is one frequently encountered in the literature of Canadian federalism.[4] It also crops up dangerously among the professional constitutional actors where more skepticism and prudence might better be expected.

I remember, for example, encountering such a complacent view from a senior Federal-Provincial Relations Office official during an interview over the ratification of the Meech Lake Accord. He remained convinced that, despite the many expressed reservations of Atlantic governments, they would in the end swallow their principles and come on board the Meech Lake express in compliance with the will of Ottawa and the other powerful governments at the centre. Atlantic Canadians were described as basically "good natured and amiable," whereas the objections of Manitobans were immediately given more credence. Such self-serving complacency doubtless supported the long federal strategy of ignoring Premier Clyde Wells of Newfoundland or of underrating his concerns and those of Premier McKenna of New Brunswick. It also clearly contributed to federal and Quebec confidence in the utility of veiled economic threats to try to secure Atlantic ratification of the accord. Yet, as events later demonstrated, this image of the region's compliant constitutional politics was seriously flawed.

How are we to account for this intellectual vacuum of understanding? We might begin by examining the legacy of intellectuals like George Rawlyk, and his followers, who decades ago began the now venerable tradition of treating the constitutional politics of Atlantic Canada with undisguised contempt. His essays in several critical collections on the future of Canada were presumably meant to explain Atlantic Canada's constitutional politics to the rest of the country; in the end, he merely produced a caricature that conveniently reinforced and sanctioned an already existing perception of the region held by national historians at the centre for many years.[5] After summarily dismissing the size of the land mass and population of the maritime provinces in an early essay in 1971, for example, he went on to give this blunt and probably accurate account of how other Canadians then viewed the region:

> For many Canadians, the seemingly unimportant Maritime area is considered to be an economic, political, intellectual, and social backwater. Events of crucial "national consequence" have apparently (or so it is argued) passed the backwater by. The main thrust of Canadian historical development after 1873, when Prince Edward Island finally entered Confederation, owed little, if anything (or so it seems), to events or persons in the three Maritime Provinces.[6]

The alleged "trauma" of marginalization as an historical and actual backwater in Canada was all the more painful for the people of the region still living the memory of their pre-Confederation golden age of "wooden ships and iron men." Unable to account "rationally" for this calamity, the Rawlyk diagnosis soon has Maritimers in the paranoid mode — shrill, despairing — in search of villains to blame for their feelings of "collective inferiority and bitterness." From here the gradual twentieth-century descent into numb and quiet dependency upon federal handouts is an easy, seemingly inevitable outcome — a fitting ending for a defeated people whose anti-Confederation resistance had been broken. Ultimately, we are told, these Maritimers developed a "love-hate" relationship to Canada, capable over time of developing genuine affection for Canada and yet deeply resentful of past injustices and current indignities.

These sullen wards of the state, Rawlyk suggests, when faced with the prospect of Quebec separation, now can "give the impression that they are eager to be more Canadian than the most vociferous Upper Canadian."[7] Their constitutional politics are said to be status quo and centralist, protective of federal powers that feed their dependency. Most fearful of Quebec separation, most economically and geographically vulnerable, most conservative, and most compliant to federal interests, their constitutional politics by this account turn out to be predictably pedestrian. Only superficially drawn to the struggle over language rights and the charter, it is argued, Maritimers are said to be motivated by "bread and butter issues." Rawlyk concludes by declaring that their dependency will lead them to cling even to a truncated "East Pakistan" Canada, because they believe that "as Canadians they are something — removed from Canada, they are next to nothing."[8]

Wonderfully sado-masochistic, these scholarly themes, developed largely in the late 1960s and early 1970s during a quieter period of constitutional activity in English-speaking Canada generally, crop up repeatedly in the subsequent literature on Atlantic Canadian constitutional politics. Robert Finbow has recently produced a careful review of these themes and tested their adequacy against the actual record of the Atlantic provinces in constitutional discussions from 1967 to 1990.[9] He has concluded that "the principles expressed and positions taken [of the Atlantic provinces] belie the stereotypical portrayal of political life in these [allegedly] quiescent, stagnant peripheries."[10] The actual constitutional record offers little empirical support for the proposition that Atlantic Canadian provinces have been docile dependents, nor for the proposition advanced by Simeon and Elkins that the constitutional politics of these governments simply mirror the traditionally conservative regional political culture.[11] Hence, even if the Simeon and Elkins analysis is valid — and there is increasing reason to question the relevance of these old portraits of Atlantic political culture dating back to the mid-1970s[12] — the constitutional evidence adduced by Finbow over almost a quarter century does not appear to validate it. This conclusion comports perfectly with my own practical experience working with the constitutional politics of two governments of varying political stripe in the region in 1980-81 and again in 1991. In my judgement, it is doubtful that the conventional stereotype can do much justice to the actual constitutional politics of the provinces in this part of Canada, particularly after the reemergence of regionalism as a powerful constitutional force in the mid-1970s.

The stereotype appears to retain some modest plausibility for the 1967-71 period when Atlantic provinces came to the negotiating table largely with equalization payments and regional economic development on their collective minds. Yet, even here, the record shows an aggressiveness to put their constitutional concerns on the agenda unbecoming mere satrapies. Moreover, the insistence that equalization and regional economic development be constitutionally recognized and "guaranteed" also reflected the preference of the Atlantic provinces for a modern juristic approach to entitlements rather than relying upon old-fashioned federal charity for their security. At the same time, at least two of the provinces in the region — Nova Scotia and Prince Edward Island — were responsive to provincial concerns over the abuse of the federal spending power and were prepared to see reasonable limits placed upon it. In that respect, they were not much different in their approach from provinces like Manitoba and Saskatchewan, though the record shows that they worried far less than the western provinces over proposed restrictions to the federal spending power.[13] As for Rawlyk's label of an Atlantic "bread and butter" constitutional vision, this was scarcely atypical of provinces in English-speaking Canada, all of whom approached these early constitutional discussions with decidedly little enthusiasm. It may well be that the stereotypical regional view, here as elsewhere, misses what is *really* important, such as the interesting *variation* of constitutional response among governments in the region, particularly the genuinely warm reception that the federal reform proposal on official bilingualism had in the province of New Brunswick.

The problem with the neocolonial framework is that it organizes the analysis along regional lines — sometimes including Newfoundland, sometimes not — without demonstrating either the existence or coherence of such a regional political culture or constitutional posture.[14] Secondly, the approach pays scant regard to the fact that it is *provinces*, represented by first ministers in all their eccentricities, not regions, that are the constitutional actors and these actors have *not* normally adopted common approaches to the varying items on the constitutional agenda from patriation to Meech Lake and beyond. Indeed, apart from common support for inclusion of the decidedly uncontroversial principles of equalization and regional economic development in the constitution, there is hardly a subject upon which the Atlantic provinces have not disagreed over the years.

As Table 1 indicates, on many subjects either of special interest to Ottawa or on which a special regional interest might be expected, there has been little agreement among Atlantic governments. Test the dependency theory with the asterisked items in the table. For example, in Atlantic Canadian responses to Prime Minister Trudeau's key concerns in the comprehensive discussions in 1980: patriation, the Charter of Rights and Freedoms, an amending formula, and new federal powers over the economy. Neither in the discussions in 1978 nor in 1980-81 did Atlantic governments provide Ottawa with the support that it sought, although New Brunswick under Premier Hatfield was in general more accommodating than the others. For that matter, neither did Atlantic premiers respond favourably to Ottawa's constitutional concerns during the Meech Lake ratification process. In short, there is no uniform pattern of centralization in Atlantic constitutional goals, particularly from the late 1970s on.

Table 1
Atlantic Government Responses to Constitutional Agenda, 1980

Item	Newfoundland	Nova Scotia	New Brunswick	P.E.I.
Patriation	Opposes unilateral patriation	Opposes unilateral patriation	*Supports unilateral patriation	Opposes unilateral patriation
Charter	Supports entrenchment of fundamental freedoms & democratic rights	Opposes charter	*Supports charter	Opposes charter, especially property rights
Amending formula	Vancouver consensus	Vancouver consensus	*Victoria formula	Vancouver consensus
Power over economy	Opposes federal proposals	*Supports federal proposals	Opposes federal proposals	Opposes federal proposals
Fishery	Concurrency with provincial paramountcy over allocating provincial quotas in coastal fishery	*Federal control over quotas in coastal fishery	*Federal control over quotas in coastal fishery	Concurrent say over coastal fishery
Offshore	Provincial ownership in constitution	Provincial ownership through administrative agreement	Newfoundland ownership as special case	Provincial ownership in Constitution

* Indicates support for federal position on the item.

When one looks at issues of unusual regional concern beyond the entrenchment of equalization and regional economic development, there is the same varied pattern. Take, for example, the differences in jurisdiction over fisheries; consensus on this issue has quite eluded these coastal provinces. Even the offshore question that in 1980 managed to bring all provinces in support of Newfoundland, the regional consensus was shaky; such a consensus was not present earlier in the 1970s nor did it persist long after patriation. This is hardly surprising when even the provincial constitutional agenda itself so frequently changed over the years. The province of Newfoundland reversed itself sharply on the question of the fishery and other subjects when Premier Wells replaced

Peckford; Prince Edward Island, too, shifted from a Triple-E position on Senate reform under Conservative premiers McLean and Lee to relative indifference under Liberal premier Joe Ghiz. Much of this variation can be accounted for, not by party platforms that have rarely pronounced on constitutional issues, but by the different occupants of the first minister's chair.

But some issues do seem to have been persistently high priorities in certain Atlantic provinces *whatever* the changes in government. Such issues are often peculiar to a province's history or demography. Take, for example, the united posture of all Island parties and premiers against the inclusion of property rights in the charter from 1980-81 onward *despite* continuing federal enthusiasm for the idea. The struggle for local legislative control over land against outside private ownership has been at the centre of Prince Edward Island history and identity for centuries; similarly, there can be no compromise over the question of legislative protection of agricultural lands in the name of the family farm and the Island way of life. Therefore, it does not much matter whether Conservative leader Angus McLean or Liberal Joe Ghiz is in power, the answer is still the same — never will the Prince Edward Island legislature risk losing this legislative right to regulate land to protect this small province and its residents. The issue has already been before the courts in an earlier Supreme Court decision that supported the validity of the province's nonresident land legislation against a constitutional challenge raised by an American; there would be no wish to see the issue return again, this time as a charter challenge.[15] One looks in vain, however, for the issue to take on any serious resonance elsewhere in the region.

It is the same with the question of language rights in the province of New Brunswick. One would have to be blind to this province's demography and history to ignore the centrality of language to the constitutional preoccupations of this province. Whether under premier Robichaud, Hatfield, or McKenna, there can be no question that this issue has always been front and centre. How could it be otherwise when one-third of the population of the province is comprised of Acadians, proud of their language and distinctiveness? Far from being a "superficial" issue, as Rawlyk tried to argue in his broadbrush maritime perspective, language politics has been at the nerve centre of New Brunswick constitutional politics, most often overshadowing so-called "bread and butter issues." Hence, it was New Brunswick that acted early to promote bilingualism, encouraged the development of autonomous schools and school boards in 1974, and in 1981 passed An Act Recognizing the Equality of Status of the Two Official Communities (Bill 88). Premier Hatfield was a steady supporter of Trudeau's constitutional efforts to entrench official bilingualism in the constitution; indeed, he was the *only* premier in Canada who went further to accept official bilingualism as a constitutional requirement for his province in 1982. Premier McKenna too has continued to make language central to the constitutional politics of the province both with his criticisms of the Meech Lake Accord, and with his efforts to constitutionalize Bill 88. There is little reason to expect that the same will not be true in this province's continuing constitutional endeavours. One looks in vain elsewhere in the Atlantic region for the same constancy and concern over language issues.

A regional perspective is oblivious to that reality, and cannot in the final analysis do justice either to recurring constitutional patterns in certain Atlantic provinces or to the bewildering changes in provincial constitutional agendas in Atlantic Canada arising from a changing cast of Atlantic premiers. But the objection to a regional dependency approach to constitutional analysis for Atlantic Canada goes deeper. As a dangerously simplistic, almost mechanical, caricature, it distorts history and provides poor guidance on the present and future patterns of constitutional activity in the region. For example, the assumed psychological link between extreme dependency upon federal transfers and constitutional docility is flatly contradicted by the constitutional politics of the federation's poorest province, Newfoundland, under both premiers Peckford and Wells; if the provincialist leader Peckford is any guide. Faulty, too, is the theory's presumed centralist bias of have-not provinces. Even Premier Wells's role as a plausible defender of the centre hardly confirms a status quo position — on the contrary, he has become a vigorous champion of a full Triple-E Senate for reasons that would be well understood in Calgary or Vancouver. In English-speaking Canada, he is now by far the most vigorous and popular advocate of the concept of provincial equality as a principle in the federation, of individual rights under the charter, and of official bilingualism against Quebec's distinct society. How could this politics be grasped by a dependency model that insists on painting Atlantic Canada as a poor, docile and conservative backwater?

It is time that our models of constitutional explanation took into account the obvious modernization that has taken place in the Atlantic region.[16] Lawyers like Clyde Wells or Frank McKenna are products of a new urban middle class here, while Joseph Ghiz of Prince Edward Island, himself a Harvard graduate in law and a Canadian of Lebanese extraction, is the first representative of Canada's multicultural communities to become a first minister of the Crown. One could hardly anticipate a premier of Lebanese background appearing in Anne of Green Gables land, before western leaders with multicultural credentials like Vander Zalm in British Columbia or Romanow in Saskatchewan, but it surely indicates how far reality is outpacing old clichés and images. These leaders preside over an increasingly educated and mobile population that share, through television and other media of communication, values typical of Canadians outside the region. What then is the point of clinging to outdated and insulting images?

It is a trifle difficult, also, to see the relevance of the dependency model to Atlantic Canadian politics on any of the major federal-provincial constitutional crises of the last decade. Many of the governments of Atlantic Canada were not shy in demanding the transfer of federal powers to the provinces, especially over the offshore, or asserting the equality of provinces, or insisting on the restructuring of national institutions to give the provinces more powers at the centre. In what discernible ways were they any less independent than the other provincial players? If anything, Atlantic Canadian governments took the lead on many subjects — Newfoundland on the offshore and the fishery, New Brunswick on bilingualism, and Prince Edward Island on Senate reform when it stood alone among governments in first advancing the notion of a Triple-E Senate. Such postures were hardly the actions of conservative compliant regimes.

And where were the alleged wards of the federal state during the subsequent heady days of federal unilateralism under Trudeau? Three of the four provinces in the region joined the "gang of eight" in political and court challenges to unilateral patriation of the constitution. It was a Newfoundland court responding to a Newfoundland government reference in the spring of 1981 that stopped Trudeau's unilateral resolution in its tracks. These governments were influential, too, in achieving the final bloc-trading compromise once negotiations resumed in earnest in November, and in insisting on qualifications on mobility rights in the charter.

But it was only with the Meech Lake debacle that the Atlantic Canada dependency theory over the constitution received its final côup de grace. For here, two of the three holdouts in ratification of the accord were none other than Atlantic provinces. Small in size and population, these provinces nonetheless exercised their constitutional prerogatives with more independence than could ever have been anticipated by conventional wisdom. Ironically, it was the traditionally most supportive federal friend of Ottawa — New Brunswick — that until the eleventh hour held up ratification of the accord and demanded changes in a companion resolution; it was Newfoundland that first used the power in the amending formula to rescind its earlier consent to the accord and refused to accept federal pressure to take another final vote after it had become clear that the Manitoba legislature had adjourned hours before the deadline. While these provinces were supported in their independence by strong national public opinion, they faced an indignant array of powerful interests in Ottawa, Quebec City, Montreal, Toronto, Edmonton and Vancouver demanding that the small, poor provinces ought not to hold up the nation. Quite a performance for the proverbial provincial backwater!

Whatever the constitutional future of Canada and Quebec after Meech Lake, no historian will ever again be likely to say that events of crucial "national consequence" have passed the Atlantic region by nor that "Canadian historical development ... owes little, if anything to events or persons" in the Atlantic provinces. It is fitting that it is the premier of the poorest province of Canada that, on Meech Lake, chose to stand on principle and declare his constitutional course *despite* the economic risks that presented to his province. History will judge whether such constitutional roulette was brave or unspeakably foolish. But his defiant stand to take that risk even if "Newfoundlanders end up as paupers" because "we will have our dignity and self-respect," remains a permanent rebuke to the theory of constitutional dependency.[17]

Notes

1.   For a brief review of the dependency debate and its link to federal-provincial relations in Atlantic Canada, see Donald J. Savoie, "The Atlantic Region: The Politics of Dependency," in R.D. Olling and M.W. Westmacott, *Perspectives on Canadian Federalism* (Scarborough: Prentice Hall, 1988), 291-303. A political economy perspective might best be seen in Ralph Matthews, *The Creation of Regional Dependency* (Toronto: University of Toronto Press, 1983).

2.   According to Savoie, for example, the only exception to this rule is Newfoundland in the late 1970s and early 1980s when the prospect of offshore oil for this "distinct society" produced an uncharacteristic aggressiveness in federal-provincial relations.

3.   Cited in George A. Rawlyk, *The Atlantic Provinces and the Problems of Confederation* (St. John's, Newfoundland: Breakwater, 1979), 32.

4.   See, for example, the acceptance of the dependence theory vis-à-vis Ottawa in Donald Smiley's classic work, *Canada in Question: Federalism in the Eighties*, 3rd edition (Toronto: McGraw-Hill Ryerson, 1980), 67

5.   See G.A. Rawlyk, "The Maritimes and the problem of the Secession of Quebec," in R.M. Burns, ed., *One Country or Two* (Montreal/London; McGill-Queen's University Press, 1971), 205-30; George Rawlyk, "Quebec's Separation and the Atlantic Provinces," in Richard Simeon, ed., *Must Canada Fail?* (Montreal/London: McGill-Queen's University Press, 1977), 85-92.

6.   Rawlyk, "The Maritimes and the Problem of the Secession of Quebec," 205.

7.   Ibid., 206.

8.   Rawlyk, "Quebec's Separation and the Atlantic Provinces," 92.

9.   Robert Finbow, "The Atlantic Provinces in the Constitutional Reform Process, 1967-1990," paper presented at Canadian Political Science Association annual meeting, Queen's University, Kingston, Ontario, June 1991.

10.   Ibid., 30.

11.   See Richard Simeon and David Elkins, "Regional Political Cultures in Canada," *Canadian Journal of Political Science* 7, no. 3 (September 1974), 420-21. See also David J. Bellamy, "The Atlantic Provinces," in David J. Bellamy et al., eds., *The Provincial Political Systems: Comparative Essays* (Toronto: Methuen, 1976), 3-18.

12.   See the reappraisal of the thesis, for example, in Ian Stewart, "Simeon and Elkins Revisited: Regional Political Cultures in Canada," paper presented to the Atlantic Provinces Political Science Association, St. John, New Brunswick, 26 October 1991.

13.   It was the same story at the Meech Lake negotiations where the champions of the federal spending power, contrary to the stereotype, were provinces like Manitoba and Ontario, not the Atlantic provinces.

14.   For a careful dismissal of the notion of a maritime political culture, see J. Murray Beck, "The Maritimes: A Region of Three Provinces?" Transactions of the Royal Society of Canada, Series IV, Vol. 15, 1977, 301-13. That was also the conclusion of a symposium on Atlantic Canada and the constitution held at Acadia University, 2-4 July

1980. See J.R. winter, ed., *The Atlantic Provinces in Canada: Where Do We Go From Here?* (Wolfville, Nova Scotia: Acadia University, 1980).

15. Morgan v. A.G. of P.E.I. [1976] 2 S.C.R. 349.

16. This is a point that Robert Finbow raises too in his very thoughtful paper, ''The Atlantic Provinces in the Constitutional Reform Process.''

17. Clyde Wells, Government of Newfoundland and Labrador, *Meech Lake Accord Rescission Debate: Hansard Record*, 27 March 1990, R72.

18

The Prairies and Atlantic Canada: Constitutional Common Ground?

Thérèse Arseneau

The study of Canadian politics has tended to emphasize the cleavages which divide the country. In particular, much is made of Canada's territorial-based diversity. For instance, Canada is frequently labelled "a country of regions"[1] and Canadian politics as regional politics.[2] Yet upon closer examination even these "regions" do not hold together. Murray Beck, for example, has described Atlantic Canada as a figment of Ottawa's imagination, "a contrivance based on convenience or budgetary considerations" and not discernable from within the so-called region itself.[3] Roger Gibbins argues that prairie regionalism is in decline.[4] It would appear then that Canada is not merely divided into five or so regions but more fundamentally into ten provinces and two territories. Hence many experts now believe that the more important units of analysis are the provinces.[5] Others are quick to add that in addition to the differences between the provinces within the Atlantic and the prairie regions, important differentiations exist within the provinces as well.[6]

While Canada is undoubtedly a diverse and fragmented country, the purpose of this paper is, to paraphrase Robert Frost, to take "the road less travelled." It will focus on what potentially unites rather than divides Atlantic and prairie Canadians, on what is similar rather than different between the regions. It would appear from first glance that the basis for any such commonalty could stem from the shared experiences of the two regions as political and economic hinterlands. Thus the study starts with an examination of traditional Atlantic and prairie grievances. In short, while it is generally accepted that there is "western alienation," is there also "eastern alienation," and if so, does it resemble its western counterpart? When studying this alienation the complaints of the two peripheral regions are separated into two categories — political and economic.

More specifically the focus of the paper is the possibility of a shared prairie-Atlantic approach in constitutional negotiations. Given the similar, but not identical, economic and political complaints, is there correspondingly a list of common constitutional demands? It will be argued that in terms of suggested "political" constitutional reforms the East and West do indeed share common ground. But in terms of reforms meant to deal with the economic complaints stemming from the hinterland status of these provinces, there is a definite split in the group of seven. On economic constitutional issues the critical grouping is "have" versus "have-not" provinces, not the fact that the provinces are part of the periphery. Hence Alberta maintains a different position on what constitutes an appropriate level of federal government involvement in the economy to the Atlantic provinces and Manitoba, recipients of federal government largesse. Saskatchewan is a province in transition — sometimes "have," sometimes "have-not." Its position is therefore less fixed, siding with Alberta on issues such as provincial control over natural resources but remaining committed to federal involvement in the economy. Yet while those in the "have-not" group seek a more centrally dominated economy than does Alberta, contrary to popular perception they are not uncritical of Ottawa's fiscal policies. What these provinces seek to entrench therefore is central, but regionally sensitive, economic direction.

Having established the likely constitutional position of the Atlantic and prairie provinces, the paper concludes with a brief examination of the federal government's proposals contained in *Shaping Canada's Future Together*. Although it is too soon to predict with certainty what position the seven provincial legislatures will take on this document, given their past records, certain preliminary observations will be made.

WESTERN ALIENATION AND EASTERN ALIENATION COMPARED

The Prairies
    It has been argued that the three prairie provinces have less in common today, and hence act less like one region, than they did when they were predominantly agrarian-based.[7] Yet Roger Gibbins asserts that still today there exists a common regional mythology, one that "infuses itself into every nook and cranny of Prairie political life" and which he has labelled "western alienation."[8] He defines it as:

> a political creed of regional discontent which embodies a socially shared, generated and transmitted set of interrelated beliefs, a set of beliefs with at least some degree of cultural embodiment and intellectual articulation, with a recognized history and constituency and recognized spokespersons and carriers of the creed.[9]

David Elton claims this shared disaffection with the federal government has become so embedded in the western political culture that it persists in the West regardless of the party in power or the number of prairie MPs on the government side in the House of Commons.[10] What fuels this regional discontent is a broad range of federal government policies which, while meant to be in the "national interest," have not been beneficial to the western region.

    Many of the initial objections emanating from the region were traditional agrarian complaints. The tariffs featured in Sir John A. Macdonald's National Policy were perhaps the prime agrarian grievance and contributed more than any other single policy to the farmers' estrangement from the federal government.[11] The tariff wall effectively drew a line across the North American continent in order to promote east-west rather than north-south trade. While the policy was meant to encourage the development of industry and provide jobs for Canadians, western farmers believed these benefits were only felt in central Canada. On the Prairies the effects were negative — higher prices on all imported goods. These higher prices could not be passed on to the consumer since the farmers sold their product on the highly competitive world market. These higher prices might have been acceptable to the farmers had the region been the recipient of some of the benefits of tariff walls, namely the development of industry.

This was not the case though largely due to the equally contentious federal transportation policy of "fair discrimination." This specified that in areas of competing transportation facilities freight rates would be set at a competitive level, even if it meant the railroad would operate at a loss. These operational losses were recouped in an area where there was no competition — the Prairies.[12] What made the CPR's high freight rates particularly damaging was the fact that, aside from not having any other modes of transport (water or road), the CPR was also granted a monopoly in the West preventing any other rail competition. This was one of the conditions insisted upon by the central-Canadian CPR syndicate before it would agree to build the railroad. Since one-half of the all-Canadian line would pass through land where little or no traffic could be expected, most notably north of Lake Superior and through the Rockies, and given that in the area where there was the most traffic there was also the most competition, the syndicate members realized that only high freight rates in the west would make the project viable. A western monopoly was thus needed to force all the prairie traffic onto the CPR line. The result was the federal government conceded the enticements needed for the syndicate to undertake the construction of the railroad — trememdous land grants and a twenty-year monopoly in the West.

The defenders of the National Policy did not think that this arrangement was unfair. They argued that if it were not for the granting of this monopoly, the West would not have had a railroad at all. By the same reasoning, it was only right that the West pay for the operating losses of the CPR since "the entire line from Ottawa west had been built to open up and develop the West."[13] What this argument failed to consider was that the operating losses occurred due to Macdonald's insistence on an all-Canadian route which was far more expensive to construct and operate than a more direct line south of Lake Superior. The West would have preferred the cheaper, more direct railroad. Furthermore:

> The 'national' Lake Superior section was not built merely as a service to the West. It was accepted as the instrument which would tie the western traffic to the Canadian metropolitan centres in the St. Lawrence lowlands. Far from being a generous and magnanimous gesture to the West, the Lake Superior

line was also an instrument of Canadian nationalism and eastern Canadian economic imperialism.[14]

The price of shipping wheat from the West to central Canada was almost three times that for comparable distances in the eastern areas.[15] The Alberta farmers were doubly hurt by these high freight rates: since they exported primarily unprocessed goods (wheat), they had to pay the highest freight rates charged to ship the unprocessed grain to export ports at Vancouver or Thunder Bay and then pay the highest rates again to have processed goods (flour and flour products, manufactured goods) shipped back to Alberta. The Crow's Nest Pass Agreement of 1897, which provided a federal transportation subsidy for the exportation of western wheat out of the region and for the importation of central Canadian manufactured goods into the region, seemingly addressed these complaints. But the long-term effect of the agreement was to discourage the development of industry in the West. "Because it was cheap to export grain, specialization in agriculture was encouraged. Because it was cheap to bring manufactured goods in, the growth of manufacturing industry in the west was discouraged."[16] In 1925 the subsidy for the importation of manufactured goods was removed but by this time central Canadian industry already enjoyed a significant competive advantage. Consequently prairie industry did not develop; the region remained a resource hinterland.[17]

Another major area of dispute was natural resources. Initially the point of contention was the federal government's decision to retain control over the Crown lands and natural resources of the three prairie provinces, thus denying these new provinces a jurisdiction granted the four original provinces in 1867, and British Columbia when it joined in 1876.[18] Alberta, Saskatchewan and Manitoba interpreted this move as Ottawa's refusal to grant the Prairies equal status with the other provinces. Even though the federal government did transfer control over property and natural resources to the three provinces in 1930, according to prairie rhetoric, the only reason the federal government agreed to give up the jurisdiction then was because it believed there was nothing worth keeping.[19] Whether or not this perception is accurate is open to question but there appears to be at least some truth in this claim: by 1930 a large part of the productive Crown lands had been lost to private ownership, the wheat economy had ceased its expansion phase, and the bonanza of oil and gas had not yet been discovered.

The federal-provincial disputes over natural resources continued throughout the 1960s, 1970s, and early 1980s but the intensity of involvement in these disputes varied by province in the region. Manitoba, for instance, was generally sympathetic to the complaints of its prairie neighbours concerning federal government intrusion in natural resources, especially since it was the jurisdiction all three provinces had fought so hard to gain. According to Larry Pratt and John Richards:

> Westerners of all classes came to perceive Ottawa as an imperial govern-
> ment, a complex of institutions organized by central Canadian elites for the
> purpose of dominating and plundering the hinterlands. The provincial ad-
> ministration, whatever its colouration, became the indispensible agent for
> attacking political colonialism and bargaining with external interests.[20]

The three prairie provinces therefore typically shared the perception that
Ottawa's regulation of this industry was a symbol of its colonial mentality
towards western Canada.[21] Yet Manitoba, unlike Alberta and Saskatchewan, did
not have large oil and gas reserves and thus tended to view the debate more like
a consumer than a producer.[22] The province was therefore unsupportive of the
push for world prices for domestic oil.[23]

Saskatchewan was more acutely involved in the battles with the federal
government over natural resources. Premier Allan Blakeney was highly critical
of the price ceilings on oil and gas first set by Ottawa in 1973:

> Historically in Canada, resources and their benefits have been unreservedly
> provincial. Until recent years no one has even suggested that it should be
> any other way. When the power potential of Niagara Falls was harnessed at
> the turn of the century, the total benefits of cheap power went to Ontario.
> And that involved an international river — certainly reason enough for the
> Government of Canada to step in.

> And at that time, prairie people were paying four or five times as much for
> electricity as were Ontario people. And these higher costs were true up to
> the 1950s. But there was no national policy of equalizing energy costs
> then...

> We in the West find it passing strange that the national interest emerges
> only when we are talking about western *resources* or eastern *benefits*. If oil,
> why not iron ore and steel products? If natural gas, why not copper? If
> uranium ... why not nickel?[24]

Blakeney joined Peter Lougheed as a firm critic of the National Energy Program
(NEP), announced in the October 1980 federal budget. The NEP was seen as an
unveiled attempt by the Trudeau government, which had just been re-elected on
a platform of selling the West's energy resources cheaply, to take over the
region's oil and gas. It seemed to the citizens of Alberta and Saskatchewan that
Trudeau had few qualms about "plundering" a region which, although rich in
natural resources, was poor in votes.[25] The budget was perceived as being calculated against one particular region — the West — and yet another example of the
fact that federal policies were designed to exploit and drain the West, in spite of
the objections of the region. Blakeney and Lougheed were also united in their
aggressive approach to constitutional negotiations taking place against the backdrop of the NEP; enhanced provincial ownership in Sec. 92 was their prime objective. At issue for Saskatchewan was the province's mineral income tax and
royalty surcharges passed by the legislature in 1973, and the province's ability to

proration potash production, both of which were declared *ultra vires* by the courts. Blakeney sought constitutional changes which would give the province the authority to legislate in these policy areas.

Yet even though Blakeney was deeply involved in the wranglings over natural resources, Lougheed and the province he represented were the federal government's principal antagonists. Alberta was more specifically focussed on oil and gas production and pricing than was Saskatchewan. In terms of both frequency and intensity of conflict with Ottawa, Lougheed was the undisputed leader of the prairie revolt against federal resource policy. Lougheed also led prairie criticism in other areas of complaint such as the federal government's bilingualism policy; Trudeau's plans to unilaterally patriate the constitution; and the federal government's lack of initiatives in the areas of agriculture, transportation and secondary industry. But overall the major complaint was the region's perceived unequal treatment within Confederation.

The Atlantic Provinces

The Maritimes were not enthusiastic supporters of Confederation. Maritime delegates were fearful of the political and economic ramifications of such a union. Politically they recognized that, due to their relatively small population, they would be swamped by central Canada in the House of Commons where their contingent "would have scarcely more weight and dignity than the City Council."[26] When their worst fears were realized in the early years of Confederation, Nova Scotia threatened secession.

Like the West, the Maritimes faced some hardship due to the national tariff policy. As S.A. Saunders observed the Maritimes, along with the western provinces, bore more of the burden of higher commodity prices than did central Canada due to the greater per capita reliance on imports of these peripheral regions.[27] According to Robert Brym "this amounts to stating that consumers in the Maritimes and in the west subsidized the growth of industry in central Canada by paying for a disproportionately large part of the tariff bill."[28] Unlike the West however, in the medium term (1879 to the early 1920s), secondary industry in the Maritimes flourished. This was largely due to a transportation eastbound price differential. This differential was designed by the privately built and operated Intercolonial Railway, the undisputed rate-maker between the Maritimes and central Canada.[29] It allowed maritime shippers to export products to central Canada at a rate approximately 12 percent less than it cost central Canadians to reciprocate; the savings were even greater the further west the goods were shipped.[30] The effect of the policy was to encourage the development of secondary industry in the Maritimes since it allowed the manufacturers to get their products to the centre at a competitive price. The further advantage of the differential was that it simultaneously safeguarded the Intercolonial's profits on goods travelling eastward, hence raising the price of central Canadian products in the Maritimes and, as a consequence, it also provided the infant maritime industries with a degree of protection in their home markets.[31] Once secondary industry was established in the region, the burdens of the tariffs, e.g. high prices on imported goods, were more than offset by the benefits — the protection of maritime industry from foreign competition. Hence due to the combination of the National Policy and cheap freight rates the maritime economy boomed. In the 1880s, Nova Scotia per capita growth in manufacturing was the highest in the country; major industry including steel plants, rolling mills, glass works, cotton mills, sugar refineries and rope factories settled in the region.[32] According to Brym, so spectacular was the growth that many people at the time were predicting that Nova Scotia, with the only known supply of coal in the Dominion, would become the heartland of Canada.[33]

Yet at the same time that the Intercolonial's freight rates were helping to sustain a booming economy, the region's political influence in the House of Commons, and hence its ability to defend the policy, was steadily declining as the balance of power shifted westward.[34] The more numerous and powerful populations of central and western Canada were able to pressure the federal government into withdrawing the special freight rates for the Maritimes, thus eliminating the region's ability to compete.[35] The East-West price differential was abolished in 1912, the Intercolonial Railway was placed under the management of the board of directors of the Canadian Northern Railway in 1918 and by 1920 the Intercolonial's regional office had been dismantled and its intricate rate schedule demolished.[36] As a result, maritime manufacturers could no longer get their products to markets at a competitive price, the benefits of the tariff system were erased and deindustrialization of the region ensued. The maritime economy has never recovered; reliance on the service sector and on the monopolization of trade has led to chronic underdevelopment in the region.[37]

An area of heated exchange between the federal government and Nova Scotia and Newfoundland (in particular) has been offshore resource jurisdiction. Nova Scotia settled with Ottawa in 1982 while Newfoundland, under the leadership of Premier Brian Peckford, entered into a more protracted battle with the federal government. Driven by the prospect of using the development of the offshore to break the province's cycle of economic weakness and dependency, there was a surge of "neonationalism" in Newfoundland reminiscent of a similar sentiment prominent in Alberta throughout the 1970s and early 1980s. Although the dispute resulted in the signing of the Atlantic Accord in 1985, which, like the previously signed Nova Scotia agreement, retained ownership of the resources for the federal government with the province sharing in the revenue and management, Newfoundland remained highly critical of Ottawa and more determined than ever to promote provincial competence.[38]

More contentious has been the continuing battle over the fisheries. The constitutional jurisdiction is divided between the federal and provincial governments; the former controls and manages the region's offshore while the latter have jurisdiction over the inshore. Although there is not consensus across the region as to whether or not the federal government should withdraw from the offshore — Newfoundland generally favours increased provincial control over the offshore while Nova Scotia, New Brunswick and Prince Edward Island are more inclined to support continued federal government involvement — all four provinces do advocate a more regionally-sensitive and high-profile federal approach to the fisheries. The governments of the Atlantic region are united in their criticism of what they perceive as Ottawa's policy of trading foreign access to the fisheries for the continued admittance of central Canadian manufactured goods into foreign markets.[39]

Most complaints inevitably return to the region's economic difficulties and, more specifically, to the belief that the region is underdeveloped by federal government design.[40] Ottawa's policies adopted to alleviate the fiscal hardships, including equalization grants, conditional grants in health care, education and social services and regional development programs, have not silenced these complaints for two reasons. First, according to Brym, the policies have not been incredibly successful.[41] The per capita income gaps between the "have" and "have-not" regions, for instance, have actually broadened,[42] and even though there have been some gains in incomes and jobs, analysts like Ralph Matthews argue that the negative consequences of the federal policies — such as the institutionalization of regional economic underdevelopment — outweigh any benefits.[43] Corporations which do make profits under the federal assistance programs to private industry usually do so by paying the local labour force lower wages than paid at the centre and typically transfer their profits out of the region. The result is a state-assisted method of transferring wealth from the periphery to the centre.[44] Ironically then, Ottawa's regional development policies actually increase the region's dependency on the centre rather than reduce it.[45] Further complaints include the misdirection and inappropriateness of programs, inefficiency of delivery mechanisms and the overall inadequacy of funding.[46] A second reason why Atlantic premiers have remained ungrateful and unpacified by federal handouts is that they believe the programs are in place not because of the Atlantic region's economic plight but more because of Quebec's economic and political troubles. Many believe had it not been for Quebec's need, Ottawa would not have introduced special regional development policies.[47] The westward shift in focus of federal financial resources is often offered as evidence of the federal government's fixation with the centre: economically buoyant Ontario receives federal resources annually for federal-provincial regional development agreements equivalent to similar funds given New Brunswick and Newfoundland;[48] and while the Atlantic received 53 percent of DREE's spending in 1969-70, by 1984-85 it had dropped to 16.1 percent with Quebec receiving 42.6 percent and Ontario 23 percent.[49]

East and West Compared

When comparing eastern and western alienation it is obvious that there are some important differences. For instance, the western version has been more forcefully and continuously articulated through the use of third parties and western premiers. Nelson Wiseman argues that the history of prairie protest reveals a broader spectrum of ideological responses to the same perceived injustices:

> Like Atlantic Canada, the West has been a peripheral economic hinterland for central Canada; but it is quite unlike Atlantic Canada in its legacy of social heterogeneity and frontier openness. This fed a contentious ideological component in Western Canadian politics, whereas Atlantic Canadian party politics has never risen far above contests between "ins" and "outs" with like differentiation in terms of platforms, programs and philosophies. Unlike Atlantic Canada ... the West has produced third parties throughout this century.[50]

Furthermore, at first glance at least, mineral-rich Alberta, and to a lesser extent Saskatchewan, seem to have little in common with the chronically deprived Atlantic. The landlocked Prairies do not share the Atlantic's dependence on the fisheries and similarly agriculture is not as high a priority in the East as it is in the West. Last, the Prairies with its polyglot ethnic mix is said to have a different political culture from the more traditional, homogeneous east.[51]

Yet more striking than these differences are the similarities shared by East and West. Vitally, the complaints expressed are more than random grievances against certain federal government policies. Rather, they constitute a far-reaching critique of the economic and political structures of Canadian federalism.

Many of the eastern and western "economic" grievances issue from the fact that the regions are hinterland economies. Donald Smiley characterizes the devices and principles of such an economy as follows: metropolitan policies confine the hinterland to primary industry, whether based on fishing, agricultural or natural resources, with the products exported from the region in a raw or simi-processed state; metropolitan policies ensure that the hinterland buys manufactured goods from the industrial heartland; capital development of the hinterland is controlled by institutions in the core; in external economic relations the good of the hinterland is sacrificed for the benefit of the heartland; transportation facilities which link core and periphery are controlled by and operated for the benefit of the former; and, many of the crucial aspects of hinterland-heartland relations have been carried out through the instrumentalities of big business organizations protected by the heartland authorities from both foreign and hinterland competition.[52]

Both regions display these characteristics. In the case of the Prairies, this status was very much by design, since they were created to grow food for the metropolitan area while at the same time provide a market for the heartland's manufactured goods. Many conclude from this that "the west was always intended as a sort of colonial hinterland in permanent economic vassalage to the dominant urban centres of Canada."[53] But it is obvious that those who migrated West did not believe this status was meant to last otherwise why leave Ontario to be exploited on the Prairies? Besides, with its great potential due to its vast acres of prime wheat-growing land, prairie settlers expected their region to be central to the Canadian economy and as such, an equal partner with the metropolitan area. They therefore believed that the region remained a periphery, not by accident, but because of central Canadian design.

The Atlantic provinces make the same claim as to the origin of their hinterland status — the result of central Canadian design rather than the product of nature. J. Kenneth Galbraith is quoted as saying: "The Maritime provinces are on the main path from Europe to the United States — right on the greatest seaway ... how in the world did it happen that development jumped right over them?"[54] According to maritime historian W.S. MacNutt the explanation lies in the effect of Confederation on the region's economy: "Ontario would dominate, and untold sums of money extracted from the Maritime Provinces would be expended in developing the West," to which Brym adds, "for the principal benefit of Ontario."[55] The region's boom years, quashed only as the result of the federal government acquiescing to central (and western) Canadian pressure to alter the Intercolonial's freight rate structure, is offered as evidence.

Hence both regions interpret the history of Canada as a history of the federal government "being used by powerful central Canadian economic interests to drain wealth from the weak peripheral or hinterland regions such as the Prairies and the Maritimes."[56] As E.A. Partridge emphatically stated in 1925:

> The history of Canada since Confederation — the outcome of a politico-commercial, or a commerico-political conspiracy, if consequences are any indication of motive — has been a history of heartless robbery of both the people of the Maritimes and of the Prairie sections of Canada by the Big "Vested" Interests — so called from the size of their owners' Vests — of the politically and financially stronger Central Provinces.[57]

Many analysts, including the staples theorists, are critical of this perception of the federal government as being culpable. They believe the underdevelopment of the peripheries to be the inevitable result of geography and that government actions had few, and relatively insignificant negative affects.[58] For them, grievances are only directed at the federal government for want of a better target.[59]

This interpretation would be irrefutable if the federal government had never intervened and simply allowed market forces to take their natural course. This has been shown not to be the case in Canada; tariff and transportation policies alone constitute major interventions and were responsible for protecting inefficient and uncompetitive industries at the centre, while impairing the peripheries. The Free Trade Agreement is unlikely to alter the already established pattern of industrialization at the center and underdevelopment in the peripheries. The infant industries in the hinterlands will have difficulties competing with their more established competitors in central Canada. Yet this pattern of national growth might have been quite different had the federal government not intervened or if this intervention had been more helpful rather than detrimental to the periphery. The amount of federal government intervention was designed to suit the needs of the more stable, and populous, metropolitan economy. Typically however, what is suited to the heartland is not what is needed in the periphery.[60]

Yet while there is a degree of sympathy and empathy for Atlantic Canada as an economically deprived region, these sentiments are less forthcoming for mineral-rich Alberta and, to a lesser extent, Saskatchewan. For many Canadians the discontent and complaints of these provinces concerning their peripheral status are enigmatic. For them, the spectacle of Alberta, a province with no sales tax, the lowest provincial income taxes and huge governmental surpluses complaining of its treatment within Confederation is difficult to comprehend.[61] The complaints are more easily understood when two considerations are taken into account. First, despite the wealth accruing from oil and gas, Alberta and Saskatchewan have remained essentially "hewers of wood and drawers of water"[62] — primary producers with comparatively little secondary industry. According to Wiseman, the percentage of westerners engaged in manufacturing is lower than that of Atlantic Canadians and, despite frequent provincial government intervention, the economy of the region has been neither diversified nor strengthened.[63] In essence then they are still dependent on a very vulnerable one-crop economy. Second, the complaints of Alberta and Saskatchewan are only difficult to comprehend if one believes that their grievances are only a matter of "dollars and cents." This is a misconception. It cannot be denied that economic grievances do exist and are partially responsible for discontent in these two provinces. Similarly it is not disputed that these economic grievances are important factors in the formation of western alienation. However, they do not constitute the crucial cause for they are not at the base of the western, nor the Atlantic, sense of grievance.[64]

What is crucial is the complaint which lies at the heart of the grievances of the two regions — lack of political voice in the central government. Whether rich or poor, the seven provinces experience the same feelings of political powerlessness. Once this is recognized it is easier to understand why western alienation has persisted and even intensified in Alberta and Saskatchewan during the prosperous years — economic power has not converted into political power. Equally though, the five poorer provinces — Nova Scotia, New Brunswick, Prince Edward Island, Newfoundland and Manitoba — express their dissatisfaction with national political institutions and, more specifically, with their lack of political voice in central decision making. The impact of federal decisions on the poorer provinces is more obvious; given their dependence on federal financial aid, these provinces need effective access to the federal decision-making process. But even the citizens of Alberta and Saskatchewan have found that retreating behind the bulwarks of their provincial governments, a line of defense often advocated by the premiers of the two provinces, is only a partial remedy. During the 1980s an increasing number of people in these provinces became convinced that no matter how much they withdrew behind their seemingly strong provincial governments, Ottawa would still exercise powers key to their interests such as taxation, international trade, transportation, social policy and defense.

Fundamental to the sense of political powerlessness on the Prairies and in Atlantic Canada is their relatively small and scattered populations. This small population is partly detrimental in that it results in the regions having very little effect in deciding the partisan composition of the federal governments. Quebec and Ontario, with 174 of 295 seats, dominate in the House of Commons. Manitoba and Saskatchewan, on the other hand, have fewer MPs than the greater Toronto area;[65] the four Atlantic provinces have a mere thirty-two seats. This means that governments can be, and frequently are, decided without input from either region. This lack of political clout was demonstrated on the Prairies during the Pearson and Trudeau years when, despite the region's rejection of the Liberals, the party continued to win office, except for Clark's nine-month sojourn. This doubly exacerbated the region's feelings of political powerlessness — not only did their rejection have no fundamental affect on the election outcome but further the result was a government with few Liberal MPs so prairie interests were underrepresented.

The cause of the region's sense of political powerlessness is more fundamental than failure to vote for the winning side; the Mulroney government, with an abundance of western MPs has not allayed western grievances. Similarly, despite a steady flow of government MPs and prominent cabinet ministers from the region, Atlantic Canadians also continuously express their complaint of lack of political voice. The cause of this complaint is even more fundamental than the region's meagre share of seats in the House of Commons. At the root are certain structural factors at the very heart of Canadian federalism.

In most federal systems there is an inevitable collision between, on the one hand, the belief that each province, irrespective of demographic weight or resources, is essentially equal and, on the other hand, the liberal democratic principle of representation by population.[66] Federalism is meant to be a system of equal partnership between the constituent units thus suggesting the need for special recognition of each constituent polity in national government decision making.[67] In Canada the Senate, with its more equitable provincial representation, was formed for just this purpose.[68] It was to be the central institution which would act as the protector of the federal principle. However, because the Senate "was appointive in a society with a growing democratic consciousness, it was handicapped from the beginning and has become the appendix of the Canadian body politic."[69] The failure of the Senate to perform the function originally intended for it has resulted in the absence of a counteracting force in the central government to offset the dominance of the core region by virtue of its population.

The Canadian system is therefore inherently flawed. This defect is exacerbated by other structural factors, most notably the use of the parliamentary-cabinet system. This form of government has been derived from, and is appropriate to, a unitary state. The backbone of the cabinet model is the primacy of party discipline over all other considerations, including regional loyalties. In such a system territorial interests, particularly those of the scantily populated hinterlands, cannot take precedence. Even though the representative principle of cabinet selection normally ensures the presence of regional representatives in the executive, it does not follow that regional interests regularly dominate or are even articulated in cabinet. Hence the cabinet model is fundamentally incongruous to a federal state which must by definition accommodate regional interests. A modified cabinet system which introduces some counterbalancing factor in the central government in favour of the provinces would work in theory, but in practice in Canada this has not happened. As a result prairie premiers (in particular) and their Atlantic Canadian counterparts have used First Ministers Conferences to highlight their regional concerns. In this forum the Prairies constitute 30 percent and the Atlantic provinces 40 percent of the membership. But the premiers would prefer a more equitable intrastate federal institution.

In sum, eastern and western alienation are chronic and not susceptible to quick remedies. As long as the Atlantic and prairie provinces remain hinterlands, lacking in population in a majoritarian parliamentary system with few counterbalancing mechanisms protecting federalism in central decision making, then the regional complaints of political powerlessness will persist. Crucially then what interlocks the provinces within the Atlantic and prairie regions, and, in turn, what links East and West is the belief that they are outgunned in national politics, and that *as a consequence* they have been economically exploited by central Canada.[70]

ATLANTIC AND PRAIRIE CONSTITUTIONAL POSITIONS

There are common prairie and Atlantic economic grievances which are the result of more fundamental political complaints; but the focus here is whether or not this similarity in peripheral protests leads, in practice or in potential, to significant constitutional common ground between the regions. Each region's position on constitutional reforms (allowing for provincial differences within each region) will be examined concluding with a comparative study of these positions.

The Atlantic

The stance taken by successive Atlantic premiers in constitutional debates is frequently overlooked and misinterpreted. The traditional depiction of Atlantic Canadian involvement suggests that the region has adopted a pliant attitude towards constitutional negotiations largely due to its economic dependence on Ottawa and its unwillingness to bite the hand that feeds it.[71] Robert Finbow, in the most comprehensive analysis of recent positions taken by Atlantic premiers at constitutional conferences, compellingly argues that this traditional depiction is inaccurate.[72] He contends that Atlantic premiers have consistently maintained a dualistic approach to constitutional reform. On the one hand the provinces have normally been staunch supporters of centralized, but regionally sensitive, economic power. On the other hand, the provinces simultaneously favoured channelling federal power into patterns more agreeable to the region (such as entrenched guarantees of equalization payments) and to enhance the autonomy of the provinces in development and resource fields.

Finbow traces this dualistic approach from the 1967 Confederation of Tomorrow Conference, through the patriation round, and up to the failure of the Meech Lake Accord. In what he labels as "the first round" (1967-71), Finbow states that the Atlantic premiers used the process to gain national attention for their economic woes by demanding that regional economic disparities be included on the agenda, and by opposing the decentralization of federal economic and taxing powers on the grounds that it would put equalization, cost sharing and regional development programs in jeopardy. In the same round the premiers also expressed their concern about the lack of consultation by Ottawa when spending money in provincial jurisdictions. Thus the premiers' support for a centralized economic regime did not extend to support for a general grant of power to the federal government to act without consulting the provinces.[73]

In the patriation round (1979-82), despite some different approaches within the region, what was most striking according to Finbow was the constancy displayed by the Atlantic premiers. Economic issues were stressed and once again the premiers used the constitutional negotiations as a forum to focus concern over the region's economic difficulties. Entrenchment of equalization and regional development programs were again sought; so too was greater intergovernmental consultation and coordination in these development policies. All Atlantic premiers were wary of what they saw as the expansionist tendencies of the federal government, and they extended their search for the constitutional competence and fiscal resources to move out of have-not status.[74] They opposed Ottawa's proposal to create a common market by enhancing mobility rights on the grounds that the restriction of mobility was the "affirmative action" used by the region to protect local workers and producers.[75] According to the Prince Edward Island position paper, a common economy meant that "it is common for some sections of the country to prosper and for others to cope with built-in economic disadvantage."[76] The promise of offshore oil and gas reserves helped Nova Scotia and Newfoundland to persuade the Atlantic premiers to seek control of the continental shelf. Newfoundland premier Brian Peckford was more strident in his demands to assert provincial control over resources, including the fisheries, a measure not fully shared by his three Atlantic counterparts.

Yet economic concerns were not the only priority; Atlantic premiers once again expressed their concern about the region's political powerlessness in national political affairs and the need for the equality of provinces. There was however some disagreement as how to best redress the situation: Nova Scotia and Prince Edward Island supported an enhanced regional role in the selection of senators and Supreme Court justices; Newfoundland advocated an "equal" Senate; New Brunswick was opposed to regionalizing national institutions for fear it would leave "outer Canada" even more vulnerable.[77]

In the end, Finbow contends that the patriated constitution contained many concessions which appealed to the region: the amending formula recognized the equality of provinces; equalization was entrenched in the constitution; exceptions were permitted in mobility rights to allow economically disadvantaged areas local-preference policies; and Newfoundland secured protection for its Labrador boundary and church-dominated school system. On the other hand the federal government did not extinguish its claim to offshore resources; there were no significant intrastate reforms to central political institutions; and the commitment to the principle of equalization was a somewhat vague guarantee.

The involvement of certain Atlantic premiers in the Meech Lake round was more notorious. Nova Scotia premier John Buchanan and Prince Edward Island premier Joe Ghiz staunchly supported the accord. They accepted that the deal was imperfect but believed that accommodating Quebec was of paramount importance. However, the premiers of New Brunswick and Newfoundland, Frank McKenna and Clyde Wells respectively, were strong critics of the accord. Both premiers feared the accord would erode the federal spending power because of the "opting out" provision; there would be little political mileage for Ottawa if the richer provinces opted out of future federal initiatives, thus reducing federal government incentives to initiate new programs. Wells and McKenna were equally concerned about what they perceived as the threat of reduced regional political influence due to the Meech Lake Accord. For Wells, the distinct society clause, by providing Quebec with special status, violated the equality of provinces essential, he believed, to federalism. McKenna felt that Ottawa, by handing over the powers to promote and protect bilingualism to Quebec, was downplaying his province's proper role in these policies. Both premiers sought Senate reform as a means to redress the political imbalance. For Wells this entailed a Triple-E model; McKenna became less insistent on Senate reform in the later stages of the debate but still sought the body's reinvigoration in future constitutional rounds.[78] The premiers were also critical of distinct society on the grounds that it could infringe on rights protected in the charter; both sought to protect the rights of women, Natives and multicultural groups from the clause. Last, McKenna and Wells criticized the process of Meech Lake as being undemocratic and closed to public input.

Constitutionally speaking, what does Atlantic Canada want? According to Finbow the region's position is one of support for federal power when it suits the regional interests, normally economic policies, and demands for change when the federal policy is perceived as hurting the region. Typically this has meant strong central economic control (to maintain regional development programs) but reforms to increase input of the provinces in central decision making including greater access to federal fiscal decision making. Certainly they seek reforms which would aid them in shedding their "have-not" status. The Atlantic's preferred vision is that of a strong region in a united, regionally sensitive Canada.

The Prairies

The initial demands for constitutional reform, which led to the Confederation of Tomorrow conference and the constitutional negotiations which followed, did not originate on the Prairies. In fact, initially the premiers were caught somewhat unawares. The premiers of Alberta and Saskatchewan in particular were leery of the desire of Quebec and Ottawa to revise the constitution; they feared a revised BNA Act would embellish the federal government's powers, especially in the area of natural resources, and enhance Quebec's already powerful position in the confederation. These provinces were also suspicious of Ottawa's timing; the rules of Confederation were to be changed just when Alberta and Saskatchewan had been "winning" for a short time.[79] Even so the prairie premiers generally agreed that a reshaping of the constitution was necessary to make it more sensitive to regional and provincial needs and less inclined towards centralization. Hence they used the constitutional conference to air traditional grievances regarding Ottawa's lack of attention afforded regional interests, and to voice their concern over the proposals of Quebec and Ottawa concerning language, a charter of rights and the division of powers between governments.[80]

In the patriation round prairie premiers were anxious to place a number of issues important to the region on the agenda. Their approach, given the backdrop of the NEP, was a defensive one. Blakeney and Lougheed aggressively sought enhanced provincial control over natural resources. In this regard they were successful; Sec. 92A of the Constitution Act allows the provinces to collect indirect taxes on resources and to regulate resource production even though this may affect interprovincial and international trade. The provinces were limited in the jurisdiction by the proviso that provincial taxation and regulation practices had to be applied equally across the country. The general amending formula, originally proposed by Lougheed, recognized the western vision of the equality of provinces by denying any one province a veto power. The concerns of western premiers to maintain parliamentary sovereignty were addressed through the notwithstanding clause. Yet one of the fundamental positions of these premiers, the need to reform central political institutions, was not addressed; the constitutional act did not include parliamentary reforms designed to effect regional representation at the centre. At the time, however, while there was regional consensus that reforms were needed there was no such consensus as to what the reforms should entail. British Columbia's support for the Triple-E Senate had not yet spread through the Prairies.

After 1982 there was solidification of a regional constitutional approach, at least in regards to political issues. The regions had long nursed a sense of unease with the two-nation perception of Canada, the federal government's policy of bilingualism and biculturalism and Quebec's influence in national politics. According to Wiseman the Prairies' ethnic mix and distance from Quebec potentially explain the antipathy found there to the dualistic conceptualization of Canada and to the extension of French-language rights across the country. "The attitude of many European-origin pioneers was that if they could assimilate into the anglophone majority, so should the French, who, at least in terms of numbers, did not warrant a 'special status'."[81] Thus with every further entrenchment of French-language rights on the Prairies and with the CF-18 contract being given to an "inferior" Quebec firm, the western Canadian perception that the rules of the national political system were stacked against them, and in Quebec's favour, were bolstered.[82] To counter the dominance of Quebec and Ontario at the centre the region increasingly embraced Senate reform, and more specifically the Triple-E version. The fact that Mulroney seemed fixated with maintaining support at the centre, even if it was at the expense of western interests and support, led many westerners to believe "that regional representation cannot be achieved through party mechanisms alone, that any party with national ambitions will necessarily downplay the regional concerns of western Canadians in the search for seats in Ontario and Quebec."[83] Institutional reform was therefore needed.

This two-pronged regional approach was apparent in the public reaction, but not in the official government reaction, to Meech Lake. It was criticized publicly on the grounds that it compounded, rather than eleviated, both regional concerns. First, the Meech Lake round was billed as the Quebec round and the accord was thought to extend Quebec's powers (especially through the distinct society and immigration clauses) and once again placed western constitutional issues on the backburner.[84] Second, the pervailing view on the Prairies, a view not shared by Don Getty or Grant Divine, was that ultimately the accord would have spelt the death of effective Senate reform. The unanimity clause, and the predicted unwillingness of the premiers to give up the patronage gem gained by the nomination process outlined in the accord, were cited as the reasons why the accord was damaging to Senate reform.

Yet despite a widespread regional consensus on these two constitutional issues what also became apparent during the Meech Lake round was the diversity of governmental constitutional positions within the region. The Saskatchewan government, led by the conciliatory Devine, was the most steadfast supporter of the accord. His government's "special relationship" with the federal government was widely believed to be the result of Mulroney's last-minute financial aid to Saskatchewan farmers just prior to the 1986 provincial election.[85] Many saw Devine's unswerving support as the payback.[86] But the constitutional negotiations were not a high priority for Devine. His party believed that the Blakeney government had been defeated due to its obsession with the constitution. The new Conservative government focussed more on provincial politics; its approach in intergovernmental relations was cooperative rather than conflictive. Overall the government did not play a significant role in the constitutional debates.[87] The Manitoba government, originally a majority NDP government led by Howard Pawley and after the 1988 provincial election a minority Conservative government led by Gary Filmon, was committed to public consultation prior to ratification. Manitobans expressed a desire to include the issues of northern participation in national institutions and aboriginal government in constitutional discussions. They disliked the restrictions placed on the federal spending power as they were perceived as a threat to Ottawa's ability to respond to "the universal needs of Canadians."[88] Conversely, Alberta welcomed control on the federal spending power and the general decentralist nature of the accord.

Constitutional Common Ground?

The Atlantic region and the Prairies share common economic and political complaints stemming from their peripheral status. Both regions have also been energetic participants at recent constitutional conferences, each premier pressing his provinces constitutional wish list.[89] But have the common complaints led to similar eastern and western constitutional positions? And even more significant in terms of the next round, are there still unsatisfied common demands for constitutional reform emanating from both regions?

In reference to the sought after political reforms of the East and the West, the answer to both questions is yes. The common political theme running through the constitutional positions of both regions starting in 1967, through the patriation round and up to Meech Lake is a desire to reform the central political institutions to enhance their influence in national policies. Although the regions have not always shared a common vision of how this would best be achieved, nevertheless Atlantic and prairie leaders consistently sought to strengthen their relatively weak regional voice at the centre. While all Atlantic premiers agreed on the objective of more regionally sensitive policy making, they were particularly vague on the "how to." Premiers Wells and McKenna expressed support for a reformed Senate during the Meech Lake debates but it seems that, so far at least, Wells is the only Atlantic premier firmly committed to the Triple-E version. Conversely, by the end of the Meech Lake round prairie premiers were far more clear and united on the specifics of institutional reform — a Triple-E Senate. The "equal" component of the three "Es" incorporates the eastern and western belief in the inherent equality of provinces. For them, central Canada has not earned the right to completely dominate by virtue of its population. Nor should Quebec's unique culture be used to sanction its preponderance at the expense of western and Atlantic Canada; a Quebec veto would be unacceptable to both regions. Yet despite a growing consensus in both regions on the issue of political reform, as of yet these demands have not been resolved or even fully addressed at the national level. Ottawa's *Shaping Canada's Future Together* attempts to redress this omission.

As was discussed above, the hinterland economic status has led to similar demands for more fair federal policies to allow or encourage the growth of secondary industry in both the East and West. Yet interestingly, these common hinterland complaints have not translated into similar economic constitutional demands. In constitutional negotiations the "have" versus "have-not" classification of provinces supplants the common hinterland status as the determinant of position on economic reforms. Nova Scotia, New Brunswick, Prince Edward Island and Manitoba are chronically "have-not" provinces as determined by the federal-provincial equalization formula. Saskatchewan is described as a swing province — a recipient some years and not others[90] — making its approach a mixed one, sometimes having more in common with its neighbour to the east and sometimes united with its neighbor to the west. The prime objective of the "have-not" provinces, whether Atlantic or prairie, is a "longing to shed the humiliation of dependence and charity."[91] According to Finbow, the Atlantic provinces, Manitoba and even Saskatchewan share a common approach in constitutional negotiations — the desire "to maximize the prospects of an escape from have-not status."[92] These provinces, on the whole, favour a strong central government with the financial resources and necessary policy tools to combat regional economic disparities.

Donald Savoie points to a seeming contradiction in this approach:

> On the one hand, political leaders in Atlantic Canada argue that a major reason — perhaps the most important reason — for the region's under-development is discriminatory federal policies and national programs. The region has often pointed out that it does not carry much political weight on the national scene... Yet, on the other hand, the region's provincial premiers by and large prefer a strong central government and have said so publicly on many occasions.[93]

Even though Savoie was writing about the Atlantic specifically the same could be applied to Manitoba and Saskatchewan.[94] Although seemingly contradictory, the position becomes more congruous when examined in tandem with the political reforms also requested. The regions are attempting to combine the advantages of federal and provincial state intervention; "the main thrust remain[s] a desire for enhanced federal ability to combat disparities, coupled with increased provincial authority to promote economic development."[95] Hence they support a strong, but reformed, regionally sensitive federal government.

Alberta is the consistently aberrant "have" province. While the other six provinces more generally support a fiscally strong federal government, Alberta tends to view Ottawa's handling of the economy with disdain, laying charges of federal mismanagement with damaging effects in the West.[96] They therefore advocate the transfer of policy responsibility to the provincial government accompanied by the taxing power to finance it.[97] As the APEC study points out, in this regard, the Alberta position is similar to Quebec's. The fundamental difference is that while many Albertans view this restructuring as a way to reduce government at all levels, Quebec's demands for greater provincial autonomy do not seem to include this vision of a diminished public sector.[98] But irrespective of whether or not Alberta's position is compatible with Quebec's, of significance here is the fact that it differs greatly from what the have-not Atlantic and prairie provinces envisage. Hence, while there is significant common ground on political reforms, in reference to "economic" constitutional demands, Alberta normally stands apart from the other six. There are exceptions to this rule — Peckford supported more decentralization, Blakeney's position was more in line with Alberta's — but generally oil-rich Alberta, a province subsidizing the have-not provinces of Canada through equalization payments, views economic issues and the proper level of federal fiscal involvement in a different light from its prairie and Atlantic counterparts.

SHAPING CANADA'S FUTURE TOGETHER : ATLANTIC AND PRAIRIE RESPONSE

Given this similar, but not identical Atlantic and prairie constitutional approach, it is important to conclude with an examination of their likely reaction to the latest federal government constitutional proposals contained in the paper *Shaping Canada's Future Together*. Will the seven provinces be satisfied with the economic and political reforms contained therein? It would be folly to underestimate the ramifications of this question. Joe Clark and Brian Mulroney contend that if these, or similar proposals, are not accepted by the nine English-speaking provinces, and presented to the Quebec government for its consideration, then Quebec will separate and "Canada" will cease to exist, at least in any recognizable form. If they are correct in their assertion, and if we can expect a somewhat similar Atlantic-prairie position on political and, to a lesser extent, on economic reforms, then the answer to the question posed above is of vital importance. These seven provinces may feel insignificant in the House of Commons where they hold a minority of seats, but since the amending formula needed to adopt the federal government's proposals requires the approval of *seven* provinces with 50 percent of the population some peripheral support is essential.

Part II of the federal proposals includes a host of reforms designed to "revitalize" Canada's political institutions to make them more effective, fair and responsive.[99] The federal government is more elaborate on what it hopes the reforms will achieve than on the actual details of the reforms *per se*. For example, it is recognized that the parliamentary system is too partisan and conflictive and that changes are needed to rectify this. The federal government therefore promises to "commit itself to a process of further parliamentary reform to give individual MPs more free votes and to reduce the application of votes of confidence."[100] It appears that these reforms *could* be popular in the East and the West since the peripheries resent the fact that partisan loyalties take precedence over regional concerns in the House of Commons. Yet until there is more detail such a prediction remains purely spéculative.

This lack of particulars also hampers predictions as to whether or not the Senate-reform proposals will meet with the approval of the Atlantic and prairie provinces. According to Gibbins:

> Senate reform is the symbolic key that Western Canadians will use to unlock the federal government's complex constitutional proposals. At first glance, they should be pleased with what they see.
>
> Admittedly, the proposed Senate is not Triple-E, but it is elected, and it is more effective than anyone might have expected. It is not equal, only more "equitable."[101]

He goes on to argue that the acceptability of the package in the West will most likely depend on the third and as of yet undefined "E" — equal. Quebec, it seems, would not accept equal. Yet it will be onerous to satisfy the Prairies with anything much less. The Atlantic provinces, which are overrepresented in the present Senate, have perhaps the most to lose in this debate; New Brunswick and Nova Scotia with ten senators each are better represented than the more populous Alberta with its six senators. A "more equitable" distribution would probably reduce the Atlantic's share of senators. The federal government plans to leave it to a special joint committee of Parliament to decide on the number and distribution of Senate seats.

Although the government paper's proposed upper house is described as a 2½ "E" version (meaning elected, effective but only equitable) whether or not it warrants a full "E" for effectiveness is open to question. Once again the package is short on detail. Even though it states that "as a general rule, in order for measures to become law, approval of both the Senate and House of Commons should be required," it also declares that the lower house will "remain the primary legislative body" and that "since the Senate is not a confidence chamber, the Senate would have no legislative role in relation to appropriation bills and measures to raise funds including borrowing authority."[102] Furthermore, the Senate would only have a six-month suspensive veto on all matters of "national importance"; how broadly this will be defined is yet to be seen. On the whole there appear to be major differences of opinion on how effective this Senate would be. Clark, for example, claims that it would be a strong, regional force; others feel that given the proposed Senate's inability to deal with money bills and the seeming ban on it initiating legislation, the new upper house will be a rather ineffectual body which would merely give the impression of enhanced provincial input in central decision making.

The package is also ambiguous as to the purpose of the Senate. Is it primarily to be a house of the provinces, an intrastate federal institution? The paper declares that "the impetus for Senate reform stems first and foremost from the conviction ... that federal decision making is not sufficiently responsive to regional diversity."[103] Yet the proposals also state that the electoral system selected for the Senate should "give expression to the social diversity of the

Canadian population, keeping in mind the history of the inadequate political representation of women, Aboriginal peoples and ethnic groups,"[104] suggesting that it also become a house of charter groups. It is ironic that Ottawa should mandate this elected Senate to try to become more culturally and gender representative of Canada when both Conservative and Liberal federal governments have done little in this regard themselves. The representative nature of the House of Commons is often blamed on the voting behaviour of Canadians; this of course ignores the relative dearth of minority and women candidates nominated by the Liberals and Conservatives. But in terms of the present Senate, appointed as it is by the federal government, there is no such excuse. It is interesting then that Ottawa should only become interested in representative balances once it is relinquishing its control over Senate patronage appointments.

The "council of the federation," although not identified in the proposals as an institutional reform *per se*, could become a significant new level of government. The minimalist reading would be that the council would merely formalize the existing practices of executive federalism. The more liberal prediction would foresee a more substantial council using its power to vote on proposed federal legislation "to enhance the functioning of the economic union" in such a broad way so as to become a dominant new branch of government. If this were to happen, the council would rival the Senate as the effective voice of regional interests at the centre.

The economic proposals, which combine more centralized economic authority with the decentralization of legislative jurisdictions, would appear to have mixed blessings for the "have" versus "have-not" groupings differentiated above. The "have" province of Alberta predictably could be more supportive of the decentralizing aspects of the economic proposals and critical of the increased centralization of economic authority. The "have-not" contingent however should be relieved that Ottawa did not drastically decentralize its economic authority since significant decentralization would reduce the federal government's capacity to effect redistribution of wealth.[105] Less appealing however is the renewed commitment to "opting out." There are indications that some people in the "have-not" peripheries are also uncertain of the impact of common-market proposals on their vulnerable economy.

CONCLUSION

In terms of hinterland complaints and desired constitutional reforms there is significant common ground between the Prairies and Atlantic Canada. The peripherial complaint of political powerlessness in central decision making is evident in the demands for entrenched political reforms of central institutions articulated by all seven provinces. The precise nature of these reforms, although still not definitively outlined, is increasingly centred on Senate reform in both regions. There is no such consensus on constitutional reforms dealing with the provinces' economic ´ complaints. Although all seven lament the lack of secondary industry in the regions and condemn the prejudicial federal policies which they believe are responsible for creating this situation, essentially this is where the commonality ends. Alberta is certain of its own ability, were it given the relevant jurisdictional and taxing authority, to redress this situation and therefore supports more decentralized economic policy making in Canada. The other six generally believe that such decentralization would be harmful to them.

Whether or not this common ground will be sufficient to unite the prairie and Atlantic provinces in the present constitutional round is yet to be seen. There are other reforms included in the federal proposals, and not discussed here, which could potentially divide the regions — aboriginal self-government and the distinct society clause, for example. The have-not provinces will probably have a stronger commitment, stemming from a sense of self-preservation, to maintaining some semblence of the status quo, particularly the principle of regional redistribution. Alberta, although equally committed to "Canada," could be more supportive of Quebec's vision of a looser, more decentralized vision.

This present round is certain to be different to the "Quebec round." This already is evident in the prairie and Atlantic provinces. All seven provincial governments are sure to be better prepared for these constitutional negotiations due to more wide-ranging consultations, not only with the so-called experts, but with the general electorate as well. These discussions are more focussed on the details of reform rather than just the broader issue of the need to keep Quebec in Canada. If this round is to end with an agreement, then the federal government must learn from the mistakes of Meech Lake and accept that the provinces want to discuss the actual specifics of proposed constitutional reforms. There are some indications that Ottawa has recognized this. *Shaping Canada's Future Together* is far more detailed than was the Meech Lake Accord; in particular it attempts to place parameters on the distinct society clause.

There are other indications however that the federal government's approach has not altered significantly. In a recent speech in Halifax, amazingly reminiscent of speeches given by Mulroney in the last days of the Meech Lake ratification process, Clark passionately urged those present to accept the government's reform proposals not because they would be good for the Atlantic or would improve the operation of the federation, but because Quebec will leave if they do not. There was little reference to specifics, just an attempt to appeal to Nova Scotians "nationalism." Further, in the government's proposals, when addressing the question of how do we get to the point of shaping our future together, the authors of the federal document include a quote from Sir John A. Macdonald presumably as a blueprint of the route they propose:

> If we had not felt that, after coming to this conclusion, we were bound to set aside our private opinions on matters of detail, if we had not felt ourselves bound to look at what was practicable, not obstinately rejecting the opinions of others nor adhering to our own; if we had not met, I say, in a spirit of

conciliation, and with an anxious, overruling desire to form one people under one government, we never would have succeeded.[106]

This is a course not acceptable to the Atlantic and the Prairies. What is needed are discussions of details and how the proposals will affect the two regions. More specifically the government must show that the reforms address the demands of the peripheral regions, and not just those of Quebec, for an altered federation.

Notes

1. David Jay Bercuson, "Canada's Burden of Unity: An Introduction," in David J. Bercuson, ed., *Canada and the Burden of Unity* (Toronto: Macmillan, 1977), 1.

2. Richard Simeon and David Elkins, "Regional Political Cultures in Canada," in Richard Schultz et al., eds., *The Canadian Political Process*, 3rd edition (Toronto: Holt, Rinehart and Winston, 1979), 15.

3. J.M. Beck, "The Maritimes: A Region or Three Provinces?" *Transactions of the Royal Society of Canada* 15 (1977): 301.

4. Rober Gibbins, *Prairie Politics and Society: Regionalism in Decline* (Toronto: Butterworths, 1980).

5. See Simeon and Elkins, "Regional Political Cultures"; Peter Boswell, "The Atlantic Provinces," in Michael Whittington and Glen Williams, eds., *Canadian Politics in the 1990s*, 3rd edition (Scarborough: Nelson, 1990), 119.

6. Boswell, "The Atlantic Provinces," 119.

7. See Gibbins, *Prairie Politics and Society*.

8. Roger Gibbins, "The Prairie Provinces," in Whittington and Williams, eds., *Canadian Politics in the 1990s*, 60-61.

9. Roger Gibbins, "Western Alienation and the Alberta Political Culture," in Carlo Caldarola, ed., *Society and Politics in Alberta* (Toronto: Methuen Press, 1979), 145.

10. David Elton, "Federalism and the Canadian West," in R.D. Olling and M.W. Westmacott, eds., *Perspectives on Canadian Federalism* (Scarborough: Prentice-Hall, 1988), 350.

11. Grace Skogstad, "Farmers and Farm Unions in the Society and Politics of Alberta," in Caldarola, ed., *Society and Politics in Alberta*, 225.

12. See T.D. Regehr, "Western Canada and the Burden of National Transportation Politics," in Bercuson, ed., *Canada and the Burden of Unity*.

13. Ibid., 114.

14. Ibid.

15. Ibid., 118.

16. Robert J. Brym, "An Introduction to the Regional Question in Canada," in Robert J. Brym, ed., *Regionalism in Canada* (Toronto: Irwin Publishing, 1986), 11.

17. See Paul Phillips, "National Policy, Continental Economics, and National Disintegration," in Bercuson, ed., *Canada and the Burden of Unity*, 70-71; and Regehr, "Western Canada and the Burden."

18. It added salt to the wound that British Columbia joined one year later than Manitoba and yet was granted the jurisdiction denied to Manitoba the year before.

19. Doug Owram, "Reluctant Hinterland," in Larry Pratt and Garth Stevenson, eds., *Western Separatism: The Myths, Realities and Dangers* (Edmonton: Hurtig, 1981), 54.

20. John Richards and Larry Pratt, *Prairie Capitalism: Power and Influence in the New West* (Toronto: McClelland and Stewart, 1979), 17.

21. Elton, "Federalism and the Canadian West," 349.

22. Ibid., 353.

23. Nelson Wiseman, "The West as a Political Region," in Alain G. Gagnon and James P. Bickerton, eds., *Canadian Politics* (Peterborough: Broadview Press, 1990), 320.

24. Allan Blakeney, "Resources, the Constitution and Canadian Federalism," in J. Peter Meekison, ed., *Canadian Federalism: Myth or Reality?* (Toronto: Methuen, 1977), 180-81.

25. Allan Tupper, "Mr. Trudeau and the West," in Pratt and Stevenson, eds., *Western Separatism*, 92.

26. J.M. Beck, *Joseph Howe: Voice of Nova Scotia* (Toronto: McClelland and Stewart, 1964), 174-75.

27. S.A. Saunders as quoted in Brym, "An Introduction to the Regional Question," 9.

28. Brym, "An Introduction to the Regional Question," 9.

29. Ernest R. Forbes, "Misguided Symmetry: The Destruction of Regional Transportation Policy for the Maritimes," in Bercuson, ed., *Canada and the Burden of Unity*, 64.

30. Ibid.

31. Ibid.

32. See T.W. Acheson, "The National Policy and the Industrialization of the Maritimes, 1880-1910," *Acadiensis* 1 (1972): 3-28.

33. Brym, "An Introduction to the Regional Question," 10.

34. Forbes, "Misguided Symmetry," 65.

35. Ibid.

36. Ibid., 66-67.

37. Gary Burrill and Ian McKay, eds., *People, Resources, and Power: Critical Perspectives on Underdevelopment and Primary Industries in the Atlantic Region*. Gorsebrook Studies in the Political Economy of Atlantic Canada, No. 1. (Fredericton: Acadiensis Press, 1987), 4.

38. Robert Finbow, "The Atlantic Provinces in the Constitutional Reform Process, 1967-

1990," Canadian Political Science Association Annual Meeting, June 1991. Cited with permission.

39. Boswell, "The Atlantic Provinces," 124.

40. See Donald Savoie, "The Atlantic Region: The Politics of Dependency," in Olling and Westmacott, eds., *Perspectives on Canadian Federalism*; and Brym, "An Introduction to the Regional Question."

41. Brym, "An Introduction to the Regional Question," 11.

42. Ibid.

43. Ralph Matthews, *The Creation of Canadian Dependency* (Toronto: University of Toronto Press, 1983), 99-117.

44. Brym, "An Introduction to the Regional Question," 12-13.

45. Savoie, "The Atlantic Region," 292.

46. Boswell, "The Atlantic Provinces," 126.

47. See David G. Alexander, "Canadian Regionalism: A Central Problem," in David Alexander, ed., *Atlantic Canada and Confederation* (Toronto: University of Toronto Press, 1983), 75; and Savoie, "The Atlantic Region," 295.

48. Savoie, "The Atlantic Region," 295.

49. APEC, *Atlantic Canada Today* (Halifax: Formac, 1985), 124.

50. Wiseman, "The West as a Political Region," 312.

51. See Simeon and Elkins, "Regional Political Cultures."

52. Donald Smiley, *Canada in Question: Federalism in the Eighties*, 3rd Edition (Toronto: McGraw-Hill Ryerson, 1980), 263.

53. Doug Owram, "Reluctant Hinterland," in Pratt and Stevenson, eds., *Western Separatism*, 51.

54. As quoted in Savoie, "The Atlantic Region," 291.

55. W.S. MacNutt, *New Brunswick: A History 1784-1867* (Toronto: Macmillan, 1963), 461.

56. Brym, "An Introduction to the Regional Question," 8.

57. As quoted in ibid.

58. Ibid., 11.

59. See David Elton and Roger Gibbins, "Western Alienation and Political Culture," in Schultz et al., eds., *The Canadian Political Process*, 88.

60. Garth Stevenson, "Western Alienation in Australia and Canada," in Pratt and Stevenson, eds., *Western Separatism*, 131.

61. Owram, "Reluctant Hinterland," 45.

62. J.F. Conway, "The Recrudescence of Western Canadian Separatist Sentiment: Political and Economic Background," Canada House Lecture Series, 1982, p. 20.

63. Wiseman, "The West as a Political Region," 315.

64. Owram, "Reluctant Hinterland," 45.

65. Wiseman, "The West as a Political Region," 318.

66. Stevenson, "Western Alienation in Australia and Canada," 131.

67. See Bercuson, "Canada's Burden of Unity"; and Stevenson, "Western Alienation in Australia and Canada."

68. Bercuson, "Canada's Burden of Unity," 6.

69. Ibid.

70. Gibbins, "The Prairie Provinces," 61.

71. See G.A. Rawlyk, *The Atlantic Provinces and the Problems of Confederation* (St. John's, Newfoundland: Breakwater, 1979), 32.

72. The following discussion comes from Finbow, "The Atlantic Provinces in the Constitutional Reform Process."

73. Ibid., 8.

74. Ibid., 12.

75. Ibid., 13.

76. P.E.I., *Position Statements: Constitutional Conference, Sept., 1980* (Charlottetown, 1980), 4.

77. Finbow, "The Atlantic Provinces in the Constitutional Reform Process,"16.

78. Ibid., 20-21.

79. Peter Lougheed, *Canada News Facts*, 1980, 2394.

80. Elton, "Federalism and the Canadian West," 357.

81. Wiseman, "The West as a Political Region," 314.

82. Gibbins, "The Prairie Provinces," 72.

83. Ibid., 73.

84. Ibid.

85. Howard Leeson, "Saskatchewan in Transition," in R.L. Watts and D.M. Brown, eds., Canada: The State of the Federation 1990 (Kingston, Ontario: Institute of Inter-governmental Relations, Queen's University, 1990), 183.

86. Ibid., 185.

87. See ibid., 195.

88. Kathy Brock, *A Mandate Fulfilled: Constitutional Reform and the Manitoba Task Force on Meech Lake*, December 1990, 109.

89. McKenna more aggressively than Hatfield, Blakeney more so than Divine, Lougheed more so than Getty.

90. Wiseman, "The West as a Political Region," 310.

91. Alexander, "Canadian Regionalism," 91.

92. Finbow, "The Atlantic Provinces in the Constitutional Reform Process," 24.

93. Savoie, "The Atlantic Region," 299.

94. Finbow, "The Atlantic Provinces in the Constitutional Reform Process," 24.

95. Ibid., 23.

96. See Canada West Foundation, "A Strategy for Canadian Nationalists," *Western Perspectives.*

97. APEC, "Restructured Federalism and its Impacts on Atlantic Canada," prepared for the Atlantic Forum, 30 September-1 October 1991, p. 10.

98. Ibid.

99. See *Shaping Canada's Future Together: Proposals* (Ottawa: Supply and Services Canada, 1991), 15.

100. Ibid., 53.

101. Roger Gibbins, "2½ E's May Not Be Enough," *Globe and Mail*, September 1991.

102. *Shaping Canada's Future Together*, 53-54.

103. Ibid., 17.

104. Ibid., 18.

105. APEC, "Restructured Federalism," 10.

106. *Shaping Canada's Future Together*, 49.

Contributors

James N. McCrorie: Canadian Plains Research Center, University of Regina

Martha L. MacDonald: Gorsebrook Research Institute, Saint Mary's University

Gerald Friesen: University of Manitoba

Margaret Conrad: Acadia University

Paul Phillips: University of Manitoba

Tim O'Neill: Atlantic Provinces Economic Council

Isabel B. Anderson: University of Saskatchewan

Edward J. Chambers: University of Alberta

Michael B. Percy: University of Alberta

Harold Chorney: Concordia University

William E. Schrank: Memorial University of Newfoundland

Noel Roy: Memorial University of Newfoundland

Rosemary Ommer: Memorial University of Newfoundland

Blanca Skoda: Memorial University of Newfoundland

Wade MacLauchlan: Dalhousie University

Alvin Finkel: Athabasca University

Stephen G. Tomblin: Memorial University of Newfoundland

Léon Thériault: Université de Moncton

J. Peter Meekison: University of Alberta

Jim Silver: University of Winnipeg

James Bickerton: St. Francis Xavier University

Howard A. Leeson: University of Regina

David Milne: University of Prince Edward Island

Thérèse Arseneau: Saint Mary's University